Praise fo

MASTER OF THE

"Wiencek carefully probes the historical record, parsing the enormous body of Jefferson literature. His work is a thoughtful and well-documented contribution, offering a powerful reassessment of our third president."
—Kevin J. Hamilton, *The Seattle Times*

"An engrossing investigation . . . *Master of the Mountain* is narrative history wrapped around an incendiary device: surely, political pundits and Jeffersonians will be wrestling over Wiencek's explosive interpretations of the historical evidence—some of it newly discovered—for years to come . . . One of the incontestable strengths of Wiencek's book is the way it transports readers deep into the hierarchical world of Jefferson's Monticello."
—Maureen Corrigan, *Fresh Air*

"[Wiencek] reviews Jefferson's record like a prosecutor, hammering away at the evasions, rationalizations, and lies that have preserved Jefferson's reputation as a profoundly decent man trapped by the conventions of his own times . . . [He] does not reargue the tawdry details of the Sally Hemings affair. Rather, he invites readers to reflect seriously on one famous man's stunning refusal to provide moral leadership for a nation that desperately needed it . . . Wiencek reminds us that political courage requires more than the articulation of noble principles. It assumes a willingness to act on them."
—T. H. Breen, *The American Scholar*

"A remarkable re-creation of Monticello's economy and culture . . . Whether you agree or disagree with Wiencek's provocative analysis, it's a book worth taking seriously as we continue to struggle with slavery's legacy."
—Anne Bartlett, *BookPage*

"[A] meticulous account . . . Wiencek's vivid, detailed history casts a new slant on a complex man."
—*Publishers Weekly* (starred review)

Tom Cogill

Henry Wiencek

MASTER OF THE MOUNTAIN

Henry Wiencek, a nationally prominent historian and writer, is the author of several books, including *The Hairstons: An American Family in Black and White*, which won a National Book Critics Circle Award in 1999, and *An Imperfect God: George Washington, His Slaves, and the Creation of America* (FSG, 2003), which won a Los Angeles Times Book Prize. He lives in Charlottesville, Virginia.

ALSO BY HENRY WIENCEK

Mansions of the Virginia Gentry

Plantations of the Old South

The Smithsonian Guides to Historic America:
Southern New England and *Virginia and the Capital Region*

The Moodys of Galveston

National Geographic Guide to America's Great Houses
(with Donna M. Lucey)

Old Houses

The Hairstons: An American Family in Black and White

An Imperfect God: George Washington, His Slaves,
and the Creation of America

MASTER OF
THE MOUNTAIN

MASTER OF
THE MOUNTAIN

Thomas Jefferson and His Slaves

HENRY WIENCEK

Farrar, Straus and Giroux

New York

For my mother and father, with love

Farrar, Straus and Giroux
175 Varick Street, New York 10014

An excerpt from *Master of the Mountain* originally appeared, in slightly
different form, in *Smithsonian*.

The Library of Congress has cataloged the hardcover edition as follows:
Wiencek, Henry.
    Master of the mountain : Thomas Jefferson and his slaves
/ Henry Wiencek. — 1st ed.
        p.   cm.
    Includes bibliographical references and index.
    ISBN 978-0-374-29956-9 (alk. paper)
        1. Jefferson, Thomas, 1743–1826—Relations with slaves.
2. Monticello (Va.)—History.   3. Slaves—Virginia—Albemarle
County—History.   4. Plantation life—Virginia—Albemarle
County—History.   I. Title.

E332.2. W54 2012
973.4'6092—dc23

                                                2011052231

Paperback ISBN: 978-0-374-53402-8

Designed by Jonathan D. Lippincott

Our books may be purchased in bulk for promotional, educational,
or business use. Please contact your local bookseller or the Macmillan
Corporate and Premium Sales Department at 1-800-221-7945, extension 5442,
or by email at MacmillanSpecialMarkets@macmillan.com.

www.fsgbooks.com
www.twitter.com/fsgbooks • www.facebook.com/fsgbooks

5 7 9 10 8 6 4

Contents

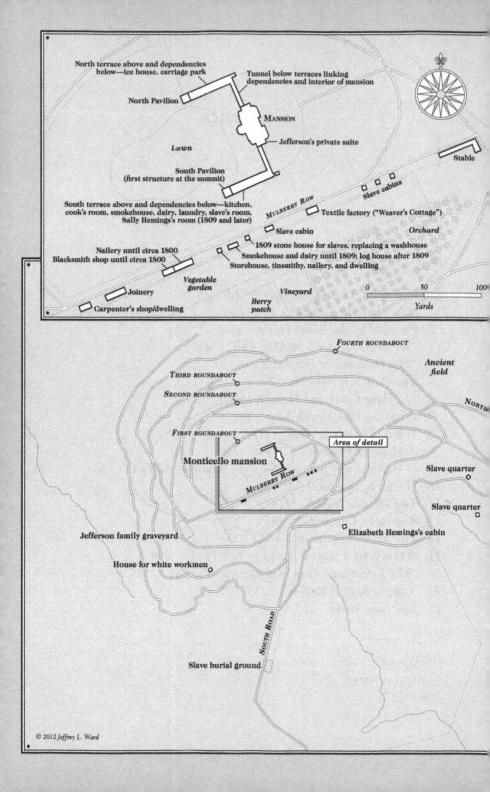

North terrace above and dependencies below—ice house, carriage park

Tunnel below terraces linking dependencies and interior of mansion

North Pavilion

MANSION

Jefferson's private suite

Lawn

Stable

South Pavilion
(first structure at the summit)

Slave cabins

MULBERRY ROW

Textile factory ("Weaver's Cottage")

Orchard

South terrace above and dependencies below—kitchen, cook's room, smokehouse, dairy, laundry, slave's room, Sally Hemings's room (1809 and later)

Slave cabin

1809 stone house for slaves, replacing a washhouse

Nailery until circa 1800

Blacksmith shop until circa 1800

Smokehouse and dairy until 1809; log house after 1809

Storehouse, tinsmithy, nailery, and dwelling

Vegetable garden

Vineyard

Joinery

Berry patch

0   50   100

Carpenter's shop/dwelling

Yards

FOURTH ROUNDABOUT

Ancient field

THIRD ROUNDABOUT

SECOND ROUNDABOUT

NORTH

FIRST ROUNDABOUT

Area of detail

Monticello mansion

Slave quarter

MULBERRY ROW

Slave quarter

Jefferson family graveyard

Elizabeth Hemings's cabin

House for white workmen

SOUTH ROAD

Slave burial ground

© 2012 Jeffrey L. Ward

Monticello Plantation

c. 1800–1826

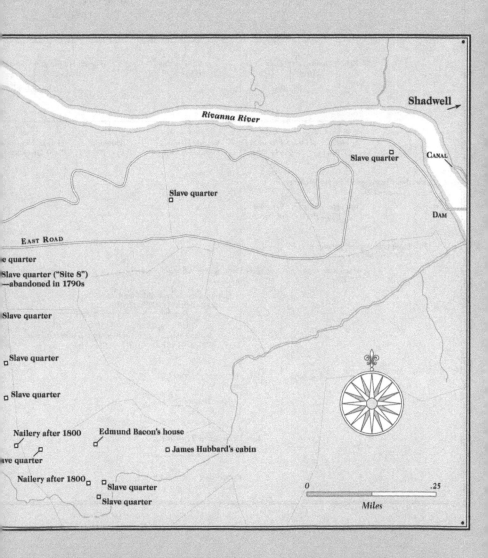

Shadwell

Rivanna River

CANAL

Slave quarter

DAM

Slave quarter

EAST ROAD

e quarter

Slave quarter ("Site 8")
—abandoned in 1790s

Slave quarter

Slave quarter

Slave quarter

Nailery after 1800   Edmund Bacon's house

James Hubbard's cabin

ave quarter

Nailery after 1800   Slave quarter

Slave quarter

0   .25

Miles

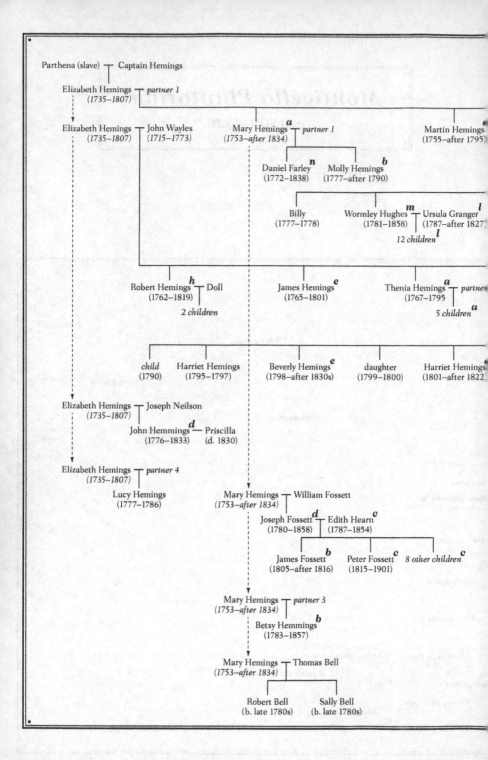

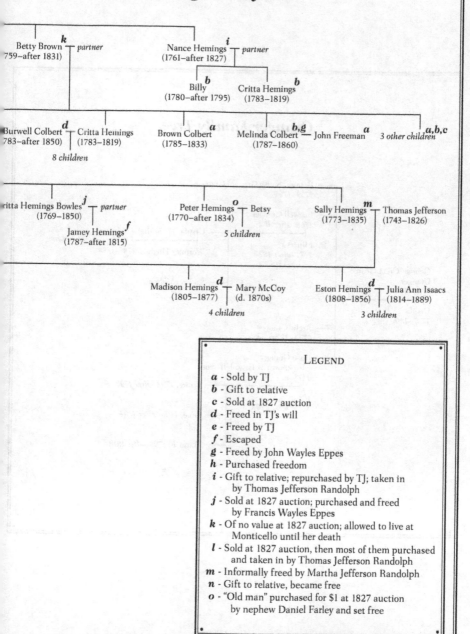

Hemings Family Tree

Betty Brown *k* — *partner* Nance Hemings *i* — *partner*
759–after 1831) (1761–after 1827)

Billy *b*   Critta Hemings *b*
(1780–after 1795)   (1783–1819)

Burwell Colbert *d* — Critta Hemings   Brown Colbert *a*   Melinda Colbert *b,g* — John Freeman *a*   3 other children *a,b,c*
783–after 1850)   (1783–1819)   (1785–1833)   (1787–1860)

8 children

ritta Hemings Bowles *j* — *partner*   Peter Hemings *o* — Betsy   Sally Hemings *m* — Thomas Jefferson
(1769–1850)   (1770–after 1834)   (1773–1835)   (1743–1826)

Jamey Hemings *f*   5 children
(1787–after 1815)

Madison Hemings *d* — Mary McCoy   Eston Hemings *d* — Julia Ann Isaacs
(1805–1877)   (d. 1870s)   (1808–1856)   (1814–1889)

4 children   3 children

LEGEND

a - Sold by TJ
b - Gift to relative
c - Sold at 1827 auction
d - Freed in TJ's will
e - Freed by TJ
f - Escaped
g - Freed by John Wayles Eppes
h - Purchased freedom
i - Gift to relative; repurchased by TJ; taken in
      by Thomas Jefferson Randolph
j - Sold at 1827 auction; purchased and freed
      by Francis Wayles Eppes
k - Of no value at 1827 auction; allowed to live at
      Monticello until her death
l - Sold at 1827 auction, then most of them purchased
      and taken in by Thomas Jefferson Randolph
m - Informally freed by Martha Jefferson Randolph
n - Gift to relative, became free
o - "Old man" purchased for $1 at 1827 auction
      by nephew Daniel Farley and set free

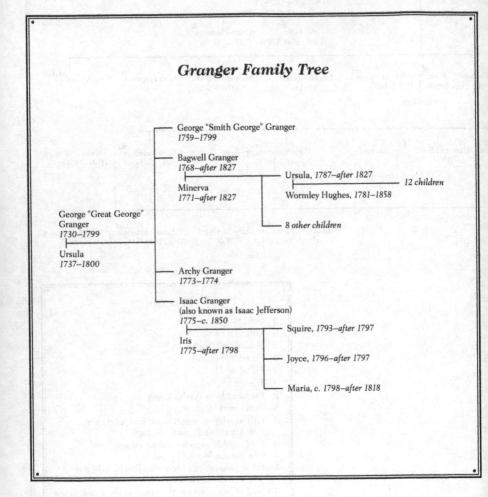

Granger Family Tree

George "Great George" Granger
1730–1799

Ursula
1737–1800

George "Smith George" Granger
1759–1799

Bagwell Granger
1768–after 1827

Minerva
1771–after 1827

Ursula, 1787–after 1827

Wormley Hughes, 1781–1858

12 children

8 other children

Archy Granger
1773–1774

Isaac Granger
(also known as Isaac Jefferson)
1775–c. 1850

Iris
1775–after 1798

Squire, 1793–after 1797

Joyce, 1796–after 1797

Maria, c. 1798–after 1818

Jefferson/Randolph Family Tree

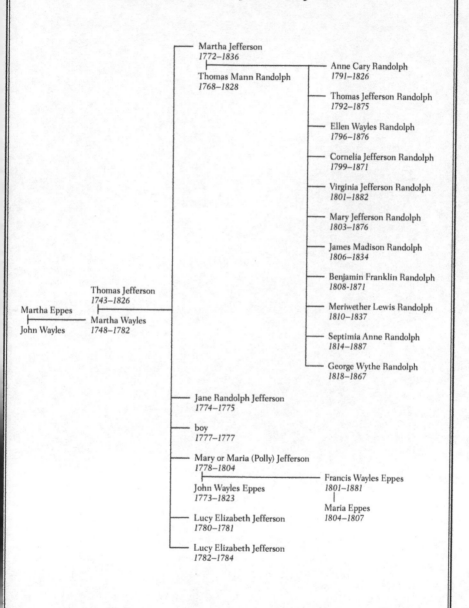

MASTER OF
THE MOUNTAIN

Introduction:
"This Steep, Savage Hill"

Thomas Jefferson's mansion stands atop his mountain like the Platonic ideal of a house: a perfect creation existing in an ethereal realm, literally above the clouds. To reach Monticello, you must ascend what a visitor called "this steep, savage hill," through a thick forest and swirls of mist that recede at the summit, as if by command of the master of the mountain. "If it had not been called Monticello," said another visitor, "I would call it Olympus, and Jove its occupant." The house that presents itself at the summit seems to contain some kind of secret wisdom encoded in its form. Seeing Monticello is like reading an old American Revolutionary manifesto—the emotions still rise. *This* is the architecture of the New World, brought forth by its guiding spirit.[1]

Under a churning gray sky on a ferociously hot July afternoon not long ago, a guide was telling a story about the plantation to a group of tourists. It was a story not of Jefferson but of a child slave and his impossible deliverance—an account of eleven-year-old Peter Fossett, sold here at auction. As the woman moved through Fossett's story, the wind rose and thunder erupted, crashing around the mountaintop—Nature's god attempting the *Eroica*. The guide and her group were jammed together under a shelter in the slave quarter just below the summit, and she said that anyone nervous about the approaching storm could run to the old tunnel beneath the house. But having heard the beginning of Fossett's story, no one moved.

Peter Fossett was sold in 1827 and split from his family in the enormous auction of 140 Monticello slaves after Jefferson had died. His new master promised to release him if he was paid enough money, but broke that promise. Forbidden to read on pain of the whip, Fossett defied the master and practiced his reading and writing at night in the dim glow of fading embers. He did this to save himself and his fellow slaves. The son of another slave said, "Peter Fossett taught my father to read and write by lightwood knots in the late hours of night when everyone was supposed to be asleep. They would steal away to a deserted cabin, over the hill from the big house, out of sight."[2] Having taught himself to read and write, Fossett did precisely what the slave masters feared he would do: he forged "free papers." These fake emancipation documents allowed his sister and others to escape Virginia. He ran away himself and was caught and brought back to Charlottesville, but he could not be stopped: "I resolved to get free or die in the attempt." He fled again and was caught again, and this time he was taken in handcuffs to the Richmond slave traders to be disposed of: "For the second time I was put up on the auction block and sold like a horse."

But there was an intervention—"God raised up friends for me."[3] When word of the sale reached certain people in Charlottesville, they bought Fossett and sent him to Ohio a free man. There, he became a businessman, a Baptist minister, and a smuggler of fugitives through the Underground Railroad. In his old age he had one wish, to see Monticello again, which lived in his memory as "an earthly paradise." The members of his church collected the necessary funds, and one last time Peter Fossett ascended Jefferson's mountain, to the spot where we were standing and listening to his story, and again he saw this place where his family had lived in slavery for four generations, washed clean of slavery by war.

From where our group stood in the old slave quarter, on the slope below the summit, I could just see the upper level of Jefferson's mansion and "the high cerebral dome" atop it.[4] Fossett's story hinted at the obvious ironies in this place. Up there lived the author of the Declaration of Independence; down here lived Peter Fossett, forger of emancipation papers that enacted the Declaration. On any plantation, irony is thick, but this story contained reversals that plunged deeper than mere irony.

I had read Peter Fossett's story, but that afternoon, when I *heard* it, I discovered elements in it I had missed. Told under a darkening sky and accompanied by the fortissimo booms of a looming storm, Fossett's powerful narrative of heroism, forgiveness, and transcendence shone as a victory over slavery. But in that setting his story also raised a brooding moral question. The visitors heard the lost chord: as one, they gasped when they heard that after being sold in 1827 at the age of eleven, Fossett remained a slave for another twenty-four years; it seemed impossible to them that a person like Peter Fossett could be held as a slave. In that wordless gasp, past and present, slave and free, black and white, imploded into one instant of human recognition.

The visitors had committed the sin of "presentism," judging the past by the standards of the present, but they couldn't help themselves: Fossett's story tore at their sense of justice and humanity. More than that: his courage, perseverance, and unshakable faith revealed the true character of a people who Thomas Jefferson had once said were inferior and had no place in America. How could these people have been held in slavery? It was an abomination, a betrayal of the very ideals Jefferson stood for. How could Jefferson not see it?

Actually, he did see it.

It is no great secret that an important part of the Declaration of Independence went missing during the debates in the Continental Congress, but if you look at one section drafted by Thomas Jefferson and then deleted by the Congress, it will tell you a lot about both Jefferson and the foulness he then saw in slavery: "a market where MEN should be bought & sold," a loathsome system, a precursor of what Walt Whitman would call "the seething materialistic and business vortices of the United States, in their present devouring relations, controlling and belittling everything else."[5]

Every summer, slave ships made their landings along the James River in Virginia, unloading their tragically diminished cargoes, for many slaves suffered, as Jefferson wrote, "miserable death in their transportation"; every vessel tossed overboard twenty, fifty, a hundred corpses in its passage across the sea. Jefferson most likely learned of this shrinkage of inventory from his father-in-law, John Wayles, who was one of the traders.

Jefferson might have seen other miseries with his own eyes. From the wharves, grim coffles of chained Africans were marched by the traders into the interior and offered for sale to planters and speculators who were vying for land and labor in a mad scramble of "grab, grab, grab," a triplet written by the old-line historian Douglas Southall Freeman, a Virginian not known for his radical views.[6]

When Jefferson courted the beautiful Martha Wayles, he spent evenings by the fire with her father, old John, who undoubtedly talked business with the young suitor, discoursing on slaves and the peaks and
valleys in the market for them. The incoming tide of slaves washed up
against the steps of the county courthouses. Every late summer and fall
the lawyers and magistrates had their routine of land transactions and
debt collections interrupted when overseers herded gangs of newly delivered African children into the courthouses for the magistrates to scruti-
nize, their task being to assign each child an age. When children reached
sixteen, they became taxable, so the planters had an interest in low estimates. Entered on the rolls of "tithables," the children got new names
provided by the master—Bobb, Mary, Phil, Cupid, Monkey. By one estimate, about a sixth of every slave-ship cargo consisted of children.[7]

They were Africans but they were human beings—Jefferson said so.
He stood aghast at "this execrable commerce . . . this assemblage of
horrors," a "cruel war against human nature itself, violating its most sacred rights of life & liberties," as he wrote in the deleted part of the
Declaration of Independence.[8] Several years earlier, shielding his own
identity, he had submitted an emancipation bill to the Virginia House of
Burgesses through a cousin, whom he then heard denounced and belit-
tled as someone who must hate America, "an enemy of his country."
Under his own name, as the Revolution approached in 1774, he floated a
radical idea in his manifesto *A Summary View of the Rights of British
America*: If only the country would stop the slave trade, it could proceed
to "the enfranchisement of the slaves we have." Some enslaved families
had been in America for generations. Jefferson's own wife had six half
siblings who were slaves. Then in his soaring, damning, fiery prose he
denounced the "execrable commerce" in the Declaration; but the Continental Congress struck the passage because South Carolina and Georgia,
crying out for more slaves, would not abide shutting down the market.

Somewhere in a short span of years during the 1780s and into the
early 1790s, a transformation came over Jefferson. "One cannot question the genuineness of Jefferson's liberal dreams," writes the historian
David Brion Davis. "He was one of the first statesmen in any part of the
world to advocate concrete measures for restricting and eradicating Negro slavery." But in the 1790s, Davis continues, "the most remarkable
thing about Jefferson's stand on slavery is his immense silence." And

later, Davis finds, Jefferson's emancipation efforts "virtually ceased."[9] In the early 1780s, Jefferson formulated theories about black inferiority, so it has seemed plausible that this brilliant, admirable Founder slid from his Olympian idealism as he was slowly overcome by racism. Yet when he was in France in 1789, years after first setting forth his racial theories, Jefferson wrote that on his return to Virginia he planned to train slaves to set them free in the certainty they would become "good citizens."[10]

"Citizens" . . . "enfranchisement of the slaves"—these are not words that a lawyer and statesman, the author of the Declaration, would use lightly. Nor are these the rash effusions of a young man; Jefferson was forty-six when he outlined his scheme to train Monticello slaves and usher them into the status of citizens. But then he changed.

We can be forgiven if we interrogate Jefferson posthumously about slavery. It is not at all "presentist" to do so. Many people of his own time, taking Jefferson at his word and seeing him as the embodiment of the country's highest ideals, appealed to him: *Give us a plan; take the lead; show the country how to end slavery.* When he evaded and rationalized, his admirers were frustrated and mystified; it felt like praying to a stone. The Virginia abolitionist Moncure Conway, noting Jefferson's enduring reputation as a would-be emancipator, remarked scornfully, "Never did a man achieve more fame for what he did not do."[11]

The historian Joseph Ellis advanced the intriguing counterintuitive theory that Jefferson's involvement with his slave Sally Hemings might explain the disappearance of his emancipationist fervor: "If Jefferson's relationship with Hemings began in the late 1780s, it would mean that he began to back away from a leadership position in the anti-slavery movement just around the time that his affair with Sally Hemings started."[12] It is a good theory, but it cannot answer the $20,000 question.

Descendants of Monticello slaves passed down an intriguing fragment of oral history that surfaced in the 1940s. According to the oral history, Jefferson "misused large sums of money entrusted to him for the benefit of the Negroes."[13] This isolated shard of evidence seemed at first glance to be palpably false, a vindictive fabrication made by embittered people. But as it happened, Jefferson's friend and fellow Revolutionary War hero Thaddeus Kosciuszko offered him nearly $20,000 in his will to free as many Monticello slaves as that sum would buy and send them anywhere Jefferson wanted, with equipment to start life on their own.

The offer seemed to satisfy Jefferson's needs and wishes: he could pay off some debts and fulfill his stated intention of sending freed slaves to Africa or the West Indies or anywhere else. But he left the money on the table. Clearly, some very powerful motive was at work to make him keep his slaves.

In seeking some clarity in his universe, we find instead a murky place, not just strange, but very nearly mad. The system deranged even language; or rather, language could not contain the reality it was compelled to describe. For instance, this utterance from Jefferson's grandson Jeff Randolph takes several readings to decode: "Having the double aspect of persons and property the feelings for the person was always impairing its value as property." In that garbled sentence Jeff pointed toward a governing principle of this universe: the execrable commerce had taken control, devouring human relationships.

As Jefferson was counting up the agricultural profits and losses of his plantation in a letter to President Washington in 1792, it occurred to him that there was a phenomenon he had perceived at Monticello but never actually measured. He proceeded to calculate it in a barely legible, scribbled note in the middle of a page, enclosed in brackets. What Jefferson set out clearly for the first time was that he was making a 4 percent profit every year on the birth of black children. The enslaved people were yielding him a bonanza, a perpetual human dividend at compound interest. Jefferson wrote, "I allow nothing for losses by death, but, on the contrary, shall presently take credit four per cent. per annum, for their increase over and above keeping up their own numbers."[14] His plantation was producing inexhaustible human assets. The percentage was predictable.

In another communication from the early 1790s, Jefferson takes the 4 percent formula further and quite bluntly advances the notion that slavery presented an investment strategy for the future. He writes that an acquaintance who had suffered financial reverses "should have been invested in negroes." He advises that if the friend's family had any cash left, "every farthing of it [should be] laid out in land and negroes, which besides a present support bring a silent profit of from 5. to 10. per cent in this country by the increase in their value."[15] We might not grasp a world where a man can own his wife's siblings as slaves, but investments, markets, "silent profit"—these we can recognize.

The irony is that Jefferson sent his 4 percent formula to George Washington, who freed his slaves precisely because slavery had made human beings into money, like "Cattle in the market," and this disgusted him.[16] Yet Jefferson was right, prescient, about the investment value of slaves. A startling statistic emerged in the 1970s when economists taking a hardheaded look at slavery found that on the eve of the Civil War, enslaved black people, in the aggregate, formed the second most valuable capital asset in the United States. As David Brion Davis sums up their findings: "In 1860, the value of Southern slaves was about three times the amount invested in manufacturing or railroads nationwide."[17] The only asset more valuable than the black people was the land itself. The formula Jefferson had stumbled upon became the engine not only of Monticello but of the entire slaveholding South and the Northern industries, shippers, banks, insurers, and investors who weighed risk against returns and bet on slavery. The words Jefferson used—"their increase"—became magic words.

Jefferson's 4 percent theorem threatens the comforting notion that he had no real awareness of what he was doing, that he was "stuck" with or "trapped" in slavery, an obsolete, unprofitable, burdensome legacy. The date of Jefferson's calculation lines up with the waning of his emancipationist fervor. Ellis is probably right when he speculates that Hemings had something to do with Jefferson's deciding that he could live with slavery, but we must add this corollary: Jefferson began to back away from antislavery just around the time he computed the silent profit of the "peculiar institution."

I suppose that if you squint at this world with one eye closed, you might claim that Jefferson was a progressive master, with training programs and incentive plans calculated to instill good character, diligence, and discipline. But this innovator, a Henry Ford of slavery, presided over a world that was sealed: *Work as hard as you like—there is no way out.*

And this world was crueler than we have been led to believe. A letter has recently come to light describing how Monticello's young black boys, "the small ones," aged ten, eleven, or twelve, were whipped to get them to work in Jefferson's nail factory, whose profits paid the mansion's grocery bills. This passage about children being lashed had been suppressed—deliberately deleted from the published record in the 1953 edition of Jefferson's *Farm Book*, containing five hundred pages of plantation papers and an introduction that asserts, "Jefferson came close to creating on his own plantations the ideal rural community."[18] That edition of the *Farm Book* still serves as a standard reference for research into the way Monticello worked.

Peter Fossett's story suggests that Monticello was a carefully crafted illusion. Fossett was a Hemings and thus enjoyed extraordinary privileges on the mountain. He said that as a child he owned a fancy suit and a silver watch and that "as a matter of fact we did not need to know that we were slaves." But then came the day when even he, a Hemings, instantly, shockingly, became aware of what he had always been: part of the silent profit, something less than a man and more "like a horse." In a trice he was devoured, he became money, and his innocent world was gone—it had all been an illusion. The slaves had an expression for this: at any time the master could "put you in his pocket."[19]

The sale smashed the illusions that Jefferson's grandson had nurtured about Monticello. Thomas Jefferson was in his grave when the plantation and its people were auctioned, but his grandson Jeff Randolph saw Peter Fossett, his mother, and his siblings go on the block. He wrote a brief, melancholy remark about that day on the mountain when people he had known well, including some who were related to him, were sold and dispersed. He could not shake the emotion of the event, and an image from the remotest past came to him to describe this occasion that should not be occurring: he said it was a scene like "a captured village in ancient times when all were sold as slaves."[20] It is as if he had never thought of these people as slaves until that moment when the auctioneer's hammer came down and they were taken away. The scales fell from his eyes. There were processes at work that Jeff had not quite grasped. He was an owner, a master—he was in charge—but he was one of the "economic overlords of society," as Reinhold Niebuhr writes, "who wielded a form of power so covert that it betrayed them into sentimental illusions."[21]

Nothing at Monticello was straightforward. How could Peter Fossett call Monticello "an earthly paradise" when it was the domain of slavery?

In a place where the small ones are whipped, memory finds paths away from a humiliation too terrible to accept. Picture it: your child is lashed and no god raises up a friend but the whole world tells you that you are inferior, that you deserve what you get, that you are serving a Founder. *It is not Jefferson's fault; he is a very great man and we are poor ignorant creatures. No one must ever know.* This was the inner architecture of slavery.

The very existence of slavery in the era of the American Revolution presents a paradox, and we have largely been content to leave it at that, since a paradox can offer a comforting state of moral suspended animation. Oddly enough, embracing paradox has become a badge of tough-minded realism. Thus Joseph Ellis derides a historian whom he labels "neo-abolitionist" for refusing to join him in accepting what he calls the "muddled reality" of the founding era.[22] It is an old impulse. When abolitionism was gathering climactic force in the 1850s, Herman Melville put a similarly soothing sentiment on the lips of one of his characters: "The past is passed; why moralize upon it? Forget it."[23] But Melville wrote with bitter irony.

Jefferson animates the paradox. Somehow he rationalized an abomination to the point where an absolute moral reversal was reached and he made slavery fit into America's national enterprise. This book is about that process.

1

"Let There Be Justice"

The thunderstorm that shook the mountain during the telling of Peter Fossett's story passed. We tourists were deposited back into the present, with shafts of sunlight illuminating a peaceful scene—a broad pathway stretching into the distance, disappearing over the curve of the hillside. Jefferson named it Mulberry Row for the fast-growing shade trees he planted here in the 1790s. One thousand yards long, it was the main street of the African-American hamlet atop Monticello Mountain. The plantation was a small town in everything but name, not just because of its size, but in its complexity. Skilled artisans and house slaves occupied cabins on Mulberry Row alongside hired white workers; a few slaves lived in rooms in the mansion's south dependency wing; some slept where they worked. Most of Monticello's slaves lived in clusters of cabins scattered down the mountain and on outlying farms. In his lifetime Jefferson owned more than 600 slaves. At any one time about 100 slaves lived on the mountain; the highest slave population, in 1817, was 140.[1]

The labyrinths of Monticello mirror the ambiguities of its maker. As you approach the house, you are taken in by one of Jefferson's cleverest tricks: through the artful arrangement of windows he achieved the illusion of having his three-story building appear to have only one floor. He *had* to have a house like the ones he'd seen in Paris when he was the U.S. minister there. "All the new and good houses are of a single story," Jefferson said, in the tone of someone who has discovered a new law of physics.

So in the 1790s he tore apart his first house—eight rooms, two floors—and began work on a twenty-one-room mansion, ingeniously concealing its bulk. Its innovations included skylights, indoor privies, and a system of drainpipes and cisterns to capture rainwater. He brainstormed on novel solutions for ventilating smells and smoke, such as tunnels to carry away the odor of the privies and an underground piping system to direct the smoke of cooking fires away from the house. He built the privy tunnels, through which a slave had to crawl once a month, for a dollar, to clean them; he dropped the idea of the underground pipes, considered smoke-stacks in the shape of obelisks, and finally settled on just having chimneys.[2]

One feature that Monticello does not have is a grand staircase, usu-ally the centerpiece of a Virginia squire's entrance hall. A waste of space, Jefferson thought, and in any event he didn't need one, because he rarely went upstairs. He had everything he needed in his private, L-shaped suite of rooms on the main floor—the bedroom, the study or "cabinet," the book room, and the greenhouse, with its access to a private terrace and the lawns. A visitor called this spacious domain Jefferson's "sanctum sanctorum." His extended family—beloved daughter, impecunious son-in-law, widowed sister, grandchildren, nieces, and nephews—packed themselves into the second and third floors, reached by an extremely nar-row, steep, and winding staircase—a treacherous ascent for anyone and doubly dangerous for someone carrying a load or a squirming infant. Jeff Randolph recalled the cramped quarters allotted him as a child: "I slept a whole winter in an outer closet."[3] The granddaughters, desperate for private space where they could read and write, improvised their own sitting room out of an architectural gap over a portico, contending with wasps for control of the room.[4]

Jefferson grasped the ways geometry talks to the eye and mind, and in his hands that arid specialty yielded visual music. He imparted an uncanny sense of motion to the inanimate mass of bricks, glass, and wood, playing variations on geometrical themes. The facades of Monti-cello and many of its rooms have no real corners, which puts the eye, expecting right angles, off-balance. (His design for his country retreat, Poplar Forest, which he started in 1806, called for a pure octagon con-taining a cube.) Today we are accustomed to skylights, but in his time people did not expect to stand indoors in gentle sunlight coming from above, banishing the expected shadows and making others.

So innovative and eccentric in its irregularities and geometric illusions, Monticello not only baffled but irritated people of Jefferson's time, who expected something more conventionally pompous. "This incomprehensible pile," grumbled one visitor, calling the house "a monument of ingenious extravagance . . . without unity or uniformity." Another visitor, granted a rare tour of Jefferson's private suite of rooms by the master himself, pronounced herself "much disappointed in its appearance, and I do not think with its numerous divisions and arches it is as impressive as one large room would have been." Having heard the murmurings, Jefferson had to acknowledge that his "essay in architecture" was derided as being "among the curiosities of the neighborhood."[5]

Then as now, people were charmed by gadgets, and Monticello was full of them. "Everything has a whimsical and droll appearance," said one guest.[6] One enters the parlor through an automatic double door in which both doors open or close when just one is pushed, being linked by an unseen chain under the floor. A visitor to his sanctum sanctorum would have found telescopes, a microscope, thermometers, surveying equipment, and an astronomical clock for predicting eclipses. "His mind designs more than the day can fulfill," a visitor remarked. Laid up one day with rheumatism, Jefferson passed the hours "calculating the hour lines of a . . . dial for the latitude of this place."[7] To satisfy an omnivorous mental appetite, he designed an ingenious revolving book holder that accommodated five open volumes at a time. Reclining on a chaise, he composed his voluminous correspondence at a polygraph, a two-pen, two-sheet proto–copying machine that produced a duplicate of a letter as it was written. Even his bed is an item of interest. He placed it in an alcove with open sides—on one side lay his dressing room, on the other his study—but the reason for the open alcove arrangement was not to provide convenient access to one room or the other from the bed but to create a "breezeway" through which the cool night air would flow with increased speed. It is often said that he invented the polygraph, which he did not, and to this day the rumor persists that his bed could be raised on ropes into a hidden compartment in the ceiling—a false story that expresses the abiding belief that Jefferson practiced all manner of disappearing tricks.

Indeed, a great deal went on here out of sight. In designing the mansion, Jefferson followed a precept laid down two centuries earlier by Palladio: "We must contrive a building in such a manner that the finest and most noble parts of it be the most exposed to public view, and the less agreeable disposed in byplaces, and removed from sight as much as possible."[8]

The mansion sits atop a long tunnel through which slaves, unseen, hurried back and forth carrying platters of food, fresh tableware, ice, beer, wine, and linens while above them twenty, thirty, or forty guests sat listening to Jefferson's dinner-table conversation. At one end of the tunnel lay the icehouse, at the other the kitchen, a hive of ceaseless activity where the enslaved cooks and their helpers produced one course after another.

During dinner Jefferson would open a panel in the side of the fireplace, insert an empty wine bottle, and seconds later pull out a full bottle. We can imagine that he would delay explaining how this magic took place until an astonished guest put the question to him. The panel concealed a narrow dumbwaiter that descended to the basement. When Jefferson put an empty bottle in the compartment, a slave waiting in the basement pulled the dumbwaiter down, removed the empty, inserted a fresh bottle, and sent it up to the master in a matter of seconds. Similarly, platters of hot food magically appeared on a revolving door fitted with shelves, and the used plates disappeared from sight on the same contrivance. Guests could not see or hear any of the activity, nor the links between the visible world and the invisible that magically produced Jefferson's abundance.

Looming above Mulberry Row was a long terrace where Jefferson appeared every day at first light, walking alone with his thoughts. A slave looking up from Mulberry Row would see a very imposing figure outlined against the magnificent architectural features of his mansion. Jefferson was a tall man, over six feet two inches, well muscled, and "straight as a gun barrel," his overseer Edmund Bacon said; "he had an iron constitution and was very strong."[9] One of his slaves, the blacksmith Isaac Granger, remembered his master as "a tall, strait-bodied man as ever you see, right square-shouldered . . . a straight-up man, long face, high nose."[10] Jefferson owned a spring-driven strength tester called a dynamometer that he imported from France to gauge the force needed to pull a new plow he was designing. He and his neighbors decided to test their own muscles on this proto-Nautilus machine. His son-in-law

Colonel Thomas Mann Randolph could out-pull all contestants, but Jefferson beat him.[11]

From his terrace Jefferson looked out upon an industrious, well-organized enterprise of black coopers, smiths, nail makers, a brewer, cooks professionally trained in French cuisine, a glazier, painters, millers, and weavers. Black managers, slaves themselves, oversaw other slaves. A team of highly skilled artisans constructed Jefferson's coach. The household staff ran what was essentially a midsized hotel, where some sixteen slaves waited upon the needs of a daily horde of guests.

Below the mansion there stood John Hemmings's* cabinetmaking shop, called the joinery; a dairy; a stable; a small textile factory; and a vast garden carved from the mountainside—the cluster of industries Jefferson launched to supply his plantation and bring in cash. "To be independent for the comforts of life," Jefferson said, "we must fabricate them ourselves." He was speaking of America's need to develop manufacturing, but he had learned that truth on his plantation.[12]

Jefferson looked down from his terrace onto a community of slaves he knew very well—an extended family and network of related families that had been in his ownership for two, three, or four generations. Though there were several surnames among the slaves on the mountaintop—Fossett, Hern, Colbert, Gillette, Brown, Hughes—they were all Hemingses by blood, descendants of the matriarch Elizabeth "Betty" Hemings, or Hemings relatives by marriage. "A peculiar fact about his house servants was that we were all related to one another," Peter Fossett said. Jefferson's grandson Jeff Randolph observed, "Mr. Js Mechanics and his entire household of servants . . . consisted of one family connection and their wives."[13]

At dawn the cooks Edith Fossett and Fanny Hern would already be at work preparing breakfast for the household in the kitchen beneath the terrace, right below Jefferson's feet. When he was president and they were teenagers, Jefferson had personally selected them to live in the White House as apprentices to his French chef. Edith was the wife of the blacksmith Joseph Fossett, the son of Mary Hemings.

Mary Hemings's younger sister Sally would be cleaning Jefferson's private suite, removing the chamber pot and the tub of cold water in which the master soaked his feet every morning upon awakening. In

---

*John spelled the name "Hemmings."

the other rooms of the mansion, Jefferson's daughter's family was stirring. He had asked them to move into Monticello when his presidential term ended—Martha had been with her father in Washington and before that in France—so in 1809 Monticello became the residence of Martha and her husband, Colonel Randolph, and their eight children, with three more children to come in the next few years.

Jefferson's grandchildren knew the slaves on the mountaintop very well. They were devoted to John Hemmings and he to them. John and his wife, Priscilla, had no children, but to the presidential grandchildren Priscilla Hemmings was "Mammy" and John Hemmings "Daddy." The grandchildren felt perfectly at ease descending on "Daddy" Hemmings in his joinery. "All other amusements failing," one granddaughter remembered, "there was a visit to 'Daddy' in the carpenter's shops to beg for nails and bits of wood, or to urge on the completion of 'a box for my drawings,' or a table, or stand, or a flower box. 'Yes yes! my little mistises, but Grandpapa [Jefferson] comes first! There are new bookshelves to be made, trellises for the roses, besides farm work to be done.' This reply brought a clamor of tongues and 'You know Daddy you promised!'"[14]

A relic of one of these visits turned up in an archaeologist's sieve. In Hemmings's joinery the diggers found a three-inch-long, jagged shard of broken slate, inscribed with an enigma, a passage of cursive writing:

Beneath . . .
As ugly B. . . .
Short . . .

The slate had snapped apart, leaving only those words of a text that might have been part of a poem. Jefferson's grandchildren taught some of the slaves to read and write, and this might be a remnant of a lesson in the carpentry shop. Jefferson countenanced his grandchildren teaching the favored slaves (sixteen-year-old Cornelia gave John Hemmings a dictionary!) but did not entirely approve of it.[15] "He was in favor of teaching the slaves to learn to read print and no more," one slave remembered; "to teach them to write would enable them to forge papers [and] they could no longer be kept in subjugation."[16] But writing was more than a tool for would-be escapers. It was the era of the Enlightenment, and "the very idea of writing oneself free was typical of the eighteenth century, when writing seemed to be the visible sign of reason and imagination," writes one historian.[17] Archaeologists have found writing slates and pencils all over the mountain, suggesting that many people tried to make themselves literate there.

For decades archaeologists have been scouring Mulberry Row, finding mundane artifacts that testify to the ways life was lived in the workshops and cabins. They have found saw blades, a large drill bit, an axhead, blacksmith's pincers, a wall bracket made in the joinery for a clock in the mansion, scissors, thimbles, locks and a key, and finished nails forged, cut, and hammered by the nail boys.

A large fragment of animal bone showed the marks of a gouge used for punching out buttons. It had been partly used and then discarded, evoking the image of a particular day in the distant past when someone had her bellyful of making buttons and just threw the damned thing away.

There were marbles, dominoes, and a toy tea bowl left by the children—perhaps by Peter Fossett—as well as part of a Jew's harp and part of a violin neck. One Christmas, Cornelia was walking outside when she was stopped short by music. She turned and saw a "fiddler as he stood with half closed eyes and head thrown back, with one foot keeping time to his own scraping in the midst of a circle of attentive and admiring auditors."[18]

The archaeologists also found a bundle of raw nailrod—a lost measure of iron handed out to a nail boy one dawn. Why was this bundle found in the dirt, unworked, instead of forged, cut, and hammered the way the boss told them? Once, a missing bundle of rod had started a fight in the nailery that got one boy's skull bashed in and another sold south to terrify the rest of the children—"in terrorem" were Jefferson's words—"as if he were put out of the way by death."[19] Perhaps this very bundle was the cause of the fight. But the whole episode, showing the underside of the smoothly functioning plantation machine, is for later in this book.

Weaving slavery into a narrative about Thomas Jefferson usually presents a challenge to authors, but one writer managed to spin this vicious attack and terrible punishment of a nailery boy into a charming plantation tale. In a 1941 biography of Jefferson for "young adults" (ages twelve to sixteen), the author wrote: "In this beehive of industry no discord or revilings found entrance: there were no signs of discontent on the black shining faces as they worked under the direction of their master. . . . The women sang at their tasks and the children old enough to work made nails leisurely, not too overworked for a prank now and then." It might seem unfair to mock the misconceptions and sappy prose of "a simpler era," except that this book, *The Way of an Eagle*, and hundreds like it shaped the attitudes of generations of people about slavery and African-Americans. *Time* magazine chose it as one of the "important books" of 1941 in the children's literature category, and it gained a second life in America's libraries when it was reprinted in 1961 as *Thomas Jefferson: Fighter for Freedom and Human Rights*.[20]

In describing what Mulberry Row looked like, William Kelso, the archaeologist who excavated it in the 1980s, writes, "There can be little doubt that a relatively shabby Main Street stood there."[21] Kelso notes that "throughout Jefferson's tenure, it seems safe to conclude that the spartan Mulberry Row buildings . . . made a jarring impact on the Monticello landscape."

It seems puzzling that Jefferson placed Mulberry Row, with its slave cabins and work buildings, so close to the mansion, but we are projecting the present onto the past. Today, tourists can walk freely up and down the old slave quarter, and they have computer-generated images and sounds magically transmitted into their smartphones. But in Jefferson's time guests didn't go there, nor could they see the cabins from the mansion or the lawn. Only one visitor left a description of Mulberry Row, and she got a glimpse of it only because she was a close friend of Jefferson's, someone who could be counted upon to look with the right attitude. When she published her account in the Richmond *Enquirer*, she wrote that the cabins would appear "poor and uncomfortable" only to people of "*northern* feelings."

There is a scene from the construction of Monticello that would make an excellent diorama, one of those old-fashioned museum exhibits that make you feel you are actually looking through a window into the past.

Jefferson moved onto Monticello Mountain as a twenty-seven-year-old bachelor in November 1770. During a snowstorm on a bitterly cold day he went to observe the digging of a cellar. Wrapped in a coat, the young master watched a sixteen-year-old girl dig into frozen clay. The crew consisted of four men, two sixteen-year-old girls, and "a lad"—all slaves hired by his contractor.[22] He wrote a description of the work, taking note of the crew's output for the day, which lasted about eight and a half hours in the frigid weather. Half-frozen, the slaves took frequent breaks to warm up by a fire. An instinctive engineer and calculator, Jefferson measured their output, a hole about 3 feet deep and 132 feet square. He was not commenting on slavery but making engineering and labor notes, setting down for future reference how much digging could be accomplished by youthful laborers on a terrible day.

Our diorama depicting the harsh reality of slave labor—teenage girls and a boy digging frozen clay in a snowstorm to make the cellar of a great mansion—might stir a sense of injustice in our modern breasts and inspire us to wonder what the young Jefferson might have thought about this scene.

Perhaps we think we know the answers: he inherited slavery; it was the accepted system; he believed that black people were inferior; it was impossible to get anything done in Virginia without slaves. Attempting to quiet debate on this vexing, politically charged subject, Dinesh D'Souza echoes this sentiment when he writes, "Jefferson and the founders faced two profound obstacles. The first was that virtually all of them recognized the degraded condition of blacks in America and understood it posed a formidable hurdle to granting blacks the rights of citizenship."[23]

But if we push an imaginary button on our imaginary diorama, we will hear a voice-over narration in Jefferson's own words. After describing the work in his notebook, he wrote down a verse from Alexander Pope expressing his own condition: "Let day improve on day, and year on year; / Without a pain, a trouble, or a fear." So it might seem that D'Souza was right, that Jefferson had no moral qualms about what he saw. But the voice-over continues: after copying Pope's optimistic, forward-looking verse, Jefferson wrote an aphorism in Latin—"Fiat justitia, ruet coelum"—"Let there be justice, even if the sky falls."[24] Years later he would call this his guiding maxim.

Violent contradictions roil the pages—a turmoil of doubts, loathings, self-recrimination, all vying with the imperative to create a productive plantation and the imperative to have peace and justice on the mountain. Jefferson had lately read a savage indictment of slavery by the English poet William Shenstone, a subversive, damning attack by a troublesome foreign intellectual, an attack on the American system that Jefferson did not ignore or rebut but copied into his notebook. He copied out the lines proclaiming that the country of the slave master is "stain'd with blood, and crimson'd o'er with crimes." He copied the sentiment that the master is "the stern tyrant that embitters life." In Shenstone's poem, the voice of a slave, torn from his native land, denounces the masters, their cruelty, and their hypocrisy: "Rich by our toils, and by our sorrows gay, / They ply our labours, and enhance our pains."

The pages of Jefferson's notebook offer a diorama of the young man's psyche—the architect and planter struggling against the moralist, seeking a way to absorb this foul, repugnant system into his interior landscape and into the exterior landscape he is shaping. Jefferson planned a mountaintop cemetery where he would bury both blacks and whites in common ground—"one half to the use of my own family; the other of strangers, servants." The graveyard would pay everlasting tribute to the slaves: "On the grave of a favorite and faithful servant might be a pyramid erected of the rough rock stone, the pedestal made plain to receive an inscription."[25] He wrote out an "Inscription for an African Slave" using Shenstone's verse that calls the master a tyrant, making a monument of self-denunciation.

It is highly ironic that Jefferson planned a common burying ground for blacks and whites. Much of the bitterness over the question of Sally Hemings and her relation to him arose from the wish of some slave descendants to be buried in the Jefferson family cemetery on the mountaintop—a request that was rejected by the "documented" Jefferson descendants who own the cemetery. Yet their distinguished ancestor had envisioned everyone resting together for eternity. As it turned out, Monticello ended up with separate cemeteries.

Jefferson's inner debate continues in the pages of his notebook. His copying a passage from Horace, the great Roman poet of the pastoral life, suggests that he is taking moral refuge in the knowledge that he was an heir to classical slavery. "Happy the man who, far from business cares . . . works his ancestral acres."[26] Horace's character, a moneylender, retires to the countryside after a strenuous, stressful life. The

Bro, this is so wrong.

future that Jefferson envisions for himself at Monticello is like that of Horace's Roman in his villa: "what joy to see the sheep, hurrying homeward . . . to see the wearied oxen . . . and the home-bred slaves, troop of a wealthy house."

Jefferson had grown up among "home-bred slaves." As a child, he had been conditioned to feel safe among the black household servants, enveloped in a relationship of trust, loyalty, and intimacy. They were his guardians. He preserved a memory, from the age of two, of being lifted into the arms of a slave who held the young master safely through a long journey—"he often declared that his earliest recollection in life was of being . . . handed up to a servant on horseback, by whom he was carried on a pillow for a long distance."[27]

Archaeology has yielded an insight into the psychology of the slavery Jefferson grew up with. From his mountaintop Jefferson could look down on the site of his old family home, Shadwell, a modest frame house. Marks in the ground show that a fence separated it from four slave cabins housing some thirty people. A handful of trusted slaves lived in a cabin and kitchen building within the pale, but fences and gates kept most of the slaves at a distance.*[28] Jefferson wrote down a vivid recollection of someone bullying or beating a slave: "The parent storms, the child looks on, catches the lineaments of wrath, puts on the same airs in the circle of smaller slaves, gives loose to his worst of passions, and thus nursed, educated, and daily exercised in tyranny, cannot but be stamped by it with odious peculiarities." He did not identify "the parent," but the scene is so vividly described that it was likely Jefferson's own mother or father.[29]

As he grew into manhood, Jefferson said that he'd felt virtually alone in believing that the Africans were more than just the equivalent of livestock. He wrote in 1814 to a fellow Virginian:

→ okay but you're still treating them like livestock if you OWN them!

From those of the former generation who were in the fulness of age when I came into public life, . . . I soon saw that nothing was to be hoped. Nursed and educated in the daily habit of seeing the degraded condition, both bodily and mental, of those

---

*Jefferson's father, Peter, gave his slaves only a pot and a pothook; everything else they had to get for themselves.

unfortunate beings, not reflecting that that degradation was very much the work of themselves & their fathers, few minds have yet doubted but that they were as legitimate subjects of property as their horses and cattle. The quiet and monotonous course of colonial life has been disturbed by no alarm, and little reflection on the value of liberty.[30]

A Virginia law enacted in 1723 forbade owners to free a slave "upon any pretence whatsoever," with one exception. A slave who performed some meritorious service could be freed, but the manumission had to be approved by the governor and the governor's council.[31] Though slaves were private property, the government interfered with an individual's right to manumit that property because private choice could undermine the institution of slavery. If owners could free slaves at will, there would be no stopping the growth of a class of free blacks. Thus the maintenance of slavery required the imposition, by the government, of rigid class discipline among the slave owners. The Virginia government, entirely controlled by slaveholders, policed their peers to ensure that no emancipationist mavericks rose up among their number.

Jefferson determined to do something about a system that treated people like cattle. After his election in 1769 to Virginia's House of Burgesses, as he writes in his autobiography, "I made one effort in that body for the permission of the emancipation of slaves." In his 1814 letter he describes what happened:

> In the first or second session of the Legislature after I became a member, I drew to this subject the attention of Colonel Bland, one of the oldest, ablest, & most respected members, and he undertook to move for certain moderate extensions of the protection of the laws to these people. I seconded his motion, and, as a younger member, was more spared in the debate; but he was denounced as an enemy of his country, & was treated with the grossest indecorum.[32]

He blamed a hidebound mentality for the vociferous rejection of his emancipation idea. The lawmakers were deaf to principled argument: "during the regal government, nothing liberal could expect success."

Jefferson made his emancipation proposal around the same time he took on an intriguing legal case, *Howell v. Netherland*, that illuminates the shifting, increasingly ambiguous racial borderland in colonial Virginia, where strict enforcement of racial laws could have the effect of making white people black.

In the winter of 1769, Samuel Howell, a mixed-race indentured servant who had escaped from his master, sought a lawyer in Williamsburg to represent him in suing for freedom. His grandmother was a free white woman, but his grandfather was black, so Howell had become entrapped in a law that prescribed indentured servitude to age thirty-one for certain mixed-race people "to prevent that abominable mixture of white men or women with negroes or mulattoes."[33] Howell, aged twenty-seven, was not indentured forever, since he would be freed in about four years, but nonetheless Jefferson felt angry enough over this denial of rights that he took Howell's case pro bono.

Jefferson later became famous for his diatribes against racial mixing, but his arguments on behalf of Howell, made more than a decade before he wrote down his infamous racial theories, suggest that the younger Jefferson harbored doubts about the supposed "evil" of miscegenation. The word "seems" in the following sentence suggests that he did not quite accept the prevailing racial ideology: "The purpose of the act was to punish and deter women from that confusion of species, which the legislature seems to have considered as an evil."

Having just one black grandparent, Howell probably appeared very nearly white. But with the full knowledge that Howell had African blood, Jefferson argued to the justices that he should be immediately freed. He made his case partly on a strict reading of the original law, which imposed servitude only on the first generation of mixed-race children and could not have been intended, Jefferson argued, "to oppress their innocent offspring." He continued: "it remains for some future legislature, if any shall be found wicked enough, to extend [the punishment of servitude] to the grandchildren and other issue more remote." Jefferson went further, declaring to the court: "Under the law of nature, all men are born free," a concept he derived from his reading of John Locke and other Enlightenment thinkers, the concept that would later form the foundation of the Declaration of Independence. In the Howell case, Jefferson deployed it in defense of a man of African descent.

Jefferson's close reading of the statutes and his invocation of the law of nature left the justices unmoved. At the conclusion of Jefferson's argument the opposing attorney stood up to begin his response, "but the Court interrupted him," as Jefferson recalled, and issued a summary judgment against Howell.

The young Jefferson was not finished with his campaign against "unremitting despotism." In a few short lines he sketched out a solution: free the slaves and make them citizens. "The abolition of domestic slavery is the great object of desire in those colonies, where it was unhappily introduced in their infant state. But previous to the enfranchisement of the slaves we have, it is necessary to exclude all further importations from Africa." So wrote Jefferson in the summer of 1774. He wove that declaration into a statement intended for presentation to a gathering of Virginia's dissidents, then to a national congress of colonial representatives, and ultimately to King George III. It rehearses many of the points Jefferson later put into the Declaration of Independence. As he worked through the process of writing the nation into existence, he envisioned not only freedom for the slaves but also their "enfranchisement," their incorporation into the citizenry. Given his later history and the tenor of his times, the formula sounds preposterous, but that is what he proposed. He was trying to pull the people far beyond where they thought they could go. His cousin Edmund Randolph, who heard the document read aloud in Williamsburg, commented that "it constituted a part of Mr. Jefferson's pride to run before the times in which he lived."[34]

A moment of political crisis had inspired Jefferson. Virginia's royal governor, Lord Dunmore, had just dissolved one legislature for its radical tendencies and was refusing to seat another, so the legislators decided to meet unofficially in Williamsburg. A gathering of freeholders in Albemarle County chose Jefferson as one of their two delegates to the Williamsburg conference and voted their approval of a set of resolutions he laid before them. He forged these talking points into a fiery manifesto, *A Summary View of the Rights of British America*.

Jefferson's "glowing sentences" in *Summary View*, observes Dumas Malone, were "written in the white heat of indignation." Declaiming the doctrine of natural rights, Jefferson "regarded himself as the spokesman of a free people who had derived their rights from God and the laws."[35] Ascending to a "prophetic" tone, Jefferson "grounded his argument on the nature of things—as they were in the beginning and evermore should be." Jefferson was not in a compromising mood, and his statement, Malone says, "left no place . . . for tyranny of any sort."[36]

Jefferson himself said that *Summary View* was "penned in the language of truth" and free from "expressions of servility."[37] In his passionate defense of liberty he staked out an extreme position. Edmund Randolph thought that *Summary View* offered "a range of inquiry . . . marching far beyond the politics of the day."[38] A modern historian concurs: "Broader and even more prescient are references to the rights of 'human nature,' which Jefferson daringly ascribed even to the chattel slaves."[39] *Summary View* makes no mention of exiling the blacks after freeing them. The clear implication is that people of African descent had natural rights and deserved a place in this country as free people.

Randolph reported that *some* sections of the document were received with enthusiasm, others not. "I distinctly recollect the applause bestowed on [most of the resolutions], when they were read to a large company. . . . Of all, the approbation was not equal." But the whole document was embraced by "several of the author's admirers," who paid to have it printed and circulated as a pamphlet.*[40] *Summary View*, its incendiary provision about slavery intact, won Jefferson a wide reputation as an eloquent spokesman for liberty and led to his selection to write the Declaration of Independence.

The Howell case and *Summary View* cast light on the enduring question of the meaning of the phrase "all men." When Jefferson wrote in the Declaration of Independence that "all men are created equal," could he have possibly meant to include the slaves? The usual answer is no. It has seemed evident that Jefferson expected the word "white" to be silently added before "men." But when he wrote *Summary View*, he included the Africans under the law of nature, and when he argued for Howell, he declared that *all* men are born free, without qualification.[41]

In his original draft of the Declaration, Jefferson denounced the slave trade in terms that summon to mind the two-step process of

---

*Randolph remarked on the pervasive, indeed defining influence of slavery upon a society, writing that colonies with few slaves were "dissimilar . . . in manners, habits, ideas of religion and government from the states abounding in slaves." James Monroe made a similar remark to Edward Coles (see Chapter 16).

emancipation he had proposed in *Summary View*: first, the abolition of the slave trade; second, the "enfranchisement of the slaves we have." John Chester Miller writes: "The inclusion of Jefferson's strictures on slavery and the slave trade would have committed the United States to the abolition of slavery."[42] Thus when the Continental Congress deleted Jefferson's attack on the slave trade, it drained out the full implications of "all men are created equal."

Jefferson had overthrown millennia and set everyone free. He had undone Aristotle's ancient formula—"from the hour of their birth, some men are marked out for subjection, others for rule"—which had governed human affairs until 1776.[43] In search of "original intent," we can gather evidence from original hearers. Massachusetts freed its slaves on the strength of the Declaration of Independence, weaving Jefferson's language into the state constitution of 1780, giving it the force of law. A court in Massachusetts affirmed this end to slavery in 1783 because the state constitution had "ratified the doctrine that all men were created free and equal," as John Chester Miller writes.[44] The Vermont Constitution had abolished slavery even earlier, in 1777.

The meaning of "all men" sounded equally clear, and so disturbing to the authors of the constitutions of six Southern states that they emended Jefferson's wording. "All *free*men," they wrote in their founding documents, "are equal." The authors of those state constitutions knew what Jefferson meant, could not accept it, and sought to nullify the Declaration's intent within their borders.[45]

As Edmund Randolph observed, it was Jefferson's pride "to run before the times in which he lived." We do not quite grasp how far in advance of his times he was running. We tend to look at Jefferson backward, projecting his later statements onto the young man; but the young Jefferson was a firebrand. Jefferson's first two public declarations of natural rights were both linked to the rights of people of color. His third pronouncement, the Declaration itself, flowed from the first two. The celestial notion of natural rights gained sufficient hold over him to overpower any aversion he had to what Virginia law called "abominable mixture." The racial barrier had been breached long ago, and it was "wicked" to defend it any longer.

Another, more personal absolute may have weighed on his conscience. For two years, since his marriage in 1772, he had been the owner of his wife's blood kin, for Martha Jefferson had six slaves who were her half siblings and therefore now his in-laws. This was an absolute of blood, a parallel genealogical reality of in-laws not recognized in law. His marriage had thrust him very deeply into the realm where people had the "double aspect" of being both humanity and property. This erased any clear-cut sense of separation between the races and any comfortable notion of who was destined to be a slave and who was destined to be free.

2

Pursued by the Black Horse

Jefferson married Martha Wayles Skelton on New Year's Day 1772 at the Forest, her father's plantation outside Williamsburg. Jefferson was then twenty-nine; the bride, though only twenty-three, was already a widow. At age eighteen she had married Bathurst Skelton, who died in 1768, less than two years into their marriage. An early biographer described Martha as "distinguished for her beauty, her accomplishments, and her solid merit . . . a little above medium height, slightly but exquisitely formed. Her complexion was brilliant." She had large eyes "of the richest shade of hazel—her luxuriant hair of the finest tinge of auburn."[1] Martha rode, danced, played the spinet and harpsichord, and shared her husband's love of literature.

The couple left the Wayles plantation in a carriage during a light fall of snow; by the time they reached Monticello, the snow was eighteen inches deep. Their daughter later described the "horrible dreariness" of the scene. At that time Monticello was little more than a construction site. One small building had been completed—a one-room brick pavilion that still stands at the end of the south terrace. On the mountain all was dark and silent. The couple had to step carefully to avoid tumbling into the unfinished pit of Monticello's cellar, outlined in snow. The next morning Jefferson went out to measure the snow—three feet, which remains the heaviest snowfall ever recorded in Virginia. Nine months later Martha gave birth to their first child.[2] In the next ten years she gave birth to six children, but only two survived to adulthood and had children.

Martha Wayles brought Jefferson a rich inheritance of land and slaves as well as a dowry of another sort—emotional and blood ties to her enslaved half siblings. After the death of his third wife in 1761 (when Martha was twelve), John Wayles had begun a relationship with his mixed-race slave Elizabeth "Betty" Hemings; it lasted until Wayles's death twelve years later.[3] Born about 1735 to a slave woman and an English sea captain, Elizabeth Hemings was in her mid-twenties when her relationship with Wayles began. She already had four children, Mary, Martin, Betty Brown, and Nance, whose father, or fathers, are not known. With Wayles she had six children—Robert, James, Thenia, Critta, Peter, and Sally. And she had two more children, John and Lucy, at Monticello.[4]

Betty Hemings's family was fortunate to remain intact when Wayles died. All of them came into Jefferson's possession. The Granger family, whom Martha felt very close to, had been separated and sold away. But Martha was determined to reunite them. Just after the marriage, she told Jefferson that she was "very desirous to get a favorite house woman of the name of Ursula."[5] So he traveled fifty miles to an estate auction to bid on Ursula Granger and her two sons, George and Bagwell, who were fourteen and five years old.

Acceding to his wife's wishes cost Jefferson a great deal of money, since he had to pay £210 for Ursula and the children. As it happened, Ursula's owner had died owing money to the estate of Martha's late husband, Bathurst Skelton. Eager to recoup as much of this debt as possible, Bathurst's brother Meriwether turned up at the auction. Knowing that his former sister-in-law was set on having Ursula, he engaged Jefferson in a bidding war, converting Martha Jefferson's feelings for the Grangers into cash. Jefferson later complained that Meriwether had "run me up to 210£, an exorbitant price."[6] From another owner in another distant county Jefferson retrieved Ursula's husband, George, for £130. He became known at Monticello as "Great George." The Grangers became cornerstones of the Monticello establishment.

Jefferson, too, had a connection to a particular slave. He had grown up with Jupiter, born at Shadwell the same year as he. If they followed the custom of the time, the two of them were playmates and companions in fishing and hunting, though Jefferson left no recollection of this. When Jefferson attended the College of William and Mary in

Williamsburg, Jupiter went with him as his personal servant. (Decades later, when Jefferson drew up regulations for the University of Virginia, he forbade students to have their slaves with them, which he thought ruined the character of young white men.) Jefferson and Jupiter, who likely had the surname Evans, married women from the same plantation, Jefferson marrying Martha Wayles and Jupiter marrying Suck, a Wayles slave. Their courtships took place simultaneously; Jupiter met his future wife when he accompanied Jefferson to the Wayles plantation as valet.[7]

Jupiter lost his position when the Hemings family arrived at Monticello and took over most of the household posts. Twelve-year-old Robert Hemings became Jefferson's personal servant, and Jupiter was put in charge of the plantation's horses and coach. He may have had a better knack with horses than anyone else and may have preferred more manly, physical work than shaving, dressing, and following his master about. But the decision to shift assignments may have been Martha's; she might have preferred to have a young Hemings she knew well bustling around the private rooms rather than a man her husband's age.

Jupiter won Jefferson's trust to a truly extraordinary degree. When cash had to be delivered or collected, Jefferson often sent Jupiter. Cash is one thing; gunpowder is quite another. Jupiter became Jefferson's explosives expert, skilled at pulverizing rock, quarrying limestone, and general construction blasting. Had he been so inclined, Jupiter could have blown up Monticello. Jefferson bought the indenture of a white stonecutter and apprenticed Jupiter to him. Jupiter then shaped the four Doric limestone columns still standing at the main entrance to Monticello.[8]

Although the Hemingses are the best-known family among Monticello's enslaved people, the Grangers and Evanses also had very close ties to the Jeffersons that lasted generations. There is no indication that Jefferson had even a distant kinship tie to these two families, but they held posts of trust and responsibility.

In the winter of 1774, Jefferson started his Farm Book, the plantation ledger he would keep until his death, writing out a census of the 45 slaves he received from his parents, the 135 from the Wayles estate, and 5 he had purchased. He owned the future: the census included the astonishing total of 79 children under the age of fourteen. About 40 percent of Jefferson's slaves were children.*[9]

It is always dangerous to read too much into small details, but in studying Jefferson's Farm Book, I was struck by the calligraphy. Most of the ledger showed a cramped, businesslike script on pages jammed with names and dates, as the master struggled to keep up with the business of running the plantation—births and deaths, work assignments, allotments of food and blankets, purchases and sales. But at the beginning, when Jefferson first set down the names of the people who had come into his possession, the writing is beautiful, and the pages have an elegant copperplate look. Pride of possession? Perhaps—but it seemed more likely a sign of respect, or rather recognition, as Jefferson recorded the families.

Jefferson's architectural papers contain an intriguing document, probably dating to the mid-1770s, when the Monticello household was taking shape. Jefferson sketched out plans for a row of substantial, dignified neoclassical houses with stone or brick hearths and ample windows for "George and his family" and "Betty Hemings and her family." On the list of possible occupants he put the names of slaves and white workmen, having in mind an integrated row of residences.[10]

The buildings were going to have identical facades and two different interior arrangements. Interior "No. 1" would have four bedrooms around a central hall with a communal fireplace; such a dwelling would be appropriate for "Betty Hemings and her family." Interior "No. 2" could house two slave families, with a single large room for each family, heated by a fireplace, and no central hall. No. 2 would also be appropriate for unmarried white workers.

It was no small thing to use architecture to make a visible equality of the races. Jefferson's theoretical vision of natural rights inherent in everyone, regardless of race, would have become real on his mountain had he actually built this row of houses, but he did not. Perhaps they

---

*From his parents Jefferson inherited ten families and nine individuals. Five of these families had a father and mother; the other five family groupings listed children under a woman's name only. From John Wayles he inherited eighteen families headed by a man and woman, six by a woman only, and twenty-three unconnected individuals. Some of the one-parent families might have been "abroad" marriages, with the husband owned by another master. He actually began the Farm Book with several pages of horse-breeding notes.

were too expensive, or too radical. Later he backed away from equality in housing and always gave whites the larger, more solid, and more comfortable accommodations.[11]

It was not unusual for slaves to sleep where they worked. It saved money on housing, made them efficient, and had the psychological effect of making them identify totally with what they did. But it also separated them from their families. One of Monticello's cooks, Ursula Granger, had responsibility for the smokehouse and washhouse. Her son Isaac recalled, "She was pastry cook and washerwoman; stayed in the laundry"—and by "stayed" he meant that she slept there. Ursula's husband, George, probably slept elsewhere, since he was needed in the fields at first light. Young Isaac slept alone, apart from his parents, in a pavilion where the white children had their schoolroom. His job was to light the fire before dawn so the room would be warm when "the scholars" came in. Other slaves on Mulberry Row bedded down and ate their meals in the tiny dairy room and in the nailery storeroom.[12]

For more than twenty-five years Ursula was a "mammy" to Thomas Jefferson's children, whom she wet-nursed, and then to his grandchildren. When an infant became ill, Jefferson recorded the child being restored to health "almost instantaneously by a good breast of milk" from Ursula.[13] Martha's health was poor from the first year of the marriage, when a doctor came to see her almost once a month. In ten years Martha gave birth six times; gaps of weeks or months in her accounts suggest that she was often too weak to attend to the household. Jack McLaughlin writes, "Throughout much of her ten-year marriage to Jefferson, she was either pregnant, nursing, grieving the death of an infant, or sick from the complications of childbirth." He notes that she bore up under these strains during "the difficult years of the American Revolution and in an unfinished house, littered with workmen's debris, while simultaneously undergoing the physical and emotional stress of multiple pregnancies and infant death."[14]

Martha's account books show that when her health permitted it, she oversaw the brewing of immense amounts of beer; the slaughtering of ducks, geese, and hogs; weaving, sewing, soapmaking, and candlemaking. Her accounts record the production of fabrics in a spectrum of quality, depending on who would wear them: "fine linen shirts [for] Jefferson," "fine mixt cloth for the children [her own]," "mixt cloth for the house servants," and, for the "out negroes," "hemp linen" and "coarse linen." She bartered bacon to the slaves in exchange for their chickens. She supervised the preparation of meat for her own family and for the white workers: "packed up for our own eating 28 hams of bacon 21 shoulders 27 middlengs. packed up for workmen 40 hams 50 shoulders."[15] Every day, as Isaac recalled, she descended to the kitchen to give instructions to Ursula: "Mrs. Jefferson would come out there with a cookery book in her hand and read out of it to Isaac's mother how to make cakes, tarts, and so on."[16]

When Ursula looked after the Jefferson children and grandchildren, she sang to them and told them folktales "to pass away the long lonely winter and cheer up the evenings."[17] Repeated endlessly on an endless chain of winter nights, these songs and stories became fixed in the memory of Jefferson's daughter Martha. In 1816 she sang five songs from memory and dictated two lengthy folktales to a visiting Frenchman. Another family member commented that "although Jefferson's ears seemed to be closed to all but the European mode, his daughter Martha kept her ears open. She had a large store of songs and tales that she had picked up from the black people around her. It was authentic material, of which the later minstrel shows were no more than a caricature."[18] For example, young Martha learned a "corn song," a tune with a repetitive chorus sung "when the negroes were employed in extracting the grains from the ears of corn," and a song with verses about slaves taking the master's horses on nighttime excursions away from the plantation.

The folktales Ursula told had their origins in Africa. In one, a character named Mammy Dinah escapes a demon by climbing into a tree and humming a song to summon her fierce guard dogs, which possess supernatural powers. Just as the demon is about to devour Dinah, the dogs arrive: "They fell upon the evil genie and tore him to pieces, thus delivering Mammy Dinah forever from her mortal enemy." In another tale a devious fox talks his way into the home of a rabbit and then casually announces, "I am in a hurry to feast on some of your tender bones." Keeping his presence of mind, the rabbit tricks the fox into hiding in a box and then drenches his trapped enemy in boiling water, "which ended his days."

In addition to these allegories of the struggle between good and evil in the world, Ursula sang the children a song called "Captain Shields," about the real-life depredations of a Richmond policeman:

I was an old hare, I was born in the snow,
I was pursued by the black horse of Shields.
Grass grows green, tears roll down my cheeks,
Still Shields is mayor of the town.
Oh! Mr. Koon, you come too soon,
Just let us rest until tomorrow.

As the Frenchman explained in his notes to this song, "For a time, Captain Shields of Richmond's City Police, was a severe and vigilant man, and who in the exercise of his functions, came often to trouble the negroes in their excessive noisy pastimes. So they held him in horror, and their only possible means of vengeance was to make him the theme of their songs, in which they represented him as a hunter and themselves as hares and marmots or raccoons."

In the long succession of evenings with songs and stories by the fireside, an intimate, enduring relationship took shape among the Jeffersons, Hemingses, Grangers, and Evanses. The Jeffersons owned everyone, but human attachments softened the underlying brutality of slavery. The care of children brought the families together. When Martha was sick, the Hemingses tended her and kept the household running; Ursula took over wet-nursing the Jeffersons' infants as she gave birth to her own children.

We cannot fully know the nature of these relationships—everything here, even the birth of children, had multiple meanings—but we can see outward signs. Several Monticello slaves left personal recollections of Jefferson and his family that suggest emotional bonds founded upon the shared experience of living in the same place for decades. Asked to reminisce about Jefferson, several slaves summoned up warm memories of their master. On the other side of the divide, however, Jefferson left no intimate account of the Monticello slaves.

The families grew in tandem, and they knew each other's lineages directly, by the entries in the master's ledger book and by oral history. Thus George and Ursula's son Isaac could summon from memory, as late as 1847, the lineage of his long-dead mistress, whom he had known when he was a small child: "Mrs. Jefferson was named Patsy Wayles, but when Mr. Jefferson married her she was the Widow Skelton, widow of Batter [Bathurst] Skelton."[19] On the one hand, he knew this as one knows the details of a title search, because the Grangers had passed through the ownership and auctions of those families. But on the other hand, as an old man Isaac kept in his mind's eye the images of the whites he had grown up with: "Mrs. Jefferson was small. . . . Patsy Jefferson was tall like her father. Polly low like her mother and longways the handsomest, pretty lady jist like her mother."[20]

Madison Hemings, at an even later date, could summon up the story of Thomas and Martha Jefferson's courtship, which had occurred more than thirty years before Madison was born, but his elders had watched closely and passed down the account of it: "Thos. Jefferson was a visitor at the 'great house' of John Wales. . . . He formed the acquaintance of his daughter Martha . . . and intimacy sprang up between them which ripened into love, and they were married."[21] That phrase "ripened into love" bespeaks a close eye for human feelings; the slaves had seen arranged marriages, and this was not one of them.

As Thomas Jefferson had grown up alongside Jupiter, his grandson Jeff Randolph grew up alongside Jupiter's son, Phil Evans, about two years older than he. Jeff said that Evans "was my companion in childhood and friend throughout life," describing him as "small, active, intelligent, much of a humourist."[22]

The bonds formed in childhood proved lasting. In 1819, when Jeff was viciously attacked by his drunken, half-mad brother-in-law, Charles Bankhead, in the courthouse square in Charlottesville, Phil Evans galloped to get a doctor from a distant town, there being none available in Charlottesville. During Jeff's difficult recovery from the attack, Evans held him in his arms when his master became feverish and passed out. When Jeff regained consciousness, "Phil was holding me in his arms with his eyes streaming with tears."

The lore and literature of plantations show time and again that people held in slavery formed profound attachments to the families who owned them. These relationships baffled outsiders, who saw the fact of enslavement but not the decades of intimacy that led to the slaves' extraordinary acts of kindness and loyalty. After the Civil War a visiting Northerner, astonished at the stories she had heard, asked a former slave how he could risk his life for the family that enslaved him. The answer was that the slaves had not lost a sense of common humanity. "Often we left our own wives and children during the war in order to take care of

Dude! what else were they gonna do?

the wives and children of our absent masters. And why did we do this? Because they were helpless and afraid, while our families were better able to take care of themselves, and had no fear."[23] When they saw their "oppressors" stricken with fear, they did not rise up in vengeance but offered help.

In his recollections of the slaves he had grown up with, Jeff Randolph declared, "they would run any risk for my protection." When the Revolutionary War brought life-or-death moments of crisis, Jefferson's slaves also ran those risks for him.

Elected governor of Virginia during the Revolutionary War, Jefferson moved his family first to Williamsburg and then to Richmond, taking an entourage of Hemingses, Grangers, and other slaves to run his household and look after Martha and the Jeffersons' three small children. Isaac recalled the wartime events many years later. He was only about five years old at the time, but records confirm the accuracy of many of his recollections. Speaking of himself in the third person, he said, "Isaac remembers coming down to Williamsburg in a wagon at the time Mr. Jefferson was Governor. He came down in the phaeton, his family with him in a coach and four. Bob Hemings drove the phaeton; Jim Hemings was a body servant; Martin Hemings the butler." Ill after childbirth, Martha Jefferson needed all the assistance she could get from her servants.

In January 1781 the turncoat Benedict Arnold landed in Virginia with a powerful invasion force of British soldiers and began to lay waste. Much of Virginia's militia was occupied far to the west of the state fighting Indians, and the defense forces available to Governor Jefferson were scattered and poorly equipped. Learning of the approach of the British raiders, Jefferson sent his family out of Richmond and then returned to the governor's house in the capital. Isaac Granger remembered that Jefferson took a spyglass up to the attic window to watch for the invaders.

A relief column unexpectedly appeared and set up several cannon, to the delight of Richmond's inhabitants, who greeted the rescuers with hearty hurrahs. But then the cannon boomed, and, as Isaac recalled, "everybody knew it was the British." As cannonballs knocked the top off a butcher's house, "the butcher's wife screamed out and holler'd and her children too and all." The ensuing panic was instant and total. Isaac remarked: "In ten minutes not a white man was to be seen in Richmond." Jefferson called for his strongest horse, Caractacus, and galloped off.

The arrival of the invaders, to the grim beating of drums, terrified young Isaac: "it was an awful sight—seemed like the Day of Judgment was come." Isaac remembered that his mother "was so skeered, she didn't know whether to stay indoors or out." But his father, George, kept calm and turned his attention to the task of saving Jefferson's most valuable possessions. He went through the house gathering all the silver, which he laid in a bed tick "and hid it under a bed in the kitchen." When the British marched up, Granger was prepared.

"Whar is the Governor?" demanded a mounted officer.

"He's gone to the mountains," Granger replied, giving a vaguely accurate but perfectly useless answer.

"Whar is the silver?"

"It was all sent up to the mountains."

The British searched the house, smashed Jefferson's wine bottles, emptied the corncrib for their horses and the smokehouse for their own knapsacks, but they did not find the Jefferson silver.

Assuming that his family would be safe, Granger left them in Richmond and set off west to aid his master's family. But the day after sacking the governor's house, the British returned and grabbed little Isaac. "When Isaac's mother found they was gwine to car him away, she thought they was gwine to leave her. She was cryin' and hollerin'." The British took her as well.

The British hunted Governor Jefferson fruitlessly, raiding the plantation west of Richmond where he had hidden his family, only to find the quarry gone. After placing Martha and the children at a farm deeper in the interior, Jefferson tried to organize Virginia's defenders as best he could. The British withdrew to the east, carrying off many slaves, leaving Richmond a shambles, and permanently scarring Jefferson's reputation as a wartime leader. The tumultuous winter ended with a personal tragedy: the Jeffersons' infant daughter Lucy died in April.

The following month the British returned, more determined than before to hunt Jefferson down. Once again British raiders swarmed into Richmond, forcing Jefferson and the legislature to abandon the capital and reconvene seventy miles west in Charlottesville. The British commander, Lord Cornwallis, ordered Colonel Banastre Tarleton to lead his elite unit of dragoons on a lightning raid to "disturb the assembly."[24] Tarleton's column halted at a country tavern, where a burly young militiaman, Jack Jouett, correctly guessed that they were on their way to seize the governor and the legislators. He galloped through the night to warn the Jeffersons.

Once more, the frail Martha Jefferson and her two small daughters climbed aboard a carriage to be trundled over rough mountain roads to a hideout. A second man who had gone up to Monticello to warn Jefferson found the governor "perfectly tranquil," though he was hastening to pack up as many private papers as he could.[25] Jefferson barely escaped capture, leaping onto Caractacus just as the dragoons were closing in.

What happened next became part of the oral tradition of the Jefferson family. Jefferson's grandchildren Ellen Coolidge and Jeff Randolph eagerly shared the story in the 1850s with the biographer Henry Randall, who noted that the grandchildren had "repeatedly heard all the particulars from [Jefferson's] lips."

When the raiders swarmed into the house at Monticello, it quickly became apparent that once again Jefferson had eluded them, but they knew he could not be very far off. So one of the dragoons jammed a pistol into Martin Hemings's chest and said he would shoot if Hemings did not tell them where the governor had gone.

"Fire away, then," Hemings replied, and refused to say anything else.[26]

Martin Hemings was not one of the half siblings of Mrs. Jefferson. His mother had borne him before she began her relationship with John Wayles, so his kinship tie to the Jeffersons was not as direct as that of his younger siblings fathered by Wayles. As the Jefferson grandchildren recounted the story, Hemings stood his ground, "fiercely answering glance for glance, and not receding a hair's breadth from the muzzle of the cocked pistol." Unbeknownst to the British, another servant named Caesar lay in silence beneath their feet under the floor of the portico with silver he and Martin had just finished hiding when the raiding party rushed in.

As Hemings stared down the dragoons, his owner made his escape, galloping down obscure mountain paths. Jefferson gathered up his family from a plantation outside Charlottesville. Together they made their way west and then south. Not everyone along the route was eager to help the rebellious governor and author of the Declaration of Independence. According to Jeff Randolph, when Jefferson knocked at a house seeking refuge, the owner "refused to take him in, fearing he might be . . . punished for harboring him."[27]

Traveling alone, Jefferson made a brief return to Monticello, where he learned what Hemings and Caesar had done for him. With the British still hunting him, Jefferson went to ground with his family at his farm ninety miles southwest, Poplar Forest, a property he had inherited from Wayles.

George Granger's heroism may have led Jefferson to set him free, but the record is ambiguous. In his memoir, Granger's son Isaac said that his father "got his freedom by it. But he continued to sarve Mr. Jefferson and had forty pounds from Old Master and his wife." There is no direct evidence for this manumission in the records, but Jefferson's list of taxable servants includes two free people, one of whom might have been George Granger.[28]

Hiding out at Poplar Forest, Jefferson resumed work on a manuscript that would be his only book, *Notes on the State of Virginia*. With the loyalty and heroism of Granger, Hemings, and Caesar still fresh in his mind, Jefferson considered the future, pondering the questions, Who will live in this new country? Who is an American and who is not?

3

"We Lived Under a Hidden Law"

Notes on the State of Virginia is the Dismal Swamp that every Jefferson biographer must sooner or later attempt to cross, the infamous tract in which Jefferson claims that blacks are inferior, notoriously remarking that African women copulated with apes. With fabrications, hypocrisies, and ludicrous "twistifications"[1] (that marvelous Jeffersonian word), Jefferson puts the blame for slavery on the slaves.

Jefferson began writing *Notes* in the midst of the wartime chaos in Virginia. With the British on his trail and the duties of government weighing upon him, Jefferson cleared time to write detailed answers to a questionnaire sent out by an official of the French legation in Philadelphia to representatives of each American state. Eager for information about the new nation taking shape, the French diplomat posed twenty-three "Queries" on such points as each state's borders, rivers, ports, mountains, mines, climate, population, laws, religion, and manners. In the fall of 1780, Jefferson had begun gathering notes and formulating his answers, taking great pleasure in a task that was "making me much better acquainted with my own country than I ever was before."[2] Chased by British raiders from Richmond and then from Monticello to his refuge at Poplar Forest, Jefferson still managed to complete a draft of his answers, which he sent to the French official late in 1781.

Writing as an American scientist and philosopher, and a Virginian, to the tight community of French scientists and philosophers, Jefferson did not anticipate that the manuscript would become public. A few years later he expanded and revised his responses, intending to have a small private printing made in Philadelphia for acquaintances who had asked to see his work, but the cost was prohibitive. After many second thoughts and misgivings, he had *Notes* published in France, where he was sent in 1784 as U.S. minister, and later in England.[3] Later in life he shed his misgivings and urged abolitionists to read *Notes* for an accurate and unchanging expression of his views.

Jefferson wrote *Notes* as a defense against allegations of American inferiority. He took up the task and pursued it despite so many difficulties and distractions because in his view some French intellectuals had slighted and slandered the New World. The noted naturalist and *philosophe* Georges Louis Leclerc, Comte de Buffon, had put forth, as Jefferson wrote, "this new theory" which held that the plants and the Native people of the New World were runts. The Native Americans, Buffon proclaimed, were weak, not fully developed, defective, and poorly endowed in a very crucial aspect: "The savage is feeble, and has small organs of generation." No wonder that Jefferson rushed to the New World's defense.

Buffon had written that the Native American "is also less sensitive, and yet more timid and cowardly; he has no vivacity, no activity of mind; the activity of his body is less an exercise, a voluntary motion, than a necessary action caused by want; relieve him of hunger and thirst, and you deprive him of all his movements; he will rest stupidly upon his legs and lying down entire days."

Another Frenchman, the Abbé Raynal, advanced the very disturbing theory that white people deteriorated when they emigrated from Europe to the New World. As proof the abbé pointed out that "America has not yet produced one good poet." In *Notes*, Jefferson responded that it had required great expanses of time before "the Greeks . . . produced a Homer, the Romans a Virgil, the French a Racine and Voltaire, the English a Shakespeare and Milton," so America should be given some time.

As for the charge that the New World had not yielded "one able mathematician, one man of genius in a single art or a single science," Jefferson pointed to the accomplishments of George Washington, Benjamin Franklin, and the Philadelphia scientist David Rittenhouse, the last ranking "second to no astronomer living . . . in genius he must be the first, because he is self-taught." In many fields of endeavor, Jefferson declared, "we might shew that America, though but a child of yesterday, has already given hopeful proofs of genius. . . . We therefore suppose, that this reproach is as unjust as it is unkind."

Jefferson did not have to mention slavery at all, since the questionnaire did not ask about it. But he addressed this uncomfortable subject because the persistence of slavery in the land of liberty put the new nation in a very awkward position. Virginia's revolutionaries "found themselves partners in the liberal vanguard of their times, and were properly embarrassed at a stigma from which their other partners were free," as the historian Robert McColley observes.[4] Having accused King George of attempting to enslave them, American leaders laid themselves open to the charge of hypocrisy by their failure to end slavery in their own country. Samuel Johnson jibed, "How is it that we hear the loudest yelps for liberty among the drivers of negroes?" Slavery had been outlawed in England's home island, though not in its colonies, in the landmark 1772 *Somerset* decision by an activist judge, who concluded that enslavement was such an egregious denial of rights that slavery had to be specifically authorized by law, and Parliament had never done so. When there were calls for Parliament to pass enabling legislation for black slavery, the proposal was derided in a widely circulated joke, which was eventually published in *The Virginia Gazette*: "If Negroes are to be Slaves on account of colour, the next step will be to enslave every mulatto in the kingdom, then all the Portuguese, next the French, then the brown complexioned English, and so on until there be only one free man left, which will be the man of palest complexion in the three kingdoms."[5]

In the opening lines of the Declaration of Independence, Jefferson had written that "a decent respect to the opinions of mankind" required Americans to state their case for independence. Though most of *Notes* is a detailed description of Virginia, in several sections it becomes a public-relations tract aimed at the international intelligentsia, explaining to a candid world the persistence of slavery in a nation taking shape upon the foundation of universal natural rights.

Jefferson did not attempt to paint a benevolent portrait of slavery. He acknowledged that the existence of slavery in Virginia had exerted "an unhappy influence" on the manners of white people, making them tyrants, destroying their morals: "The whole commerce between master and slave is a perpetual exercise of the most boisterous passions, the most unremitting despotism on the one part, and degrading submissions on the other." Young white Virginians were "nursed, educated, and daily exercised in tyranny . . . stamped by it with odious peculiarities. The man must be a prodigy who can retain his manners and morals unde-praved by such circumstances."*[6] Slavery destroyed the industriousness of whites: "no man will labour for himself who can make another la-bour for him. This is so true, that of the proprietors of slaves a very small proportion indeed are ever seen to labour."

Jefferson made it plain that his country trampled upon the rights of the slaves. Who could blame them if they stole? "That disposition to theft with which they have been branded, must be ascribed to their situ-ation, and not to any depravity of the moral sense. The man, in whose favour no laws of property exist, probably feels himself less bound to respect those made in favour of others."

In the infamous passages of *Notes*, Jefferson speculates that blacks were in some ways, possibly, inferior to whites, but in any case were unquestionably *different*, and the difference was "fixed in nature." They looked different, they smelled different, they thought, felt, and loved dif-ferently from whites.

"The first difference which strikes us is that of colour." Speaking as a naturalist, he had to admit that he did not know precisely where "the black of the negro resides." It might be "in the reticular membrane be-tween the skin and scarf-skin, or in the scarf-skin itself." He did not know what caused it—"whether it proceeds from the colour of the blood, the colour of the bile, or from that of some other secretion." In any case, "the difference is fixed in nature," and it was "real."

"Is this difference of no importance?" Jefferson asked rhetorically. He claimed that color had tremendous importance because skin color was the foundation of human beauty, and because black skin rendered the slaves impenetrable to the master's gaze, made their responses and thoughts inscrutable; "eternal monotony . . . reigns in the countenances"; an "immoveable veil of black . . . covers all the emotions."†

---

*In another passage he mentioned the "mild treatment our slaves experience, and their wholesome, though coarse, food."

†This discussion of the black face may have been inspired by the Shenstone poem Jefferson planned to inscribe on the Monticello grave monument, in which the slave narrator describes the beauty of the white face and its concealment of hypocrisy.

Jefferson said that white people's "flowing hair" and "more elegant symmetry of form" made them more sexually attractive than blacks. He claimed that all blacks lusted after whites. In triumphant proof, he wrote the ill-famed phrase—that black people seek sex with white people "as uniformly as is the preference of the Oranootan for the black women over those of his own species." Jefferson had extracted this tidbit from Buffon's report of travelers' accounts of apes kidnapping and raping African women. Jefferson probably summoned up the fantastical image of an ape mating with an African woman to deflect attention from the actual reality of Virginia society—the pervasive rape of black women by white men.

Seeming to assume that his readers in the French community of Encyclopedists and *philosophes* might have seen very few Africans, Jefferson presented a scientific description: "there are other physical distinctions proving a difference of race. They have less hair on the face and body. They secrete less by the kidneys, and more by the glands of the skin, which gives them a very strong and disagreeable odour. This greater degree of transpiration renders them more tolerant of heat, and less so of cold, than the whites." Blacks seemed to be indefatigable—"they seem to require less sleep"—though not in a productive way: "A black, after hard labour through the day, will be induced by the slightest amusements to sit up till midnight, or later, though knowing he must be out with the first dawn of the morning."

He enumerated racial differences in the emotions: "They are more ardent after their female: but love seems with them to be more an eager desire, than a tender delicate mixture of sentiment and sensation." He declared that "their griefs are transient," that the "numberless afflictions" of their lives "are less felt, and sooner forgotten with them," which led him to the conclusion: "In general, their existence appears to participate more of sensation than reflection."

In memory he judged "they are equal to the whites," but "in imagination they are dull, tasteless, and anomalous" and "in reason much inferior," advancing as proof that it would be all but impossible to find a black person "capable of tracing and comprehending the investigations of Euclid." (One might ask how many white Virginians could comprehend Euclid.) By this very imperfect logic Jefferson concluded that blacks were innately mentally inferior: "It is not their condition then, but nature, which has produced the distinction." It was essential to Jefferson's purpose that he establish in the minds of his readers that *nature* had produced the distinction and Jefferson was merely observing it, that he prove that black inferiority sprang from nature, whose laws ruled existence. But as John Stuart Mill observed: "Was there ever any domination which did not appear natural to those who possessed it?"[7]

Having stated his contention, Jefferson backed away from it: "Further observation" was needed to verify the "conjecture" of inferiority, to be sure that "nature has been less bountiful to them in the endowments of the head." Elsewhere he wrote that it was only "the opinion, that they are inferior in the faculties of reason and imagination," and "a suspicion only." These conjectures, opinions, and suspicions "must be hazarded with great diffidence." To achieve certainty, the subject under discussion, in this case, human beings, had to be "submitted to the Anatomical knife, to Optical glasses, to analysis by fire, or by solvents," and Jefferson the scientist was not prepared to go that far. He contradicted himself in another section where he wrote that slavery compels the concealment of talents, that the slave "must lock up the faculties of his nature."

Though he argued that the griefs of the blacks were transient, he admitted that the slave had the ability to see into the future, where he could perceive "his own miserable condition" passed perpetually to "the endless generations proceeding from him."

Jefferson wrote *Notes* at a time when Revolutionary fervor made some leading Virginians question slavery, while others began freeing their own slaves because of religious principles. Quakers and the new "dissenting" sects of Baptists and Methodists campaigned against slavery as an affront to the Almighty.

Virginia came close to outlawing the continuation of slavery. When its legislature was putting together a new state constitution—just before Jefferson wrote the Declaration of Independence—George Mason submitted a draft that stated "all men are born equally free and independant, and have certain inherent natural Rights, of which they can not by any Compact, deprive or divest their Posterity." This declaration would have ended perpetual, hereditary slavery in Virginia. But when

Mason's text was put to a vote, the legislature added a qualification that men take possession of their rights "when they enter into a state of society," thus eliminating slaves, who were not adjudged part of society. It later sharpened this point when it limited citizenship to "all white persons born within the territory of the commonwealth." But then, remarkably, it reversed course somewhat a few years later to include black people as citizens if they were already free; it deleted "white" from the citizenship definition and declared that "all free persons" born in Virginia were citizens.[8]

As the historian Eva Sheppard Wolf writes, "Several Revolutionary-era Virginia laws seemed to signal a shift toward anti-slavery policies that could have led to universal emancipation." Clashing notions of race and liberty "created turbulence and disarray out of a much more settled and ordered colonial world." At this critical moment, Jefferson broke from the dominant progressive thinking of his time to construct an image of the black person as the Other, a being with no place in American society. Putting a scholarly sheen on the rationalizations of slaveholders, Jefferson made himself the theorist and spokesman for the reactionaries. "Jefferson was not as torn as he is taken to be," writes the historian Michael Zuckerman. "He was not as confined by his culture as his apologists have often claimed. . . . In regard to race as in regard to so much else, he was a leader." In a letter to a newspaper one Virginian referred to slaves as "the greatest part of the property of thousands of our best citizens, most of whom have acquired their slave property at the expence of much labour or risk." Another Virginian said that what is useful for the majority is legal: "General utility is the basis of all law and justice, and on this principle, is the right of slavery founded." Another Southerner wrote to a Pennsylvania newspaper to insist that emancipation was "totally blind to our ease and interest . . . the certain consequence would be that we must work ourselves."[9]

Jefferson's intellectual peers in Europe and America rejected the idea that black people could be legitimately held as slaves. Montesquieu derided the notion that racial difference could justify slavery: "That all black persons might be slaves is as ridiculous as . . . that all red haired persons should be hanged."[10] On the subject of slavery Samuel Johnson remarked to his biographer James Boswell that "men in their original state were equal" and that although many countries may have had slavery in the past, he doubted whether slavery "can ever be supposed the natural condition of man." A criminal or prisoner of war could be enslaved, "but it is very doubtful whether he can entail that servitude on his descendants."[11]

In *Notes*, Jefferson compiles an overwhelming bill of indictment against the black race that unavoidably creates the impression that their enslavement is justifiable, but he never explicitly comes to that conclusion—he leaves it to the reader's judgment. When Jefferson sent the manuscript of *Notes* for comment to Charles Thomson of Pennsylvania, who had served as the secretary of the Continental Congress and inherited slaves and a tobacco plantation, Thomson clearly discerned the thrust of Jefferson's argument. He suggested deletions: "though I am much pleased with the dissertation of the difference between the Whites and blacks & am inclined to think the latter a race lower on the scale of being yet for that very reason & because such an opinion might seem to justify slavery I should be inclined to leave it out." Thomson and his wife freed their slaves.[12]

One of Jefferson's closest intellectual acquaintances, Dr. Benjamin Rush of Philadelphia, also took a careful scientific look at race and, as a result, helped establish the Pennsylvania Society for Promoting the Abolition of Slavery. In keeping with many other thinkers of the time who speculated on the effects that environment might have on humans, Rush postulated that the heat of the African climate had made its inhabitants indolent in mind and body; he also theorized that the Africans were dark-skinned because they suffered from genetic leprosy, which not only darkened the skin but thickened the lips, flattened the nose, made hair tightly wired, and increased the libido. Rush and others were certain that the American climate would eventually "cure" the Africans of their dark skin.

Yet Rush insisted that, dark-skinned or not, indolent or not, the Africans were as human as whites: "Human Nature is the same in all Ages and Countries; and all the difference we perceive in its Characters in respect to Virtue and Vice, Knowledge and Ignorance, may be accounted for from Climate, Country, Degrees of Civilization, form of Government, or other accidental causes." Furthermore, he declared, "all the claims of superiority of the whites over the blacks, on account of their color, are founded alike in ignorance and inhumanity."[13]

While Jefferson pleaded for extra time for America to develop its geniuses and strengths, he consigned the blacks to perpetual inferiority. They had already enjoyed exposure to white society and had not shown any signs of uplift. Though "most of them indeed have been confined to tillage, to their own homes, and their own society," Jefferson said that some slaves "have been liberally educated . . . and have had before their eyes samples of the best works from abroad. . . . But never yet could I find that a black had uttered a thought above the level of plain narration."

He had to backtrack immediately to account for the most famous and most acclaimed poet in America, Phillis Wheatley, who was, very unfortunately for Jefferson's argument, unquestionably black. She had been brought to Boston as an enslaved African at the age of about six, learned English and Latin as a child, and began writing poetry as a teenager. Her published works earned accolades on both sides of the Atlantic. Among her admirers were Voltaire, who praised Wheatley's "very good English verse," George Washington, Benjamin Franklin, and even the naval hero John Paul Jones, who addressed her as "the celebrated Phillis the African favorite of the Nine [Muses] and Apollo" when he sent her some of his own verses. Dr. Rush cited her as a proof of black ability, listing her accomplishments when he wrote in 1775, "We have many well attested anecdotes of as sublime and disinterested virtue among them as ever adorned a Roman or a Christian character."[14] Franklin went to see Wheatley when she was in London, a literary celebrity on book tour. The acclaim irked Jefferson: "The compositions published under her name are below the dignity of criticism."[15]

To account for this apparent refutation of his inferiority argument, he redefined poetry, insisting that a poem had to be about love—a definition that would exclude a large portion of the world's literature. He then declared that Wheatley, who seems to have enraged him, could not be a poet because she wrote about religion.

One of Wheatley's most famous works not only undermined Jefferson's contention that blacks could not write but stood as proof of African-American loyalty to the American cause. In 1775, Wheatley wrote a long paean to the American army facing the British in Boston and sent the verses to General Washington, who personally arranged for the poem's publication and invited Wheatley to his headquarters.

Elsewhere in *Notes*, Jefferson suggested it was impossible that blacks could be patriotic because slavery had irreparably destroyed their "amor patriae," and without love of country blacks could never live in America. A patriotic Wheatley compromised his argument as much as Wheatley the poet did.

One verse of Wheatley's poem in praise of Washington's army challenged Jefferson's philosophy on a deeper level, advancing the notion that love of country and love of liberty transcended racial divides to create a new American identity under God, a new class of people the poet called "freedom's heaven-defended race." Wheatley's formula—simple, powerful, hopeful, and self-evident—linked the idea of freedom with divine Providence, with *E pluribus unum*.[16]

In *Notes*, Jefferson described the status of blacks as fixed by nature and unalterable, but he shifted his thinking about Native Americans depending on the political situation. In the Declaration of Independence he had railed against the depredations of "the merciless Indian Savages" whom the king had unleashed against white Virginians. Their mode of warfare, he wrote, "is an undistinguished destruction of all ages, sexes, and conditions." As governor, Jefferson instructed his military commander in the West, George Rogers Clark, to unleash Anglo-Saxon ferocity: "If we are to wage a campaign against these Indians [the goal] should be their extermination, or their removal beyond the lakes of the Illinois river."[17] He followed with a remark that echoed his views on blacks: "The same world will scarcely do for them and for us."

But by the time he wrote *Notes*, the military crisis had passed, Indians would never again threaten Virginia, and his attitude toward them softened. They were, he thought, of the same species as whites. He praised Native American artworks, oratory, and even tobacco pipes: "The Indians, with no advantages of [association with white society], will often carve figures on their pipes not destitute of design and merit." He judged "their reason and sentiment strong, their imagination glowing and elevated." He went further in a letter written in 1785: "I beleive the Indian . . . to be in body and mind equal to the whiteman."[18] As president, Jefferson adopted a program of civilizing the Indians, believing that if they adopted white customs, then the two races could live together in the same world. In remarks he made to Indians while he was president, he said: "You will mix with us by marriage, your blood will run in our veins, and will spread with us over this great island."[19] Invoking the image of harmony that was so crucial to his worldview, he envisioned a joint future for whites and Native Americans: "The ultimate point of rest and happiness for [the Indians] is to let our settlements and theirs meet and blend together, to intermix and become one people."[20]

Jefferson may have welcomed Native Americans into the brotherhood of races because he was already kin to them. He had a family tie to Native Americans through his Randolph cousins at Tuckahoe plantation, who were descended from Pocahontas. The relationship came closer to Jefferson when his daughter Martha married Thomas Mann Randolph of Tuckahoe, mingling the bloodline of the Founder with that of the Powhatans. On a sheet of paper found among Jefferson's records, Thomas Mann Randolph charted his family tree back to Pocahontas.[21] Randolph left no explanation on the sheet, so we do not know if he calculated out of genealogical curiosity or racial anxiety, but he worked out the degree of Indian blood in each generation. Though the relationship was distant, the Randolphs bore its mark. Jefferson's overseer Edmund Bacon commented that three of Jefferson's grandchildren "had the fresh rosy countenance of the Jefferson family. The rest of the family, as far as I can remember . . . had the Randolph complexion, which was dark and Indianlike. You know they claim to be descended from Pocahontas. Virginia and Cornelia [Jefferson's granddaughters] were tall, active, and fine-looking, with very dark complexions."[22]

Addressing the *philosophes* of France in defense of the rising nation, Jefferson thus turned the troublesome subject of slavery on its head and presented a progressive image of Virginia—*yes, we have slavery, but we are working to get rid of it.* He described in detail an emancipation plan he had helped to draft that Virginia's legislature would soon consider.[23] Ecstatic at the news, the Paris intelligentsia heaped praise on the plan to abolish this "horrible practice, the shame of humanity," and hailed Jefferson as a *philosophe.*[24]

Under the plan as Jefferson accounted for it in *Notes*, enslaved adults would continue to toil as slaves their entire lives, but their adolescent children would be taken from them and put into training, at public expense, in "tillage, arts or sciences, according to their geniusses."* When women reached age eighteen and men twenty-one, they would be equipped by the state with "arms, implements of household and of the handicraft arts, feeds, pairs of the useful domestic animals, &c." and sent away to a place to be determined, where the United States could "declare them a free and independant people, and extend to them our alliance and protection, till they shall have acquired strength." Jefferson did not specify where the people would be sent. To replace the lost labor, the state would dispatch fleets of vessels to find white immigrants, lured by "proper encouragements."

Jefferson knew that this elaborate and costly plan—a plan cruel to the people who would be wrenched from their families and exiled—would seem entirely unnecessary to a foreigner: "It will probably be asked, Why not retain and incorporate the blacks into the state, and thus save the expence of supplying, by importation of white settlers, the vacancies they will leave?" He hastened to explain his reasons. He imagined that keeping blacks in Virginia would lead inevitably to a race war: "Deep rooted prejudices entertained by the whites; ten thousand recollections, by the blacks, of the injuries they have sustained; new provocations; the real distinctions which nature has made; and many other circumstances, will divide us into parties, and produce convulsions which will probably never end but in the extermination of the one or the other race."

Jefferson phrased the other compelling reason to expatriate blacks in philosophical terms: "Will not a lover of natural history then, one who views the gradations in all the races of animals with the eye of philosophy, excuse an effort to keep those in the department of man as distinct as nature has formed them? This unfortunate difference of colour, and perhaps of faculty, is a powerful obstacle to the emancipation of these people."

A few brief passages in *Notes* give the impression that as Jefferson was writing them, he glanced toward his window and a bright shaft of reality's

---

*A noteworthy Jeffersonian self-contradiction: elsewhere in *Notes* he expressed doubt that blacks could have a "genius" for anything except brute labor and music, but in this passage he said that almost any endeavor was within the natural talent of the Africans.

light penetrated his room. Right after a complex sentence concerning the "structure in the pulmonary apparatus" that makes blacks radically different from whites, he continues abruptly, "They are at least as brave, and more adventuresome." Perhaps he might have glimpsed one of the slaves who had lately risked his life on his behalf, facing down the British at Monticello. Further on he writes, "We find among them numerous instances of the most rigid integrity . . . of benevolence, gratitude, and unshaken fidelity." In these fleeting phrases, he seems to acknowledge the humanity of the people and to stress it for the reader; we get the sense that there is more to this world than Jefferson's philosophy. His prediction that "ten thousand recollections" of injustice would provoke a race war flew in the face of the unshaken fidelity he had recently experienced. Despite widespread fear among the slaveholders, no uprising had materialized during the Revolution.

At the outbreak of the war Virginia's royal governor, Lord Dunmore, threw the state into a panic by promising freedom to slaves who would fight for the king. The British army additionally recruited some blacks and offered refuge to runaways. It is often said that in Virginia alone thirty thousand slaves ran to the British during the Revolution. The source for this number is Jefferson, and he made it up. He also said that some twenty-seven thousand slaves died of smallpox in British camps during the Revolution; he made up that number as well. The historian Cassandra Pybus, who researched the relevant documents, found that the actual figures were far smaller. Where, then, did Jefferson get his estimates? Pybus found that in a letter detailing the losses from his own plantations, Jefferson wrote that thirty of his slaves had run away and twenty-seven had died of smallpox. He simply took his private numbers and added zeros to create the Virginia numbers.[25]

Dunmore's offer in fact attracted some two or three hundred slaves, not the thousands Jefferson imagined, and many of the people who ran to the British were noncombatant women and children. The most reliable estimate for the total number of "disloyal" slaves is around five thousand men, women, children, and elderly in Virginia and Maryland combined. Some blacks did fight for the British, but Virginia's masters and mistresses were not murdered in their beds. Some slaves did conspire against their owners and were executed for it; others were whipped but not severely, which suggests that the authorities were not convinced of the seriousness of their offenses. In the atmosphere of crisis, the whites imagined more threats than existed. "There have been many Rumours here of the Negroes intending to Rise," a man in Williamsburg wrote, but he thought the reports were "without much foundation."[26]

Such was the loyalty of Virginia's blacks that James Madison proposed an emancipation incentive for slaves who would fight for the state.[27] About a third of the seamen who served in Virginia's navy were black. But it was disloyalty and slacking among whites that presented a much greater problem. Draft resisters rioted, landowners refused to pay taxes, and Jefferson denounced one county as a nest of "delinquents." Given a quota to fill in Washington's army, Virginia could muster only about a quarter of the troops it promised.[28] Some slaveholders dispatched slaves to serve in their stead and then re-enslaved them after the war. Tasked with defending the state against the British invaders, General Lafayette faced a critical shortage of horses and resistance from Virginians who could have helped him. Virginia's planters refused to let him take their mounts, and Governor Jefferson backed the planters. "Stud horses and brood mares will always be excepted" from requisition, he told Lafayette, because "to take them would be to rip up the hen which laid the golden egg."[29] Nevertheless, after the war the supposed disloyalty of *blacks* loomed ominously in Jefferson's memory as an obstacle to their ever becoming citizens, or at least that is what he strongly implied in *Notes*.

If we are to believe what Jefferson claimed in *Notes*, the greatest barrier to emancipation was the risk of blacks "staining the blood" of the masters. "When freed," he wrote, "he is to be removed beyond the reach of mixture." But the subversion of the natural order had already taken place: his own wife's father, among many others, had mingled the races and destroyed the separation ordained by nature. Years later his friend William Short tried to get Jefferson to modify his views on racial mixing since it had already taken place: "Even in our own country there are some [white] people darker than the gradual mixture of the blacks can ever make us." As an example Short pointed to Jefferson's relatives in the Randolph family.[30]

Jefferson gave his blessing to an interracial marriage just a few years after writing *Notes*. He sold one of his slaves, a mixed-race woman, to a white man in Charlottesville so that they could live as husband and wife. The husband was an esteemed business acquaintance of Jefferson's, a man of substance in Charlottesville. The couple and their free, mixed-race children, technically the offspring of "abominable mixture," lived together openly, and the family often went up to Monticello to visit their enslaved relatives and bring gifts.* It is doubtful that Jefferson supplied his overseers and white workmen with copies of *Notes* so that they would abstain from relationships with enslaved women. White workmen fathered two of his top enslaved craftsmen, Joseph Fossett and John Hemmings.

White women, however, had to be policed. When he revised Virginia's slave code after the Revolution, Jefferson proposed extreme punishment for a white woman who gave birth to a mixed-race child: if she refused to leave the state, she was to be outlawed, meaning that she was outside the protection of the laws, legally exposed to any punishment devised by a mob or aggrieved husband. The legislature refused to adopt Jefferson's draconian measure, which suggests an authoritarian streak harsher than the norm of this harsh age and a layer of anxiety over loss of control. As the historian Jon Kukla writes, "Jefferson regarded women's sexual appetites as equal to or even stronger than men's, and he felt a deep-seated fear of women as threatening both to his own self-control and to the proper ordering of society. . . . Jefferson exhibited a deep distrust of women's capacity to disrupt their homes and his world."[31] The severity of the punishments Jefferson suggested in the revision to Virginia's criminal code shocked one of his contemporaries, John Armstrong Jr. (whom President Jefferson appointed minister to France in 1804). In his copy of *Notes*, Armstrong commented in the margin, "This Code has not been adopted and 'tis well it has not. . . . Death & mutilation show it to be the work of a man quite ignorant of the progress of truth, or quite indifferent to it."[32]

Notes leaves a great deal unsaid. Jefferson never alluded to his own kinship to slaves through his wife and her father. He stressed, rather, eloquently and passionately, that slavery presented an unutterable horror

---

*The marriage of Mary Hemings and Colonel Thomas Bell is discussed in Chapter 11.

and must be eradicated. Only the most careful reader would perceive the unspoken but crucial connection between the section of *Notes* that concerns slavery and another section where he makes it plain that slavery was essential to the survival of the new nation. Slaves formed a bulwark against an existential threat to liberty, because as long as America had slaves, the Old World mobs of white working people could be left on the other side of the Atlantic.

In the section of his book concerning slavery, he wrote of replacing slaves with whites, but in another section he withdrew his proposal of "proper encouragements" and proposed a total ban on immigration for twenty-seven years, the span of time he calculated it would take for the existing population to double. After that hiatus newcomers might be more safely absorbed, resulting in a government "more homogeneous, more peaceable, more durable," but these newcomers would have to be carefully screened.

Jefferson firmly opposed admitting a particular class of people that we might regard as the vanguard of entrepreneurship—artisans, mechanics, and other independent workers who made their livings by their skills. He looked upon this class of people as inherently debased, a danger to the Republic as grave as slavery. "Corruption of morals," he wrote in *Notes*, was the indelible "mark" set on people who depended for their sustenance on the "caprice of customers." His use of the word "mark" is striking, because it was commonly used when referring to the mark of race, or the mark of "corruption of blood" attributed to felons. In his view dependence on customers "begets subservience and venality, suffocates the germ of virtue, and prepares fit tools for the designs of ambition." So, he concluded, "Let us never wish to see our citizens occupied at a work-bench, or twirling a distaff. . . . [L]et our work-shops remain in Europe."

Insisting upon banning artisans from Virginia, Jefferson brushed aside the added cost of importing manufactured goods from Europe, a premium that, he said, "will be made up in happiness and permanence of government." This was far better than dealing with the "inconveniences" caused "by the importation of foreigners." He wrote: "It is for the happiness of those united in society to harmonize as much as possible," particularly under a form of government "conducted by common consent." The principles of American government "perhaps are more peculiar than those of any other in the universe. It is a composition of the freest principles of the English constitution, with others derived from natural right and natural reason." Europeans immigrating to the New World came from absolute monarchies, and they would "bring with them the principles of the governments they leave, imbibed in their early youth; or, if able to throw them off, it will be in exchange for an unbounded licentiousness, passing, as is usual, from one extreme to another. It would be a miracle were they to stop precisely at the point of temperate liberty. These principles, with their language, they will trans-mit to their children."

Jefferson recoiled from the prospect that foreigners and their chil-dren would get the vote and "share with us" the power to affect legis-lation: "They will infuse into [the law] their spirit, warp and bias its direction, and render it a heterogeneous, incoherent, distracted mass." The future of the nation, and of Virginia especially, presented a grand prospect, but only if the nature of the population could be controlled. John Armstrong made a marginal note on this subject as well: "Mr. [John] Jay is said to have had the same dread of foreigners when he disfigured the Constitution of N.Y. by making their admission to citi-zenship in that State both tedious and difficult." Pointing to the Ger-mans of Pennsylvania as examples of people "as fond of freedom and as tenacious of equal government as Mr. J. himself," Armstrong suggested that all those who share Jefferson's and Jay's dread "should recollect that in politics almost every speculative truth is a practical falsehood."

But soon enough Jefferson found that he could not let his workshops remain in Europe, and at Monticello he built them with slaves occupy-ing the workbenches and twirling the distaffs. Because these skilled people were slaves, they did not disrupt the happiness and permanence of society. An Englishman who visited Virginia in the early nineteenth century and stopped to see Jefferson at Monticello noted that demo-graphic phenomenon. In Virginia, "the mass of people, who in other countries might become mobs, [were] nearly altogether composed of their own Negro slaves."[33]

Notes contains an electrifying jeremiad that might have moved the ston-iest heart in the assembly had Jefferson ever delivered it. He foresaw

Virginia, "my country," in wreckage because Virginians refused to give up slavery: "Can the liberties of a nation be thought secure when we have removed their only firm basis, a conviction in the minds of the people that these liberties are of the gift of God? That they are not to be violated but with his wrath? Indeed I tremble for my country when I reflect that God is just: that his justice cannot sleep for ever."

Jefferson was haunted by the vision that God might be on the side of the slaves, that the turning of fortune's wheel "may become probable by supernatural interference! The Almighty has no attribute which can take side with us in such a contest," and "under the auspices of heaven" a racial revolution might bring the "extirpation" of the masters. In this lightning flash of terror, the master of Monticello is once more the child of Shadwell, coddled by the slaves he knows but nervously eyeing the fence line, wondering what could be in the minds of the unknown mass of blacks beyond the pale, kept in check by unremitting despotism. As he would do so often, Jefferson articulated what was inarticulate—in this instance, the persistent Anglo-Saxon fear of being overwhelmed by darker people in a horrific, apocalyptic battle like the future ones at the Alamo or Little Bighorn, when the races collide on a frontier.

The racial sections in *Notes* captured the predicament of blacks in America and the multiple layers of reality they had to contend with. Jefferson spoke and wrote disparagingly of them in the abstract, when in practice he routinely placed his trust in them, gave them significant responsibilities, exulted over the abilities and output of his slave craftsmen, allowed a surprising degree of autonomy to some slaves, paid some of them for good work, and was related to them. As a matter of day-to-day reality, the slaves could perceive Jefferson's trust, the responsibilities they discharged, the loyalties they felt and displayed, and most of all the blood kinship they had with him. But these made up just one layer of reality.

As an African-American said a century and a half later, after segregation had fallen: "We lived under a hidden law which we did not understand."[34] The most powerful force in the plantation world resided within the mind of the man in charge, concealed by the same "immoveable veil" that Jefferson attributed to blacks. The Jefferson scholar Merrill Peterson once remarked on "the Negroes' . . . subtle ways of confounding the white folks," but the slaves were powerless against the fantasies that white people could concoct about them.[35] Jefferson's racial theorizing strikes many modern eyes as irrational and illogical or simply repugnant. If asked, Jefferson could explain every clause, but intellectual consistency was not the point. His philosophy was a tool of control over others and himself. If you have a governing philosophy, you can summarily exclude exceptions, like a Phillis Wheatley, as a hanging judge excludes evidence as it suits him.

Jefferson made a brief observation in another section of *Notes* that shows his ability to absorb contradiction. In the section on "public revenue and expenses" he states, "The value of our lands and slaves . . . doubles in about twenty years. This arises from the multiplication of our slaves, from the extension of culture, and increased demand for lands." So on the one hand, black people are inferior, disloyal, and dangerous, and they grow in number alarmingly; but on the other, they are extremely valuable assets and multiply most profitably. Should we believe the philosophy or the calculation? They worked together. His assets reliably compounding, his philosophy rendering him deaf to the appeals of humanity, he plowed through any contradiction. He wielded a species of power that made its own reality.

4

"The Hammer or the Anvil"

The sufferings endured by the American people in the Revolution seized one of Jefferson's early biographers with emotion: "Our fabric, such as it is, is a blood-cemented one. Groans, and tears, and woes unutterable, accompanied every step of its foundation."[1] He declared the crucial importance of telling and retelling the stories of the Revolution—"Let every coming generation of Americans understand these facts"—because only then could the nation be forever knit together by shared emotion.

The suffering of the people is written in Jefferson's Farm Book. What makes these woes especially unutterable is that so many of the lives lost were those of children. Next to the names of two girls aged about eight and six Jefferson wrote: "joined enemy & died," as if they had betrayed him and had been punished.[2] Their names were Flora and Quomina. They fled Jefferson's Elk Hill plantation with their mother, Black Sal, and their brother Jemmy, aged ten. They ran because the British promised freedom. Very little is known of Black Sal. She was not a house servant and had no special skill. In Jefferson's records she is a single mother marked down as the lowest kind of worker, a "labourer in the ground."

The commander of the British forces, Lord Cornwallis, hunting for Jefferson and laying waste everywhere in Virginia, during the month of June 1781 made his headquarters at Elk Hill, a plantation fifty miles from Monticello. In American history the name Cornwallis is synonymous with tyranny and terror, but to the enslaved people of Virginia he was the Liberator. So that summer Black Sal put her family's fate in the hands of the British army. Flora and Quomina died of disease in the British camp. Disheartened, Sal returned with Jemmy to the plantation, where she and her son shortly died.

Though it was known that the British camps were dangerous, two other laborers in the ground, Hannibal and his wife, Patt, gathered up their six children, all under the age of twelve, and ran to the British to get freedom. All of them died of disease.[*3]

The Revolutionary War ended with a mass emancipation of slaves, a landmark event that Americans have largely forgotten because it was enacted by the British, and partly because it puts the taint of treason on African-Americans. This liberation culminated in 1783 as a matter of military honor for British field commanders. They rejected the compromises of the diplomats, applied their own interpretation to the peace treaty, and fulfilled their promise to give freedom to everyone who had reached their lines. In the final months of the Revolutionary War some eight to ten thousand black Americans embarked on British ships from New York and ports in the South. The British emancipation of slaves—most of whom were from Virginia—became a political issue. The Virginia Assembly instructed its congressional delegation to demand reparations from the British government.

The story of Black Sal and her children, of Hannibal and Patt and their children, does not quite fit into our "blood-cemented" fabric. When Jefferson's biographer Henry Randall summoned the memory of "woes unutterable" and called for "groans, and tears," he did not have these people in mind. Their humanity cries out, but they ran to the wrong flag. We can only imagine the desperation and the hope of these parents who took their small children to a military camp on the move. It is a mark of their despair at what they thought the future would otherwise hold; they were fleeing a dead zone where the Declaration of Independence cast no light, and they never made it onto the ships.

When Randall evoked groans and tears, he surely had in mind a passage in Jefferson's papers:

---

*Disease killed thousands of these runaway slaves, as it killed thousands of British and American soldiers. British doctors inoculated newly arrived slaves against smallpox as fast as possible but could not keep up with the speed of the terrible epidemic sweeping the Eastern Seaboard.

When the measure of their tears shall be full, when their groans shall have involved heaven itself in darkness, doubtless a god of justice will awaken to their distress, and by diffusing light and liberality among their oppressors, or at length by his exterminating thunder, manifest his attention to the things of this world, and that they are not left to the guidance of a blind fatality.[4]

Jefferson was writing about the travail of the slaves, and in his entire canon there is nothing more moving than this passage. From the date when he wrote it, June 1786, until Lincoln's second inaugural address, no American leader so powerfully condemned the American enterprise for violating God's justice. Jefferson possessed a sharp sensitivity to injustice and inequity. Massive social disparity appalled him. He recoiled at the vision of a world without justice, ruled solely by power, in which "every man . . . must be either the hammer or the anvil," of society divided in two, with a gilded class resembling "god and his angels in splendor" lording over "crouds of the damned trampled under their feet . . . suffering under physical and moral oppression."[*5]

Few biographical tasks are more frustrating than trying to assemble a montage of quotations from Jefferson's written work that make sense of his stance on slavery. Among the completely contradictory points he advanced about slaves and slavery, we have: the institution was evil; blacks had natural rights, and slavery abrogated those rights; emancipation was desirable; emancipation was imminent; emancipation was impossible until a way could be found to exile the freed slaves; emancipation was impossible because slaves were incompetent; emancipation was just over the horizon but could not take place until the minds of white people were "ripened" for it.

Laid end to end, his utterances present a rolling paradox of contradictions that inspire his detractors to call him a hypocrite, his defenders to call him compartmentalized, and baffled onlookers to call him "human." In Joseph Ellis's well-known observation, "He had the kind of

---

*In his advice to Americans traveling in Europe he wrote: "Take every possible occasion of entering into the hovels of the labourers . . . see what they eat, how they are cloathed, whether they are obliged to labour too hard; whether the government or their landlord takes from them an unjust proportion of their labour" ("Jefferson's Hints to Americans Travelling in Europe," June 19, 1788, in *Papers*, vol. 13).

duplicity possible only in the pure of heart." Ellis argues that Jefferson possessed, and in some ways was victimized by, "daunting powers of self-deception," defends him against the charge of lying, and does not see evidence of a conflicted soul or guilty conscience that others have detected. John Chester Miller finds a "harrowing sense of guilt." Fawn Brodie writes, "Still, there was guilt," and suggests that Jefferson urgently examined his conscience, conducting "scrutinies into the heart of man."[6]

Jefferson appears out of focus because he was not static; we are seeing a process unfolding. There was the young man, heir to the slave system, who planned a common cemetery for blacks and whites with a monument that condemned his own mastery. There was the fiery revolutionary who denounced the "execrable commerce" of the slave trade, declared that Africans possessed natural rights, and then in 1785 sold thirty-one slaves to keep his creditors at bay. During the post-Revolutionary decade, from 1783 to the early 1790s, Jefferson's misgivings over slavery seem to fade. Blacks still have rights, but the prospect of their emancipation recedes. The "scrutinies" involve not only the heart but also the microeconomics of slavery at Monticello and the macroeconomics of slavery in the emerging nation. The young, unmarried idealist, the disgusted heir of slavery, ages into the father worried over making "provision for my children" and enlarging "that capital which a growing family had a right to expect."[7] He is a man holding a crystal ball in which he simultaneously sees a golden future and a moral abyss, and is thus confronted with a choice.

Jefferson's process mirrored the one taking place in the whole country, so this span of years from the 1780s into the 1790s is crucial. Given the ideals of the Revolution, it was difficult to admit that slavery had a place in the new nation. The racial integration of George Washington's army had raised hopes for a general emancipation of black slaves. Under pressure from extreme progressives—notably the Quakers—the Virginia legislature in 1782 had passed a remarkable law allowing individuals to free slaves, but it stopped short of mandating a general emancipation. Then, as tobacco cultivation faltered in eastern Virginia, it boomed in southern Virginia, North Carolina, and Kentucky. "The Western people are already calling out for slaves for their new lands, and will fill that country with slaves," George Mason declared during the Constitutional Convention.[8]

Revered as the chief spokesman of liberty, Jefferson received many appeals from abolitionists foreign and domestic to explain and expunge the contradictions. When the British abolitionist Richard Price, a Unitarian minister, arranged to have a pamphlet on emancipation hand-delivered to South Carolina's Speaker of the House, he was told that the Speaker "thought himself almost affronted by having the pamphlet presented to him."[9] To whom did Price turn for an explanation of this blatant betrayal of American ideals? To Jefferson, of course. Price wrote, "I have made myself ridiculous by Speaking of the American Revolution in the manner I have done; it will appear that the people who have been Struggling so earnestly to save *themselves* from Slavery are very ready to enslave *others*; the friends of liberty and humanity in Europe will be mortify'd, and an event which had raised their hopes will prove only an introduction to a new Scene of aristocratic tyranny and human debasement."

Jefferson admitted that the new nation presented the "interesting spectacle of justice in conflict with avarice and oppression," but he raised hope for the future. He told Price that "the sacred side" in the conflict over slavery was "gaining daily recruits from the influx into office of young men."[10] This was one of a series of responses he composed in the 1780s to defend himself and his country for America's inexplicable delay in ending injustice. To borrow from Joseph Ellis, there is duplicity here and a strange species of purity, because it was vital to Jefferson that he make everything America did seem good.

The lives of Flora and Quomina put a human face on the woes suffered by slaves during the Revolution. They also put a human face on aspects of slavery often omitted from discussions of the Founders but very much on Jefferson's mind. The fate of these girls is known because they were assets that Jefferson listed in his Farm Book, along with the names of the rest of Monticello's war dead, as lost property. That crowded corner of the ledger page has a blank feel to it, empty of any remark on the human travail it records. On this page the people are listed not as freedom seekers but as absconded assets, and Jefferson pressured the British government for reparations.

It is still said that slavery was a dying, unprofitable institution after the Revolution, although the historian Robert McColley debunked that myth in the 1970s. The myth remains useful because it averts attention from the fact that slavery was extremely profitable—so profitable in so many ways that, as McColley demonstrated, it was not dying but expanding, well before the cotton boom. Then as now, no one liked to admit that questions of "sacred" human rights are determined by financial considerations.

And without the financial factor, Jefferson's protest against Britain's mass evacuation of freed slaves seems inexplicable, given that the British precisely fulfilled the wish he expressed in *Notes* that African-Americans be colonized to distant places beyond the reach of mixture. If *Notes* is to be believed, the king's generals had done America, and Jefferson himself, a huge favor.[11]

But Flora and Quomina, young as they were, owed Jefferson money. In his legal writings he referred to "a debt contracted from the infant to the master."[12] All unknowing, the girls contracted this debt through their mother, as did every enslaved child through every enslaved mother: "being the property of the master, it is impossible she [a slave mother] should maintain it [her child] but with her master's goods." This formula was universally recognized by slaveholders.* Slaves came into this world, and into the consciousness of their masters, not only as property but in a debtor relationship, as if they had a contract. Every time a child was born into slavery, a debt was incurred. Their relationship to the master was not just as brute laborers but as shadow players in the economic landscape, quasi-people who could incur obligations, duty-bound to pay for their own upkeep.

This way of thinking put a legal footing under perpetual slavery, as if there existed a contract between Jefferson and his family, on the one hand, and their slaves, on the other. The slaves formed the critical mass of the capital his family had a "right" to expect. Thus redefining his relationship to his slaves, he moved it away from "slavery," which was loathsome to him because it was a theft of their rights, and toward a framework he felt comfortable with, a framework formed by legalisms of debt and reciprocal obligation, which acknowledged in theory (at

---

*The emancipation laws of Northern states required slaves to work into adulthood to pay off the master's expense for having maintained them as children. Having died before being able to work off their debt, Flora and Quomina departed this life with their account unbalanced.

least to his satisfaction) the rights of his slaves. Their rights were not abrogated, merely suspended. By being born at Monticello, slaves became part of the legacy that Jefferson's children had a right to expect. In this decade of Jefferson's decision-making, thirty-five girls were born into indebtedness at Monticello.

His dealings with Monticello's slaves express an idea of reciprocity. One of his most important terms is "happiness" (familiar from the Declaration of Independence), both his and the slaves'. He writes, "I have my house to build, my feilds to farm, and to watch for the happiness of those who labor for mine."[13] For his part, he is obligated to act as benefactor of the slaves. He stated to his plantation manager without a trace of irony: "I am governed solely by views to their happiness." He never explained the existence of this contract to his slaves, but he expected they would perceive its effect and be inspired to reciprocate his benefactions with diligence and loyalty. Those who did not act according to the unspoken contract could be punished.

Jefferson's sense of his slaves' obligation to him was sharpened by what the British did to him when the Revolution ended, when he and his fellow Virginia planters confronted once more the debts they owed to British merchants from before the war. Their grace period was over, and it had not really been a grace period after all. They were shocked to learn that their creditors had added interest during the war. Freed from Great Britain politically, they became enslaved financially. "These debts had become hereditary from father to son for many generations, so that the planters were a species of property annexed to certain mercantile houses in London," he wrote.[14] When Jefferson was living in Paris as U.S. minister plenipotentiary in 1784–89, he sought some way out from the debts that he and his countrymen owed.

Jefferson's British creditors were pressing hard for payment of a debt that had been passed to him from the estate of his wife's father, John Wayles. In negotiations with his creditors in 1786, Jefferson raised the issue of Flora, Quomina, and the other dead souls, claiming that the slaves and other property he had lost "would have paid your debt, principal and interest."[15] It is not quite proper to say that Jefferson could "lie," but here he was twisting the truth. He claimed a loss of thirty slaves, though by his own count he had lost eighteen. (Some returned to Monticello, and later he sold or gave away at least five of those.) He questioned Cornwallis's motives, saying that the general "would have done right" if his intention had been "to give them freedom"—in fact, that *was* Cornwallis's intention. It is worth noting that during the war Governor Jefferson never proposed freeing African-Americans who would agree to bear arms for the United States.

Coldly making the case for what we would call a wrongful-death claim, Jefferson accused Cornwallis of intentionally planning "to consign them to inevitable death from the small pox and putrid fever then raging in his camp." In any humane calculation the melancholy deaths of the families who fled to freedom can only be called an accident of war, and if anyone had fault, it was Jefferson. But he passed blame to the British for his own failure to inoculate his slaves against smallpox, as Washington had done. Jefferson's pleas left his creditors unmoved.*[16]

Tossing in Paris "on a bed of thorns," haunted in his sleep by the nightmarish face of the debt collector, he has a liberating revelation: it is the slaves who are responsible for the debt. It is not his fault. The laborers in the ground must compensate him by making greater exertions than ever before—they must work harder, very much harder.[17]

In July 1787 he writes to his manager at Monticello:

> I cannot decide to sell my lands. I have sold too much of them already, and they are the only sure provision for my children, nor would I willingly sell the slaves as long as there remains any prospect of paying my debts with their labor. In this I am governed solely by views to their happiness which will render it worth their while to use extraordinary exertions for some time to enable me to . . .

At this point one expects that Jefferson will write "set them free." But he writes: "put them ultimately on an easier footing,† which I will do the moment they have paid the debts due from the estate, two thirds of which have been contracted by purchasing them."[18]

---

*Having failed to lift the debt burden as a private citizen, as secretary of state he argued in 1791 and 1792 that debts to British creditors should be expunged because British generals had violated the peace treaty by evacuating freed slaves.

†In December 1786 he wrote almost the same words to his manager at Monticello: "I am miserable till I shall owe not a shilling: the moment that shall be the case I shall feel myself at liberty to do something for the comfort of my slaves."

His slaves in fact had nothing to do with this debt, so it is hard to put a properly descriptive word to this final sentence, which is a turning point in Jefferson's embrace of slavery. One could call it a lie, or an evasion, or a delusion. In any event, it is completely untrue, and Jefferson knew it to be untrue because he was immersed in the legalities of that debt.[19] His father-in-law had taken a speculative plunge into the slave market and lost his shirt to a crowd of rich Virginia planters.

Wayles was "one of those wholesale chaps," as an aristocratic planter described the traders, middlemen, and debt collectors who flocked to the slave trade when the market rose. He and a partner had brokered the sale of a consignment of slaves arriving aboard the *Prince of Wales* in 1772. The shrinkage of inventory en route was 30 percent—only 280 people out of 400 survived the passage, and of these Wayles and his partner sold 266.[20] But when Wayles tried to collect payment from his wealthy customers, they were "not at home." The tobacco market had collapsed; the planters had no ready cash; and in any case they were accustomed to evading bills tendered by the lower sort of chap. So Wayles and his partner were on the hook to their London agents for the total payment for the shipload of people. Jefferson got stuck with the bill when he inherited the Wayles estate in 1773.[21]

The phrase "blaming the victim" is a modern coinage, but it approximates the frame of mind Jefferson constructed. The slaves Jefferson inherited from Wayles were not the people who had been imported for sale. They were Virginia-born people, but because they were black, he considered that they bore a communal responsibility for the debt Wayles had incurred by trading in black people. Jefferson's letter to his manager shows a deft, magical shifting of blame away from himself, from his father-in-law, from the planters, from the big traders in London—all of whom had bet on the market and lost. Ensnared in obligations by a market so deranged that money had become, Jefferson said, "like oak leaves," he blames the slaves—*their situation is their own fault, and they are obliged to pay off my debt because I am the victim.*[22] His laborers became harnessed to a virtuous undertaking; they would save him; and their obligation for his debts quieted his moral conflicts.

5

The Bancroft Paradox

Slavery followed Jefferson abroad. Sent by Congress to France in 1784 as minister plenipotentiary to forge "a powerful link of commercial connexion" between the United States and France, Jefferson carried in his head a vital statistic: more than one-third of all U.S. exports consisted of tobacco. He estimated the total annual value of American exports at $80 million, and of this "thirty [million dollars] are constituted by the single article of tobacco."[1] Not far behind tobacco was rice. Both crops were raised and harvested mainly by slaves.

Without the French fleet, French troops, and French loans, the United States might well have lost the War of Independence. France now held the key to the financial survival of the fledgling republic, locked in a commercial struggle with Great Britain. So Jefferson appealed to the French foreign minister, the Comte de Vergennes, stating his hope that "the whole of this [the tobacco crop] be brought into the ports of France" to overcome the "serious obstacle [of] our debt to Great Britain." With the proceeds of tobacco and rice sales to France, American planters could make payments on their British debts. Furthermore, importing French products for sale in the United States would stimulate the American economy, allowing the British debt to be paid off entirely.[2]

Jefferson's personal predicament at Monticello mirrored the national predicament. He wrote letters to the foreign minister and to his manager at Monticello in the same week, and the messages were essentially the same; in both the micro- and the macroeconomies, the slaves would be harnessed indefinitely to the task of paying off British debt.*

Jefferson found himself in an extremely awkward position in his dealings with the French government on this issue. The representative of a weak new nation, he could gain access to royal officials only through the intervention of America's friends at court, and all of them were abolitionists. Like his predecessor, Benjamin Franklin, Jefferson took up a public-relations campaign to persuade our most valued foreign partner that his newly fledged nation did not have a human-rights problem.

The "Americanists" at the French court believed in the ideals of the Revolution and its extraordinary promise for the future of humanity, and they expected Jefferson to do something to end slavery. These were men who had marshaled military and financial backing for the American Revolution. The Marquis de Lafayette is the one best remembered today; other supporters were the Marquis de Condorcet, the Marquis de Chastellux (who had visited Monticello in 1782), and the Duke de La Rochefoucauld-Liancourt (who translated the U.S. Constitution into French). Lafayette and Chastellux had crossed the ocean to risk their lives for the American cause, the former as a general in the Continental army, the latter as an officer in the French expeditionary force. Now that independence had been won but slavery remained, they wondered what they had fought for.

These men took America at its word, particularly the words of Jefferson. Gazing across the Atlantic in hope and expectation, Condorcet declared, "The spectacle of the equality that reigns in the United States and which assures its peace and prosperity can be useful in Europe. . . . What had been for [European liberals] only words and paper had, in America, become flesh and blood."[3] What Americans had accomplished made European hopes soar: "everything tells us that we are bordering the period of one of the greatest revolutions of the human race."[4]

The equality was not universal. When the fighting subsided during the Revolutionary War after the Battle of Yorktown, Chastellux had taken the opportunity to visit Jefferson at Monticello. On his way he

---

*The proceeds of tobacco had already paid much of the expense of fighting the Revolutionary War. "To a large degree it may be said that Americans bought their independence with slave labor," writes Edmund Morgan in *American Slavery, American Freedom.*

saw that in Virginia the planters had impoverished free whites working alongside still enslaved blacks. Chastellux wrote that he had never, "since I crossed the sea," seen white poverty in America to compare with what he found in this slave state:

> Humanity has still more to suffer from the state of poverty in which a great number of white people live in Virginia. It is in [Virginia], for the first time since I crossed the sea, that I have seen poor people. For, among these rich plantations where the Negro alone is wretched, one often finds miserable huts inhabited by whites, whose wan looks and ragged garments bespeak poverty. At first I found it hard to understand how, in a country where there is still so much land to clear, men who do not refuse to work could remain in misery; but I have since learned that all these useless lands and those immense estates, with which Virginia is still covered, have their proprietors. Nothing is more common than to see them possessing five or six thousand acres of land, but exploiting only as much of it as their Negroes can cultivate. Yet they will not give away or even sell the smallest portion of it, because they are attached to their possessions and always hope to eventually increase the numbers of their Negroes.[5]

While Jefferson served in France, a tide of anti-American propaganda poured from England's presses. In order to ruin America's chances of forming commercial alliances with the Continent, the British spread stories that the new American experiment in republican government was sinking into disorder and bankruptcy. "The British ministry," Jefferson wrote, "have so long hired their gazetteers to repeat and model into every form lies about our being in anarchy, that the world has at length believed them."[6] Naturally suspicious of republican government, many French officials were inclined to believe the propaganda. France's small circle of ardent Americanists formed a bulwark against it.

In response to British slanders, both Jefferson and Franklin emphasized America's virtue, enlightenment, liberality, and commitment to equality. Condorcet had declared that equality assures a nation's peace and prosperity. Jefferson wrote that agricultural pursuits made the United States "more virtuous, more free, and more happy."[7] In his campaign to break the traditional, royal-sponsored monopolies that governed the European economy, Jefferson argued a liberal ideology, pressing the notion that free trade emerged from intellectual enlightenment and the advance of "liberal sentiment," whereas monopolies had their roots in "remote and unenlightened periods."[8]

But to keep the support of the Americanists, Jefferson had to confront an ideology of human rights purer than his own. An outspoken opponent of slavery (and a distinguished mathematician and economist), Condorcet wrote that the slave owner "abjured his own rights" and that "to reduce a man to slavery, to buy him, to sell him, to keep him in servitude, all these are real crimes that are worse than stealing."[9] He insisted, in direct contradiction of Jefferson, that "Nature has endowed [blacks] with the same genius, the same judgment, the same virtues as the Whites." Addressing the slaves directly, Condorcet wrote, "I know how often your fidelity, your probity, your firmness have put your masters to the blush."[10] He advanced a proposal to compel the French government to "examine the means of destroying the slave trade and preparing for the destruction of black slavery."[11]

With men such as Condorcet in mind, Jefferson created the impression in *Notes* that a sweeping emancipation law would very soon be passed in Virginia, but that was not the case at all. (Thus he was deeply afraid of having the antislavery statements he tailored for the French circulated in America.) He succeeded in convincing Condorcet of the imminence of change. Condorcet wrote, "It is true that Negro slavery still exists in some of the United States; but all enlightened men feel its shame, and its danger, and this blemish will not long continue to sully the purity of American laws."[12]

Jefferson assiduously courted the editor of a major encyclopedia, a publication that was to be widely circulated and would shape opinions about the United States for decades to come, so that he could propose changes in the draft for the entry on the United States. The editor, Jean Nicolas Démeunier, had described Virginia's slave laws and pointed out that the gradual emancipation act whose imminent passage Jefferson had promised in his book had not been enacted. Realizing that this failure put the United States, and Virginia especially, in a very poor light, Jefferson hastened to explain the reason, which he hoped Démeunier would add to the entry: "Persons of virtue and firmness" in the Virginia Assembly had decided that the time was not right; "they saw that the moment of doing it with success was not yet arrived, and that an unsuccessful effort, as too often happens, would only rivet still closer the chains of bondage, and retard the moment of delivery to this oppressed description of men."*[13]

Jefferson omitted mentioning that the Virginia legislature had liberalized the slave laws so as to enable individual owners to free people at will, for Démeunier would then have asked why persons of virtue and firmness had not yet freed their slaves, particularly why Jefferson had not freed his. Jefferson also did not mention that in revising the slave code, he had suggested a law compelling a white woman who bore a mixed-race child to leave Virginia or be placed "out of the protection of the laws."[14]

Painfully aware that French hands were bloody from slavery, Lafayette helped to form the Society of Friends of the Blacks in 1788 with the purpose of abolishing slavery in French colonies and elsewhere. The group included the famous chemist Lavoisier and, of course, Condorcet, who was elected president.[15] Among the other founders were some of America's most avid supporters, including the Marquis de Chastellux and the Duke de La Rochefoucauld-Liancourt. Jefferson declined to join the society while expressing fulsome support for its goals: "You know that nobody wishes more ardently to see an abolition not only of the trade but of the condition of slavery: and certainly nobody will be more willing to encounter every sacrifice for that object." But in order to ensure his effectiveness as an antislavery activist in the United States, "prudence" required that he "avoid too public a demonstration of my wishes."[16]

During his tenure as America's spokesman in Europe, Benjamin Franklin had trod the same fine line as Jefferson, as the historian David Waldstreicher discovered when he took a fresh look at Franklin's diplomatic career: "He played very carefully with antislavery to gain peace and favorable trading conditions—including access to the Caribbean islands—for the new nation. Whether [Franklin] believed that North

---

*Satisfied with Jefferson's response, Démeunier invited him to rewrite the encyclopedia's entry on the United States, which Jefferson expanded to a length nearly forty pages longer than the article on Great Britain.

American slavery was being eliminated or not . . . it was extremely useful to say it was." Waldstreicher continues: "Everything Franklin did in France reflected the need to depict America as virtuous."[17]

Though wary of Lafayette, finding him vain and ambitious, Jefferson cultivated his relationship with him, since Lafayette had vital connections at court. Lafayette helped persuade the foreign minister to establish an "American Committee" to examine trade issues. To ensure that American interests would be strenuously represented, Lafayette arranged to get himself appointed a member.[18] When he argued the case for importing tobacco from the United States, someone submitted to the committee a persuasive set of agricultural statistics in support of the American position. The author of these complicated statistical tables is not known, but the quality of the work has led scholars to speculate that Condorcet compiled the statistics. Persuaded that slavery would soon be expunged, the abolitionist mathematician quietly used his talent in service to America.[19]

One of Jefferson's most damning pronouncements about black people—on a par, perhaps, with his speculation that African women copulated with apes—is that it was impossible to free them because they were like children. The key sentence reads: "to give liberty to, or rather, to abandon persons whose habits have been formed in slavery is like abandoning children." Given Jefferson's experience managing slaves, many observers have felt comfortable taking this as the well-considered opinion held not only by Jefferson but by "virtually all" of the Founders.[20] But the full context of this remark puts it in a vastly different light. It was not a statement of the impossibility of emancipation but the preamble to a plan for emancipation. So we have reversed Jefferson's meaning, and we have stepped into the Bancroft Paradox.

This famous assessment came out of a dinner party at a country house outside Paris, attended by officials in a position to advance American trading interests. Whatever Jefferson said at this dinner would soon be repeated at court, not only in Paris, but in London as well. Pestered by questions about the injustice of race relations in the United States, Jefferson did what Southerners would do for the next two centuries: he painted a picture for these outsiders of the difficulties and burdens of a white man living among black people.

The dinner took place at the country house of the Chevalier de La Luzerne, who had been France's wartime ambassador to the United States. The king's minister of household affairs, a well-known lawyer named Malesherbes, was also at the table. Jefferson regarded him as a "good and enlightened minister," an important ally at court to whom he personally sent a copy of *Notes on the State of Virginia*. Also present was Edward Bancroft, an American with connections at the highest levels of British society and officialdom. Bancroft also had ties to important French progressives and to English abolitionists. The signal fact about his career in France at this time was, unfortunately, that he was operating not only as a spy for the Americans but also as an agent for the British, playing them off against each other.

Jefferson addressed the delicate question of why there had not yet been a general emancipation in the cradle of liberty. Emancipation had actually been tried in Virginia, he said, and had failed, not because the white people did not have the right spirit, but because the blacks were incompetent. Worse, it turned out that many blacks—the most sensible ones, Jefferson said—actually preferred slavery. Given their freedom, they found it very difficult to handle and asked to be taken back as slaves.*

We know what was said at this dinner because Bancroft recapitulated the conversation in a letter to Jefferson, seeking additional information:

> You mentioned the Case of a Gentleman in Virginia, who had benevolently liberated all his Negroe Slaves and endeavoured to employ them on Wages to Cultivate his Plantation; but after a tryal of some time it was found that Slavery had rendered them incapable of Self Government, or at least that no regard for futurity could operate on their minds with sufficient Force to engage them to any thing like constant industry or even so much of it as would provide them with food and Cloathing and that the most sensible of them desired to return to their former state.[21]

Bancroft had repeated the table talk, as Jefferson expected, in England. The abolitionists Bancroft knew were keenly interested in getting an

---

*Variations of this scenario pop up on Internet discussions today.

exact statement of the circumstances, as they were then campaigning for the emancipation of West Indian laborers "who have been long habituated to Slavery." Not discouraged by Jefferson's account, they hoped rather to learn from the Virginia experiment.[22]

Jefferson replied to Bancroft with a long letter, offering his assessment of "the experiments which have been made," when "many quakers in Virginia seated their slaves on their lands as tenants." The experience ended very badly, he said. And then he formulated the oft-quoted creed: "to give liberty to, or rather, to abandon persons whose habits have been formed in slavery is like abandoning children."

He offered persuasive details:

> I remember that the landlord was obliged to plan their crops for them, to direct all their operations during every season & according to the weather. But what is more afflicting, he was obliged to watch them daily & almost constantly to make them work, & even to whip them. . . . These slaves chose to steal from their neighbors rather than work; they became public nuisances and in most instances were reduced to slavery again.*

He asked Bancroft "to make no use of this imperfect information," but on the other hand he released Bancroft to spread the story by word of mouth, "in common conversation."

Jefferson did everlasting damage with his dinner-table story about the incompetence of black people. He knew it would circulate widely, but he could not have known that his comparison of blacks to children would resound for centuries. And it was a lie.

A group of Quakers in Virginia had indeed freed their slaves in the 1770s, alarming slaveholders across the region. As one of the emancipators, Warner Mifflin, wrote, "Great stir was made, as if the country was going to be overturned and ruined. It seemed as if the living spirit had gone forth, to deceive the people." He continued: "When the subject of setting the blacks free [arose], the prevailing opinion was, that negroes

---

*In this letter Jefferson absolved the slaves from any guilt for stealing, as he had in *Notes*: "A man's moral sense must be unusually strong, if slavery does not make him a thief. He who is permitted by law to have no property of his own, can with difficulty conceive that property is founded in anything but force."

This whole page is good b/c it contradicts the excuse of "people were a product of their time" because even then many people were abolitionists

were such thieves, that they would not do to be free. . . . this was chiefly the plea of slave-holders." Not only did the Quakers declare that it was God's wish "that the Black People should be free as well as the White people in society," but they held, more ominously, that God had made all people "of one blood."[23]

Warner Mifflin's father, Daniel, had freed ninety-one slaves on Virginia's Eastern Shore in 1775, inspiring a spate of emancipations by Quakers in that region—all of which were illegal at the time. One emancipator appealed directly to Governor Patrick Henry for relief from the "meddling people," local officials who seized the freed people and put them back into slavery. So *successful* were the manumissions that the Virginia legislature eventually ratified these extralegal acts after a petition from the Quakers, and they even turned aside individual requests from disgruntled heirs to invalidate manumissions. In 1782, Quakers spent fifteen days in Richmond lobbying the assembly for the emancipation law allowing owners to manumit their property at will. Governor Henry supported them.[24] Jefferson was no longer governor, but he could not have been ignorant of the extraordinary lobbying effort, and of the law that was its result.[25]

Southern planters reacted hysterically to this early success of the abolitionists, as Warner Mifflin recounted, and set out "to deceive the people." The empire of slavery made its own reality in a propaganda war against the Quakers. It was essential to the preservation of slavery to discredit anyone who actually did set slaves free, smothering dissent in a cloud of rumor. Jefferson obliquely acknowledged the shakiness of his sources, admitting he "never had very particular information." It is possible that Jefferson knew the actual results of the Quaker emancipation program but disparaged it in order to protect Virginia's image. He could blame the victims. Emancipation was slow in coming because the blacks were like children, not because the slaveholders lacked virtue.

And then comes the Bancroft Paradox. In the same letter in which Jefferson forcefully states that it is nearly impossible to free slaves, he says he is going to do it:

> Notwithstanding the discouraging result of these experiments, I am decided on my final return to America to try this one. I shall

endeavor to import as many Germans as I have grown slaves. I will settle them and my slaves, on farms of 50 acres each, intermingled, and place all on the footing of the Metayers [sharecroppers] of Europe. Their children shall be brought up, as others are, in habits of property and foresight, & I have no doubt but that they will be good citizens.

"Citizens"! The soaring hope summoned by that word! Jefferson had written notes eight months earlier about German farmers who "might be had in any number to go to America and settle lands as tenants on half stocks or *metairies*."[26] They typically worked plots of fifty acres each. And then Jefferson wrote to his private secretary, William Short, in great excitement about a plan involving German tenant farmers: "I have taken some measures for realizing a project which I have wished to execute for 20 years past without knowing how to go about it."[27]

The Bancroft letter connected to something Jefferson had been mulling for months, which connected to a project in his mind for two decades. Twenty years takes us back to the fiery revolutionary who had envisioned "the enfranchisement of the slaves we have." In France, Jefferson had been compelled to defend his country against the suspicion that it was delaying the justice it had promised. Jefferson counseled patience; the minds of white Americans needed to be "ripened" to accept emancipation. He explained the division in Southern society between "a respectable minority ready" for emancipation and the greater number whose consciences were "inquiet" but who needed an injection of courage to divest themselves of slaves. And there were those who had no qualms about slavery, to whom slaves were "legitimate subjects of property" on the level with "their horses and cattle."[28] Someday, he wrote to a Frenchman, God will make a better world: "we must await with patience the workings of an overruling providence."[29]

Twenty years earlier Jefferson's emancipation plan had been hooted down in Virginia. It would be painful to risk such humiliation again. But he found at least one ally in William Short, who later wrote to him about a plan "for exciting in these people [the slaves] the idea of property and the desire to acquire it, which I think would be easily done, and which when done, I think would insure the success of the experiment."[30] Among his French friends he felt the heat of an extreme passion for human rights. For Lafayette, the "blood-cemented" fabric of American liberty must enfold blacks as well as whites. From Condorcet, he received a lesson in standing up for one's beliefs against derision. In the months when he was mulling the métayer idea, Jefferson bought two copies of Condorcet's book on slavery, began to translate it, and came to these lines: "I shall insist on the laws of justice, not on the interests of commerce. Your tyrants will say that my arguments are trite, my ideas chimerical. True, [there is] nothing more trite than the maxims of humanity and justice, nor more chimerical than the proposition that man should conform to them."[31]

What if Jefferson really meant what he said about slavery being nothing more than avarice and oppression in naked conflict with justice? The cloud of rationalizations and racial theorizing parts to reveal Jefferson seized by the idea that he has finally found the way to free his slaves, to realize a hope he has held for twenty years. The strange thing is that we have become so conditioned to Jefferson the prevaricator that no one believes he meant it. Must every man be either the hammer or the anvil? The answer would come when Jefferson reached home.

6

"To Have Good and Human Heart"

In the salons of France, Jefferson conducted the equivalent of a graduate seminar on slavery as the engine of the American enterprise. Confronted for the only time in his life by abolitionists who were actually in a position to keep him from something he wanted, trading rights for the emerging nation, Jefferson went up against these progressives—men like Lafayette who had worn the uniform of the fight for liberty—matched them theory for theory, trumped them with tales of his experience dealing with slaves, and so deftly explained the peculiar, inexplicable institution that to this day no one can figure out exactly what he meant. But he concluded his time in France with an apparently clear pledge to train and free his slaves on his return to Virginia.

Other ideas were percolating in his head. While selling America's tobacco, he knew he would have to abandon planting it himself. (In a strangely modern twist, Jefferson had taken note of the measurable climate change in his region: the Chesapeake region was unmistakably cooling and becoming inhospitable to heat-loving tobacco that would soon, he thought, become the staple of South Carolina and Georgia.) He visited farms and inspected equipment, considering a new crop and the exciting prospect it opened before him. And he envisioned an ambitious engineering project, the rebuilding of a canal and mill, built by his father, that had been washed away in a flood.

He was also thinking of his mansion. French architecture had fired Jefferson's imagination. He returned bursting with ideas for building a new Monticello. To erect this Xanadu, while also shifting crops and getting a canal built, he needed both skilled slaves and common laboring slaves. All of them had to be persuaded in one way or another to go along with the master's ardor for enterprise.

Once he set foot in Virginia in 1789, Jefferson got down to business. Its morals aside, his elaborate program at Monticello in the 1790s would make an excellent case study in business schools today. Jefferson the philosopher has been endlessly parsed, but Jefferson the on-the-ground manager is most revealing, carrying us closer to the truth of slavery than anything he wrote in *Notes* or his other explications of slavery. At Monticello in the 1790s we find innovation; strategic investment; the conveyance of assets to the next generation; methods of controlling and motivating a workforce; critical turning points where conflicts must be resolved between cherished ideals and economic goals; and the revitalization of an economic, industrial, and social system supposedly pronounced dead. Owning the workers created unique possibilities for very long-term personnel planning: he could train talented adolescents for posts they would hold for twenty or thirty years. Like many other forward-thinking planters, Jefferson would reimagine an old, widely maligned system to make it fit into a modernizing nation while preserving the values, outlook, and structure of an extremely conservative society.

Nation-building on two fronts, Jefferson put in place his program for modernizing slavery at home while serving as President Washington's secretary of state. He retired from that post in 1793 to devote his full attention to Monticello but returned to the political fray in 1796 to campaign for the presidency against John Adams. Coming in second, he became vice president in 1797 but continued to manage Monticello from afar.

Jefferson had received an astonishing welcome in 1789 when he arrived home at Monticello from France. He had directed his manager, Nicholas Lewis, to extract "extraordinary exertions" of labor from the slaves to stay current with his debt payments. Some slaves had endured years of harsh treatment at the hands of strangers, for to raise cash, Jefferson had also instructed Lewis to hire out slaves.* He demanded

---

*Jefferson arrived at Monticello the week before New Year's Day, when hiring contracts began, when slaves who had been rented out would gather their possessions and be marched off.

he literally wanted old men so he could pimp out his house?!

extraordinary exertions from the elderly: "The negroes too old to be hired, could they not make a good profit by cultivating cotton?"[1] For the five years Jefferson had been gone, Lewis had struggled just to keep the people fed and clothed on farms going to ruin. So when word spread that the owner was returning at last, the slaves welcomed him as a savior. They unhitched the horses from his carriage and pulled it up the mountain themselves:

> When the door of the carriage was opened, they received him in their arms and bore him to the house, crowding around and kissing his hands and feet—some blubbering and crying—others laughing. It seemed impossible to satisfy their anxiety to touch and kiss the very earth which bore him. . . . perhaps it is not out of place here to add that they were at all times very devoted in their attachment to him.[2]

This event might seem to bolster the idea that slaves were, as Jefferson said, like children. His biographer Dumas Malone wrote: "To their simple minds it seemed that he had come home to stay, and he must have thought it good to be there—though he did not like to be the master of slaves."[3] But Jefferson observed that when you thrust people into poverty, you reduce them to "passive obedience."[4]

Jefferson had assured the French that emancipation was "gaining daily recruits" among younger Americans, and he may have had his own daughter in mind. In a note to her father in 1787, Patsy had expressed ardent abolitionist sentiments. Hearing that a boatload of slaves might be delivered to Virginia, she wrote: "Good god have we not enough? I wish with all my soul that the poor negroes were all freed."[5] But her abolitionism receded when she suddenly needed a dowry.

Within days of arriving from France, Patsy ran into a distant cousin, Thomas Mann Randolph, whom she had known in childhood. Within weeks the cousins announced their engagement, and they married at Monticello on February 23, 1790. Patsy was seventeen and Thomas Mann Randolph, later known as Colonel Randolph, was twenty-one. In the weeks leading up to the wedding, Jefferson and Randolph's father hastily negotiated a marriage settlement. The senior Randolph (also named Thomas Mann Randolph) bestowed on the couple a 950-acre plantation with livestock and forty slaves. But on close examination, the plantation turned out to be a very dubious "gift," for it came with a $2,900 mortgage. Alarmed at the onerous debt, Jefferson urged his future son-in-law to refuse the gift.[6]

Jefferson wanted Randolph to refuse the gift for another reason. The plantation, called Varina, lay near Richmond, ninety miles from Monticello, and Jefferson did not want his daughter living so far away. Nor did Patsy wish to leave her father's orbit.[7] Not even marriage weakened her attachment to her father. When Jefferson later wrote to Patsy of his plans to return to Monticello after a long absence, she replied that this news stirred in her "raptures and palpitations not to be described."[8]

After very difficult and protracted negotiations Jefferson persuaded the elder Randolph to sell young Randolph his Edgehill plantation, situated in a lovely valley just a few miles north, with a view of Monticello. This transaction took two years to complete. In the meantime, the newlyweds settled into Monticello itself. And with gifts of slaves, Jefferson set up Patsy's household to emulate his. For her personal attendant he gave her a Hemings—thirteen-year-old Molly, the daughter of Mary Hemings; for a cook he gave her Suck, the wife of his lifelong enslaved companion Jupiter. Though divided ownership put Jupiter's family at risk of permanent separation, Jefferson would not have seen these gifts as sundering black nuclear families but as consolidating the larger plantation "family."

That was the genteel face of the slave system; next he turned to the business side. The transfer of household servants might have been a sufficiently generous wedding gift, but Jefferson could see that young Tom Randolph, saddled with the Varina debt, was bankrupt on arrival. And the elder Randolph, a widower forty-nine years old, was about to marry a nineteen-year-old maiden only two years older than one of her stepdaughters-to-be. (She quickly produced another male heir, whom the patriarch named Thomas Mann Randolph III, in an act of apparent paternal hostility toward Thomas Mann Randolph Jr.) In light of this looming December-May marriage, the elder Randolph's "gift" might be more accurately characterized as a clearing of the books: he unloaded a debt onto his son, with a farm attached.

Concerned "to place them in security," Jefferson promised to give his daughter one of his "best" properties and "25 negroes little and big."[9]

The legal document solemnizing the "Marriage Settlement for Martha Jefferson" transferred a farm called Wingo's, a one-thousand-acre part of the Poplar Forest plantation some ninety miles southwest of Monticello, and twenty-seven slaves. At every level this was a family transaction. The Wingo's community consisted of five families with children, nine of them under the age of ten, and a couple. The Wingo's families were very closely related, having lived in isolation on the plantation for decades. Slaves named Tom and Billy were married to the sisters Sarah and Lucy, whose father, Lundy, also lived on the place, as did Tom's parents and Tom's brother Jeffery. These slaves formed Patsy's safety net, for Jefferson put the land and slaves in her name alone, giving her a layer of protection if Colonel Randolph ran into financial problems. And he augmented this gift with a twenty-eight-year-old slave woman and her four small children, all younger than ten.

Ownership of a critical mass of black people provided financial stability to an upper-class family, and Jefferson could not launch his daughter into marriage without "that capital which a growing family had a right to expect."[10] As Jefferson expected, Colonel Randolph repeatedly encountered financial difficulties and sold or mortgaged slaves to cover his shortfalls.

The image of slaves carrying Jefferson into his mansion is apt. They had been carrying him for years, and they had no notion of how valuable they really were. Labor was so costly and sought-after in Virginia that Jefferson's manager had been able to match the plantation's agricultural income by hiring out slaves while Jefferson was in Paris. Jefferson's eye had caught this profit in the accounts; he had written to Lewis in 1786: "Would it be better to hire more?"[11]

Again and again the sale, the hiring, or the mortgaging of black souls rescued the Jeffersons from a bad harvest, bought time from the debt collectors, and kept the family afloat while a new and grander version of Monticello took shape. Meanwhile, Jefferson embarked on other costly projects he could not afford without slave labor. Yet Jefferson, his children, and his grandchildren forever referred to these slaves as a burden, and historians have sympathetically echoed their complaints, writing that Jefferson was "trapped" or "entangled" in a system he hated.

The slaves formed Jefferson's bulwark against catastrophe. While he was in France, he ordered the sale of 31 people, from which he netted £2,300. He sold another 30 slaves in 1791, 13 more in 1792, and 9 in the next two years. "Finding it necessary to sell a few more slaves to [pay down] the debt of mr Wayles . . . I have thought of disposing of Dinah & her family," he wrote to his brother.[12] Between 1784 and 1794 he sold or gave away 160 people. But the community constantly replenished itself. In 1792 he calculated that the births of slave children produced capital at the rate of 4 percent per year: "I allow nothing for losses by death, but, on the contrary, shall presently take credit four per cent. per annum, for their increase over and above keeping up their own numbers." In the 1780s and 1790s the astounding total of 143 children were born into Jefferson's possession.

Jefferson had recrossed the ocean to Virginia with blueprints for the future of Monticello in his head, along with a startlingly modern business model. The economy was changing and he adapted. His vision for Monticello's future depended on slaves in new ways.

Actually, Jefferson had recrossed the ocean with a real blueprint—his design for an ingenious new plow blade "of least resistance" that cut and turned the earth more efficiently, requiring less force than the plows he had studied in Europe.[13] Simple in its design, the blade could be fabricated on the farm "by the coarsest workman." With this tool, "mathematically demonstrated to be perfect," he would remake his farming enterprise. "The plough is to the farmer what the wand is to the sorcerer. Its effect is really like sorcery."[14]

A species of sorcery is what he had in mind. We still hear it said that because tobacco was creating a ruined landscape of washed-out gullies, slavery would have died off peacefully if Eli Whitney had not invented his cotton gin and made fresh work for millions of enslaved black hands. But before the reign of King Cotton there was the regency of Prince Wheat. Jefferson arrived in Virginia with a plan to shift away from growing tobacco, whose cultivation he described as "a culture of infinite wretchedness." Tobacco wore out the soil so fast that new acreage constantly had to be cleared, engrossing so much land that food could not be raised to feed the workers, requiring planters to purchase rations for the slaves.[15]

The cultivation of wheat revitalized the plantation economy and reshaped the South's agricultural landscape. Planters all over the

Chesapeake region had been making the shift. (George Washington had begun raising grains some thirty years earlier because his land wore out faster than Jefferson's did.) Jefferson continued to plant some tobacco because it remained an important cash crop, but his vision for wheat farming was rapturous: "The cultivation of wheat is the reverse [of tobacco] in every circumstance. Besides cloathing the earth with herbage, and preserving its fertility, it feeds the labourers plentifully, requires from them only a moderate toil, except in the season of harvest, raises great numbers of animals for food and service, and diffuses plenty and happiness among the whole."

The machine age had arrived, promising a transformation of agriculture, and Jefferson took a keen interest in the latest innovations. In August 1791, while serving as George Washington's secretary of state, he visited a farm outside Philadelphia to inspect a newly invented threshing machine (the president went with him for a look).[16] Later in that decade he ordered models of several different designs, which he then modified himself, eventually putting three machines into operation at Monticello. Outside contractors built the machines, but he depended on slaves to operate and repair them, and that was the keystone of the new plantation system.

Wheat farming forced changes in the relationship between planter and slave. Tobacco was raised by gangs of slaves all doing the same repetitive, backbreaking tasks under the direct, strict supervision of overseers. Wheat required a variety of skilled laborers, and Jefferson's ambitious plans required a retrained workforce. When his slaves greeted him on his return, he saw not a mob of "simple minds" but a promising flock of potential millers, mechanics, carpenters, smiths, spinners, coopers, and plowmen and plow-women.

Jefferson still needed a cohort of "labourers in the ground" to carry out the hardest tasks, so the Monticello slave community became more segmented and hierarchical. They were all slaves, but some slaves would be better than others. The majority remained laborers; above them were enslaved artisans (both male and female); above them were enslaved managers; above them was the household staff. The higher you stood in the hierarchy, the better clothes and food you got; you also lived literally on a higher plane, closer to the mountaintop. A small minority of slaves received pay, profit sharing, or what Jefferson called "gratuities," while the lowest workers received only the barest rations and clothing. Difference bred resentment, especially toward the elite household staff.

Planting wheat required fewer workers than tobacco, leaving a pool of field laborers available for specialized training. Jefferson embarked on a comprehensive program to modernize slavery, diversify it, and industrialize it. Monticello would have a nail factory, a textile factory, a short-lived tinsmithing operation, coopering, and charcoal-burning. He had ambitious plans for the mill and a canal to provide water-power for it.

Training for this new organization began in childhood. Jefferson sketched out a plan in his Farm Book:

> children till 10. years old to serve as nurses.
> from 10. to 16. the boys make nails, the girls spin.
> at 16. go into the ground or learn trades.[17]

Measuring and counting everything, Jefferson devised numerous expedients for saving money and labor and for maximizing productivity. He determined, for example, that he could feed the slaves on dried fish for half the cost of pork: "a barrel of fish, costing 7.D. goes as far with the laborers as 200. lb of pork 14.D." He laid out housing to save labor: "Build the Negro houses near together that the fewer nurses may serve & that the children may be more easily attended to by the super-annuated women."[18] He put old people and the partially infirm to work, referring to the crew of gardeners as his "senile corps." He exulted that his successful textile factory "only employs a few women, children and invalids who could do little in the farm." He had a very broad definition of "invalids": on the one hand, he specified that they should "work only when they are able," but on the other hand he thought that "they will probably be equal to the hauling away the earth and forming it into a bank on the side next the river."[19]

Tobacco required child labor (their small stature made children ideal workers for the distasteful task of plucking and killing tobacco worms); wheat did not, so Jefferson transferred his surplus of young workers to his nail factory (boys) and spinning and weaving operations (girls). He launched the nailery in 1794 and supervised it personally for three years. "I now employ a dozen little boys from 10. to 16. years of age, overlooking all the details of their business myself."[20] He said he spent half the day counting and measuring nails. In the morning he weighed and distributed nailrod to each nailer; at the end of the day he weighed the finished product and noted how much rod had been wasted.

The nailery "particularly suited me," he wrote, "because it would employ a parcel of boys who would otherwise be idle."[21] Equally important, it served as a training and testing ground. All the nail boys got extra food; those who did well received a new suit of clothes, and they could also expect to graduate, as it were, to training as artisans rather than going "in the ground" as common field slaves. Some nail boys rose in the plantation hierarchy to become house servants, blacksmiths, carpenters, or coopers. Wormley Hughes, a slave who became head gardener, started in the nailery, as did Burwell Colbert, who rose to become the mansion's butler and Jefferson's personal attendant.[22] Isaac Granger was the most productive nailer, with a profit averaging eighty cents a day over the first six months of 1796, when he was twenty; he fashioned half a ton of nails during those six months. The work was tedious in the extreme. Confined for long hours in the hot, smoky workshop, the boys hammered out five to ten thousand nails a day, producing a gross income of $2,000 in 1796. Jefferson's competition for the nailery was the state penitentiary.[23]

The nailers received twice the food ration of a field worker but no wages. Jefferson paid white boys (an overseer's sons) fifty cents a day for cutting wood to feed the nailery's fires, but this was a weekend job done "on Saturdays, when they were not in school." Jefferson's grandchildren sometimes pitched in, as the overseer wrote, and worked with them "like little Turks on Saturdays, so that my boys could go with them a-fishing."[24]

Exuberant over the success of the nailery, Jefferson wrote: "My new trade of nail-making is to me in this country what an additional title of nobility or the ensigns of a new order are in Europe."[25] The profit was substantial. Just months after the factory began operation, he wrote that "a nailery which I have established with my own negro boys now provides completely for the maintenance of my family."[26] Two months of labor by the nail boys paid the entire annual grocery bill for the white family. He wrote to a Richmond merchant, "My groceries come to between 4. and 500 Dollars a year, taken and paid for quarterly. The best resource of quarterly paiment in my power is Nails, of which I make enough *every fortnight* to pay a quarter's bill [emphasis added]."[27] The success of the nail factory spurred him to develop other enterprises staffed by skilled slaves that brought in cash or made Monticello more self-sufficient.

He wrote out a plan for a harvest involving a small army of sixty-six laborers. His enslaved manager and blacksmith, Great George Granger, would ride behind the harvesters "with tools & a grindstone mounted in the single mule cart . . . constantly employed in mending cradles & grinding scythes. The same cart would carry about the liquor. . . . cradlers should work constantly." Five of the "smallest boys" would be the gatherers, supervised by a "foreman," who was one of the larger boys. Women and "abler boys" would bind the sheaves. There would be stackers, loaders, cooks, and carters; "the whole machine would move in exact equilibrio, no part of the force could be lessened without retarding the whole, nor increased without a waste of force." He estimated that this force, fueled by four gallons of whiskey, would complete a harvest in six days.[28]

A foreign visitor in 1796, the Duke de La Rochefoucauld-Liancourt, observed this human machine in operation and was deeply impressed. "I found him in the midst of the harvest from which the scorching heat of the sun does not prevent his attendance," wrote the duke, who noted Jefferson's all-encompassing attentiveness to plantation management: "He orders, directs and pursues, in the minutest detail, every branch of business."[29]

Sharing Jefferson's passion for innovative, scientific agriculture, the duke inspected the plantation with a practiced eye, noting with approval the treatment of the workers—"His negroes are nourished, clothed, and treated as well as white servants could be"—and observing with some astonishment that the blacks had mastered a multiplicity of skills: as "cabinet-makers, carpenters, masons, bricklayers, smiths, etc." He could not restrain his excitement.

The exhilaration in the duke's account arises from his perception that a breakthrough had been achieved in a remarkably short time. He could see no trace of the racial inferiority Jefferson had described in

Notes. The enslaved, who Jefferson had said in France were as simple and useless as children, were skilled, diligent workers motivated "by rewards and distinctions." So the question inevitably arose: Is *this* the moment to set the people free?

Apparently not. The duke dutifully reports to his European readers Jefferson's good intentions: "The generous and enlightened Mr. Jefferson cannot but demonstrate a desire to see these Negroes emancipated."[30] But then there is the thud of disappointment. In a tone of some bafflement La Rochefoucauld-Liancourt tries to explain why the demonstrable skills and good character of the enslaved are not sufficient, in Jefferson's view, to gain them freedom: "He sees so many difficulties in their emancipation [and] he adds so many conditions to render it practicable, that it is thus reduced to the impossible." Jefferson is determined to police the color line: "the Negroes of Virginia can only be emancipated all at once, and by exporting to a distance the whole black race. He bases his opinion on the certain danger, if there were nothing else, of seeing blood mixed without means of preventing it."

At this point an air of unreality settles over the scene, for the race-mixing Jefferson claims to dread has already taken place. La Rochefoucauld could see for himself that Jefferson had staffed his household with mixed-race slaves "who have neither in their color nor features a single trace of their [African] origin."[31]

The people of Monticello had more than fulfilled the conditions Jefferson had set down in a letter written in 1791 to the black mathematician-astronomer Benjamin Banneker:

No body wishes more than I do to see [proof] that nature has given to our black brethren, talents equal to those of the other colours of men. . . . I can add with truth that no body wishes more ardently to see a good system commenced for raising the condition both of their body & mind to what it ought to be.[32]

The roster of skills acquired by the Monticello slaves is remarkable. Historians have compiled a list of their occupations: plowmen and plow-women, gardeners, shepherds, millers, charcoal burners, sawyers, carpenters, joiners, cabinetmakers, wheelwrights, carriage makers, coopers, basket makers, blacksmiths, nail makers, tinsmiths, spinners, weavers, dyers, seamstresses and tailors, shoemakers, brickmakers and bricklayers, stonecutters and stonemasons, glaziers, plasterers, painters, roofers, launderers, cooks, dairy workers, brewers, soap makers, candlemakers, butlers, barbers and hairdressers, maids and valets, midwives, coachmen, hostlers, wagoners, and watermen.

The conversation of the duke and the Founder on that blazing June day at Monticello is an archetypal scene in Southern life—the visit to a plantation by an outsider who gazes and listens in increasing bafflement as the evidence of his eyes is contradicted by what he is told. Here Jefferson takes on the part of a universal figure—the master called upon to explain a central mystery of American life. With the diligence and skill of the slaves fully evident, Jefferson explains that *despite what you see, these people are degraded and different and they have no place in our country.* He establishes that slavery is mysterious, that on this borderland of races the master alone comprehends the processes taking place: dangerous primal struggles despite the apparent tranquillity.

Arguing with such a man was futile. Tossing up *so* many difficulties, *so* many conditions, the master trumps the outsider with his esoteric knowledge of the race mystery. But like the duke, we must take a close, interrogating look at the systems Jefferson put into operation on his mountain. Indeed, there were processes invisible to the duke.

The people gathering the sheaves and sharpening the scythes in the hot sun of a Virginia afternoon were soon to be owned in Amsterdam. Jefferson was conducting negotiations with a Dutch merchant-banking house to finance the recapitalization of Monticello's operations and the construction of its new mansion. The people La Rochefoucauld-Liancourt watched at work were about to become bundled and collateralized assets in an international banking transaction.

The deal was finalized in the solemn legal language of "Witnesseth" in a financial instrument between Thomas Jefferson of Albemarle in Virginia on the one part and Nicholas Van Staphorst, Jacob Van Staphorst, and Hubbard of Amsterdam in the United Netherlands, merchants and partner:

whereas the said Van Staphorsts & Hubbard have now lately and since the dates of the said deeds lent to the said Thomas the further sum of two thousand dollars . . . he hath given granted and conveyed unto the said Nicholas and Jacob Van Staphorsts & Hubbard all his right and equity of redemption in the said hundred and fifty negro slaves in full and absolute right and dominion.[33]

In his approach to the Dutch bankers, with whom he had had dealings in Europe, Jefferson reported that his estate was "much deteriorated" after his absences but that "an advance of from one to two thousand dollars would produce a state of productiveness."[34] Determined to fight off his debts, Jefferson bought time by selling people, and then he realized he could take on debt *to expand*, to acquire new machinery and erect a new house. He showed the plans to La Rochefoucauld, who thought "his house will certainly deserve to be ranked with the most pleasant mansions in France and England."[35] The Dutch bankers opened an equity line backed by Jefferson's slaves for $2,000.[36]

It was around this time that Jefferson chided a neighbor who had suffered financial losses, saying he "should have been invested in negroes," and urged the neighbor's family to invest "every farthing" of their available cash "in land and negroes, which . . . bring a silent profit of from 5. to 10. per cent in this country by the increase in their value." The slaves had condemned themselves: the more skilled they became, the more valuable they became, and the more they tightened the chains of their enslavement.[37] With the machine functioning in equilibrium, the owner would never dismantle it. Jefferson had also calculated that it was vastly cheaper to feed, house, and clothe a slave than hire a free white worker, if he could find one.[38] Yet when questioned by an outsider about freeing slaves, a master never said *they are too valuable*; it was much easier to say *they are like children*.

The duke was present at a transitional moment in American history. Like many other planters in the South, Jefferson was trying to devise a "rational and humane" plan not to end slavery but to reshape it and bring it into the new republic as an acceptable, indeed respectable component of the economy and society. This is what slaveholders called "amelioration." Traveling through the Chesapeake country at about this time, the Irishman Isaac Weld noted that slaveholders "have nearly everything they can want on their own estates. Amongst their slaves are found tailors, shoemakers, carpenters, smiths, turners, wheelwrights, weavers, tanners, etc."[39] Mainly a business plan, amelioration included a psychological component—persuading slaves that it was rational and humane for them to be enslaved. This is what Jefferson, Washington, and the other revolutionaries had most feared that the British would do to the white people of America: persuade them or trick them into submitting to a form of slavery that had invisible chains.[40]

The psychological underpinning of amelioration might be found, perversely, in the Declaration of Independence and Jefferson's sources for it. Jefferson wrote of a fearful apparition, *the sufferable evil*, a concept he derived from John Locke's observation that people "are more disposed to suffer than right themselves by resistance." Jefferson rewrote this in the Declaration as, "all experience hath shewn, that mankind are more disposed to suffer, while evils are sufferable, than to right themselves by abolishing the forms to which they are accustomed." The ameliorated version of slavery looks very much like the sufferable evil Jefferson warned of, clothed in "prevarications and artifices" masking a design to reduce the people "under absolute Despotism."[41]

The slaveholders were fashioning a transition from the system of slavery they had inherited, which Jefferson portrayed as a burdensome legacy bequeathed by the dead hand of the past, to a new, refined system of deliberate enslavement. With Virginia's liberal manumission law of 1782 still on the books, owners could free their people at will, but that law was quietly gathering dust, a vestige of Revolutionary fervor now burning out. Very few planters relinquished their slaves, as Jefferson had predicted in *Notes*: "Mankind soon learn to make interested uses of every right and power they possess."

Another outsider rose up. As if from the grave of the Revolution, a stalwart veteran of the cause, the Polish general Thaddeus Kosciuszko, called upon Jefferson for help in composing a last will and testament. The memory of what he had fought for was on his mind. Leaving America for Europe in 1798 to take up the cause of Polish independence,

Kosciuszko wished to ensure that the long-delayed payment he had just received for his Revolutionary service in the American uniform would be put to a revolutionary use. Kosciuszko's command of English was not perfect, so he asked Jefferson, in whom he had complete faith, to sit down with him to compose a will that would stand up in an American court. In preparation, Kosciuszko drafted the following document in his own hand, in imperfect English. It reads like a farewell address to America and Jefferson:

> I beg Mr. Jefferson that in case I should die without will or testament he should bye out of my money so many Negroes and free them, that the [remaining] Sums should be sufficient to give them education and provide for their maintenance. that is to say each should know before, the duty of a cytysen in the free Government. that he must defend his Country against foreign as well internal Enemies. . . . to have good and human heart sensible for the sufferings of others. each must be married and have 100 ackres of land, wyth instruments. Catle for tillage, and know how to manage and Gouvern it as well as how to behave to neybourghs. always with kindness and ready to help them. Themselves frugal, to their Children give good education. I mean as to the heart and the duty to their Country.[42]

Kosciuszko had one request to make of the people he expected to free: "in gratitude to me to make themselves hapy as possible."

The word to which every writer on slavery must eventually resort is "irony." When Jefferson had gone to inspect the new threshing machine near Philadelphia, George Washington went with him. One irony is that Washington was turning in his mind plans for freeing his slaves, which he would eventually do in his will after his family had thwarted his earlier effort. On the issue of slavery, Jefferson emerges poorly in a side-by-side moral comparison with Washington, but in hindsight we can see which Founder more truly reflects the times and the character of the country. The public would little note, and did not long remember, Washington's emancipation of his slaves. In hindsight, George

Washington's "inflexible" sense of justice and insistence on "a common bond of principle" seem antique, as dull and disapproving as his portrait on the dollar, when set beside the ingenuity, vision, and entrepreneurial energy on full display at Monticello. The future belonged to Jefferson.

7

What the Blacksmith Saw

When the Duke de La Rochefoucauld-Liancourt toured Monticello in 1796, he was shown the industrious, apparently tranquil surface of a smoothly functioning system. But the duke saw right through it. *What happened to your ideals? When will you free the people?* Patiently, Jefferson explained to the duke that yes, the enterprise is patently unjust, but it is temporary. Soon we shall find a way to exile these people, and the moral problem will be solved. In the meantime, the system works well, and no one seems to object. No slaves complain to the duke. The moral universe of the Revolution has been upended, yet everyone seems satisfied, so perhaps he is wrong to impose his values on this strange society.

And so La Rochefoucauld wrote an account of the "generous and enlightened" plantation master, which has echoed through the histories and biographies. His description of harvest time at Monticello is one of the strongest pieces of evidence that Jefferson had been able to fashion a humane version of slavery. But what the duke saw was a carefully constructed illusion.

Rarely did plantation insiders break ranks and tell the truth about slavery, unless something deeply shocking jolted them into an awareness they had suppressed. After decades of managing Monticello for his father-in-law, managing his own farm at Edgehill, and observing slavery's operation at its most enlightened and progressive, Colonel Randolph wrote a wrenching private letter saying that the whole "Southern system" was "a hideous monster" ruled by brutality and fear. The event that jolted Tom Randolph into writing this letter was the discovery of a man's body dangling from a tree at a neighbor's plantation near Monti-cello.[1]

He knew the man. The attributes Randolph ascribed to him in the letter, a eulogy to a slave, were bravery, intrepidity, trustworthiness, resoluteness, and "despising pain and not knowing fear"—attributes not usually ascribed to African-Americans by people of Randolph's class. The man had committed suicide after being whipped. Unable to bear the humiliation, he had lynched himself.

No one is to blame. "In this particular case both Master and over-seer are humane men, and the latter of proven fortitude, as well as moral worth." The enterprise is cruel, but no one stops it. The system is amoral and seems to run by itself, and it functions, perversely, under a veneer of humanity and moral worth. The blame is nowhere, but it is everywhere; people live as if in a miasma. In his haunted mood Ran-dolph writes of a "sooty atmosphere," an extraordinary, Melvillean meta-phor of filthy, choking air that stinks of corruption. It is the air of hell, and Randolph was breathing it in Virginia. But one gets used to it, espe-cially when you are utterly dependent on making the machine work, as Randolph was.

When Jefferson told the duke that he animated slaves with rewards, he was fabricating an illusion for his visitor and perhaps for himself. In the first place, he was speaking of a very small number of people. Only a very small minority of the slaves received a share of profits and what Jefferson called "gratuities." The rest were animated by fear of the over-seers. And La Rochefoucauld was not shown everything on his tour of inspection. The system had a less tranquil operation just across the Rivanna River at the farm where Jefferson's overseer William Page was acquiring a reputation as a "terror" with free use of the whip to maintain productivity.

The favored slaves, whom the duke did see, labored so industriously because they were desperate to remain in the master's favor, to stay on the mountaintop and not be sent below, where the overseers were in charge. Amelioration did not trickle down. Writing about a girl who was not performing well in the textile mill, Jefferson said, "I have given her notice that she shall have some days trial more, and if there be no im-provement, she must cease to spoil more cloth and go out to work with the overseer."[2]

Perhaps the master's greatest power was his control over family life. It was Jefferson's general policy to keep families together, partly because he did have feelings of humanity, though he sometimes referred to the marriages among slaves as "connections," which he thought were rather easily broken. Keeping families intact was also in his interest: "Certainly there is nothing I desire so much as that all the young people in the estate should intermarry with one another and stay at home. They are worth a great deal more in that case than when they have husbands and wives abroad" (meaning on another plantation and owned by someone else).³ Housing, food, clothing, work assignments, family unity—all benefits flowed from the master. But to receive these benefits, one must stand in the master's favor, encouraging a permanent posture of dependence and gratitude.

When the duke inspected the Mulberry Row nail factory, he saw twenty-year-old Isaac Granger pounding hard at a forge, setting an example of efficiency for the younger nail boys. Granger belonged to one of Monticello's leading families. His father and brother, both managers, were crucial gears in the Monticello machine, men who stood in Jefferson's favor. Isaac left a memoir in which he calls Jefferson "a mighty good master," an assessment that has echoed through the Jefferson biographies.⁴ But the blacksmith left many things out.

For some thirty years Jefferson depended on the Grangers to help him run Monticello. The Grangers owed Jefferson a very deep debt. As mentioned earlier, they were separated after John Wayles's death and would never have seen each other again had Jefferson not reunited them at Monticello through two costly purchases. When Jefferson was in France and ordered his manager, Nicholas Lewis, to hire out slaves—which put the slaves at great risk of mistreatment—he specifically exempted the Grangers along with the Hemingses: "Great George, Ursula, Betty Hemings not to be hired at all."*⁵ And when Jefferson rented a farm to the cruel overseer William Page, he first moved Great George's son Bagwell and his family away from the place.

---

*Jefferson regarded renting slaves as very risky because he expected they would be abused: "Would it not be well to retain an optional right to sue [renters] for ill usage of the slaves or to discontinue it by arbitration?" Later he limited slave-hiring contracts to one year "so that I may take them away if ill treated" (TJ to Nicholas Lewis, July 11, 1788, in *Papers*, vol. 13; TJ to Thomas Mann Randolph Jr., Feb. 18, 1793, in *Papers*, vol. 25).

Jefferson sized up the Grangers as accomplished, loyal, hardworking people. Great George could read and write. They possessed skills in high demand that would have allowed them to support themselves in Virginia or elsewhere. As individuals and as a family, they were perfect candidates for the citizenship Jefferson spoke of in his pledge to train slaves for freedom. But they were also perfect candidates for high-ranking positions in the Monticello establishment.

When Jefferson returned from France, he spent less than a year at Monticello, having been summoned to serve as secretary of state by President Washington. Before he left, he placed direct management of the mountaintop farm in the hands of Great George, under the loose supervision of Colonel Randolph, who would be residing at Monticello in Jefferson's absence. Before he left for Philadelphia in the fall of 1790, Jefferson walked around Monticello with Granger and gave him instructions about what he wanted built for the Randolphs. As he put it in a memo for Colonel Randolph: "A wash house . . . to be built and placed where I pointed out to George. . . . A stable to be built . . . where I have pointed out to George."[6] He expressed the highest confidence in Granger: "George . . . will be sufficient to see that the work is done, and to take all details off of your hands."[7]

Jefferson appointed Great George the foreman of laborers at Monticello, sought his advice on crops and livestock, and paid him £20 a year, which was much less than the wages of white overseers. He paid £35 a year and five hundred pounds of pork to William Page.[8] As farm manager, Granger had good years and bad. One season he brought in a harvest that Jefferson judged "extraordinary." Jefferson made the Grangers, the father and later a son, buffers between himself and the workforce that labored at the forges and "in the ground." Jefferson told Colonel Randolph to exempt Granger from the lowest tasks: "I consider George as their foreman, and should not require him to lay his hand to the hardest work."[9]

As early as 1774, Jefferson had recognized the qualities of the oldest Granger son, also named George, and made him an apprentice to a hired white blacksmith. After two years "Smith" George, as he became known, took over the forge, saving Jefferson the expense of the hired white man. Smith George ran the Monticello blacksmith shop for more than fifteen years.[10] Jefferson also put him in charge of the nailery. When

Jefferson was away, Colonel Randolph reported, "I scarcely look to the Nailery at all—George I am sure could not stoop to my authority & I hope and believe he pushes your interests as well as I could."[11]

The Grangers were the beneficiaries and victims of Jefferson's long-term planning. Too important to release, four generations of Grangers served Jefferson in skilled positions. Multigenerational service of one family to another was not unusual in the plantation world and imparted the feeling that the institution of slavery had some relationship to eternity.

The manuscript of Isaac Granger's memoir, along with a daguerreotype portrait of him, came to light only in the 1940s. The twenty-four-page, handwritten document had been set down by a white historian, Charles Campbell, who had sought out the blacksmith in the 1840s and spoke with him at some length about his experiences. Then in his seventies, Isaac was a free man living in Petersburg, Virginia. The daguerreotype shows a robust, well-muscled man wearing a white work shirt and a leather apron—apparently, the blacksmith was still working. Campbell described him as "rather tall, of strong frame, stoops a little, in color ebony; sensible, intelligent, pleasant."[12] It is not entirely clear how the blacksmith got to Petersburg as a free or semi-free man.

The blacksmith's memoir conveys snippets of conversation with Jefferson and verbal snapshots of Jefferson and daily life on the mountain. Isaac got to know his master rather well, it seems, and Jefferson, who had an instinctive affinity with artisans, seemed to take a liking to him. With Isaac as his helper, Jefferson tinkered at various projects in a small metalworking shop. As a young boy, Isaac had learned to be an adept forgeman, a maker of fire. He told of crawling into a "great big bake oven" in Williamsburg, where he worked as a boy of six or seven years old: "Isaac would go into the oven and make fire. . . . Isaac used to go way into the oven."[13] (Throughout the account Isaac refers to himself in the third person.) The baker who hired him commended his skills to Jefferson: "This is the boy that made fire for me."[14]

As a workingman, Isaac made a point of giving credit to other laborers, both white and black, even if no one might be interested in hearing it. He did it instinctively: "Mr. Jefferson came down to Williamsburg in a phaeton made by Davy Watson. Billy Ore did the ironwork."[15] With Isaac's help Jefferson fabricated small metal items he needed around the house: "My Old Master was neat a hand as ever you see to make keys and locks and small chains, iron and brass. He kept all kind of blacksmith and carpenter tools in a great case."[16]

Isaac's father could read and write, so young Isaac had a sense of the power of literacy, took note of Jefferson's machine for copying his writings, and was impressed by the "abundance of books" heaped and strewn on the floor of the study—"sometimes would have twenty of 'em down on the floor at once." He recalled that whenever someone asked Jefferson a question, "he go right straight to the book and tell you all about it."[17] One wonders if Isaac himself put any questions to the master. The vividness of Isaac's recollections suggests that he spent a surprising amount of time in Jefferson's presence. He noticed when Jefferson began to wear glasses and recalled when Jefferson had a swelling in his legs which made walking so difficult that he and John Hemmings would have to roll the master around the farm on a wheelbarrow. He noted that Jefferson sang when he went about his fields and that his master "bowed to everybody he meet; talked with his arms folded." Interestingly, this was a posture of authority. The polite way to present oneself to equals was with arms hanging loosely at one's side with the forearms very slightly raised. Formal eighteenth-century men's clothing was tailored to hold the arms in this position. Isaac was describing a gentleman's manner of presenting himself to people he regarded as his inferiors.[18]

Isaac went along as a servant on Jefferson's hunts for partridge and hare, noting with approval that his master would never shoot game that was sitting, "would give 'em a chance for thar life." Isaac gazed in wonder at the dramatic beauty of the landscape surrounding the mountaintop, leaving a word portrait of Monticello that is remarkably like Jefferson's well-known comment on seeing weather fabricated at his feet: "From Monticello you can see mountains all around as far as the eye can reach; sometimes see it rainin' down this course and the sun shining over the tops of the clouds."[19] He remembered the portraits Jefferson had in the parlor, including "pictures of Ginral Washington and Marcus Lafayette." Granger had actually met Lafayette—"saw him fust in the old war in the mountain with Old Master." Later, when Isaac was living in Petersburg, he went to see Lafayette on his triumphal visit to Richmond in 1824. He walked right up to the hero "and talked with him and made him sensible [reminded him] when he fust saw him in the old war."[20]

Granger vividly recalled Monticello as a place of music, that Jefferson "kept three fiddles" and that he "fiddled in the parlor" in the afternoon and evening. He heard one of the daughters playing the spinet and tried to chat up the Frenchmen who came to tune the fortepiano: "Isaac never could git acquainted with them; could hardly larn their names." He recalled his master constantly singing as he rode or walked around the plantation—"hardly see him anywhar outdoors but what he was a-singin'. Had a fine clear voice."[21] As night fell, a different voice could be heard—that of Isaac's mother, Ursula, singing the Randolph children to sleep.

Isaac's story of the courtship of Polly Jefferson* is one of the most charming and touching scenes of Monticello life that we have. Told in deft, almost cinematic strokes, the anecdote reveals the emotional connection slaves felt for their young masters and mistresses:

> Billy Giles courted Miss Polly, Old Master's daughter. Isaac one morning saw him talking to her in the garden, right back of the nail factory shop; she was lookin on de ground. All at once she wheeled round and come off. *That* was the time she turned him off. Isaac never so sorry for a man in all his life—sorry because everybody thought that she was going to marry him. Mr. Giles give several dollars to the servants, and when he went away dat time he never come back no more. His servant Arthur was a big man. Isaac wanted Mr. Giles to marry Miss Polly. Arthur always said that he was a mighty fine man.[22]

We can picture the servants, clustered behind buildings, peering from cabin doors, tenderly observing this sweet scene. But between the lines there is another story: as he watched this scene unfold, Isaac may have been wondering, *Is this the man who will own me?* Isaac had been earmarked as part of Polly's dowry, so when she married, he would become the property of Polly's husband. Isaac quietly approached Giles's valet, Arthur, the "big man." He asked about the character of his master

---

*Polly was a nickname of Mary Jefferson, also known as Maria.

and was assured that Giles was "mighty fine." But now Isaac would have to wait longer to see what kind of master Polly's romantic inclinations would bring him. It could be someone "mighty fine" like Giles, or more like another visitor to Monticello, a man of habitual, instinctive cruelty.

As a boy, Isaac had frequent, unpleasant encounters with a friend of Jefferson's who often stopped at Monticello, Colonel Archibald Cary, "as dry a looking man as ever you see in your life. He has given Isaac more whippings than he has fingers and toes." When Cary visited Monticello, it was Isaac's job to stand by the plantation's gate to open it the second the colonel appeared. As Cary made his way along the circuitous roads that looped up the mountain, Isaac would run straight uphill to open two more gates so that the colonel would not have to stop or even pause. "Whenever Isaac missed opening them gates in time, the Colonel soon as he git to the house [would] look about for him and whip him with his horse-whip. . . . Colonel Cary made freer at Monticello than he did at home; whip anybody."[23] The colonel could do whatever he wanted, and no one stopped him. A small boy being horsewhipped by a visitor was just part of the background of the bustling plantation scene, like the tiny figure of Icarus fallen from the sky in Brueghel's panorama of Dutch life. Evidently, Jefferson made no effort to persuade Cary to cease. To compensate, Cary distributed very generous tips.

Isaac had been a diligent worker from the time he was a small child, working alongside his mother in the kitchen and laundry—"toted wood for her, made fire, and so on"—and arising before dawn to build a fire in the room where the white children had their lessons.[24] When Jefferson left for Philadelphia in the fall of 1790, he took the fifteen-year-old boy with him to learn tinsmithing, with the idea of setting up a tinning shop at Monticello to produce and sell utensils. Jefferson bound the teenager as an apprentice to an ironmonger whom Isaac described as "a short, mighty small, neat-made man; treated Isaac very well." The first week he learned to cut and solder tin and began making "little pepper boxes and graters and sich, out of scraps of tin, so as not to waste any. . . . Then to making cups." Isaac lived with the ironmonger and visited Jefferson on Sundays to report his progress: "Old Master used to talk to me mighty free and ax me, 'How you come on Isaac, larnin de tin business?'"[25] It seems that it never occurred to Isaac that he could escape slavery in Philadelphia.

Soon Isaac was taking three or four cups to show his master every Sunday, and eventually he was turning out four dozen pint cups a day and had learned to tin copper and sheet iron. Finally, Jefferson pronounced himself "mightily pleased" and told Isaac it was time to go back to Virginia and start the Monticello tin business, which lasted but a short time; so Isaac went to work in the nailery under his brother Smith George. The brothers worked so hard and so devotedly that Jefferson paid them £32 in 1795. The next year Jefferson paid Smith George $42, a 6 percent commission on the nailery's profits.[26] By then Isaac had a wife and two small children to support, so after a full day at the nailery he put in extra hours by night at the blacksmith shop, hammering out lengths of chain, for which Jefferson paid him a penny and a half apiece.

In his memoir Isaac describes the incentives Jefferson offered the nailers: "Gave the boys in the nail factory a pound of meat a week, a dozen herrings, a quart of molasses, and peck of meal. Give them that wukked the best a suit of red or blue; encouraged them mightily."[27] Not all the slaves felt so mightily encouraged. It was Great George Granger's job, as foreman, to get those people to work. Without molasses and suits to offer, he had to rely on persuasion, in all its forms. For years he had been very successful—by what methods, we don't know. But in the winter of 1798 the system ground to a halt when Granger, perhaps for the first time, refused to whip people.

Colonel Randolph reported to Jefferson, then living in Philadelphia as vice president, that "insubordination" had "greatly clogged" operations under Granger.[28] A month later there was "progress," but Granger was "absolutely wasting with care."[29] He was caught between his own people and Jefferson, who had rescued his family, given him a good job, allowed him to earn money and own property, and shown similar benevolence to Granger's children. Now Jefferson had his eye on Granger's output.

Jefferson noted curtly in a letter to Randolph that another overseer had already delivered his tobacco to the Richmond market, "where I hope George's will soon join it."[30] Randolph reported back that Granger's people had not even packed the tobacco yet but gently urged his father-in-law to have patience with the foreman: "He is not careless . . . tho' he procrastinates too much."[31] It seems that Randolph was trying to protect Granger from Jefferson's wrath. George was not procrastinating; he was struggling against a workforce that resisted him. But he would not beat them, and they knew it.

At length, Randolph had to admit the truth to Jefferson. Granger, he wrote, "cannot command his force." The only recourse was the whip. Randolph reported "instances of disobedience so gross that I am obliged to interfere and have them punished myself."[32] Randolph would not have administered the whip personally; they had professionals for that. Most likely he called in William Page, the white overseer who ran Jefferson's farms across the river, the man notorious for his cruelty.

A stunning catastrophe started to unfold in the autumn of 1798 when Smith George began to show signs of a serious ailment, "a constant puking, shortness of breath and swelling first in the legs but now extending itself."[33] He sought out a black healer who lived twenty miles to the south in Buckingham County.[34] Jefferson, though always very wary of physicians, paid for the treatment. George died in June 1799, marking the start of a mysterious cluster of deaths among Monticello slaves who managed other slaves.

In December of that year, Jefferson set out from Monticello for a journey to Philadelphia; he planned to travel on horseback with a servant to Fredericksburg, where he would board a stage to the North. Despite illness, his attendant Jupiter insisted on riding with him as was customary, pronouncing himself much disturbed that his master was going to use another servant. He feared losing his place at Jefferson's side, just as many years earlier he had been replaced by a Hemings as Jefferson's personal valet. But after a day of winter traveling it was clear to Jefferson that Jupiter was very ill; he urged his man to return home, but Jupiter would not hear of it. He made it to Fredericksburg, then returned to Monticello, worn out by the trip. Jefferson's daughter Patsy wrote to her father that Jupiter "conceived himself poisoned."[35]

Jupiter went to see the same healer who had treated Smith George. He gave Jupiter a mixture that, he said, "would kill or cure." After taking the dose, Jupiter "fell down in a strong convulsion fit which lasted from ten to eleven hours, during which time it took three stout men to hold him. He languished nine days but was never heard to speak from the first of his being seized to the moment of his death."[36]

Then Great George and Ursula began showing signs of the same ailment that had carried off their son Smith George. The illness seemed to wax and wane, and Granger carried on as best he could. One day he was working as usual; the next day he was dead. Not long afterward, Ursula rapidly declined. Alarmed, Patsy wrote, "Ursula is I fear going in the same manner with her husband and son." Jefferson responded with concern and perplexity: "the state of Ursula is remarkable. The symptoms & progress of her disease are well worthy [of] attention. That a whole family should go off in the same and so singular a way is a problem of difficulty." There was some optimism in April 1800, when Colonel Randolph reported, "Ursula is better tho still confined in bed & greatly swelled," but Ursula succumbed.[37]

It is impossible to know with certainty what caused this "singular" cluster of fatalities, but the similarity of symptoms suggests a common cause. It could have been something as simple as chronic lead poisoning, brought on by cooking in a pot containing lead, which caused untreatable kidney failure. When I described the symptoms to a physician, he replied that kidney failure "would cause all those symptoms in the terminal phase."[38]

Or the Grangers were poisoned. The Monticello historian Lucia Stanton took note of Jupiter's remark that he "conceived himself poisoned." The immediate cause of his fatal seizure was the "medicine" given him by the country healer, but he had been seriously ill for days before receiving the fatal dose. Stanton suspected that Jupiter might have been right. All the deceased held positions of high status at Monticello. Great George and Smith George were bosses in the field, the nailery, and the forge. Jupiter ran the stable and had at least one run-in with another slave. And poison was the weapon of choice for settling scores on plantations. A Monticello slave later tried to poison an overseer, and a slave at Poplar Forest was accused of poisoning other slaves. The favors and power bestowed on Jupiter and the Grangers might have made them targets of jealousy and resentment, and they paid with their lives.[39]

Isaac constructed a history he could live with, and he could do that only by leaving some things out. He had very kind words for Colonel Randolph: "Treated Isaac mighty well—one of the finest masters in Virginia."[40] With that pronouncement Isaac truly reached the limit of what could be safely or comfortably said. Only when you look at the record do you find what the blacksmith left out: Colonel Randolph, desperate for cash, sold Isaac's daughter Maria, who was taken away to

Kentucky and probably never seen again. Why would he leave that out? Perhaps he did not wish to share a painful story with a white man, or perhaps he did tell it and Campbell left it out. Perhaps it was just unremarkable. People got sold all the time; it was the system, the sooty air, a filthy gust that snatched your Maria, and you can't blame a wind that has no soul.

8

What the Colonel Saw

Throughout Jefferson's plantation records there runs a thread of indicators—some direct, some oblique, some euphemistic—that the Monticello machine operated on carefully calibrated violence. Some people would never readily submit to being slaves. Some people, Jefferson wrote, "require a vigour of discipline to make them do reasonable work."[1] That plain statement of his policy has been largely ignored in preference to Jefferson's well-known self-exoneration: "I love industry and abhor severity."[2] Jefferson made that reassuring remark to a neighbor, but he might as well have been talking to himself. He hated conflict, disliked having to punish people, and found ways to distance himself from the violence his system required. He was the owner, but nothing was his fault. Thus he went on record with a denunciation of overseers as "the most abject, degraded and unprincipled race," men of "pride, insolence and spirit of domination."[3] Though he despised these brutes, they were hardhanded men who got things done and had no misgivings. He hired them, issued orders to impose a vigor of discipline, and then spread a fog of denial over the whole business.

In *Notes on the State of Virginia*, Jefferson had denounced violence against slaves, which he had good reason to hate because he had seen too much of it. A woman named Hannah, whom Jefferson knew, was beaten to death in "a cruel whipping" by an overseer at his brother's plantation.[4] He wrote the vivid description in *Notes* of someone, probably his father, beating a slave. As a boy, he witnessed other scenes he did not describe; the historian Susan Kern has found an advertisement taken out by Jefferson's father for a runaway named Robin who "had on his Neck when he went away an Iron Collar."[5] A modern reader might think this was some item of adornment, but the collar was very different. A Civil War soldier described one of these infernal devices, which he removed from a man's neck: "On either side of the collar was riveted a spike about four inches long, so arranged that one of the spikes stuck up behind each ear, and held the head as in a vice. Any attempt to turn the head ever so slightly resulted in a prod from one of these spikes."[6]

Small wonder that Jefferson called slavery "unremitting despotism," having witnessed his father's overseer, or his father himself, collaring a slave. But from his post in France, Jefferson ordered his manager to elicit "extraordinary exertions," and the manager's expense accounts in 1791 include a line item for the purchase of "collars."[7]

In the first decade of his ownership of Monticello, Jefferson leased farms for three years to Thomas Garth, whom he characterized as "excessively severe." When Garth's lease expired in 1775, Jefferson nevertheless hired him as overseer of all his holdings in Albemarle County. Garth set a standard of cruelty Jefferson did not want to see matched: when he evaluated potential overseers some thirty years later, he rejected one candidate because the man "has been brought up in the school of the Garths . . . his severity puts him out of the question."[8]

From 1790 until 1803, Colonel Randolph acted as Monticello's "executive overseer," supervising a series of overseers when Jefferson's public duties took him away from Monticello for months at a time. Like George Washington, Jefferson ran a country and a plantation simultaneously. Both issued highly detailed orders from a distance to their plantation managers. Both possessed virtually photographic memories of their properties by the square foot, held agricultural calendars in their heads, and could summon clear mental images of the work that needed to be done, precisely where and how it needed to be done, and by whom. Both felt seized by anxiety that as they labored in the capital for the public good, their personal substance was draining away at home. Both commanded their managers to maintain production.

When Nicholas Lewis left Monticello in 1792, Jefferson and Colonel Randolph exchanged letters about choosing his replacement. Their discussion suggests that both men knew that harsh treatment had been the standard under Lewis's command and that they hoped for improvement. Randolph proposed hiring a man named Manoah Clarkson because he thought he combined "Goodness" with "firmness and vigor." After Clarkson had worked for a while, Randolph reported, "The skill and activity of Clarkson are sufficiently manifested allready to make us hope that your affairs in Albemarle will be better conducted than they have ever been. I know it will give you real pleasure to hear that he has a valuable art of governing the slaves which sets aside the necessity of punishment allmost entirely. Contentment reigns among them."[9] Jefferson shared Randolph's optimism: "Your account of Clarkson's conduct gives me great pleasure."[10]

In his response to Randolph, Jefferson also wrote, "My first wish is that the labourers may be well treated."[11] But what appears at first glance to be an ironclad declaration of principle turns out to be just what Jefferson said it was, a "wish," and it was qualified by a second wish—"that they may enable me to have that treatment continued by making as much as will admit it."

This seemingly simple statement contains an enormous amount of information. First, this was Jefferson's contract with the slaves: *I wish to treat you well, but if you do not produce enough, there will be harsh measures.* As with his earlier unspoken compacts, the slaves had no idea that this governing principle had been declared, although they could certainly sense its effects.

Second, it was Jefferson's contract with himself. Having made this mental compact with the slaves, he could absolve himself from blame for anything unpleasant. The slaves were at fault.

Third, we get a flickering, on-and-off sighting of Jefferson the man. The benevolent paterfamilias is dominant, but in the background stands a darker figure, harder to discern, emerging only briefly in flares of wrath, which we instinctively discount because it does not fit with the image we want to have.

Fourth, these were standing orders to the hapless son-in-law charged with managing the unmanageable—barely controllable overseers and laborers who resisted control. The heir of ruinous debts, Randolph depended on Jefferson's largesse to survive, and his wife was utterly devoted to her father. Randolph had no explicit authority over the overseers, but he was the owner's son-in-law; Jefferson told the overseers to ask him for advice, but Randolph should not intervene except in "extremities."

Randolph's letters, generally a model of clarity and erudition (he attended college in Edinburgh), sometimes degenerate to gibberish when he is forced to discuss the disciplining of slaves with his father-in-law, as if he were stammering in front of the commander in chief. In a garbled sentence that takes several readings to untangle, Randolph described his peculiar position as middleman in a chain of command as tangled as his syntax: "I have been frequently called on and have not hezitated to interfere tho' without authority I have made known to all I had none that my interference if not productive of wholesome effects might be rejected."

One letter to Jefferson abruptly opens with a declaration of loyalty and then an ambiguous hint that some overseer, unnamed, has crossed the line into severity, what Randolph calls euphemistically "strict command." Randolph would like to put a stop to something unspecified, but he thinks that strict command ("the motives upon which you depended") is what his father-in-law wants, and a change in policy presents risks. Oblique and obscure, the account apparently made sense both to Randolph and to Jefferson: "I am confident I could have served you considerably but I thought it better to trust to the motives upon which you depended than risk the consequences of a sudden relaxation of strict command."[12]

A point-counterpoint runs through Randolph's reports to Jefferson in the winter of 1798, when output sagged at the precise moment when Jefferson was urging speed. Jefferson had sent instructions that "George should be hurried to get his tobacco down. I have never learned whether he & Page have delivered all their wheat & how much."[13] This was the season in which the enslaved foreman Great George Granger faced insubordination and wasted away with care because he was too lenient, while the harsh regime of the "terror" William Page provoked "discontent." Randolph told Jefferson that Page was "peevish & too ready to strike."[14] But Jefferson had known Page's temperament when he hired him and had taken the precaution of removing Granger's son Bagwell and his family from the farm Page would manage; he had a cabin hastily constructed for them on the Monticello farm, where Bagwell would be under his father's supervision.[15] When he received the report of insubordination under one manager and discontent under the other, Jefferson loftily advised Randolph that "George needs to be supported &

Page to be moderated," but offered no advice on how that might be achieved, and later remarked, vaguely, "I am in hopes that Page & George will give you but little trouble."[16] In any event, output had to be maintained; he had his eye on delivery dates to the Richmond market.

"I am not fit to be a farmer with the kind of labour we have," Jefferson exclaimed in 1799, in an oft-quoted diatribe against the uselessness of slaves, suggesting a heroic struggle on his part to wring productivity out of them.[17] He was chief scribe in the propaganda war against African-American laborers. Despite their difficulties, Granger and Page managed to produce an excellent crop of tobacco, which Jefferson had resumed planting. Several years earlier he had exulted: "We have had the finest harvest ever known in this country. Both the quantity and quality of wheat are extraordinary."[18] He had the slaves to thank for this, the weather to blame for other problems—drought and frost destroyed the next wheat crop—and only himself to blame for the setback that inspired his outburst against the laborers. As one historian discovered, "Although the American economy was in trouble in 1798, Jefferson had a particularly good year, selling his tobacco in Richmond for $13 a hundred weight."[19] He did so well that he was able to pay off $2,000 in back debts and, because the economy was slack, to hire, at a bargain rate, a top-quality house joiner in Philadelphia, James Dinsmore, who went on to complete Monticello. He also bought his daughter a Kirchmann harpsichord, one of the finest and most expensive brands.

In 1799 he had plenty of tobacco to sell, but he bet against the market, holding back from selling in the certainty that commodity prices would rise. The market fell. By the time he decided to sell, he got only $6 a hundredweight. And when he wrote his blast against the slaves and their useless labor, the market was in free fall—not their fault, but someone had to take the blame for his embarrassment and bear the burden of repairing the damage wrought by a ruthless market.

The physical punishment of slaves presented a potential embarrassment to the plantation world and to Jefferson. When a British poet wanted to mock Jefferson, he composed a verse saying, "The patriot . . . retires to lash his slaves at home." During his presidency Jefferson received an anonymous letter about a report circulating in Washington that he had been seen at Monticello personally lashing a female slave. The charge was most likely baseless, but even the hint of such an incident could stain Jefferson's reputation.[20]

Among themselves, the planters expected and accepted a certain level of violence, but there were limits. When the Duke de La Rochefoucauld-Liancourt visited Monticello, he learned of a commotion among the planters about a heinous act by one of their own:

> I witnessed the indignation excited in all the planters of the neighborhood by the cruel conduct of a master to his slave, whom he had flogged to such a degree as to leave him almost dead on the spot. Justice pursues this barbarous master, and all the other planters declared loudly their wish, that he may be severely punished, which seems not to admit of any doubt.[21]

Jefferson's man William Page evoked the same disgust. His methods of control at Jefferson's farms unnerved the whole county. In the judgment of Albemarle's white citizens, Page was a "terror." Though Colonel Randolph told Jefferson about the slaves' "discontent" with Page's free use of the lash, Jefferson retained the peevish overseer's services for another two years.[22] Jefferson's other son-in-law, John Wayles Eppes, alluded to "the publick sentiment against him." Making his own deal with the devil, Eppes hired Page, balancing the overseer's known cruelty against "his skill and industry." But when Eppes sought to hire slaves from other Albemarle planters, nobody would do business with him: "the terror of Page's name . . . prevented the possibility of hiring them."[23]

A year after he hired Manoah Clarkson, Jefferson's estimate of that overseer's goodness had been deflated, though not to the degree that he would fire the man: "I shall perhaps propose [a project] to Clarkson . . . unless I could find a person more kind to the labourers."[24] Jefferson hired another violent overseer with an "unfortunate temper," William McGehee—"to those under him he is harsh, severe and tyrannical," so tyrannical that when McGehee was working on another plantation he had to carry a gun "for fear of an attack from the negroes."[25]

In the 1950s a tiny fragment of information about the Monticello system so shocked one of Jefferson's editors that he suppressed it in the record. The standard source for our understanding of life at Monticello has been the edition of Jefferson's *Farm Book* edited in the early 1950s by Edwin Betts, with a five-hundred-page compendium of letters and other documents describing in minute detail the day-to-day lives of master and slaves. When Betts was editing one of Colonel Randolph's plantation reports, he confronted a taboo subject: Randolph reported to Jefferson that the nailery was functioning very well because "the small ones" were being whipped. Being ten, eleven, or twelve years old, they did not take willingly to being forced to show up in the icy midwinter hour before dawn at the master's nail forge. And so the overseer, Gabriel Lilly, was whipping them "for truancy."[26]

Betts decided that the image of children being beaten at Monticello had to be suppressed, so he deleted the offending line from Randolph's letter. He had an entirely different image in his head; the introduction to the book declared, "Jefferson came close to creating on his own plantations the ideal rural community."[27] Betts couldn't do anything about the original letter, but no one would see it, tucked away in the archives of the Massachusetts Historical Society. The full text did not emerge in print until 2005.

Betts's omission was important in shaping the scholarly consensus that Jefferson managed his plantations with a lenient hand. Relying on Betts's editing, the historian Jack McLaughlin noted that Lilly "resorted to the whip during Jefferson's absence, but Jefferson put a stop to it."[28] "Slavery was an evil he had to live with," Merrill Peterson wrote, "and he managed it with what little dosings of humanity a diabolical system permitted."[29] Peterson echoed Jefferson's complaints about the workforce, alluding to "the slackness of slave labor," and emphasized Jefferson's benevolence: "In the management of his slaves Jefferson encouraged diligence but was instinctively too lenient to demand it. By all accounts he was a kind and generous master. His conviction of the injustice of the institution strengthened his sense of obligation toward its victims."[30] Joseph Ellis observed that only "on rare occasions, and as a last resort, he ordered overseers to use the lash." Dumas Malone stated, "Jefferson was kind to his servants to the point of indulgence, and within the framework of an institution he disliked he saw that they were well provided for. His 'people' were devoted to him."[31]

As a rule, the slaves who lived at the mountaintop, including the

Hemings family and the Grangers, were treated better than the slaves who worked in the ground farther down the mountain. But the machine was hard to restrain.

After the violent tenures of earlier overseers, Gabriel Lilly seemed to portend a gentler reign when he arrived at Monticello in 1800. Colonel Randolph's first report was optimistic. "All goes well," he wrote, and "what is under Lillie admirably."[32] His second report about two weeks later was glowing: "Lillie goes on with great spirit and complete quiet at Mont'o.: he is so good tempered that he can get twice as much done without the smallest discontent as some with the hardest driving possible."[33] In addition to placing him over the laborers "in the ground" at Monticello, Jefferson put Lilly in charge of the nailery for an extra fee of £10 a year.

Once Lilly established himself, his good temper evidently evaporated, because Jefferson began to worry about what Lilly would do to the nailers, the promising adolescents whom Jefferson managed personally, intending to move them up the plantation ladder. He wrote to Randolph: "I forgot to ask the favor of you to speak to Lilly as to the treatment of the nailers. it would destroy their value in my estimation to degrade them in their own eyes by the whip. this therefore must not be resorted to but in extremities. as they will again be under my government, I would chuse they should retain the stimulus of character." But in the same letter he emphasized that output must be maintained: "I hope Lilly keeps the small nailers engaged so as to supply our customers."[34]

Colonel Randolph immediately dispatched a reassuring but carefully worded reply: "Everything goes well at Mont'o.—the Nailers all [at] work and executing well some heavy orders. . . . I had given a charge of lenity respecting all: (Burwell* absolutely excepted from the whip alltogether) before you wrote: none have incurred it but the small ones for truancy."[35] To the news that the small ones were being whipped and that "lenity" had an elastic meaning, Jefferson had no response; the small ones had to be kept "engaged."

It seems that Jefferson grew uneasy about Lilly's regime at the nailery. Jefferson replaced him with William Stewart but kept Lilly in charge of the adult crews building his mill and canal. Under Stewart's

---

*Burwell Colbert, Jefferson's future butler, was then seventeen.

lenient command (greatly softened by habitual drinking), the nailery's productivity sank. The nail boys, favored or not, had to be brought to heel. In a very unusual letter, Jefferson told James Dinsmore that he was bringing Lilly back to the nailery. It might seem puzzling that Jefferson would feel compelled to explain a personnel decision that had nothing to do with Dinsmore, but the nailery stood just a few steps from Dinsmore's shop. Jefferson was preparing Dinsmore to witness scenes under Lilly's command such as he had not seen under Stewart's, and his tone is stern: "I am quite at a loss about the nailboys remaining with mr Stewart. they have long been a dead expence instead of profit to me. in truth they require a vigour of discipline to make them do reasonable work, to which he cannot bring himself. on the whole I think it will be best for them also to be removed to mr Lilly's [control]."[36]

An incident of horrible violence in the nailery—an attack by one nail boy against another—may shed some light on the fear Lilly instilled in the nail boys. In 1803 a nailer named Cary smashed his hammer into the skull of a fellow nailer, Brown Colbert. Seized with convulsions, Colbert went into a coma and would certainly have died had Colonel Randolph not immediately summoned a physician, who performed brain surgery. With a trephine saw, the doctor drew back the broken part of Colbert's skull, thus relieving pressure on the brain. Amazingly, the young man survived.

Bad enough that Cary had so viciously attacked someone, but his victim was a Hemings. Jefferson angrily wrote to Randolph that "it will be necessary for me to make an example of him in terrorem to others, in order to maintain the police so rigorously necessary among the nail boys."* He ordered that Cary be sold away "so distant as never more to be heard of among us. It would to the others be as if he were put out of the way by death." And he alluded to the abyss beyond the gates of Monticello into which people could be flung: "There are generally negro purchasers from Georgia passing about the state."

Randolph's report of the incident included Cary's motive: the boy was "irritated at some little trick from Brown, who hid part of his nailrod to teaze him." But under Lilly's regime this trick was not so "little." Colbert knew the rules, and he knew very well that if Cary couldn't find his

---

*In Jefferson's time "police" meant both order and the people who enforced it.

nailrod, he would fall behind, and under Lilly that meant a beating. Hence the furious attack.[37]

Jefferson's daughter wrote to her father that one of the slaves, a disobedient and disruptive man named John, tried to poison Lilly, perhaps hoping to kill him. John was safe from any severe punishment because he was a hired slave: if Lilly injured him, Jefferson would have to compensate his owner, so Lilly had no means to retaliate. John, evidently grasping the extent of his immunity, took every opportunity to undermine and provoke him, even "cutting up [Lilly's] garden [and] destroying his things."[38]

But Lilly had his own kind of immunity. He grasped his importance to Jefferson when he renegotiated his contract, so that beginning in 1804 he would no longer receive a flat fee for managing the nailery but be paid 2 percent of the gross.[39] Productivity immediately soared. In the spring of 1804, Jefferson wrote to his supplier: "The manager of my nailery had so increased its activity as to call for a larger supply of rod . . . than had heretofore been necessary."[40]

Maintaining a high level of activity required a commensurate level of discipline. Thus, in the fall of 1804, when Lilly was informed that one of the nail boys was sick, he would have none of it. Appalled by what happened next, one of Monticello's white workmen, a carpenter named James Oldham, informed Jefferson of "the Barbarity that [Lilly] made use of with Little Jimmy." Oldham reported that James Hemings, the seventeen-year-old son of the house servant Critta Hemings, had been sick for three nights running, so sick that Oldham feared the boy might not live. He took Hemings into his own room to keep watch over him. When he told Lilly that Hemings was seriously ill, Lilly said he would whip Jimmy into working. Oldham "begged him not to punish him," but "this had no effect." The "Barbarity" ensued: Lilly "whipped him three times in one day, and the boy was really not able to raise his hand to his head."[41]

Flogging to this degree does not persuade someone to work; it disables him. But it also sends a message to the other slaves, especially those, like Jimmy, who belonged to the elite class of Hemings servants and might think they were above the authority of Gabriel Lilly. Once he recovered, Jimmy Hemings fled Monticello, joining the community of free blacks and runaways who made a living as boatmen on the James

River, floating up and down between Richmond and obscure backwater villages. Contacting Hemings through Oldham, Jefferson tried to persuade him to come home but did not set the slave catchers after him.[42]

There is no record that Jefferson made any remonstrance against Lilly, who was unrepentant about the beating and the loss of a valuable slave; indeed, he demanded that his salary be doubled to £100. This put Jefferson in a quandary. He displayed no misgivings about the regime that Oldham characterized as "the most cruel," but £100 was more than he wanted to pay. Jefferson wrote that Lilly as an overseer "is as good a one as can be"—"certainly I can never get a man who fulfills my purposes better than he does."[43]

Years of watching people get whipped did not accustom Colonel Randolph to it. Rather, he grew to hate it. He banned the whip on his own place, Edgehill; and when people committed a serious offense, he took them to court, and they were punished by a stint in jail, like a white person. Occasionally, he took a cane to people, but there was something about the whip he could no longer abide, it being the emblem of a species of power no one should have because, he wrote, "power seldom reasons well"—a Jeffersonian notion if there ever was one. He evidently had words with his fellow planters over the question of whipping and the realpolitik of plantation management. Someone must have said to him: *Well, they whip people in the army, and this is the same.* Colonel Randolph didn't think so. He had seen army discipline, and he wrote: "Tyranny in the army is mitigated by the reflexion that the brave have to submit to the brave only," whereas on a plantation "the greatest dastard" held people "entirely in his power, and dependent upon his caprice."[44]

Jefferson wrote that punishment degraded slaves "in their own eyes," which made whipping counterproductive because it would "destroy their value."[45] He was referring not to the laborers in the ground but to the high-ranking artisans and household servants. His new model of agriculture and industry required a measure of self-reliance (very carefully limited) on the part of these exceptionally important people. Jefferson wanted them to display "character," but that emphatically did *not* mean having a sense of self-worth or self-esteem. Possessing "character" meant that you were manageable. The nailers "will again be under my government" when he returned to Monticello, and he wanted to deal with contented slaves. He certainly did not want to involve himself in any unpleasant business of punishment.

If slaves could be convinced that it was in their interest to cooperate, to be good slaves, then Jefferson would not have them collared or whipped, and slavery would be a less distasteful business for everyone. This was part of Jefferson's sinister fantasy that he was a benevolent master—sinister because he believed that by manipulating behavior with threats and rewards, he could get inside a person's head and shape the "character." He could make slavery congenial to the master by creating genial slaves suited to perpetual slavery. Alexis de Tocqueville later observed this process taking place across the South, writing that the slaveholders "have employed their despotism and their violence against the human mind."[46]

Benjamin Franklin, of all people, sketched out a remarkably calculating, cold program for manipulating people into internalizing their enslavement: "Every master of slaves ought to know, that though all the slave possesses is the property of the master, [the slave's] good-will is his own, he bestows it where he pleases; and it is of some importance to the master's profit, if he can obtain that good-will at the cheap rate of a few kind words, with fair and gentle usage."[47] Kindness, fairness, and gentleness—core human values—became useful tools for enslavement.

Jefferson's system took advantage of people rooted in old ways, who clung to conventions of loyalty and gratitude. They were tightly bound to him, and their interests intersected. Everyone cherished order. For the owner, maintenance of order kept the enterprise productive. For the slaves, order kept them alive and kept their families together. They absorbed whatever evil was done to them because something worse could always happen.*[48]

The superficial tranquillity of the plantation world helped to give the impression that the slaves had willingly accepted their enslavement. But Colonel Randolph knew that this was not a tranquil world but a desperate one. The man who hanged himself on the neighboring plan-

---

*Years after segregation had fallen, an African-American reflected on how it had become such a successful system of control: "It was like sleep, it just eased up on you. You didn't see it. You're accustomed to it. . . . Your kids, they don't know anything about it. But they will."

tation had been, according to him, a slave who possessed "character," which had not been enough to save him, and Randolph genuinely mourned the loss of this person fatally engulfed in the "sooty atmosphere" of the regime. From what he wrote, it seems that Randolph must have known the man well, because the letter stares deeply into a soul tormented by fear. His "character" sprang from terror.

The man was "the most trust-worthy among them . . . being the one chosen to go on the road with the wagon always, to hand off grain and bring back supplies"; but his trustworthiness grew from a dread of being whipped. He had "seriously formed the resolution never to incur the punishment of stripes, by any misconduct." But "for some trifling misdemeanour"—people said the man had left tools behind in the field—"the young fellow received a few lashes, on his bare back." And so, that night, "he hung himself, 30 feet from the ground, in a tree near his Masters door." Randolph did not see this as the act of a coward: "The bravery of this fellow seems to have left no room in his mind for [the thought of running away]. He had made a resolution, and he marched intrepidly forward in the execution of it, despising pain, and not knowing fear."[49] The system that could kill such a man was merely "a hideous monster" behind a cheap mask of "a few kind words . . . fair and gentle usage."

"Their griefs are transient," Jefferson wrote, suggesting that the enslaved, inside, were very nearly dead. He saw African-Americans as "a captive nation," and his system was carefully designed, to borrow a phrase from Bob Dylan, to "teach peace to the conquered."[50]

9

A Mother's Prayers

Among the mundane letters in Jefferson's archive about mansions, labor, and supplies, there is one of a completely different sort. It was a prayer.

> November 15th 1818
>
> Master, I write you a few lines to let you know that your house and furniture are all safe, as I expect you will be glad to know. . . . I was sorry to hear that you was so unwell you could not come [here] it greive me manny time but I hope as you have been so blessed in this [life] that you considered it was god that done it and no other one we all ought to be thankful for what he has done for us we ought to serve and obey his commandments that you may set to win the prize and after glory run
>
> Master, I donot [think] my ignorant letter will be much encouragement to you as knows I am a poor, ignorant creature
>
> adieu, I am your
>
> humble servant
>
> Hannah[1]

Somehow Hannah had evaded Jefferson's rule against literacy and had learned to write. When she wrote this, she was a forty-eight-year-old cook living at Poplar Forest. She followed Jefferson's personal style, not capitalizing words and signing off "adieu." The similarity of her writing to the master's suggests that a Jefferson grandchild might have tutored her. The quality of her handwriting was so fine she could have forged papers for an escape, but she wouldn't have done such a thing given the tone of her letter, which is startling in its self-abasement. Twice she calls Jefferson "Master," and even though she could write far better than most white people, she calls herself "a poor, ignorant creature." She is genuinely concerned that Jefferson has been ill, but more deeply grieved that his soul may be lost. "Set to win the prize and after glory run" had the ring of a quotation, not from the Bible, but from somewhere else; and sure enough, an American hymnal dating back to the early nineteenth century contains "Evening Shade" with the verses: "May we set out to win the prize / And after glory run." Hannah might well have sung those verses on the day she wrote the letter (Sunday, November 15) at the African Meeting House near the plantation.

Hannah lived at Jefferson's country retreat, Poplar Forest, some ninety miles from Monticello, near Lynchburg. Depending on conditions and the determination of the traveler, it could take from two to eight days to get there. Hannah did the cooking when Jefferson visited; at other times she sewed and worked "in the ground" as a common field hand. Jefferson had known Hannah from her infancy: he first wrote her name in his Farm Book when she was four, and he recorded the births of her children.[2] She was born at Monticello in 1770, and Jefferson sent her when she was a teenager to Poplar Forest, where she married her first husband, Solomon, and had three children. Solomon disappears from the records without explanation. Hannah then married Hall, the Poplar Forest blacksmith, hog keeper, and foreman of labor.

Hannah had a teenage son, Billy, who did not adopt the cooperative posture of his mother and began to attract the master's attention in an alarming way. Jefferson wrote to an overseer in 1817, "I send Bedford Billy down to be put to work with the Coopers under Barnaby. . . . Billy is found too ungovernable for Johnny Hemings."[3] The "ungovernable" Billy remained so, despite attempts to reform him. He failed at Monticello's cooper shop, was demoted to work "in the ground," and was sent back to Poplar Forest, where the manager Joel Yancey wrote, "I had at one time great hopes of reclaiming him, but . . . I despair of making anything of him, he is certainly the most consumate, bloody-minded Villan that I ever saw of his age, and he becomes more and more daring as he increases in strength."[4]

The inevitable confrontation came in October 1819, a year after Hannah wrote her letter to Jefferson. One Saturday night Yancey took the measure of the weather, saw signs of frost, and resolved to get all hands into the field at first light to gather in the tobacco. But when Yancey got to the cabins in the morning, he found almost all the people gone: they had either headed into Lynchburg for market day, as was their custom, or, more likely, gone to the African Meeting House, as Hannah probably did. In any case, having Sunday off was an inalienable right for slaves; for six days their labor was taken, and the seventh was theirs.[5]

Yancey ordered the hands he could find into the field. Later in the day another overseer saw Hannah and Billy coming back to the plantation and ordered them into the fields, but Billy "positively refused" and "a battle ensued." With his mother looking on, Billy grabbed rocks in each hand and struck the overseer, who took several blows before he could pull away a rock and hit back. In the hand-to-hand fight Billy got the overseer to drop the rock by biting his hand, and then he fled.

Here the account takes a surprising twist. Hannah went to Yancey and reported what Billy had done: "Hanah saw it all, and told me Billy had bitt and struck the overseer." She may have thought that the only way to save her son was to bring him back into the good graces of the system. She may also have felt that she was the cause of the fight, that Billy's anger had flared at seeing his mother ordered to work on the Sabbath, which to her would have been a grievous sin.

Billy did not escape into the hills but went to Monticello to beg Jefferson's forgiveness, stating his complaint that the people had been compelled to work on Sunday.[6] Perhaps for the sake of the mother, Jefferson pardoned the ungovernable son. Yancey was disgusted. "What must be done?" he pointedly wrote to Jefferson. "They run from here to you, and from you to here, I know of only one remedy." He did not specify what that remedy might be.

Billy's reprieve did not reform him. Three years later he attacked another overseer, slashing the man's face about a dozen times. Once again, Hannah witnessed her son's attack. She rushed to the overseer's aid. As one of Jefferson's relatives reported, "He would have bled to Death but . . . Hannah a Black woman who has the care of the House staunched the Blood by holding the wounds together till they sent for a

Doctor." In the preaching Hannah had heard at the African Meeting House, Moses kills the overseer and escapes to become the savior of the slaves; Hannah the cook found herself holding the overseer's bloody face in her hands as if she could undo her son's crime.[7] At that moment her world collapsed.

Billy fled for his life. Jeff Randolph put an announcement in the Richmond newspaper offering $50 for Billy's capture under the headline "A Murderer Escaped." The advertisement suggested that Billy might head to Richmond by a boat on the James River, or to Charlottesville, or to Washington. He was described as "a bright mulatto" about five feet six inches. Despite the severity of his wounds, the overseer survived the attack. In short order Billy was captured and remanded to trial in Bedford County.[8] Billy was the only one who had wielded a weapon in the attack, but he and two other Poplar Forest slaves, Gawen and Hercules, were all charged with "wickedly and feloniously having consulted upon the subject of rebelling and making insurrection against the law and government." It appears that the authorities suspected an uprising in the making.

The outcome of the trial is surprising. All three men were acquitted of the conspiracy charge. And though Billy was found guilty of stabbing, he received a very lenient sentence. He was burned in the left hand and given thirty-nine lashes, the usual punishment for theft. Given the seriousness of the crime, the acquittals and the light punishment seem strange. That fall Bedford County had executed two slaves, but somehow this incident had a different outcome.

Because of the gravity of the crime, the legal system promptly took notice of it, but the legal process might have proven costly to Thomas Jefferson. At that moment he happened to be in need of cash and wanted to sell these men. Had they been convicted of conspiring to rebel, a capital offense, they would have been hanged or transported. Since condemning slaves was legally the seizure of private property, the State of Virginia would have had to compensate Jefferson for the value of the convicted slaves, but at a much lower rate of compensation than what the open market would set.

As required by law, the defendants had an attorney, hired by Jeff Randolph. The lawyer would have explained Jefferson's position to the five gentlemen justices who sat in judgment at the court of "oyer and terminer"—the special state court that adjudicated crimes committed by slaves. Of the five judges, one was related to Jefferson by marriage and another had been on the Poplar Forest payroll as an overseer.[9] It was a simple task to persuade such judges to release these men back to Jefferson's custody. Within days, Billy, Gawen, Hercules, and another slave were "all four of them . . . chained together" and taken south to be sold by Joel Yancey and two other white men. Their destination was Louisiana, where Jefferson expected the highest price to be obtained. But the slave market was in a slump, no buyer could be found, and the men had to be hired out. Three of them soon died of disease, and Jefferson got nothing for them. Billy escaped from the plantation where he was hired out but was captured and jailed in New Orleans. What happened to him next, I could not find out.[10]

After he had the four men sent on their lethal journey, Jefferson continued to visit their home place, sitting for meals prepared by Hannah, riding and walking through fields and forests. Poisoning techniques were well known around Poplar Forest, and the farm offered a choice of blunt and sharp instruments, yet the master rode serenely about. Revenge was unthinkable.

The account of Hannah rushing to the aid of the stricken overseer is contained in an obscure letter written by Elizabeth Trist, who lived near Poplar Forest, to her grandson Nicholas, who was married to Jefferson's granddaughter Virginia. Looking through her other letters in the hope of finding more information about Poplar Forest, I made one of those discoveries that radically shifts one's perception of events. It is easy to characterize Billy as a villainous renegade, a bloody-minded resister against a system we have been told was benevolent. But Mrs. Trist wrote of Poplar Forest, "I fear the poor Negroes fare hard. I wish they were as well treated as Mr Tournillon's are."[11] The Tournillon plantation was in Louisiana, where conditions for slaves were notoriously more brutal than in Virginia, yet she thought Mr. Jefferson's Poplar Forest was worse.

10

"I Will Answer for Your Safety . . .
Banish All Fear"

The archives have their documents in abundance, but Monticello Mountain itself is one huge document: an earthen text bearing traces of uncountable stories and a past that stubbornly reasserts its mysteries. I arranged for a hike around the mountain with Monticello's archaeologist Fraser Neiman. In a single day we crossed different zones of time and morality, encountering Jefferson young and old, along with relics of the many different people who lived here, working industriously, raising families, and entangling themselves in ambiguous dramas of crime, punishment, and deception.

A dirt road led off the summit of the mountain to a low-slung building way out of the sight of visitors that looked more like some kind of repair shop than the headquarters of a high-tech archaeological team. Pickups and cars were parked in its graveled yard with various kinds of equipment scattered about. Inside, staff members shared a warren of offices and storage rooms where thousands of artifacts were warehoused and studied. Walls displayed maps, graphs, and photos with captions written in the jargon of archaeology—"protected depositional environments," meaning "storage pits"; "secondary refuse aggregates," or "garbage piles"; and "spatial auto-correlation," meaning "nearby things should be similar." Their high-flown jargon notwithstanding, the archaeology staff forms the down-and-dirty corps of the research process here. The high season for their work is also the high season for central Virginia's heat and humidity, because it is in summer that Monticello can obtain students to staff the digs. The only relief for the diggers comes when a visiting lecturer gives a talk in the refined, air-conditioned precincts of the Jefferson research library on another part of the estate. It is comical to see sweating, clay-smeared diggers, looking like lost explorers, troop into a conference room and take seats alongside the crisply dressed denizens of the archives.

Some years earlier a small group of specialists had met in a conference room at the University of Virginia to hear Neiman talk about his recent findings. A self-confessed lover of "geeky" graphs, charts, and almost any compilation of numbers, Neiman offered a broad interpretation of African-American life in the eighteenth and early nineteenth centuries based on his meticulous study of holes in the ground. He concluded, "Many Chesapeake slaves seem to have achieved modest gains in their living situations." They could do something most of them had not been able to do before: they could live together as families. I asked Neiman if he would take me around the mountain and show me some of the sites that had led him to this conclusion.

At his headquarters Neiman unrolled a map of Monticello Mountain on a worktable and ran his finger over it to outline our hike. Looking at the map, I realized how much more there is to "Monticello" than just the famous house on the summit. Jefferson intended the whole property to be a unified work of landscape art, modeled on the European idea of the *ferme ornée*, or ornamented farm. Neiman's map, which noted more than a score of African-American settlements scattered around the mountain, was laid over Jefferson's own plat of the mountain done in 1809. Jefferson had marked a few overseers' houses, slave houses, and four "Roundabouts" in a network of scenic roads laid out for carriage rides and walks, which visitors and Jefferson's family enjoyed enormously. The roundabouts took horse and carriage riders past landscape vistas and views of grazing animals and fields of crops. As his great-granddaughter recalled, "The woods around the mountainsides offered neverfailing enjoyments: to peep through the Park pales and watch the deer; to walk around the shady roundabouts."[1] These paths formed a delightful maze through the forest, through which Jefferson's grandchildren could wander on a hot summer day until they reached a cool spring at the bottom of the hillside. Neiman said we would follow the Third Roundabout to an old work road that led to an archaeological site and then pick up another roundabout to get to the remnants of a slave house.

Just a short walk from the offices Neiman paused in an open field and unrolled the map. "This is an area that we know Jefferson called the Ancient Field. This is probably the oldest cultivated piece of ground on the mountain." Here topography connected with history. All of Jefferson's fields lay on the southern side of the mountain except this one, which faces north. Three miles away stood Shadwell, the home of Jefferson's parents, Peter and Jane, where Thomas was born in 1743, six years after his father had acquired four hundred acres here. Altogether, Peter owned about seventy-two hundred acres, with his seat at Shadwell, conveniently near the Rivanna River. An explorer, surveyor, and mapmaker, Peter probably took note of the fertility of this land during one of his trips through the region. Experienced farmers, Neiman said, could judge the quality of a piece of wildland by the types of trees growing on it—poplars, for example, denote good soil with deep drainage—and he surmised that Peter Jefferson had selected this acreage by scouting the tree cover. He had his slaves cut a road in a straight line from a ford across the Rivanna River near Shadwell up to the Ancient Field, which the master could see from his house. One archaeological site we would soon pass was a small slave quarter dating to the 1740s that had been occupied by Peter's slaves.

Somewhat ruefully, Neiman pointed at a 1970s structure on the edge of the Ancient Field. It was built on top of a slave's house. No one had investigated the site before putting the building there. "There's an artifact scatter that extends through here," he said, sweeping his arm toward the structure, which "unfortunately was built in the middle of it. We know from Jefferson's surveys that by the early 1790s there were two slave houses here, one lived in by a man named Tom Shackelford, and another by a man named Phil, whose last name we don't know. They were both wagon drivers. Tom's house, we think, is pretty well preserved under this little mound here. Phil's house has not fared as well."

After Neiman came to Monticello in 1995, he launched a detailed survey, digging test pits along a grid every forty feet to search for archaeological remains. By 2011, Monticello Mountain had some twenty thousand holes punched into it, a foot in diameter to the depth of the subsoil. As each pit was dug, the archaeologists sifted the dirt for artifacts with a dogged, inch-by-inch scrupulousness that gave them a slow but rich payoff; they found sites of occupation and work never known before.

We set off again down the Third Roundabout, stopping briefly near a stand of cedar trees where crews had uncovered the stones of a cobble hearth, the remains of a log house occupied by Peter Jefferson's slaves. "One of the maddening things," Neiman said, "is that by the second quarter of the eighteenth century, log-building was the cheapest way to build. They just sit right on the surface of the ground." And when log structures were removed or disintegrated, they left no foundation lines, so "we seldom get actual measurements of dimensions." Thomas Jefferson settled slaves on this spot and at another place nearby in the 1770s when he took over Monticello and continued planting tobacco, as his father had done.

Neiman unrolled one of the computer-generated charts he was so fond of. Seeing my quizzical gaze, he said, "*Numbers*, man—numbers are our friends." He was showing me a distribution map of the ceramic shards they had found here. "So this is the white stoneware map. It was popular in the 1740s up to the Revolution, and you can see there's a big concentration of it right up here on the north end of where we are." He pointed to a pile of leaves atop black plastic sheets that covered an excavation. White stoneware was used by Peter Jefferson's slaves, and sure enough Neiman's chart indicated that as time passed and that type of stoneware fell from fashion, its occurrence here fell also. "There's a little bit on the southern side, but that's as it's going out of fashion in the 1770s."

Warming to his task, Neiman produced more charts and maps. "So then we fast-forward to the creamware map. The creamware gets popular in the 1770s. This is showing us the slave and overseer settlement in the tobacco period." His fingers darted from the charts to the clearing as he pointed out two distinct stylistic zones, with the fancier ceramics concentrated in one area. This was how the archaeology team figured out that slaves lived on the southern part of the site and someone of higher status lived where the finer shards were found. Then he played his trump card: when they consulted Jefferson's map, they found an overseer's house—"Boom! It comes out right on the edge of the site"—on the very spot where they'd found the costlier china.

We headed farther down the road through the silence of the forest. Tourists are not allowed here, so we had Monticello Mountain to ourselves. For Jefferson, the forest was a speedway. He was a wild carriage driver, as a visitor, Margaret Bayard Smith, discovered during a harrowing ride on the roundabouts with Jefferson at the reins—like a middle-aged man at the wheel of a roadster—and his granddaughter Ellen wedged into the seat with them. Jefferson talked nonstop as he maneuvered around and over rocks and fallen trees at high speed. All this was fine as long as they were on relatively level ground, but when Jefferson turned to descend the mountain, Smith wrote, "fear took from me the power of listening to him . . . nor could I forbear expressing my alarm." Jefferson tut-tutted her anxieties: "My dear madam, you are not to be afraid, or if you are you are not to show it; trust yourself implicitly to me, I will answer for your safety . . . banish all fear." But Smith was so terrified as the carriage raced toward a rock that she jumped out, while Ellen sat frozen to the bench, in fear more of disappointing her grandfather than of the looming rock: "Poor Ellen did not dare get out." Jefferson's serene confidence was due to the presence of a slave on horseback who, as they approached the rock, galloped ahead, leaped from his mount, and with great strength and skill braced the vehicle as it tilted ominously; otherwise, Smith said, "we must have all been rolled down the mountain."[2] It was the slave who answered for their safety.

As we walked down the road, I could make out some movement in a clearing up ahead. About twenty people were at work scraping dirt, pushing wheelbarrows around, and taking notes and measurements. Every summer the Monticello staff is augmented by students in a field school run jointly with the University of Virginia. They had excavated two large, shallow rectangles, exposing some scattered rocks and bricks that did not seem to promise any great historical illumination.

The earth of Monticello is the clay that has frustrated generations of Virginia farmers, and the two burnt-red excavations contrasted sharply with the grass in the clearing and the bright greenery of the surrounding forest. The archaeologists themselves seemed to have become part of this earth, as nearly all of them were smeared with clay and sweat. Dressed in khakis and a light shirt that looked resplendently clean among the mud-smeared tribe, Neiman stared intently at a blank patch of earth as if he could read it, and in fact he could. He was looking for slight differences in color that would indicate a disturbance in the earth, but it was not a good day for reading this particular patch of dirt:

"At the moment it's partially baked out and dried out, so you can't really see the differences as well."

Two hundred years earlier this forest had been a wheat field, and ten years before that a cluster of slave houses had stood here. A few yards away a small group of archaeologists worked at the spot of another house; the remains of yet other houses might lie somewhere beyond the clearing, which had the unprepossessing name "Site 8." This clearing turned out to be a hot spot for artifacts—mainly ceramics, nails, glass, and bricks but also buttons, coins, tools, and utensils—so the team focused its efforts here.

Under a canopy that protected them from the broiling sun, two female students worked amid a random scattering of rocks. Using a small trowel, one of them carefully scraped dirt onto a dustpan while the other took notes. Neiman said the rocks might have been part of a hearth that was dismantled when the slaves demolished the house and moved to another part of the mountain. About ten feet away Neiman watched someone wielding a plumb line and a ruler at the edge of a shallow pit where a neat line of bricks had been exposed.

"We're drawing," said a voice behind me. It was Sara Bon-Harper, the archaeological research manager. She explained that they make measured drawings the old-fashioned way, by hand, rather than use a computerized camera process. "You can't be too careful in your record-keeping." Like Neiman, Bon-Harper was a lover of charts, graphs, and all things computerized, but she had made an important discovery here by intuition. After the team had found evidence of one house, she scrutinized the maps of artifacts generated by a computer program and had a strong hunch there had to be another structure, but the diggers were unable to find it. "For years I kept saying, 'There's another house there, we're not finding it,' making people dig more and more holes, and they were saying, 'You're crazy,' and I said, 'Dig more holes,' and finally we dug one and came down on the corner of one of these features." Dubbed, of course, "Sara's House," it yielded the brick-lined pit that was the object that moment of the meticulous measuring and Neiman's intent gaze. Sara was very impressed with finding the brick-lined pit—"a fabulous season," she said.

"So what you have here," I said, "is a cluster of houses not too far from where the overseer lived?"

"Where there was presumably another cluster of houses, which we haven't found yet," Bon-Harper said.

"Early on, we think," Neiman added.

"So the overseer would live cheek by jowl with the slaves?"

"Exactly. That was the pattern early in the plantation. After they dispersed from these two sites, we see more spread-out and smaller settlements."

"Away from the direct supervision of the overseer."

"Exactly," Bon-Harper said.

One of the catchphrases of archaeological jargon I had seen on a poster back at headquarters—"spatial auto-correlation," meaning "nearby things should be similar"—yielded the formula for an interesting discovery here. In the upper layer of this site the artifacts were similar, suggesting that the people who lived here owned and used similar items of clothing, pottery, and utensils. But when the archaeologists dug down into an older stratum, they found different types of artifacts in the same layer, evidence of two different groups of slaves residing in the same place at the same time. History provided the answer: the archaeologists had come down to the layer from the time when Jefferson married Martha Wayles Skelton and Martha's slaves were brought to Monticello to be settled alongside Jefferson's slaves. Over time, Martha's slaves acquired the local varieties of clothing and other personal items. But where did they get these utensils, kitchenware, tools, and clothes?

"This is one of many $64,000 questions," Neiman said when I asked him. Archaeologists first assumed they were all hand-me-downs from the white family on the mountaintop, but careful dating of the artifacts suggested a different interpretation: "You see this regular turnover in stylish ceramics on the site. It's pretty clear the slaves are expending effort to acquire ceramics that are relatively up-to-date, relatively stylish."

"They participated in a consumer economy," Bon-Harper added. "They bought dishes, they bought buttons, they bought colorful fabrics. They bought all kinds of things for their houses." She hastened to add that the houses were hardly luxurious—"not a lot of furniture, and dirt floors." From her reading of the artifacts—not so much what she found as what she didn't find—she concluded that the people here spent a great deal of time outdoors. The area between the house sites was so bare of fragments that she decided it was probably a swept yard, which was an African tradition. "I think that most people who lived in tiny, unheated, unglazed, uncooled houses do as much outdoors as they can. Inside it's going to be smoky, it's going to be close, it's going to be not very well lit."

Bon-Harper was cradling something in her hand that I thought was a newly found artifact, but it was a small, quite contemporary trowel. "This is my sampling tool. I'm going to take half a dozen pollen samples." She asked someone to bring over her "high-tech, calibrated measuring device"—an old film canister. Measuring the different pollen samples was another of the "geeky" undertakings that had produced its own effusion of computer-generated charts that trace the agricultural evolution of the mountain.

Mining these sediment deposits involved digging seven-foot-deep "telephone booths" around the mountain. "We have been able to get pollen samples and put together a picture that suggests that erosion rates skyrocketed at the transition to wheat. Once you get wheat, you get permanent, clear-cut fields, deep plowing, crop rotations. It's clear that there really is an important physical difference in the kind of work that slaves are doing. Different landscapes."

What was good for agriculture is bad for archaeologists, to whom "plow zone" is a dreaded phrase. "The land was churned up," Bon-Harper said. "Plow-zone archaeology is one of the things I'm spending a lot of time in my analysis trying to sort out."

Some two hundred years after the plows did their work here, the archaeologists can still see their marks. Derek Wheeler, another archaeologist on the team, walked me over to the other house site they were excavating. Once again I stared at an utterly blank patch of bare, dry clay, which Wheeler proceeded to read for me. What I had seen as a formless blob of slightly off-color dirt, he identified as "a lot of charcoal," and he pointed out a minuscule fragment of something else: "I think that's going to be a little bit of burnt bone right there." He pointed to an irregular brown patch and admitted he was "not sure what's going on here." Being irregular, it most likely did not indicate a root cellar, but they were planning to take a deeper look. "We'll take out a little pie piece, dig down, and see what the underlying stratigraphy says." I couldn't notice anything else, but Wheeler waved his finger up and down the excavation: "See these etched brown lines? Those are plow lines, cut into the red subsoil."

The plows had not destroyed everything in their paths. "We've been finding a lot of personal items. We found a spoon last year, a thimble last year, we found a fork this year." And they also came upon a jumble of bricks. "To find this many bricks here is tantalizing. Next year we'll have to come back. Hopefully, we'll have another pit."

Back at the first house site the student archaeologists had finished measuring the line of bricks. The diggers had turned up only a small portion of a construction that remained largely hidden in the clay. It didn't look like much.

"When you see archaeology in the movies," I said, "you see them dig and find a box with all the stuff in it, and there are the secrets, right there."

"This is it!" Bon-Harper said. "This is the box with all the stuff in it and the secrets."

Overhearing these remarks, Neiman and another archaeologist said simultaneously, "It's just a big brick-lined box!"—but they were joking, and Sara had been perfectly serious. She explained that the size of the pit and the fact that it needed so many bricks "shows a certain effort to procure brick. It looks like they were taken from different building projects around the plantation. And it had a couple of inches of sand, traditionally used in root cellars." She speculated that the people who lived here built this large root cellar to store produce they had grown themselves, a surplus of food possibly for sale to the big house. The family who lived on this spot might have had their own garden and used the money they got from selling food to buy some of the artifacts that were turning up in the excavations.

The holes in the ground that the archaeologists call "sub-floor pits" would have been covered with boards. Neiman said the pits have been a mystery, "a long-standing archaeological puzzle," since they were first noticed in excavations of a slave quarter near Williamsburg in the 1960s.[3] Since then, excavations of slave quarters throughout the Chesapeake region have turned up so many of them, always located within the outlines of houses, that "sub-floor pits have become a classic sign of slave housing," according to Neiman. Archaeologists developed several theories to explain them. They thought the pits might have been a West

African tradition whose purpose is now unknown, or hiding places for stolen goods, or root cellars where food was preserved over the winter.

Neiman was unsatisfied with these explanations, however, noting in the first case that there was little evidence that sub-floor pits were common in West Africa in the era of the slave trade. The idea that the pits were hiding places for things stolen from owners or other slaves did not hold up, because everyone, including owners and overseers, knew exactly where the pits were. Neiman mentioned a 1770 entry in the diary of the Virginia planter Landon Carter: "This morning I had a complaint about a butter pot's being taken from the dairy. . . . I sent [the overseer] to search all their holes and boxes." If both Carter and his overseer knew about the pits, they would have been the worst place to hide anything.[4] It was feasible that the pits were root cellars, but Neiman said this use could not account for the fact that the size and frequency of the pits changed over time and that they had disappeared from slave housing by 1800.

Neiman theorized that these pits were personal safe-deposit boxes of the "Purloined Letter" kind—safe because they were in plain sight. Chances were good that if you lifted the boards from someone else's storage, you would be seen doing it.

Slave houses of the mid-eighteenth century had several pits, but in the 1790s there were fewer of them, and then after around 1800 there were none. Neiman's insight was that you needed a safe place for your possessions, as meager as they might be, if you shared a house with people you barely knew and didn't trust, but "individuals who could choose to live only with trusted kin and close friends would have less need for such devices." Early on, Jefferson housed many of his slaves without regard for their family ties or personal preferences. Newcomers and strangers forced to live together in close quarters felt so little connection that they habitually stole from one another. But as time went on, Jefferson allowed the slaves to choose their housemates, an unprecedented ceding of control. As families began to live together, the need for securing property declined. Indeed, the plantation documents show that by 1800 Jefferson had shifted to kin-based housing, a phenomenon seen across the Chesapeake region. In the aspect of life that was perhaps the most important—family life—the condition of the slaves was improving.

When Jefferson and other planters in the region gave up raising tobacco in the 1790s because profits were uncertain and dependent on
fluctuations in the European market, the damage done by tobacco to
Virginia's fields became more and more apparent. And Jefferson's shift
to wheat brought about a profound transformation in the lives of the
slaves. "Under the tobacco regime," Neiman said, "it was pretty much
gang labor with the overseer out there all the time." Large gangs of men
and women were out in the fields performing the same task—making
tobacco hills, transplanting, hoeing, pulling suckers, picking worms
(the task especially suited for children), topping the plants, harvesting,
and hauling. The slaves had to be both fast and careful. One overseer
and the threat of the lash could keep a whole field full of people at work
efficiently, day after day, month after month.

But the shift to wheat changed all that.[5] As Neiman wrote, "Wheat
cultivation required plows, which in turn required smithing facilities
and draft animals. Smithing required skilled smiths. Draft animals required fenced pastures, shelter, fodder crops, and attentive care. Plowing
required permanent fields, which in turn required manuring and crop
rotations to maintain soil fertility. Grain, fodder, and manure all required carting, which meant wagon makers and drivers."[6] Slaves now
worked in smaller groups and acquired special skills.

Neiman led the way farther down the mountain into a ravine, following the trace of a road laid out by Jefferson for his carriage rides. It
passed the house of Edmund Bacon, the overseer Jefferson employed
from 1806 to 1822. I had assumed that Bacon lived quite close to the
summit, but this was about a mile from the mansion. And when Jefferson retired from the presidency in 1809, he moved the nailery from the
summit—he no longer wanted to even see it, let alone manage it—to a
site downhill one hundred yards from Bacon's house. The archaeologists discovered unmistakable evidence of the shop—nails, nailrod,
charcoal, coal, and slag. Neiman pointed out on his map the locations
of the shop and Bacon's house. "The nailery was a socially fractious
place," he said. "One suspects that's part of the reason for getting it
off the mountaintop and putting it right here next to the overseer's
house."

When Bacon left Monticello with the savings from his wages, he established himself on a farm in Kentucky, like thousands of other Virginia migrants of the 1820s. Shrewd and frugal, Bacon was so tight with his wages that he was able to lend money to two presidents—Jefferson and Monroe—as well as to members of Jefferson's extended family. In the early 1860s, word of his presence reached the Reverend Hamilton W. Pierson, president of Cumberland College in Princeton, Kentucky. Realizing the historical value of the overseer's store of memories, Pierson went to see Bacon, then seventy-five years old, with a companion who promised him, "We shall not be in the house many minutes before you will be certain to hear something of Mr. Jefferson." Enthralled by what he heard, Pierson made several more visits to Bacon and recorded a long, fascinating narrative, which was published in 1862.[7] Bacon's paper trail is enormous, but he did not leave many artifacts for the archaeologists beyond a few shards of ceramics.

About six hundred feet east of Bacon's house stood the cabin of James Hubbard, a slave who lived by himself. The archaeologists dug more than a hundred test pits at this site but came up with nothing; but when they brought in metal detectors and turned up a few wrought nails, it was enough evidence to convince them they had found the actual site of Hubbard's house.[8]

Hubbard was eleven years old and living with his family at Poplar Forest in 1794 when Jefferson brought him to Monticello to work in the new nailery on the mountaintop. His assignment was a sign of Jefferson's favor for the Hubbard family. James's father, a skilled shoemaker, had risen to the post of foreman of labor at Poplar Forest, and Jefferson saw similar potential in the son. At first James performed abysmally, wasting more material than any of the other nail boys. Perhaps he was just a slow learner; perhaps he hated it; but he made himself better and better at the miserable work, swinging his hammer thousands of times a day, until he excelled. When Jefferson measured the nailery's output he found that Hubbard had reached the top— 90 percent efficiency in converting nailrod to finished nails.

A model slave, eager to improve himself, Hubbard grasped every opportunity the system offered. In his time off from the nailery he took on additional tasks to earn cash. He sacrificed sleep to make money by burning charcoal, tending a kiln through the night. Jefferson also paid

An aerial view of the Monticello summit. (Thomas Jefferson Foundation at Monticello; photograph by Leonard Phillips)

Thomas Jefferson
A Philosopher a Patriote and a Friend
Dessiné par son Ami Tadée Kosciuszko
Et Gravé par Mr. Sokolnicki

A portrait of Jefferson by Thaddeus Kosciuszko, who bequeathed substantial funds to Jefferson to free his slaves—a bequest Jefferson did not carry out. (Library of Congress)

Jefferson's private terrace off his suite of rooms, called the "sanctum sanctorum." The tall windows enclose his greenhouse, flanked by louvered "porticles" whose purpose is not clear. (Thomas Jefferson Foundation at Monticello; photograph by author)

Monticello's dining room. (Thomas Jefferson Foundation at Monticello)

Isaac Jefferson Granger, the Monticello blacksmith who left an invaluable memoir of his experiences, in a daguerreotype taken in the 1840s. (Tracy W. McGregor Library of American History, Albert and Shirley Small Special Collections Library, University of Virginia)

Edmund Bacon, Jefferson's overseer from 1806 to 1822. (Papers of Thomas Jefferson, University of Virginia Library)

Jefferson's account of the productivity of the nail boys. (William A. Clark Memorial Library, UCLA)

Ruins of the joinery, John Hemmings's workshop on Mulberry Row. (Thomas Jefferson Foundation at Monticello)

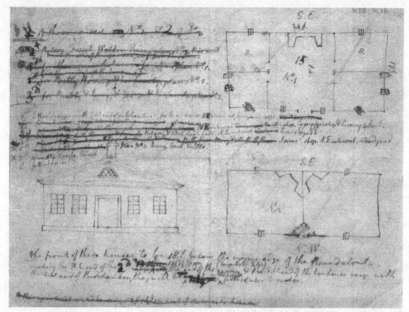

Jefferson's neoclassical design for houses to be occupied by slaves and white workers, planned for Mulberry Row but never built. (Massachusetts Historical Society)

Detail of a letter dated March 4, 1815, with Jefferson's mathematical calculations for the number of crossings with white blood required for a black person to become white. (Library of Congress)

Thomas Mann Randolph, Jr. (1768–1828), who married Jefferson's daughter Martha and acted as Monticello's executive overseer. (Virginia Historical Society)

Ellen Randolph Coolidge by Francis Alexander, c. 1836. (Thomas Jefferson Foundation at Monticello; photograph by Ed Owen)

Thomas Jefferson Randolph by Charles Willson Peale, c. 1808. (Thomas Jefferson Foundation at Monticello; photograph by Ed Owen)

The Reverend Peter Fossett (1815–1901), who left accounts of his childhood in slavery at Monticello. (From Wendell P. Dabney, *Cincinnati's Colored Citizens*, 1926; image courtesy of B. Bernetiae Reed)

RUN away from the subscriber in *Albemarle*, a Mulatto slave called *Sandy*, about 35 years of age, his stature is rather low, inclining to corpulence, and his complexion light; he is a shoemaker by trade, in which he uses his left hand principally, can do coarse carpenters work, and is something of a horse jockey; he is greatly addicted to drink, and when drunk is insolent and disorderly, in his conversation he swears much, and in his behaviour is artful and knavish. He took with him a white horse, much scarred with traces, of which it is expected he will endeavour to dispose; he also carried his shoemakers tools, and will probably endeavour to get employment that way. Whoever conveys the said slave to me, in *Albemarle*, shall have 40 s. reward, if taken up within the county, 4 l. if elsewhere within the colony, and 10 l. if in any other colony. from
                                                    THOMAS JEFFERSON.

An advertisement placed in *The Virginia Gazette* by Jefferson in 1769 offering a reward for the capture of his slave Sandy. (Library of Congress; image courtesy of B. Bernetiae Reed)

Priscilla Hemmings's tombstone, discovered atop Monticello in the 1950s. It was carved by her husband, John Hemmings. The meaning of the word at the top has eluded interpretation. (Thomas Jefferson Foundation at Monticello)

ABOVE: James Hemings's deed of manumission, 1796. (Albert and Shirley Small Special Collections Library, University of Virginia Library)

LEFT: An apothecary jar brought from Paris, discovered by archaeologists behind the site of the Mulberry Row cabin where Sally Hemings lived until 1809. (Thomas Jefferson Foundation at Monticello)

Edward Coles freeing his slaves on the Ohio River in 1819, depicted in an 1885 mural in the Illinois State Capitol. (Courtesy Illinois Secretary of State)

LEFT: The Marquis de Lafayette, depicted at the Battle of Yorktown with a slave attendant. Lafayette championed emancipation, urging both Washington and Jefferson to free their slaves. (Library of Congress)

BELOW: William Short (1759–1849), Jefferson's private secretary and close friend, who proposed an emancipation plan to Jefferson and challenged Jefferson's racial views. (Library of Congress)

Negroes alienated from 1784 to 1794. inclusive.

Jefferson's Farm Book page listing slaves he sold or gave away, 1784 to 1794. (Sol Feinstone Collection, David Library of the American Revolution, on deposit at the American Philosophical Society)

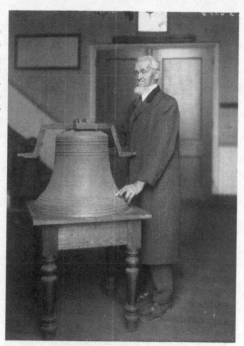

Henry Martin (1826–1915), born a slave at Monticello on the day Jefferson died, July 4. He became the bellringer at the University of Virginia. (Holsinger Studio Collection, Albert and Shirley Small Special Collections Library, University of Virginia)

The Reverend Robert Hughes (1824–1895), son of Ursula and Wormley Hughes, born a slave at Monticello. (Courtesy Union Run Baptist Church; image courtesy of B. Bernetiae Reed)

A letter to Jefferson by his slave Hannah, who lived at the Poplar Forest plantation near Lynchburg, expressing her concern for his health and spiritual welfare.

him for hauling—a position of trust because a man with a horse and permission to leave the plantation could easily escape.[9] Through his industriousness Hubbard laid aside enough cash to purchase some fine clothes, including a hat, knee breeches, and two overcoats.

And then, one day at the beginning of Jefferson's second term as president, Hubbard vanished. For years he had patiently carried out an elaborate deception, pretending to be the loyal, hardworking slave. He had done all that hard work not to soften a life in slavery but to escape it. The clothing was not for show; it was a disguise.

Hubbard had been gone for many weeks when the president received a letter from the sheriff of Fairfax County. He had in custody a man named Hubbard who had confessed to being an escaped slave. In his confession Hubbard revealed the details of his escape. He had made a deal with Wilson Lilly, son of the overseer Gabriel Lilly, paying him $5 and an overcoat in exchange for false emancipation documents and a travel pass to Washington. But illiteracy was Hubbard's downfall: he did not realize that the documents Wilson Lilly had written were not very persuasive.* When Hubbard reached Fairfax County, about a hundred miles north of Monticello, the sheriff stopped him and demanded to see his papers. The sheriff knew forgeries when he saw them and arrested Hubbard. The sheriff asked Jefferson for a reward because he had run "a great Risk" arresting "as large a fellow as he is."

Hubbard was returned to Monticello. If he received some punishment for his escape, there is no record of it. In fact, it seems that Hubbard was forgiven and regained Jefferson's trust within a year. The October 1806 schedule of work for the nailery shows Hubbard working with the heaviest gauge of rod with a daily output of fifteen pounds of nails. That Christmas, Jefferson allowed him to travel from Monticello to Poplar Forest to see his family.[10] Jefferson may have trusted him again, but Bacon remained wary.

One day when Bacon was trying to fill an order for nails, he found that the entire stock of eight-penny nails—three hundred pounds of nails worth $50—was gone: "of course they had been stolen." He immediately suspected James Hubbard and confronted him, but Hubbard "denied it powerfully." Bacon ransacked Hubbard's cabin and "every place

---

*Gabriel Lilly was illiterate, and his son's skill with words was apparently rudimentary.

I could think of" but came up empty-handed. Despite the lack of evidence, Bacon remained convinced of Hubbard's guilt. He conferred with the white manager of the nailery, Reuben Grady: "Let us drop it. He has hid them somewhere, and if we say no more about it, we shall find them."

Walking through the woods after a heavy rain, Bacon spotted muddy tracks on the leaves on one side of the path. He followed the tracks to their end, where he found the nails buried in a large box. Immediately, he went up the mountain to inform Jefferson of the discovery and of his certainty that Hubbard was the thief. Jefferson was "very much surprised and felt very badly about it" because Hubbard "had always been a favorite servant." Jefferson said he would question Hubbard personally the next morning when he went on his usual ride past Bacon's house.

When Jefferson showed up the next day, Bacon had Hubbard called in. At the sight of his master, Hubbard burst into tears. Bacon wrote, "I never saw any person, white or black, feel as badly as he did when he saw his master. He was mortified and distressed beyond measure. . . . We all had confidence in him. Now his character was gone."

Hubbard tearfully begged Jefferson's pardon "over and over again." For a slave, burglary was a capital crime. A runaway slave who once broke into Bacon's private storehouse and stole three pieces of bacon and a bag of cornmeal was condemned to hang in Albemarle County. The governor commuted his sentence, and the slave was "transported," the legal term for being sold by the state to the Deep South or the West Indies.[11] And even Bacon felt moved by Hubbard's plea—"I felt very badly myself"—but he knew what would come next: Hubbard had to be whipped. So Bacon was astonished when Jefferson turned to him and said, "Ah, sir, we can't punish him. He has suffered enough already." Jefferson offered some counsel to Hubbard, "gave him a heap of good advice," and sent him back to the nailery, where Reuben Grady was waiting, "expecting . . . to whip him."

Jefferson's magnanimity seemed to spark a conversion in Hubbard. When he got to the nailery, he told Grady he'd been seeking religion for a long time, "but I never heard anything before that sounded so, or made me feel so, as I did when master said, 'Go, and don't do so any more.'" So now he was "determined to seek religion till I find it." Bacon said, "sure enough, he afterwards came to me for a permit to go and be baptized."[12] But that, too, was deception. On his authorized absences from the plantation to attend church, Hubbard made arrangements for another escape.

During the holiday season in late 1810, Hubbard vanished again, and his story plays out like a wartime tale—one deception piled on another, clandestine meetings and deals, forged identity papers, a desperate flight through a hostile countryside. The documents about Hubbard's escape reveal that Jefferson's plantations were riven with secret networks. Jefferson had at least one spy in the slave community who was willing to inform on his fellow slaves for cash; Jefferson wrote that he "engaged a trusty negro man of my own, and promised him a reward . . . if he could inform us so that [Hubbard] should be taken." But the spy could not get anyone to talk. Jefferson wrote that Hubbard "has not been heard of." But that was not true: a few people *had* heard of Hubbard's movements. Jefferson could not crack the wall of silence at Monticello, but an informer at Poplar Forest told the overseer that a boatman belonging to Colonel Randolph aided Hubbard's escape, clandestinely ferrying him up the James River from Poplar Forest to the area around Monticello, even though the white patrollers of two or three counties were hunting the fugitive.[13] The boatman might have been part of a network that plied the Rivanna and James Rivers, smuggling goods and fugitives.

Possibly, Hubbard tried to make contact with friends around Monticello; possibly, he was planning to flee to the North again; possibly, it was all disinformation planted by Hubbard's friends. At some point Hubbard headed *southwest*, not north, across the Blue Ridge. He made his way to the town of Lexington, where he was able to live for over a year as a free man, being in possession of an impeccable, genuine manumission document.

His description appeared in the Richmond *Enquirer*:

a Nailor by trade, of 27 years of age, about six feet high, stout limbs and strong made, of daring demeanor, bold and harsh features, dark complexion, apt to drink freely and had even furnished himself with money and probably a free pass; on a former elopement he attempted to get out of the State Northwardly . . . and probably may have taken the same direction now.

A year after his escape Hubbard was spotted in Lexington. Before he could be captured, he took off again, heading farther west into the Allegheny Mountains, but Jefferson put a slave tracker on his trail. Cornered and clapped in irons, Hubbard was brought back to Monticello, where Jefferson made an example of him: "I had him severely flogged in the presence of his old companions, and committed to jail." Under the lash Hubbard revealed the details of his escape and the name of an accomplice; he had been able to elude capture by carrying genuine manumission papers he'd bought from a free black man in Albemarle County. The man who provided Hubbard with the papers spent six months in jail.[14] Jefferson sold Hubbard to one of his overseers, and his final fate is not known.

A plantation's borders might seem porous, making escape easy, so the question arises: Why didn't more slaves try to run away? Did they actually prefer the life of slavery? But they lived as if in an occupied country. As Hubbard discovered, few could outrun the newspaper ads, the slave patrols, the vigilant sheriffs demanding papers, and the slave-catching bounty hunters with their guns and dogs. Hubbard was brave or desperate enough to try it twice, unmoved by the incentives Jefferson held out to cooperative, diligent, industrious slaves.

Throughout his narrative Bacon said nothing unpleasant about slavery; his memoir purified it. A historian who studied Bacon said he "lacked a certain discrimination," and saw in him the New World version of old England's "Plain Country Fellow": "He is sensible of no calamity but the burning of a stack of corn or the overflowing of a meadow, and thinks Noah's Flood the greatest plague that ever was, not because it drowned the world, but spoiled the grass."[15]

Bacon so profoundly admired Jefferson that his idolatry became something of a joke among his fellow overseers, one of whom said to him, "Well, I believe if Mr. Jefferson told you to go into the fire, you would follow his instructions."[16] He filtered his memories of Monticello through the lens of admiration; he could not help himself, because the process was reflexive, unconscious. Merely in describing Jefferson's physical appearance, Bacon suddenly veered into a hymn: "His skin was very clear and pure—just like he was in principle."[17] Thus Bacon told the story of James Hubbard's trial and Jefferson's forgiveness to illustrate a point about Jefferson's character:

> Mr. Jefferson was always very kind and indulgent to his servants. He would not allow them to be at all overworked, and he would hardly ever allow one of them to be whipped. His orders to me were constant: that if there was any servant that could not be got along without the chastising that was customary, to dispose of him. He could not bear to have a servant whipped, no odds how much he deserved it.[18]

But in trying to suggest that punishment was virtually nonexistent under Jefferson, Bacon inadvertently reveals that it was routine—there stands Reuben Grady with the whip, prepared to dispense "the chastising that was customary"—and he reveals how Jefferson distanced himself from the ugly reality of his system. When Jefferson had personally to authorize the whipping of Hubbard, face-to-face, he shrank from it. And Jefferson's pardon amazed Grady, who "was astonished to see [Hubbard] come back and go to work after such a crime."*

On one level Bacon's memoir offers a vivid picture of the decline and fall of an old order. As the financial shadows gather and deepen, Bacon wrings his hands over Jefferson's struggles and misjudgments. But we also see the Jeffersonian vision surviving in Bacon, who embodies the rising new man of the South, the "yeoman farmer" Jefferson idealized. He expressed Jefferson's philosophy in humble terms, writing to the sage himself in 1819, "I consider it of such importance that every person who has a family should have a home and that should be of such soil as will produce well."[19] He omitted to mention slaves, but his

---

*A historian who studied Edmund Bacon in great detail wondered about the accuracy of Bacon's account, speculating that Bacon himself may have been the one to wield the whip: "One could take this account at face value. But one suspects that for the sake of morale in the nailery, the immediate supervisor, Grady, the man who had to work with the slaves day after day, would not have done the whipping. Bacon may have had the whip in hand while he and Jefferson confronted Hubbard, perhaps accounting for Hubbard's mortifications and distress. Jefferson's words—"we can't punish him"—also suggest that the punishment was to have been immediate. Bacon added that Grady was astonished to see Hubbard 'come back and go to work after such a crime,' suggesting that Grady was not expecting Hubbard to be at work that day" (Martin, "Mr. Jefferson's Business," p. liv).

memoir reveals the plain country fellow gathering human assets at bargain rates from the depleted aristocrats as he patiently lays plans for his own slave-driven plantation in Kentucky.

In his interview with the Reverend Pierson, Bacon took the opportunity to settle some old scores and as an aside leaked more revealing information. He despised the Randolphs and mocked them mercilessly. He had to compete with two generations of them for control of Monticello—Jefferson's son-in-law Colonel Randolph and the colonel's son Jeff Randolph—and he clearly did not like being second-guessed by them. "The Randolphs were all strange people," he declared.[20] In one of his rants against the family, this time against Colonel Randolph for his inability to control his finances, Bacon said, "I often loaned him money," and when the colonel was stuck, "he would be obliged to sell some of his Negroes."

On one such occasion the colonel sent an urgent note to Bacon by a slave messenger saying that he needed $150 in cash by the next day, a necessity that compelled him against his will to offer Bacon a slave from the Edgehill plantation. Overnight Bacon raised the cash. He was quite proud of his capacity, on a few hours' notice, to put cash on the barrel when the haughty Randolphs were strapped. He made the deal the next day and told the Reverend Pierson all about it: indeed, he still had the receipt! *Let me show it to you, Reverend.* As he unfolded the paper, Bacon said, "She was a little girl four years old."*[21] Her name was Edy, daughter of Fennel. The transaction was done in a trice; no hole on the mountain could hide the child.

Leaving the site of Bacon's house, we tramped into a ravine and then up again, following the Fourth Roundabout, cut into a hillside below a field. Neiman told me that the Third Roundabout was above us, running along the edge of what had been a field in Jefferson's time. He abruptly turned off the path and clambered up the slope. He paused at a tall poplar and pointed to the ground, where I could see some rocks scattered about. Nothing much here, I thought.

---

*The bill of sale is reproduced in the 1862 edition, available online, of Pierson's *Jefferson at Monticello: The Private Life of Thomas Jefferson*, pp. 98–99.

"These rocks are the hearth of Betty Hemings's house."

The poplar had long ago taken root in the middle of the hearth and broken it apart, leaving the scatter of stones in an otherwise empty forest near the edge of a field. It was not a terribly impressive site, but for some reason I found it very moving.

"We worked on this site the first summer I was here," Neiman said. "Jefferson actually mapped it, and we were able to locate it on the cheap." By "on the cheap" he meant they didn't have to dig a hundred empty holes before hitting it. On his arrival at Monticello, Neiman had looked at Jefferson's maps of the mountain and noticed a small square with the label "B.Hem" written in Jefferson's hand. The map was so accurate that it was a simple thing for the archaeology team to follow it right to Hemings's house and dig it up.[22]

"It was probably a little log house with a chimney base," Neiman said. "Actually, we found a pole for a chimney prop. There's a little artifact scatter in here—the remains of her dinner plates, et cetera." He thought the house probably took no more than about a week to build, with the workmen using scrap bricks salvaged from other work sites to build part of the hearth. She had a large garden, and the Monticello records show that even in her last years she was raising vegetables and poultry for sale to the mansion.[23]

Betty Hemings was the mother of Sally and, if one accepts the contention that Sally had children with her master, the grandmother of some of Thomas Jefferson's children. Thinking about her grandchildren made me realize why I found the site so touching. Some time earlier I had read the memoir that Betty's grandson Madison Hemings set down when he was sixty-eight, one of the prime sources in the Hemings-Jefferson controversy. Reading it closely for "evidence," I was brought up short by an aside about his childhood. Madison said that his earliest memory, from when he was about three years old, was of his grandmother: "She was sick and upon her death bed. I was eating a piece of bread and asked if she would have some. She replied: 'No, granny don't want bread any more.' She shortly afterwards breathed her last." It had no evidentiary value; it was simply a small touching fragment of humanity.

Neiman believed that Jefferson built the house for Hemings around 1795. Before that, she had been sent to an outlying farm called Tufton, "for reasons we don't understand," Neiman said. "She was a house servant. So why she's at an outlying quarter farm is not clear." But her return to Monticello in 1796 coincided with the birth of Sally Hemings's daughter Harriet. "So you think about the grandmother hypothesis," Neiman said. "She moved back here to be around as the children are born." If they were Jefferson's children, it would make sense that he would want a trusted nurse for them. She lived close enough to the mansion and Mulberry Row to be available for child care, but far enough away so that when measles broke out on the mountaintop in 1802, Jefferson thought her house would make a good quarantine for the black children who had the disease.

Jefferson built the house thirty feet from the Third Roundabout. Any passing rider could have waved to Betty Hemings and probably did. Among the artifacts the archaeologists found here were some small bits of clear glass, so the house had a glazed window. When Neiman compared Betty Hemings's porcelain with shards from the house of a white workman, he found that she had rather fancy dinnerware and a cheap tea set. He surmised that teatime was a more important social event for the white man and his family than it was for Betty Hemings, but she liked to set an attractive table for dinner.[24]

We left the house site and zigzagged down through the forest to pick up a new trail. We had walked for a few minutes when I began to hear voices and see moving shapes through the trees ahead. It was an odd sensation in the silent woods, where one could genuinely feel lost in time, and odder still when we walked a little farther and I saw we had landed at Monticello's Visitor Center, back in the present day. Hundreds of tourists were arriving and boarding vans that glided up the steep mountain road to the mansion at the top. Neiman led the way downhill through a series of parking lots to a large patch of grass and trees surrounded by pavement but set off by a split-log fence.

"This was long rumored to be a slave cemetery," Neiman said, and that's what the archaeologists believe it to be. The memory of the graveyard's existence seems to have flickered on and off at Monticello. When the parking lots were laid out and paved in the 1970s, preliminary maps marked this spot as "old graveyard," so someone knew there were graves here, and it wasn't paved over. The information that something was here may have been passed to the staff by a groundskeeper, Randolph

Crawford, who lived in a small house nearby. He had noticed that stones on this site were arranged in a way that suggested they might be markers, though there were no names on them. More intriguing to him was a mysterious circle of fieldstones. Suspecting that the site had a link to Monticello's former slaves, he spoke to an African-American housekeeper who worked at the mansion. She told him that it was indeed a burial ground and that "her people used to build a circle of stone" to use at funerals: the mourners would make a fire within the circle, seat themselves around it, and tell stories about the deceased.

Though the graveyard was spared, the memory of it faded at Monticello. "They knew the cemetery was there when they built the parking lot," Neiman said. "As people left the staff, it was forgotten about, except vaguely." After seeing the imposing Jefferson-Randolph family graveyard near the summit, where Jefferson lies buried beneath a monumental obelisk, visitors would often ask, "Where were the slaves buried?" and the answer was "We don't know."[25]

The African-American cemetery asserted its presence subtly. Whenever the mountain got a light dusting of snow (heavy snowfalls are a rarity in these parts), faint depressions revealed themselves in outline, vanishing with the melting snow. In good weather, when sunlight fell across the parking lot at a certain slant, rows of shadows appeared in the ground. For archaeologists, graves are hard to locate and just as hard to verify.

One of Neiman's predecessors, Barbara Heath, took note of the clues in 1990 and decided to investigate. The most direct approach—digging down until she struck actual burials—was immediately ruled out as a desecration. Heath began with the least intrusive method, remote sensing by magnetometry, which identifies magnetic anomalies created by the presence of human remains. The machines yielded "maddeningly ambiguous" results. The archaeologists called in a consultant, who took one look at the site and pointed to the small boulders of greenstone scattered about. Greenstone, the parent material of Monticello Mountain, is loaded with iron that deranges magnetic testing—"one of those boulders has more iron in it than a Winnebago," said the consultant. When technology failed them, Heath and her crew went back to old-fashioned methods, painstakingly mapping every tree, rock, and dip in the ground, identifying twenty-four depressions that they believed held graves.

Ten years later Neiman returned to the site with new magnetometers, but when the ambiguities persisted, he too decided to revert to old-fashioned methods, excavating in shallow squares, just deep enough to reveal the presence of grave shafts but not deep enough to disturb any burials. One of the most interesting finds was something they did not find: there was no evidence of plowing. Much of Monticello had been plowed over in Jefferson's time and later, but not this patch of ground. Neiman's crew found an old plow blade at the very edge of the cemetery, so the plowmen had gone that far but no farther. He identified twenty burial shafts, eight of which were believed, because of their small size, to hold the graves of children. Five graves had stones, but with no markings.

Because this soil is so highly acidic, it was very unlikely that any human remains, or other artifacts except coffin nails, could still exist in the shafts, but Monticello's archaeologists let a potentially valuable opportunity pass when they decided, out of respect, not to dig to the bottom. Other burials of slaves in the South have been excavated with startling results. A dig at Stratford Hall plantation, where Robert E. Lee was born, turned up thirteen African-American burials from the eighteenth century. Three black men were buried there with African-style clothing. Excavations in the Chesapeake region have discovered burials with beads and seeds, another African custom. Archaeologists in Georgia unearthed a slave's grave with remnants of a plate above the head, which fit with the custom "to place the last plate, the last glass and the last spoon used before death on the grave." Other excavations have yielded bits of crockery, upturned bottles, seashells, and particular plants with significance in African cultures. The historian Philip Morgan has explained: "All these practices were ways of propitiating the dead, of easing their journey into the spirit world, and of ensuring that they did not return to haunt the living."[26]

When the archaeologists looked at Jefferson's papers, they found that this was the very spot where Jefferson had first intended to put his burying ground—"one half to the use of my own family; the other of strangers, servants." The white Jeffersons and Randolphs ended up atop the mountain, and the slaves here.

As we were leaving the graveyard, the last stop on our trek across the mountain, I turned and saw a bouquet of flowers lying on the ground. That day, someone unknown had come and placed that remembrance here; perhaps somewhere off the mountain lived a descendant who had neither forgotten nor abandoned this place.

I asked Neiman if he thought Betty Hemings and her family might be buried here, and his answer was that the Hemingses were more likely to have been buried closer to the summit. A sign of this appeared in the 1950s in the most startling manner. Monticello's then director, James Bear, was walking in the area of the Ancient Field when, amazingly, he came upon a headstone from the 1830s wedged *in the crook of a tree*. How it got there nobody knows. One surmise is that an employee found it on the ground, put it in the tree for safekeeping, and never said a word about it. A marked headstone for a slave is very rare. Slave cemeteries are also rarely found. Indeed, given the size of the population of enslaved people—in Jefferson's time 40 percent of Virginians were slaves—so few of their cemeteries have been found that one would think that slaves never died.

The holes on the mountainside suggested an improvement in family life; the large root cellar suggested food in abundance. It has long been known that slaves raised their own crops for sale, but only recently have we begun to get an idea of the scale of this enterprise and what it means. In 1994 a Jefferson expert at the Library of Congress, Gerard W. Gawalt, published a transcription of four years of crop accounts.[27] From 1805 to 1808, Jefferson's granddaughter Anne Cary Randolph met with slaves each Sunday during the summer months and bought a wide variety of goods from them. Anne was just fourteen years old when she started the record. Conducting business transactions with slaves formed part of a young white woman's "apprenticeship" as a plantation mistress, according to Gawalt. Anne kept her records in a disused notebook of her grandfather's, his account book from his days as a Williamsburg lawyer in the late 1760s. Anne's grandmother Martha, Jefferson's wife, had used the same notebook for the same purpose. Gawalt wrote that the records reveal the "vitality" of the "entrepreneurial spirit of the slaves."

It required a farmer to find a deeper meaning in these farm records. In 2006, Monticello hired Leni Sorensen as its African-American research historian, someone with a Ph.D. in history who had also farmed in South Dakota. When she examined these crop accounts, she was struck by the "prolific" productivity of enslaved people who were obviously very skilled gardeners. Focusing on one month of late-summer records from August and September 1805, Sorensen noted an "impressive" sale of vegetables to the big house, including watermelons, cabbages, potatoes, cucumbers, and squashes, but an even more remarkable output of 47 dozen eggs and 117 chickens. With the eye of an experienced farmer, Sorensen knew that so many eggs and chickens do not simply wander onto the property: "In order to ensure a steady supply, the chicken-raisers among the slave community had to build and maintain nest boxes, food and water containers, brooding cages, and fenced chicken yards." Someone had to guard the chickens against snakes, opossums, raccoons, stray dogs, and cats. This was a very large enterprise, and it would have involved virtually everyone in Monticello's African-American community: "More than half the black adults at Monticello sold produce to the Jefferson household, and all but three adults among them also sold chickens. In fact, it is likely that all adult slaves at Monticello kept personal gardens, but that only those individuals who sold produce had occasion to appear in the records."

At first glance this presents a heartening picture of go-getting and thrift, but other numbers tell us that if the slaves had not raised their own food, they would have starved. Jefferson's rations were meager, and Sorensen calculated that the daily calorie payoff fell catastrophically short of what a working adult needed to survive. Bagwell and Minerva Granger, for example, with their five children, received a ration of sixteen dried herring and two pounds of beef—for a *month*. A modern American family of seven would consume that in three days, if the children could be persuaded to eat the herring. Pregnant and nursing women, who had to work in the fields despite their conditions and the demands on them, had special dietary needs that the Jeffersonian ration did not meet. Jefferson issued a white overseer six hundred pounds of pork a year, which is more than eleven pounds a week.[28]

For the slaves, it was plant or die, with the gardening and chicken-raising work done in the scant free time available to them in their dawn-to-dusk daily routine. Small children and the elderly had to do a lot of the work, when Jefferson did not call up the children and the "senile corps" to work for him. For the elderly, indeed, gardens were utterly essential: when slaves became too feeble to work all the time,

Jefferson cut their rations in half. From time to time, one hears the rumor that planters turned old people out to the woods to die. Cutting an elderly person's rations in half comes close to that.

Obscure and long-forgotten, Anne Randolph's farm accounts utterly demolish one of the pillars of her grandfather's racial ideology—that African-Americans were incapable of planning beyond sunset. He wrote in 1814: "For men probably of any color, but of this color we know, brought from their infancy without necessity for thought or forecast, are by their habits rendered as incapable as children of taking care of themselves, and are extinguished promptly wherever industry is necessary for raising young."[29]

At the time when his granddaughter was buying huge amounts of food for Jefferson's table from the slaves—and Jefferson the gourmand always knew precisely where his food was coming from—he wrote another letter claiming that his burden of supporting slaves was "dayly increasing."[30]

11

"To Serve You Faithful"

The recollections of the former Monticello slave Peter Fossett, from which I drew the opening of this book, contain a confusing passage: "My grandmother was free, and I remember the first suit she gave me. It was of blue nankeen cloth, red morocco hat and red morocco shoes. To complete this unique costume, my father added a silver watch." Though almost anything is possible in the slavery universe, I could not quite understand how Fossett could have had a grandmother who was free, nor did it seem plausible that a slave boy at Monticello sported a fancy suit and a silver watch given to him by a father who was a slave.

But perhaps Fossett was telling the truth. His parents were two of the most important people on the mountain. His father, Joseph, became Monticello's chief blacksmith when Jefferson had to fire his white blacksmith for chronic drunkenness in 1807. Joseph stepped into the job and expertly ran the forge for the next two decades. The overseer Edmund Bacon described him as "a very fine workman; could do anything . . . with steel or iron."[1]

It was important enough to be the son of the blacksmith, but Peter Fossett's status was further enhanced by his mother's occupation: she was Jefferson's *cook*. Edith Hern Fossett presided over the most modern culinary facility in Virginia, producing meals "in good taste and abundance" for a throng of diners, seven days a week, "in half Virginian, half French style," as Daniel Webster recalled after a visit to Monticello in 1824.[2]

Edith Fossett's extraordinary skill did not really become apparent to posterity until 2004, when the Monticello curators completed a reconstruction of the plantation's kitchen, a spacious room underneath Jefferson's private terrace in the south dependency. In Jefferson's time it was a marvel of innovation. Jefferson had ordered it built while he was president so that it would be ready, when he returned to Monticello in 1809, to produce the high-style cuisine he had become accustomed to. Since he anticipated, correctly, an unending torrent of visitors, the kitchen would also have to produce its fine food in abundance. At most plantations the cooking was done in an outbuilding in crude circumstances—dirt floor, an open hearth with a spit, and heavy cast-iron cookware.

Jefferson's new kitchen had a large hearth and a traditional bread-baking oven, but also a "set kettle," heated by charcoal, which yielded a steady, reliable flow of hot water. Along one wall stood a row of eight charcoal-heated burners called a stew stove. The heat of each burner could be individually regulated by a skilled cook, anticipating the convenience, flexibility, and utility of a modern, high-end multi-burner stove.[3]

Edith Fossett and her staff worked their culinary magic using some sixty pieces of French copper cookware, of a type seldom seen in the United States at that time—far lighter and much more efficient in conducting heat than cast-iron cookware.[4] Skilled and experienced, the cooks maneuvered these skillets, tart pans, fish cookers, and chafing dishes over the burners of the stew stove to produce the French dishes and sauces Jefferson loved. As one of Monticello's experts wrote, "The stew stove allowed cooks to regulate the heat beneath the stew pans, making possible the delicate elements of French dishes like *bouilli* with *sauce hachée*."[5]

Monticello's kitchen retained some old-fashioned features, such as a mechanical spit-jack—the eighteenth-century version of the rotisserie—and swiveling cranes to maneuver pots in and out of the fireplace. Oddly enough, the kitchen, redolent every day with smoke and cooking odors, boasted one of the most valuable items in the mansion—an extremely costly, highly accurate "kitchen timer" in the form of a tall-case clock. Jefferson wound it himself every eight days. The presence of this exquisite timepiece reveals the precise coordination and the high level of performance that created meals a visitor called "always choice, and served in the French style."[6]

It is not enough to say that Jefferson was a gourmand. As one food historian wrote, Jefferson possessed "an intense interest in food and the critical role it played in how he conducted his private life." He owned a collection of essays that included "On the Construction of Kitchen Fireplaces and Kitchen Utensils" and "Of the Construction of Saucepans and Stewpans for Fixed Fireplaces." We have ten surviving recipes that he wrote down himself, as well as his "Observations on Soup," though he had a poor understanding of how cooking was actually done.[7] As far as we know, he never visited the kitchen to offer advice, entering it only to wind the clock.

The kitchen was the domain of Edith, the head chef, and her adjutant, Frances "Fanny" Hern. (They were sisters-in-law: Fanny's husband, David Hern, was Edith's brother.) The records hint at their culinary skills, but I did not realize how extraordinary those skills were until I spoke with Leni Sorensen, the historian who shed so much light on the agricultural records. An accomplished cook herself, Sorensen narrated a typical day in this kitchen.

Every day at least fourteen people were waiting upstairs to be fed—the core of the Jefferson-Randolph household. Often the kitchen fed eighteen to twenty, sometimes as many as twenty-five; one day the kitchen fed fifty-seven people. Sorensen characterized Frances Hern as the "adjutant," a good military analogy for the highly disciplined nature of this culinary operation. Fossett and Hern would have been well aware of their owner's extreme aversion to conflict or disorder of any kind, so they would have made every effort to ensure that the kitchen operation ran smoothly. When the master emerged for his predawn stroll along his terrace, directly over the kitchen, he would not have heard shouting, cursing, or helpers being hit but the rhythmic rattling of wooden spoons as scullions beat biscuit dough, the differing tones of mechanical music made by the grinding of the day's ingredients—the master's coffee beans, his varieties of sugar (there were several), his salt, and his chocolate. He would have smelled coffee roasting.

With breakfast due on the table at 9:00, Fossett, Hern, and the scullions would have been in the kitchen by 5:30 with three meals on their minds. The cooks would start slicing yesterday's ham and getting today's different breads set up while the assistants heated the bake oven and got the fireplace going with two separate fires—a hardwood fire on the right for roasting and a charcoal bed on the left to feed the eight burners of the stew stove. Once the charcoal was ready, they could get the set kettle started for their hot water.

In addition to ham, breakfast featured three types of raised breads. The dough had to be beaten and set to rise by 7:00 or 7:30 to be out of the oven by 8:45. They brewed coffee, tea, and hot chocolate. Jefferson was particular about his coffee, so the kitchen staff roasted beans every day or every other day. Hot chocolate was also made from scratch; they would grind a block of hard chocolate and then cook it. One of the boys would tend the fires in the hearth, feeding the charcoal stoves under the direction of the cooks to maintain correct temperatures and carrying out ashes, which were saved to make soap.

As the breads and muffins were baking, one or two people would begin dinner preparation, plucking at least half a dozen fowl (chickens, ducks, or geese). By midmorning the dinner prep was fully under way. It was "like making Thanksgiving dinner every day," Sorensen said, a modern holiday feast being an "average" dinner at Jefferson's house. Every dinner would feature three or four meats and a fish dish, plus four "made dishes" of vegetables with a sauce—potatoes, peeled asparagus (served on toast), parsnips, or an elaborate stuffed cabbage, which was not considered plebeian but a tasty staple of upper-class tables: the cooks would parboil a cabbage, scoop out the center, fill it with minced meat, tie it up in a cloth, poach it, drain it, then cut it into wedges and add a sauce.

Every day they prepared a ham—soaked to get the salt out, boiled, then roasted. Jefferson's *bouilli* was a pot-roast-like dish of beef simmered with vegetables. For the fish there might be shad, or "cod sounds," a dish made from dried salt cod that Jefferson loved and ordered by the barrel. Every meal featured up to four desserts—ice cream (for which vanilla beans had to be steeped), thin cookies, custards, cakes, and perhaps baked apples in pastry.

Every day Fossett and Hern coordinated the menus and provisions with Burwell Colbert, the butler, and Wormley Hughes, the head gardener, who would keep them up-to-date on what produce his acreage was yielding, what was ripening, and what was slow in coming. Once the cooking began, one of Jefferson's granddaughters might appear from upstairs, take a seat in the kitchen, and begin reading aloud from a cookbook. In a letter Virginia Randolph Trist described herself as "seated upon my throne in the kitchen, with a cookery book in my hand."[8] It was an absurd ritual, but it was the tradition. After years of training and experience, Edith and Fanny had their routines and recipes memorized. The young mistress was actually learning from them, but the illusion of control had to be maintained.

The real function of the granddaughter was to fetch things. Everything of value had to be kept locked up. Jefferson's granddaughters rotated as carriers of the keys, serving for a month at a time, a duty they loathed. After breakfast the granddaughter with the keys would meet with the cooks and be given the list of items needed for dinner—specialty items that might include brandy, raisins, sweet oil, and costly spices such as nutmeg. Jefferson's taste had been refined in the dining rooms of France. When he returned to the Virginia wilderness from Europe, he shipped crates of items he had come to love: "mustard, vinegar, raisins, nectarines, macaroni, almonds, cheese, anchovies, olive oil, and 680 bottles of wine," as one food historian writes. He continued to replenish his stock of these rare delicacies with regular shipments from Europe.[9]

Edith Fossett and Fanny Hern held their positions as a result of Jefferson's long-term planning. He had chosen them for their future posts when they were very young; they trained for years in the White House kitchen; and Jefferson expected a lifetime of loyal service. When Jefferson was first elected president, he sought the advice of the French envoy in Philadelphia in finding a Frenchman to cook for him. He hired Etienne Lemaire as maître d'hôtel, the household administrator, and Honoré Julien as *chef de cuisine*. Taking the long view, Jefferson brought three young women from Monticello to learn the intricacies of French cuisine. One lasted only a brief time, but Fossett and Hern excelled at their demanding work.

Demanding it was. Jefferson hosted three dinners a week when Congress was in session so that he would get the chance to dine with all the nearly 150 members, believing that sitting down together at a fine meal inspired "harmony and good confidence." The daily existence of the congressmen in their Washington boardinghouses was ghastly, in the view of one Englishman; they lived "like bears, brutalized and stupefied." The Frenchmen and their enslaved pupils, augmented by a hired staff of free blacks and whites, performed heroic culinary labors. "Never before had such dinners been given in the President's House," said one guest. Jefferson's marathon meals began at 3:30 in the afternoon, and some continued well into the night.[10]

In Jefferson's estimation, one of the best servants he had at the White House was his butler, a slave named John Freeman whom Jefferson hired from an owner in Maryland. Freeman may have adopted his surname as a ferocious badge of pride: he knew he would be freed in 1815, since he had negotiated an arrangement with his owner gradually to purchase himself, and his White House pay went toward buying his manumission. Perhaps it was Freeman's pride; perhaps it was his skill and the favor it brought him from the president; but Freeman also earned the outright hostility of some of the white servants, who did not like being put on a par with a slave. They especially did not like Freeman wearing the same livery as they. One white servant complained that the president "gave preference to a negro rather than to him," but Jefferson squelched the man's complaining: "the negro whom he thinks so little of, is a most valuable servant."[11] The records show that at one point Freeman suffered a broken jaw, whether from an accident or an assault we do not know.[12]

Jefferson brought Freeman to Monticello on his vacations from office. On these visits Freeman grew acquainted with Melinda Colbert, a slave whom Jefferson had given to his daughter Maria and her husband, John Wayles Eppes, at their marriage in 1797. Freeman was at Monticello in April 1804 when he wrote the following note to Jefferson:

> Sir
>   I am sorry to trouble you with a thing of this kind though I am forced to do it: for I have been fool enough to engage myself to Melinda and I was in hope of, when I came to Virginia this time, to get her Mistress' consent with yours. I have got the Consent of her parents.*[13]

---

*I have regularized Freeman's spelling here.

Freeman made his appeal at an extremely painful moment. Melinda's mistress, Maria, had just died in childbirth at the age of twenty-five. Well aware of his master's grief, Freeman wrote to him nonetheless because Maria's death might mean that the couple's hopes to marry would be dashed: "I fear the death of her Mistress will make us miserable, unless you will be so good as to keep us both," and he went on to say that he would give his word "to serve you faithful." Freeman knew that as a hired slave he would have to return to his owner in Maryland when Jefferson no longer needed his services; so to marry Melinda, he wanted to persuade the president to acquire them both. Jefferson was willing to go halfway: he bought Freeman, even though the contract came with the proviso that he had to manumit him in 1815, but he would not buy Melinda Colbert from his son-in-law Eppes. He already had servants "in idleness" at Monticello, he said, and Freeman knew that marrying a slave woman who lived in Virginia meant, at best, long enforced separations and, at worst, a tenuous marriage.

Despite the separations and their divided ownership, Freeman and Colbert married and had several children, who became the property of Eppes. In March 1809, as Jefferson was preparing to depart Washington for the last time and wagons were moving back and forth to Monticello carrying people and possessions, Freeman wrote another pleading letter:

> Sir
>
> I am sorry to say or do any thing to displease you. I hope you will forgive me what I have done. As you wish me to go with you rather than displease you I will go and do it the best I can. I hope you will not punish me. The cart brought everything Melinda had when Davy [the Monticello wagon driver] was here last. Mr. Eppes says there is such a law as I told you. I shall be obliged to leave her and the Children.[14]

A great deal had happened in the lives of John and Melinda Freeman. Eppes had set Melinda and the children free, acting, it seems, entirely out of generosity, and the family was living in Washington. Jefferson had ordered Freeman to return with him to Monticello, but if Melinda and the children came too, they would be subject to re-enslavement or to expulsion from the state under Virginia's odious 1806 removal law. Hoping to force or at least nudge Jefferson's hand, Freeman had arranged for the Monticello wagon driver to bring Melinda's possessions to Washington, in hopes that Jefferson could be persuaded to allow him to stay there with his emancipated family.

Perhaps Freeman hoped that Jefferson would follow the example of his son-in-law and set him free, but Jefferson sold Freeman to his successor, James Madison, for $231.81. Jefferson got what he could for his butler; John Wayles Eppes took nothing when he let Melinda Colbert and her children go free. Freeman served out his time on Madison's household staff, barely escaping the White House before the British burned it in the War of 1812, and was duly manumitted in 1815. The Freemans and their eight children lived in a house they owned on K Street and joined in the antislavery campaigns of the capital's free blacks.[15]

Among the historical trivia one can turn up on the Web is that the first child born in the White House was Jefferson's grandson James Madison Randolph. It is a charming story but completely wrong. No fewer than three children were born at the White House before little James Randolph—but they were all slaves, so they haven't counted when historical time lines were drawn up. The omissions are odd because the information is in plain sight: "Edy has a son, and is doing well," Jefferson wrote from the White House in January 1803.[16]

At least five children were born at the White House to Jefferson's slaves. One wonders how Jefferson thought he could get sustained work out of young married women who—no surprise—kept having babies. Indeed, the babies required so much attention he had to hire free black nannies to look after them. In 1801 he brought the first cook-in-training to the White House from Monticello. His choice, thirteen-year-old Ursula Granger, reflected the dynastic character of slavery at Monticello. She was the granddaughter of "Queen" Ursula Granger, Monticello's cook in the 1770s.

She may not have known it, or may have hidden it, but young Ursula was pregnant when she went up to Washington. She gave birth in March 1802, when Jefferson wrote in his Memorandum Book: "Ursula exp[enses] of lying in 12.75."[17] Ursula's child, whose name is not known, was the first baby born at the White House. This birth did not escape the notice of two leading Jefferson scholars, Edwin Betts and James Bear, who edited the 1966 collection *The Family Letters of Thomas Jefferson.* They have a note for Ursula—"Her child was born in March 1802"—but they kept the significance of this birth to themselves, and in a later footnote remark that "James Madison Randolph . . . was born January 17, 1806, the first child to be born in the President's House."[18] Looking deeper into the records, we can trace Ursula's child and find some hint why this landmark event has not been made known, for it culminates in a tragedy that does not reflect well on President Jefferson.

A doctor's bill indicates that the baby received treatment in April and May 1802 at Jefferson's expense; the ailment must have been an extraordinary one to require the services of a doctor. When it was time to go to Monticello in June, Jefferson was in a quandary. He wanted his cook to go home with him, but her baby was too sick to travel: "It is next to impossible to send Ursula and her child home and bring them back again." In July, Jefferson left Washington for Monticello, and Ursula went with him but without her child. On August 17, a month later, Lemaire wrote to Jefferson, "Sir the little child . . . died on the 14th." Apparently, the baby had been born with some defect because Lemaire said that "the good d[ieu—God?] rendered a great service . . . considering that he would have been infirm all his life." It is difficult to imagine a scenario that fits all the facts except one: that Ursula's baby lay ill at the White House and Jefferson took the mother away.[19]

Though Jefferson's accounts show occasional payments of $2 to Ursula—"drink money," which he dispensed to many of his servants—and he duly recorded in his expenses that he paid for "portage of Ursula's trunk," for some reason he omitted to record the death of Ursula's child in his "deaths since 1801" column in the Farm Book.[20] Back at Monticello, Ursula alternated between the kitchen and the fields, and she married Wormley Hughes, the head gardener.

Since kitchen training at the White House presented a chance for advancement in the Monticello hierarchy, the next two young women whom Jefferson chose for the White House may have been delighted to go, even though they were married. Edith Fossett was sixteen years old and pregnant when Jefferson brought her to Washington, and she gave birth three times at the White House: a child in January 1803 who died, James in January 1805, and Maria on October 27, 1807; James was the first child born at the White House who survived infancy. The other cook-in-training brought to Washington was Fanny Gillette Hern. Her husband, the Monticello wagoner David Hern, had the unhappy task of bringing his wife to the presidential mansion in the fall of 1806—and leaving her there. Fanny would have a child in the White House who died as an infant in November 1808.

Edith's and Fanny's husbands were at Monticello, but Jefferson did not let the women return with him on his vacations from the White House,[21] though he understood only too well the torment of being separated from a spouse; he mourned the death of his own wife, and he also witnessed firsthand the hardship and strain that resulted from forced separations. Of the quarrels that nearly broke up the marriage of his Irish servants Joseph and Mary Dougherty he wrote: "The differings between man & wife, however they may affect their tranquility, can never produce such sufferings as are consequent on their separation."[22] But his concern for marital discord did not extend to his slaves.

The enforced separation of Edith and Joseph created problems in their marriage, but it was of no concern to Jefferson, who seemed to discount their marriage altogether. When he went to Monticello for a visit in July 1806, he took some White House servants with him, but not Edith. The visiting servants apparently told Joe Fossett that something untoward was going on with Edith in Washington, because within days Joe disappeared from Monticello, and it did not take long for Jefferson to figure out where he had gone. He wrote to Joseph Dougherty that "a young mulatto man, called Joe, 26. years of age . . . ran away from here . . . without the least word of difference with any body, & indeed having never in his life recieved a blow from any one."[23] Jefferson must have found out Fossett's plans from someone at Monticello because he wrote, "We know he has taken the road towards Washington." He expected that Joe would turn up at the White House surreptitiously to contact Edith "as he was formerly connected with her"—giving the impression that Joe was just a runaway looking for help from a former girlfriend, not a husband seeking out his wife.

Perhaps Jefferson feared that his habit of separating the cooks and their husbands might backfire. Both Fossett's wife *and their child* were in Washington, which meant Jefferson had no "hostage" at Monticello and there was a strong possibility that Fossett would gather up Edith and young James and run for freedom. Jefferson dispatched a workman, John Perry, to deliver his letter to Dougherty and to get Fossett and bring him back. Concerned that word might leak out that he was pursuing a runaway slave, Jefferson instructed Dougherty to "say not a word on this subject."

As Jefferson had predicted, Fossett turned up at the executive mansion, where Dougherty spotted him and "took him immediately." Since Fossett was apprehended on the White House grounds, he might not even have gotten a glimpse of his wife, let alone talked to her. Fossett spent a night in jail and then went back to Monticello in Perry's custody. In a letter to Jefferson about the incident, Etienne Lemaire characterized Fossett as a "poor unhappy" man who "was not difficult to take. He well merits a pardon for this." And Edith remained in Washington.[24]

Joseph owed his high-ranking position as Monticello's blacksmith to Jefferson's favor, and he, too, benefited from Jefferson's long-term planning, though he was also its victim. As a child, he had come within a hairsbreadth of being permanently free, except that he was dragged back into slavery as if by an icy hand.

Born a slave in 1753 on the plantation of John Wayles, Joseph was the son of Mary Hemings, the first child of Betty Hemings and a half sister of Sally Hemings's.* During Jefferson's long absence in France, she apparently enjoyed the same courtesy Jefferson extended to her siblings: in his absence she could leave the plantation to find work wherever she chose. A prosperous white merchant from Charlottesville, Colonel Thomas Bell, visited Monticello on business, fell in love with Mary, and took her off the mountain. They lived in Charlottesville as husband and wife, though the law forbade their marriage.

Bell's love for Mary Hemings had to be extraordinary. When they met, she was in her thirties and had already borne four children: she had had a child in 1772 at age nineteen, another in 1777, children whom Jefferson gave away to his sister and son-in-law; Mary then had Joseph in 1780 and Betsy in 1783. Joseph's surname suggests that his father may have been William Fossett, an English carpenter who worked at

---

*Mary Hemings's father is unknown; she was born before Betty Hemings began having children with John Wayles.

Monticello. Bell welcomed these two offspring of another father into his home. The Bells' relationship, technically an illegal "cohabitation," could have put them both in jail, but the local authorities took no notice of it, perhaps because Mary had a cover, being called a live-in housekeeper. They lived as husband and wife for nearly three years, and Mary gave birth to two children, Robert and Sally.

Then Jefferson returned from France. Just two days after arriving at Monticello in early January 1790, he visited Bell's store in Charlottesville, most likely to check on his wayward property, since a servant could have picked up for him the trifling off-the-shelf items he needed— candle snuffers. He probably saw Mary Hemings—the Bells' residence was adjacent to the store—and her two toddlers, little Robert and Sally, who were Thomas Bell's children by blood but Jefferson's property by law; he still legally owned Mary and all her "increase."

Mary Hemings Bell approached Jefferson with an offer. Thomas Bell would buy her and the *four* children—his two, as well as Joseph and Betsy, whom Bell had raised as his own. A wrenching transaction ensued, which Jefferson put in the hands of his farm manager, Nicholas Lewis: "I am not certain whether I gave you power to dispose of Mary according to her desire to Colo. Bell with such of her younger children as she chose. . . . settle the price as you think best."[25] The stipulation "younger children" stands out: it meant that Bell could buy Mary and his own children, but Jefferson wanted the older stepchildren, Joseph and Betsy, back; he had plans for them. So the youngsters went back into slavery at Monticello—Joseph, twelve, working for a while in the main house, then the nailery, and Betsy, nine, as a house girl and eventually a wedding gift for Jefferson's daughter Maria.

Jefferson also felt entitled to collect payment from Bell for the early years of his marriage. He requested that the husband pay "a conjectural sum for the hire of Mary from Jan. 1. 1787," "conjectural" because there had never been a rental agreement.*[26]

Fascinating information about the Bells came to light in the 1990s, when a Charlottesville historian, Gayle Schulman, began transcribing a

---

*Some have said that during Jefferson's absence in France, Bell leased Hemings in an arrangement made by Nicholas Lewis, but there is no rental contract in Lewis's records or any record of Bell paying Lewis for Mary's hire, though Lewis's accounts do show payments from other masters for other hired slaves.

memoir written by a local jurist, R.T.W. Duke Jr. (1853–1926).* Duke's unvarnished private remarks, written in the early twentieth century, include revealing comments on the Bells: "With the rather 'easy' morality of those early days no one paid any attention to a man's method of living & Col Bell lived openly with the woman & had two children by her"—an open relationship once tacitly sanctioned by Thomas Jefferson himself was now viewed as a symptom of "easy" morality no longer tolerable. In Duke's time, with its rigid racial caste system, there were many such hidden relationships between blacks and whites.

Bell's son, Duke wrote, was "a very handsome young man, of whom Col Bell was very proud. He sent him up North to school and college & he came back a very elegant & charming fellow"—at this point the hero narrative crumbles and the sentence continues—"tho' of course with no social status whatever." Of Mary and Thomas Bell's grandchildren, Duke wrote, in the straight-faced, absurd Orwellian locutions of his era, "They were not negroes—tho' they evidently had negro blood in their veins." He noted without comment that Jefferson's grandson Jeff Randolph tried to help the Bell grandchildren; he went to court in Charlottesville to give a statement under oath that enabled the Bells to escape Virginia's draconian race laws: "On the Court records it was proven by the oaths of Col Thos Jefferson Randolph & other citizens that they were not negroes."

The improbable scenario Peter Fossett described in his recollections—the grandmother who was free, the expensive clothes, and the silver watch—turns out to be easily explained. The suit and the watch probably came from Thomas Bell's store, gifts brought by Mary Hemings Bell on her Orwellian visits to her enslaved son and his family at Monticello†—Orwellian because the core facts of her family life were determined not by blood but by fiat from above. One son is college-bound; another hammers away at Mr. Jefferson's forge. Peter Fossett remembered his childhood in the "earthly paradise" where he did not

---

*Duke's account of Civil War events had been published in the 1940s by the Albemarle County Historical Society, but Schulman believed that a complete transcription would yield insights into Virginia society beyond the limited scope of "de Wah."

†That Peter could hold on to these precious items without having them stolen and himself beaten by the slave boys or local whites reveals the power of the invisible zone of protection that enfolded him.

even have to know he was a slave, but it all collapsed in an eerie recurrence of his father's life. Peter's childhood almost exactly paralleled that of his father, Joseph, who grew up free and was abruptly jerked back into slavery.

Through the story of Mary Hemings Bell and her family we see Jefferson's philosophy crumble before our eyes. Publicly, he condemned racial mixing in the strongest terms. Privately, he endorsed it, approving the marriage of the Bells—once he had been paid—and he even encouraged Bell to educate his mixed-race children.

Jefferson frequently spoke of the impossibility of emancipation, but in this sequence of events concerning slaves he highly valued, we can see that he bumped into emancipators at every turn and did not follow their lead. John Freeman's owner agreed to a schedule of payments enabling the man to earn his freedom. John Wayles Eppes freed Melinda Colbert and her children gratis. And Jefferson knew that emancipated people could support themselves, since they were on his payroll at the White House. Washington, D.C., had a community of free blacks that Edith and Joseph Fossett could have joined if their training and skills had not made them so valuable to him.

The story of Mary Bell also shows how the black families, owning nothing, provided a kind of subsidy for the white family. It is worth reflecting on a number: in this period Jefferson gave away eighty-five people to his heirs—gifts of black men, women, and children that were meant to ensure the financial stability and comfort of his heirs and that also perpetuated slavery into the next generations while wrecking the black families. He owned more slaves than he could possibly use, as shown by his remark, in refusing to buy Melinda Colbert, that he already had slaves "in idleness" at Monticello. These people represented not a burden but an abundance that he dispensed to his family. It was his fixed view that he and his heirs were entitled to the black children. The black mothers and fathers, possessing no such entitlement despite ties of blood and love, had to beg, abjectly, to keep their families together, and not always successfully. Mary had to yield up four of her children to Jefferson. And so, perversely, the bottom subsidized the top, not merely with their labor, but with their very selves.

12

The Double Aspect

Mary Hemings Bell had the good fortune, and the misfortune, to be a Hemings. As a Hemings, she had autonomy, which allowed her to leave Monticello in Jefferson's absence and marry a respected Charlottesville businessman. But she lost four of her children to Jefferson precisely because they were Hemingses, members of the family Jefferson valued highly for their "superior intelligence, capacity and fidelity to trusts," as Jefferson's grandson recalled.[1] Jefferson wanted those children as servants, as artisans, and as gifts, but they were also his relatives, so they occupied a hazy no-man's-land that the grandson, Jeff Randolph, struggled to describe: "Having the double aspect of persons and property the feelings for the person was always impairing its value as property."

There can be no doubt that "feelings for the person" ran deep. A touching story captures the special relationship between the Hemings family and Jefferson. When Jefferson's wife, Martha, was dying in 1782 from complications of a difficult childbirth, she was tended through her long, agonizing decline by a small group of Hemings women. According to Edmund Bacon's account, Betty Hemings and her daughters Sally, Critta, Betty Brown, and Nance "were in the room when Mrs. Jefferson died" and witnessed a poignant scene: "They have often told my wife that when Mrs. Jefferson died they stood around the bed. Mr. Jefferson sat by her, and she gave him directions about a good many things that she wanted done. . . . she wept and could not speak for some time."[2] Betty Hemings had been the mistress of Martha's father, and her daughters were Martha's half sisters. Martha might have resented Betty for being her father's mistress, but evidently not: she took Betty into her household at Monticello when she could easily have put the whole family out of sight on some distant farm, or sold them.

The kinship tie enfolded and protected the extended Hemings family. For them, Jefferson devised a quasi-slavery: he put them in responsible, highly skilled positions; he paid some of them; the Hemings men even traveled on their own (Jefferson sometimes did not know where they were). While most of the slaves at Monticello toiled "in the ground," living and working at sites scattered over the slopes of the mountain, the Hemingses lived and worked on the summit and in the house itself. Jeff Randolph said that their status "was a source of bitter jealousy to the other slaves." They wore better clothes, ate better food, and were not at the overseers' beck and call. Edmund Bacon remembered the directive he got from Jefferson regarding the Hemings women: "I was instructed to take no control of them." Unlike the other slave women at Monticello, Betty Hemings and her daughters never worked in the field, even at harvest when all hands were called out to get in the crops on a crash basis. Some of the Hemingses scarcely mingled with the people who worked in the ground. Young Hemings boys served time in Jefferson's nailery, but they were on their way up to responsible positions as artisans or in the mansion.[3]

The status of the Hemingses obviously raises doubts about Jefferson's oft-stated opposition to the mixing of the races. If miscegenation disgusted him, why did he staff his household with his mixed-race relatives? In the 1790s the brothers James and Peter Hemings were cooks; their older brother Robert was Jefferson's valet; the younger sisters Sally and Critta sewed and washed clothes, cleaned rooms, and waited on Jefferson's grandchildren; and the oldest Hemings brother, Martin, served intermittently as butler. The son of Betty Hemings and an unknown father, Martin was born before Betty began her relationship with John Wayles. Because he was a Hemings, he held an important position, but he had no blood tie to Jefferson's late wife, and his dealings with Jefferson were ambiguous and contentious. The next generation of Hemings offspring bustled around the house carrying dishes and firewood, running errands, and waiting on guests. "The boys," as they were known, included Mary Bell's son Joseph Fossett and three sons of Betty Brown Hemings—Wormley Hughes, Burwell Colbert, and Brown Colbert.[4]

Surrounding himself with these enslaved relatives—well dressed, well fed, highly trained—Jefferson created a buffer between himself and the harsher reality of Monticello's slavery farther down the mountain. Everyone in the household was utterly dependent on his favor and utterly devoted to him, bound as they were by ties of blood and affection.

John Hemmings felt an extremely close emotional bond to the white Jefferson family. In 1928 a white Jefferson descendant wrote a letter to the Monticello curator about a table made on the plantation for her grandmother Virginia Randolph Trist at the behest of Jefferson's daughter Martha: "I have a little sewing table made by the old colored cabinet maker at Monticello for my dear Grandmother, when she was a girl."[5] She passed along the story of what Hemmings had said when Martha made her request: "yes Mistis I have a piece of wood I am saving for old Master's coffin, and it is just the thing, I will take a piece of it." His remark reveals a profound regard for family connections. Being instinctively mindful of the traditions cherished by families, Hemmings knew the family would keep this child's table forever, that everything that came from this place would one day be held sacred, that when little Virginia was grown, she would be moved by a relic made from the wood of her grandfather's coffin. And that was precisely the story "Miss Virginia" passed down to her offspring.

When you walk through Monticello, you see everywhere the handiwork of John Hemmings, whose skill received the highest possible accolade from the most exacting judge. Hemmings worked alongside Jefferson's Irish joiner, James Dinsmore, in the creation of Monticello's interior. It is impossible to find any variations in the quality of the woodwork, any spots where even a sharp-eyed connoisseur could say, "here Dinsmore left off and Hemmings took over." Of this woodwork Jefferson said, "There is nothing superior in the US."[6]

Born in 1776, John Hemmings was the eleventh of Betty Hemings's twelve children; his father was Joseph Neilson, a white Monticello carpenter. Jefferson had his eye on the boy from an early age. John first worked in the fields, but at age fourteen Jefferson put him on the crew of "out-carpenters," cutting down trees and shaping logs—rough, strenuous work that served as prelude to finer skills and tasks. Two years later John joined the crew building log houses on Mulberry Row.[7] When Hemmings was seventeen, Jefferson put him to work with a recently arrived house joiner from Scotland on making window frames "exactly of the size of those now in the house and of the same mould-ings."[8] A few months later he was placed under another white artisan "for the purpose of learning to make wheels, and all sorts of work."[9] Dinsmore arrived in 1798 to work at Monticello, and he had John Hemmings under his wing. For the next decade Dinsmore and Hemmings collaborated on making Jefferson's vision of Monticello a reality. Jefferson's notes give the two men equal credit for one twelve-day task of making and installing one of the distinctive architectural features of his study or "cabinet": "Dinsmore and Johnny prepared & put up the oval arch."[10]

When President Jefferson hired Edmund Bacon to manage Monticello in 1806, he gave instructions exempting John and three other slaves from Bacon's control: "Joe [Fossett] works with Mr. Stewart; John Hemings and Lewis with Mr. Dinsmore; Burwell paints and takes care of the house. With these the overseer has nothing to do, except find them."[11] When Dinsmore left Monticello in 1809, Hemmings took over the joinery and ran it for seventeen years. The inventory of tools suggests that the Monticello joinery may have been the finest, best-equipped cabinetmaking shop in Virginia, with 125 different planes, rasps, gouges, chisels, drawing knives, saws, and other tools. Bacon said that Hemmings was "a first-rate workman, a very extra workman. He could make anything that was wanted in woodwork."[12] Recognizing Hemmings's value to him, Jefferson paid his enslaved joiner $15 in 1811, an "annual gratuity" he thereafter raised to $20.

George Washington once commented sarcastically that at Mount Vernon any complex piece of machinery would have the life span of a mushroom because neither his white nor his black workers had the brains to run such a thing, let alone repair it. The situation was quite different at Monticello. Hemmings and other skilled slaves like Joseph Fossett, David Hern, and Burwell Colbert became even more valuable to Jefferson when he shifted from planting tobacco to planting wheat; many new agricultural machines and other equipment had to be fabricated or regularly maintained by mechanics who knew what they were doing.[13] Once, Jefferson had Hemmings direct two other slaves in repairing a threshing machine, instructing him to keep an eye on the fixed thresher and "rectify it . . . if it gets out of order." He was obviously confident that Hemmings understood the workings of this device. Hemmings also rebuilt a harpsichord that had fallen apart.[14]

Bacon was right when he said Hemings "could make anything that was wanted." He fashioned bedsteads, venetian blinds, dressing tables, and a set of items Jefferson prized—several Campeche or "siesta" chairs that he found exceptionally comfortable. "I long for a Siesta chair," he wrote to his daughter from Poplar Forest. "I must therefore pray you to send . . . the one made by Johnny Hemings." Jefferson was so proud of Hemmings's handiwork that he gave some of these chairs as gifts.[15] Hemmings and Joe Fossett built Jefferson's landau, which Burwell Colbert painted. (Though Colbert's main job was butler, he was also a painter and glazier.)

We will never know the true level of Hemmings's skill because his masterpiece burned. Hemmings created all the woodwork at Poplar Forest, which suffered a catastrophic fire that gutted the house in 1845. Hemmings had labored on it for a decade (1815–25): "I am at worck in the morning by the time I can see and the very same at night."[16] A dozen letters between Jefferson and Hemmings survive from this period, when the slave was working more or less on his own on the complex task of creating the interior of a neoclassical villa for the most demanding architect in America. Following Jefferson's designs, Hemmings created neoclassical trim throughout the interior—entablatures in the Tuscan, Doric, and Ionic orders—a Tuscan entablature for the exterior, a classical balustrade, and a Chinese Chippendale railing.[17]

Another of Hemmings's creations was lost as well. When Ellen Randolph married Joseph Coolidge of Boston in 1825, John wished her to have a wedding present from him and Priscilla. He built her a writing desk, which was sent north by ship. A letter came with news that the ship had wrecked; the passengers were saved but all the cargo lost. Jefferson wrote to Ellen:

John Hemmings was the first who brought me the news. He had caught it accidentally from those who first read the letter. . . . He was au desespoir! That beautiful writing desk he had taken so much pains to make for you! Everything else seemed as nothing in his eye, and that loss was everything. Virgil could not have been more afflicted had his Aeneid fallen a prey to the flames. I asked him if he could not replace it by making another? No. His eyesight had failed him too much, and his recollection of it was too imperfect.

Ellen's mother, Martha, added further information: "The writing desk Johnny insists upon it that he has no longer eye sight to execute. He actually *wept* when he heard of the loss." Hemmings's eyesight was indeed failing. Three years earlier Jefferson had bought him a $1 pair of spectacles.[18]

The lost wedding gift symbolizes the personal connection Hemmings felt for the Jeffersons. The youngest granddaughter, Septimia, "Tim," was a special favorite of John and Priscilla Hemmings from the time she was an infant. John and Priscilla had no children of their own, and Septimia became their substitute. "She has learnt to crawl a little," her sister Cornelia wrote, "but mammy [Priscilla] dont like her to do that because she says that it makes her too dirty."[19] When "Tim" was two, Ellen wrote to her mother that "John Hemmings makes frequent enquiries after Septimia—& told me the other day that last year when he left Monticello to come here—he had cried for about five miles of the road after taking leave of her."[20] Later the young mistress and the slave corresponded: Hemmings wrote to eleven-year-old Septimia, "Your Letter came to me . . . and happy was I to embrace it to see that you take upon yourself to writ to me. . . . I hope you ar well and all the family."[21]

But a slave could rise only so high. The psychological gulf between whites and blacks is evident in Jefferson's dealings with Dinsmore and "Johnny." Jefferson wrote to Dinsmore that he "salutes him with esteem,"[22] or "tender my esteem to mr Nelson & be assured of it respectfully yourself,"[23] or "I salute you both with friendship and respect."[24] Even a hasty, dashed-off note ends, "accept my best wishes."[25] No such respectful esteem is expressed in Jefferson's letters to Hemmings. Elizabeth Langhorne, a Virginia historian descended from Jefferson and never one to suggest that Jefferson did anything wrong, was compelled to note, "Jefferson's letters to this key servant are businesslike, rather lacking in sentiment."[26] Lucia Stanton writes, "Jefferson's letters to this highly skilled workman have no complimentary closings, except for an occasional 'farewell' or 'I wish you well.'"[27]

Hemmings began doing productive work for Jefferson when he was fourteen, but he was thirty-four before he drew a paycheck. Jefferson's records usually characterize payments to Hemmings as "a gratuity" or "a donation," but in one entry he admits that he gave Hemmings one month's pay for a year of work—"the wages of one month in the year which I allow him as an encouragement."[28] Along with "encouraging" Hemmings with literacy, training, satisfying work, and payments, there was also a diminishment of the man through a careful calibration of recognition.*

Thus did Jefferson receive the services of a top cabinetmaker for $20 a year plus food. What did slavery cost the slave? It is a simple calculation to come up with a dollar figure, but there is a more compelling way of calculating the much larger loss. Imagine for a moment that John Hemmings was white and free; what would his services have earned him on the open market? When he was doing the fine woodwork at Poplar Forest—which a Monticello curator has called "incredible"—the white carpenter John Perry was doing the lesser tasks like structural work and laying a floor. Hemmings was the far better craftsman, but Perry was paid well in the marketplace open to whites: "His work on residential buildings and churches in Albemarle and surrounding counties enabled him to purchase large amounts of land, part of which he sold in 1817 to . . . the University of Virginia. A condition of the sale was that he would have carpentry and joinery contracts." Another Monticello joiner, James Oldham, earned enough money to open a public house.[29]

John Hemmings's three older half brothers, Martin, Robert, and James, enjoyed the quasi-freedom to travel around Virginia on their own and earn money off the plantation. (The average Monticello slave needed a written pass from an overseer just to attend church off the plantation.[30]) They had access to cash and many opportunities to flee.

Robert Hemings went to Annapolis with Jefferson in 1783 and had two months of tonsorial training there under a French master barber.[31] He also journeyed with Jefferson to Boston the following year when Jefferson took ship for France. With cash in hand and three of his master's horses in his care, Hemings then made his way back to the land of slavery.[32] At that time Jefferson may or may not have known that Robert Hemings and an enslaved woman named Doll were in a relationship that would culminate in their marriage. Jefferson wrote to an acquaintance in 1790 that "if you know anything of Bob," tell him to report to

---

*Recognizing the skills of Hemmings and Burwell Colbert, the overseer Edmund Bacon proposed to Jefferson that they repair and paint Bacon's carriage. Bacon would pay not *them* but Jefferson, deducting their fee from Jefferson's debt to him.

Monticello; "I suppose him to be in the neighborhood of Fredericksbg."[33] That was where Hemings had met and married Doll, who later moved to Richmond with her owner, Dr. George Stras.

With a wife and child in Richmond, Robert decided in 1794 to extract himself from Monticello with the aid of Dr. Stras. The negotiation that ensued left Jefferson feeling angry and cheated, complaining that Stras had "debauched him from me." He convinced himself that Robert's new family had nothing to do with his request to leave Monticello; rather, a conniving outsider had simply offered him a better deal. But it was his own family tie that may explain Jefferson's annoyance. Robert's kinship to Jefferson gave him leverage over his master. Kinship entangled Jefferson in a connection he could not break or evade, subverted his control of a prized servant, and breached the wall of slavery.

Despite his anger, Jefferson relented and on Christmas Eve 1794 wrote in his account book, "Executed a deed of emancipation for Bob, by the name of Robert Hemmings. He has been valued at £60."[34] Dr. Stras advanced Robert the purchase price, which was paid to Jefferson, securing Robert's release from Monticello. Robert worked for the doctor until 1799 to pay off the debt.[35]

Robert knew he was leaving Monticello under the cloud of Jefferson's disapproval. For all practical and legal purposes he was free from Jefferson for good, but he tried to repair the rupture with his kinsman as soon as he could. Right after his release, he saw Jefferson's daughter Martha in Richmond and took the opportunity to beg forgiveness. Martha wrote to her father in January 1795:

> I saw Bob frequently while in Richmond he expressed great uneasiness at having quitted you in the manner he did and repeatedly declared that he would never have left *you* to live with any person but his wife. He appeared to be so much affected at having *deserved* your anger that I could not refuse my intercession when so warmly solicited towards obtaining your forgiveness. The poor creature seems so deeply impressed with a sense of his ingratitude as to be rendered quite unhappy by it but he could not prevail upon himself to give up his wife and child.

Martha's sympathy for Robert may have arisen from their kinship; after all, he was her half uncle.[36]

After working off his indenture to Dr. Stras, Robert became fully independent and acquitted himself in a manner that confounded Jefferson's theory that freeing slaves was like abandoning children. By 1799 he was listed on Richmond's tax rolls as a property owner. Three years later he resided on a half-acre lot he purchased with the income from a livery stable he owned. He may have run a small freight-hauling operation. The Monticello family never lost touch with him. He handled a cash transaction for Jefferson in Richmond and sent a shipment of oysters to Monticello in 1809.[37]

A little more than a year after Robert left Monticello, his brother James departed as well—another great loss for Jefferson, who had invested substantially in training him. As early as 1784, Jefferson was thinking of hiring a French chef in Annapolis to come to Monticello to train a slave. But when he was dispatched to Paris as U.S. minister, he had a better idea. He took nineteen-year-old James with him "for the particular purpose of learning French cookery," arranging apprenticeships with Parisian caterers and cooks, including a pâtissier.[38] Soon Hemings was preparing meals for distinguished visitors at Jefferson's Paris residence. All did not go smoothly, however. Hemings had a violent dispute over a bill with his French-language tutor, beating and kicking the man—an outburst that may have resulted from drinking, since Hemings later showed signs of alcoholism.[39] Despite being able to claim freedom under French law, Hemings returned to the United States.

James had other opportunities to escape. He worked for Jefferson in Philadelphia, which had a large free black community (later in the 1790s two of George Washington's household slaves escaped from him in Philadelphia). As part of his household duties James got to know a former slave of James Madison's who was living as a free man with his wife, who worked for Jefferson as a washerwoman.[40] A year later Jefferson brought Hemings along when he toured New York state with Madison. At New York City, Jefferson boarded a boat for Poughkeepsie, giving Hemings expense money to bring his phaeton and horse to Poughkeepsie by land. Hemings could have escaped then and there.[41]

Jefferson fully expected that this expensively trained slave would become chef for life at Monticello, but in 1793, while serving his master in Philadelphia when Jefferson was secretary of state, Hemings decided he wanted to go off on his own. He struck a deal with Jefferson that he could go free after training his brother Peter as his replacement. The document Jefferson drew up to seal the arrangement seems calculated to instill some guilt: "Having been at great expense in having James Hemings taught the art of cookery, disiring to befriend* him, and to require from him as little in return as possible, I do hereby promise and declare" to set James free if he will train his own replacement. It took James more than two years to complete Peter's training to Jefferson's satisfaction, whereupon Jefferson drew up the manumission document "to be produced when & where it may be necessary." He also gave his freed servant $30 for travel expenses to Philadelphia. A few months later Jefferson and Hemings saw each other there, and Jefferson wrote, with evident concern: "James is returned to this place, and is not given up to drink as I had been informed. He tells me his next trip will be to Spain. I am afraid his journeys will end in the moon. I have endeavored to persuade him to stay where he is, and lay up money."[42]

It seems that Peter Hemings was not as talented in the kitchen as his brother, whom he replaced as Monticello's head chef in 1796, though Jefferson characterized him as a man of "great intelligence and diligence."[43] When Jefferson became president and the quality of White House cuisine was much on his mind, he tried to bring James back rather than entrust the presidential table to Peter. (It is also possible that Jefferson left Peter at Monticello out of respect for his family. There is evidence that Hemings had a wife and family off the plantation.)[44] The only creations of Peter's that Jefferson singled out for praise were his muffins.

When Jefferson sent word to James in Baltimore that his services would be welcome at the White House, Hemings begged off, saying he would be uneasy living "among strange servants." He briefly went back to work for Jefferson at Monticello but was dissatisfied and left, returning to a job at a Baltimore tavern. An accumulation of small bits of evidence—his fight in France with the tutor, rumors of drinking, his

---

*In Jefferson's era "friend" meant "benefactor," someone habitually rendering aid and conferring advantage; to "befriend" someone denoted one's adopting the role of such a patron. Especially in the master-slave context, the word did not imply the social relationship we associate with it today. Jefferson's granddaughter Ellen used the same word when she wrote, "I am more than ever anxious to have it in my power to befriend, and educate as well as I can, one of these children," referring to the children of a household slave who had died (quoted in Stanton, *Free Some Day*, p. 124).

wandering from place to place, his weak excuse for refusing the White House post—suggests a growing instability of some kind that in fact culminated in a tragic end. Jefferson heard shocking news from his servants and received written confirmation from an acquaintance: "The report respecting James Hemings having committed an act of suicide is true. . . . he had been delirious for some days . . . and it was the general opinion that drinking too freely was the cause."[45]

The historian Elizabeth Langhorne saw a cautionary moral in the sad fate of James Hemings: "Jefferson's interest in colonization of the blacks, and his increasing conviction that free black and white could not prosper together in the new world may well have taken its strongest impulse from the troubled career and tragic end of his servant James."[46] Such is the heavy symbolic burden borne by America's black men. She did not mention that Jefferson's white French maître d', after leaving Jefferson's service at the White House, also committed suicide. No conclusion as to the impossibility of Frenchmen living in America was drawn from that melancholy demise.

Martin Hemings, Jefferson's butler, left Monticello under very different circumstances. When Jefferson first acquired the Hemingses from the Wayles estate, he did not entirely trust Martin. In 1774 he wrote that he was keeping a count of his bottles of rum "in order to try the fidelity of Martin."*[47] As described earlier, Martin proved his loyalty during the Revolution when a detachment of British raiders ascended Monticello Mountain and swarmed about the house and Jefferson barely escaped capture. What happened next became part of the oral tradition of the Jefferson family. His grandchildren Ellen Coolidge and Jeff Randolph shared the story in the 1850s with Jefferson's biographer Henry Randall, who noted in his text that the details of the account "are given on the statements, oral and written, of several members of Mr. Jefferson's family, who repeatedly heard all the particulars from his lips, and from those of other actors on the scene." Martin Hemings

---

*From this fragment it is hard to tell if Jefferson thought Martin was drinking his liquor or stealing it; if the former, then he was the third Hemings brother to have an alcohol problem. James committed suicide after a prolonged binge, and Jefferson gave orders that John Hemmings "must have nothing to do with drink" (TJ to Thomas Mann Randolph, Feb. 4, 1800, in *Papers*, vol. 31). In contrast, Jefferson put Peter Hemings in charge of his large brewing operation without evident problems.

defied a British soldier who shoved a pistol to his chest and demanded to know where Jefferson had gone. At the risk of death, Martin refused to betray his master.[48]

The oral history of the Jefferson family preserved an image of Martin's character that does not fit the stereotype of loyal, contented slave. He was "one of those sullen and almost fierce natures, which will love and serve *one*, if worthy of it, with a devotion ready to defy anything—but which will love or serve but one." This portrait suggests a unique reciprocity between slave and master. Martin accepted enslavement only from a master who was worthy, and the judgment of worthiness was Martin's—"he served any other person with reluctance, and received orders from any other quarter with scarcely concealed anger." His relationship to Jefferson imparted a status he would yield to no other; as Jefferson's body servant, he "would suffer no fellow-servant to do the least office for his master; he watched his glance and anticipated his wants."

When Jefferson was in France in 1786, Martin found himself another temporary master of sufficiently high status to be worthy of his service. He hired himself out as an attendant to Jefferson's neighbor James Monroe, apparently without presenting any written authorization from his owner, which was customary. Monroe hired Hemings on the latter's assurance that "he was at liberty to engage for himself." Monroe took Hemings at his word, and Martin pocketed extra earnings instead of idling at Monticello for nothing. (In contrast, Jefferson hired Jupiter out for £25 a year; as trusted and valued as he was, Jupiter did not have the status of a Hemings.) Martin became accustomed to going around Virginia as he pleased when his master was not in residence. Jefferson countenanced Martin's independence as long as his servant returned to the mountaintop when needed. From New York, Jefferson wrote to his daughter Martha in 1790, "I must trouble you to give notice to Martin to be at Monticello by the 1st. of September that he may have things prepared." And when he was leaving Philadelphia for Monticello in 1792, Jefferson wrote to his tobacco agent, Daniel Hylton, "If you should know any thing of my servants Martin or Bob, and could give them notice to be at Monticello by the 20th. I should be obliged to you."[49]

Martin, James, and Robert did not marry at Monticello. It may be a coincidence, but it is likely that they knew that having a spouse owned by Jefferson might have permanently chained them to Monticello. At

least it would have vastly complicated any attempt to leave.* When
Robert married, he did not ask Jefferson to purchase his family and
bring them to Monticello; he wanted to get away.

Jefferson's requests indicate that he wanted Martin around, but the
last time the servant is mentioned in Jefferson's household financial accounts is in 1783, which suggests that Jefferson had less trust in him or
that Martin was losing interest in household management.[50] In the summer of 1792, after some twenty years on and off as Jefferson's butler,
Martin's "sullen and fierce" nature grew restive, and he did something
very, very few slaves would have dared: he argued with his owner and
insisted on being sold. In the fall Jefferson wrote again to Hylton about
Hemings in a much sharper tone than in the earlier, breezy, "where is
Martin?" note:

> Martin and myself disagreed when I was last in Virginia inso-
> much that he desired me to sell him, and I determined to do it,
> and most irrevocably that he shall serve me no longer. If you
> could find a master agreeable to him, I should be glad if you
> would settle that point at any price you please: for as to price I
> will subscribe to any one with the master whom he will chuse. . . .
> Perhaps Martin may undertake to find a purchaser. . . . I would
> wish that the transaction should be finished without delay, being
> desirous of avoiding all parley with him on the subject.[51]

Jefferson's remark suggests a power struggle between two strong-minded
men. For a master to admit having a disagreement with a slave is extraordinary, disagreement being tantamount to mutiny. The last time
Martin Hemings appears in Jefferson's Farm Book is in the roster of
Monticello slaves taken in November 1794. In January 1795, Jefferson
wrote to his daughter about two items to "be disposed of"—a carriage
and Martin. The devoted servant, the savior of Monticello, has become
another piece of surplus equipment, and he disappears.[52]

There was something very disturbing to the Jefferson family about
this final transaction. When Jefferson's grandchildren told their stories
about Martin, they said that their scant personal memories of him were

---

*Similarly, the two Hemings siblings who slipped away from Monticello in the 1820s, Harriet
and Beverly, had reached their early twenties without taking spouses or having children.

from their earliest childhood and most of what they knew had come from Jefferson and their mother, Martha. Randall wrote, "The stern Martin died so early that nothing of him but infantile recollections of his gloomy, forbidding deportment, is preserved by any of the living generation." Died? The letter from Jefferson to his daughter Martha, mother of Randall's informants, shows quite clearly that Martin had not died but been "disposed of," that is, put up for sale; the family must have disliked admitting what Jefferson had done. Jefferson himself made no note anywhere of his manservant's ultimate fate. In his records and perhaps in his conscience Jefferson resolved the problem of sullen Martin Hemings off the books.[53]

James, Robert, and Martin all enjoyed an unusual measure of independence and freedom of movement, and yet there was a stark difference among them. The first two managed to negotiate their way to freedom; Jefferson resisted and complained but granted it. That path was never open to Martin, and he knew it. He did not have the blood tie to Jefferson's wife, and he looked different from his half brothers. Isaac the blacksmith said in his memoir: "Jim and Bob bright mulattoes, Martin, darker."[54]

One task Jefferson assigned John Hemmings was to make the beautiful wooden railings along Monticello's terraces. They feature a delicate interplay of diagonals and rectangles—a casual display of geometry that Jefferson always loved—in a style known as Chinese Chippendale. The original fences deteriorated and were torn down, but they have been reproduced from Jefferson's drawings, and you can see them today. One of the best viewpoints, oddly enough, is from Mulberry Row. From that point the magnificent architectural features of the mansion seem to peek out from over the railing, offering an odd-angled, understated view of the house's greatness. This is the view the slaves had of the house from their quarter. That lovely railing, Hemmings's handiwork, is a kind of demarcation line between the worlds of the slave and the free.

On the terrace, all is beautiful, ethereal, with that majestic dome gleaming in the sun. Down below is the workaday architecture of the kitchen wing—drab in comparison, extremely plain. There is hardly any distance between these two realms. Even today one can feel the psychological state this architecture induces when seen from below—a sense of the tantalizing proximity of untouchable beauty. That railing is the emblem of an odd borderland: down here stood people who were related by blood to those up there, yet they were slaves. There is the tunnel, the dark opening on the right, where they entered the upper realm to serve the others. If you stood here two hundred years ago, you instinctively knew your place in the chain of being. Builders were acutely sensitive to how their creations would be viewed. Did Jefferson plan this contrast, as he planned everything else so meticulously? Or is it an accident of architecture and topography? Every morning he appeared behind that railing, surveying his domain. Down below, in that drab kitchen block, was the room where Sally Hemings lived.

13

America's Cassandra

From Sophocles to William Faulkner, the family has been the microcosm that reveals the society. When a plague ravages the realm of Oedipus, an oracle tells him there are murderers in his city, but the king's investigation into affairs of state soon transforms into a search through his own family history, driven by the haunting question *Who was my father?*

The search for the father in the Sally Hemings story is similarly an affair of state. For two centuries some white Americans have viewed her as a threat not just to Jefferson's reputation but to the country. Jefferson's chief scholarly defender, Professor Robert F. Turner of the University of Virginia School of Law, puts it in stark terms. Referring to the terrorist attacks of September 11, 2001, he writes:

> The events of that historic date made it all the more important that the record be set straight, because—perhaps more than any other human being in history—Thomas Jefferson is the antithesis to the bigotry and intolerance of Osama bin Laden and his terrorist followers. . . . As we seek to deal with these new threats from abroad, all Americans should cherish the traditions of human freedom Thomas Jefferson and his contemporaries bequeathed to us. . . . [Establishing] the truth in the Jefferson-Hemings controversy is all the more important in the wake of the terrorist attacks.[1]

The discovery in 1998 that DNA samples proved a link between the bloodlines of the Hemings and Jefferson families did not convince everyone that Thomas Jefferson had been the father of Sally Hemings's children. Jefferson's defenders raise the possibility that another Jefferson family member had been the father and point to Thomas's younger brother, Randolph. Given that the historical evidence is very confusing even for specialists, the defenders have been able to persuade a growing number of people that the case against Thomas Jefferson has not been proved. Several books, including one by the widely respected historian Thomas Fleming, have systematically argued Jefferson's innocence.[2]

The body of evidence in the Hemings case consists of a vexing accumulation of eyewitness and earwitness testimonies;* recollections that are biased or partially mistaken; an African-American's memoir that contradicts the Jefferson family's assertions; accounts by African-American families that contradict each other;[3] newspaper articles written in a poisonous political atmosphere; a variety of reliable, unreliable, incomplete, or partially erased documents; and many missing documents whose contents can only be surmised.

When Jefferson left for France in 1784, he took along his daughter Martha and later wrote to his sister-in-law Elizabeth Wayles Eppes requesting that she send eight-year-old Maria to France with a servant to care for her. Eppes chose fourteen-year-old Sally Hemings for the journey.

In Paris, Sally was reunited with her older brother James, whom Jefferson had with him in France to train as a chef. Almost exactly the same age as little Martha, Sally may have resided in Jefferson's house or in the convent where his daughters were being schooled. Jefferson gave her small payments from time to time and bought her clothes appropriate for a servant who went out on social occasions with her young mistress. French law did not allow slavery, so Sally and her brother could have left Jefferson's employ and lived as free people if they hired a lawyer to instigate the required legal proceeding.

Sally's son Madison later said that she became pregnant by Jefferson in Paris, did not want to return to Virginia, where she would be "re-enslaved," but made a "treaty" with Jefferson: she would return to Virginia and become his "concubine" (Madison's word) if he would agree to

*Jeff Randolph claimed that if his grandfather was having an affair with Hemings, he would have heard incriminating nocturnal sounds from Jefferson's bedroom.

free their future children when they turned twenty-one. According to Madison, Jefferson consented to the treaty, and after their return to Monticello Sally gave birth to a child who died. Aside from Madison's statement, there is no record of the childbirth. Hemings's first recorded childbirth, noted in Jefferson's Farm Book, took place in 1795, when she had a girl named Harriet, who died as a toddler. Hemings had four children who we know survived to adulthood. Her recorded childbirths are:

Harriet 1795, died 1797
Beverly 1798
unnamed daughter 1799, died 1800
Harriet 1801
Madison 1805
Eston 1808

Rumors of Jefferson having a mistress at Monticello began to float through political circles.[4] In 1800, William Rind of *The Virginia Federalist* claimed to possess "damning proofs" of an unspecified "depravity" of Jefferson's. The rumors took a bit more shape in 1801 when Rind's *Washington Federalist*, referring obliquely to a "Mr. J.," reported that a well-known figure had "a number of yellow children and that he is addicted to golden affections."[5] These charges may not have come from thin air. William Rind and his brother had been the wards of Jefferson's cousin Edmund Randolph; they had spent time around Monticello and might have heard stories of mixed-race children on the mountain.[6] In August 1802 a Hudson, New York, journalist, Harry Croswell, wrote in *The Wasp* that President Jefferson had a "wooly headed concubine." Croswell hated Jefferson, having been convicted of libel for stating that Jefferson had secretly paid a journalist to attack George Washington and John Adams in print. (The charge was true, but he lost on the prevailing legal ground that truth was no defense against libel.) One of Croswell's lawyers was none other than Alexander Hamilton, who may have been the source for the tidbit about Jefferson's "concubine."[7]

The Sally Hemings scandal erupted on a huge scale a month later, when on September 1 the Richmond *Recorder*, another Federalist paper hostile to the president, printed a claim that Jefferson had an African-American mistress and children by her. The author of the article was

James Thomson Callender, a Scottish émigré who had established himself as a political journalist in Philadelphia several years earlier. It was Callender who had taken payments from Jefferson to fund attacks on Federalists. Croswell ended up in court for publishing the truth about the payments; Callender ended up in jail, under the Sedition Act, for writing the articles. Once an ardent supporter of Jefferson's, Callender turned against him when the president refused to grant him a patronage job in Richmond.

Callender deployed a distinctive vocabulary and style: "hard-hitting, sarcastic, heavily satirical," and, on occasion, "deliberately scurrilous," according to his biographer, Michael Durey. He had the habit of taking "the most extreme position on an issue" and had a mastery of English prose "from which he extracted new forms of invective." According to Durey, Callender possessed a "misanthropy . . . so thoroughgoing as to be egalitarian. Neither wealth, nor learning, nor family background could create an elite superior to the mass of mankind. His was the egalitarianism of a common depravity, premised on the belief that no social group had the moral requirements to exercise authority." He had a "constant preoccupation with the ubiquity of corruption in American political life."[8]

One might expect that a newspaper story that looms so large over American history appeared on the front page under a banner headline, but it was tucked into the middle of page 2, under the innocuous-appearing words:

THE PRESIDENT

AGAIN.

It is well known that the man, *whom it delighteth the people to honor*, keeps, and for many years past has kept, as his concubine, one of his own slaves. Her name is SALLY. The name of her eldest son is TOM. His features are said to bear a striking although sable resemblance to those of the president himself. The boy is ten or twelve years of age. His mother went to France in the same vessel with Mr. Jefferson and his two daughters. . . .

By this wench Sally, our president has had several children. There is not an individual in the neighbourhood of Charlottesville who does not believe the story, and not a few who know it. . . .

The AFRICAN VENUS is said to officiate, as housekeeper at Monticello. When Mr. Jefferson has read this article, he will find leisure to estimate how much has been lost or gained by so many unprovoked attacks upon

J. T. CALLENDER[9]

Jefferson did not respond. He had earlier said that by the time he responded to one charge, twenty more would be printed, so the effort was useless. But two weeks after Callender's first article appeared, Jefferson's supporter Meriwether Jones fired back in the Richmond *Examiner*. Jones played down the Hemings allegation, insisting it was all just partisan politics as usual and asserting that the president's Federalist enemy Chief Justice John Marshall stood "*behind* the curtain," while Alexander Hamilton lurked in the distance. A week later Jones offered a more spirited defense of Jefferson, claiming that "not a spot [has] tarnished his widowed character"[10] and asserting that any number of white men could have fathered the Hemings children: "In gentlemen's houses everywhere, we know that the virtue of unfortunate slaves is assailed with impunity. . . . Is it strange, therefore, that a servant of Mr. Jefferson's, at a home where so many strangers resort . . . should have a mulatto child? Certainly not."[11]

In *American Sphinx* (1996), Joseph Ellis characterized the widowed Jefferson as an asexual man who directed his passions into architecture rather than women. Though Ellis later changed his thinking about the Hemings allegation, his assessment that Jefferson's "most sensual statements were aimed at beautiful buildings rather than beautiful women" still resonates because it fits so well with the received image of Jefferson as a cerebral, detached gentleman.[12] But there are well-documented episodes of Jefferson's sexual aggressiveness toward a neighbor's wife. In 1768 an old friend of Jefferson's, John Walker, asked him to look after his young wife, Betsy, and their infant daughter while Walker took off on a long frontier expedition to negotiate an Indian treaty. Walker had no idea he had invited a viper into his home. Jefferson repeatedly pressed his attentions upon Betsy, who just as repeatedly rebuffed him. With rather astonishing directness, he continued to show his ardor for Mrs. Walker after her husband's return, indeed while John was just several rooms away.

When the failed encroachments later became public, Walker wrote out a statement of what had happened, with many details as related by his wife. During a visit the Walkers made to the home of a mutual friend, the ladies retired to bed, leaving the gentlemen to talk, but Jefferson, then a bachelor, "pretended to be sick, complained of a headache & left the gentlemen among whom I was. Instead of going to bed . . . he stole into my room where my wife was undressing or in bed. He was repulsed with indignation & menaces of alarm & ran off." Later, after he was married, Jefferson

> yet continued his efforts to destroy my peace. . . . One particular instance I remember. My old house had a passage upstairs with private rooms on each side & opposite doors. . . . At one end of the passage was a small room used by my wife as her private apartment. She visited it early & late. . . . Mr. J's knowing her custom was found in his shirt ready to seize her on her way from her Chamber—indecent in manner. . . . All this time I believed him to be my best [friend] & so felt & acted toward him.[13]

When all of this got into the newspapers, Jefferson was compelled to admit the truth of the accusations. To deny them would impugn the honor of a white married woman and force a duel with John Walker. The president made his confession in a private letter to Walker, a copy of which he was forced to send to a member of his cabinet, who served as a silent witness of the confession. Jefferson never breathed a word of this admission to his family. When they asked him why they never visited their old friends the Walkers any longer, Jefferson lied, telling them that he and Walker had argued about money.

Callender printed his exposés with exquisite timing: midterm elections loomed just weeks away in October. He proclaimed that Jefferson had become the Jonah of the Republican Party, and if it did not toss him over the side, the party would be "gone forever."[14] Jefferson had a hard journey from Monticello back to Washington in October, suffering "excessive soreness all over and a deafness and ringing in the head."[15] He attributed his ailments to bad weather on the road, but the incessant ringing in his head may have been the words *Sally . . . Callender . . . Sally . . . Callender . . . Sally . . .*

Scandal sells. In the fall of 1802, with Callender at the peak of his journalistic form, skillfully piling invective on Jefferson, Federalist newspapers around the country avidly reprinted his attacks, subscriptions to *The Recorder* soared to a thousand, then to fifteen hundred, and Callender boasted that circulation "has extended from Maine to Georgia, to the remotest corners of the state of New York, to Vincennes, and to Kentucky." So many ads poured into the office that the weekly *Recorder* began to publish twice a week.[16] But Callender's fervent wish that the Republicans would toss Jefferson overboard did not see fulfillment. The electorate was not impressed by his allegations, and Republican candidates won handily in the midterm voting.

Then, within a few months, Callender's life unraveled. He was savagely beaten, in a cowardly fashion, by James Monroe's son-in-law George Hay, who came up behind him with a cudgel and struck him half a dozen blows to the head. Hay had his own quarrels with Callender, but the "Dusky Sally" campaign probably accounted for at least one or two of the blows. In the court proceeding that followed, Jefferson's nephew Peter Carr pledged bond for Hay. A small group of drunken law students invaded the office of *The Recorder* and threatened to burn it. Fearing assassination, Callender began keeping a gun, drank more heavily than ever, and talked of suicide. One Sunday morning he was seen staggering around Richmond, apparently drunk. Later that day, July 17, 1803, he was found dead in the shallows of the James River, in a spot where the water was only three feet deep. He was forty-five years old and left four sons who had recently journeyed from Philadelphia to Richmond to live with him. Within hours a coroner's jury convened, examined the body, and pronounced the journalist's death an accidental drowning, with intoxication the proximate cause.

Such swift adjudication by the local coroner was not unusual for the time, but the burial showed haste: before the sun set that day, Callender was laid in a grave.[17] To add mystery, some months earlier Meriwether Jones had made a strange, obliquely predictive remark: "Oh! could a dose of the James River, like Lethe, have blessed you with forgetfulness."[18] Either Jones could not resist a nasty parting shot at his fallen enemy, or he tried to forestall an investigation into Callender's mysterious demise. Callender was barely in his grave when Jones wrote in *The Examiner* that the death had been not an accident but a suicide, "putting a miserable end to a miserable life."*[19]

The extreme notoriety of the Hemings affair generated an enormous amount of publicity, gossip, and speculation. Much of this has come down to us in various forms to create a constantly buzzing background noise of unverifiable data. In 1811 a Vermont schoolteacher, Elijah P. Fletcher, visited Charlottesville and heard "many anecdotes much to [Jefferson's] disgrace." One of Jefferson's local detractors had the nerve to bring Fletcher to Monticello, where the ex-president courteously received them. Fletcher came down from the mountain convinced, as he wrote in a letter, that "the story of Black Sal is no farce—That he cohabits with her and has a number of children by her is a sacred truth," but Fletcher did not record a single detail of any evidence he may have spotted. Later, an Italian traveler to Charlottesville wrote, "Apropos of negresses, may I be permitted to say that . . . I was shown a pretty one—although she was no longer young—who had beautified the last days of Jefferson"; but this also is simply local chatter that proves nothing.[20]

More compelling are private remarks that were written down by one of Jefferson's good friends, John Hartwell Cocke, a wealthy planter who aided Jefferson in establishing the University of Virginia. Cocke knew Jefferson and his family well and had visited Monticello. In his diary in 1853, Cocke—a highly religious man who despised slavery and its "corruptions"—wrote about two planters who had children with slave women and decided to send the women and children to free states, one to Ohio, the other to a Northern city. He personally knew of a score of such miscegenation cases in Virginia, he continued, and had no doubt that hundreds more could be found in the state: "Nor is it to be wondered at, when Mr. Jefferson's notorious example is considered."

Cocke made another diary reference to Jefferson several years later: "All Batchelors, or a large majority at least, keep as a substitute for a wife some individual of the[ir] own Slaves. In Virginia this damnable practice prevails as much as any where, and probably more, as Mr. Jefferson's example can be pleaded for its defense."[21]

---

*In the tale of the journalist and the president, one final, ironic, and strangely comforting twist played out decades later: Callender's grandson married Jefferson's grandniece.

Jefferson's former overseer Edmund Bacon came to his employer's defense when he gave his long interview in 1862 about his life at Monticello. Bacon mentioned that Jefferson had ordered him to give money to a daughter of Sally Hemings's and to put her on the stagecoach to Philadelphia and freedom. Bacon allowed that there was a lot of talk in the neighborhood about this quiet manumission, with people saying the young woman, whom Bacon did not name, was Jefferson's daughter. But Bacon insisted Jefferson was not the father and that he knew this from the evidence of his own eyes: on "many a morning," he had seen another man, whom he did not name, leaving Hemings's room.

When the U.S. census taker came to the home of Sally Hemings's son Madison in Pike County, Ohio, in 1870, he was stunned to hear Hemings declare his lineage. "This man is the son of Thomas Jefferson!" wrote the census taker on his official return.[22] Three years later a local newspaper editor, S. F. Wetmore, interviewed Madison, who referred to Thomas Jefferson as "my father" in a first-person account published as "Life Among the Lowly, No. 1" in the *Pike County Republican* on March 13, 1873.[23] Wetmore subsequently interviewed another former Monticello slave, Israel Gillette Jefferson, who supported Madison Hemings's claim:

> I also know that his servant, Sally Hemings . . . was employed as his chamber-maid, and that Mr. Jefferson was on the most intimate terms with her; that, in fact, she was his concubine. This I know from my intimacy with both parties, and when Madison Hemings declares that he is a natural son of Thomas Jefferson . . . I can as conscientiously confirm this statement as any other fact which I believe from circumstances but do not positively know.

Some anonymous troublemaker sent a copy of Israel Jefferson's article to Jeff Randolph, who wrote a lengthy, outraged rebuttal but apparently never sent it to the newspaper; perhaps he had cooled off.[24] The statements of Madison Hemings and Israel Gillette Jefferson saw the light only in an obscure Ohio newspaper and were promptly forgotten; they might as well have been dropped down a hole.

In 1938, Madison Hemings's granddaughter Nellie E. Jones wrote to Monticello saying that she had spectacles, an inkwell, and a silver

buckle that had belonged to Thomas Jefferson and then to Sally Hemings. Though the then curator, Fiske Kimball, expressed interest in
examining the items, the foundation's president, Stuart Gibboney, did
not think the matter worth pursuing. Perhaps in an effort to get Gibboney to pay attention to Mrs. Jones, Kimball pointed out her skill at
business correspondence: "This very respectable colored woman writes
a letter much more intelligently than many of our own race." Nonetheless, Gibboney told Jones not to bother sending the artifacts, which
were sold to a dealer after Mrs. Jones's death and disappeared.[25]

After some seventy-five years in oblivion, the memoir of Madison
Hemings surfaced when an Ohio archivist found it in the early 1950s
and sent a copy to John Dos Passos, who was then working on a
book about Jefferson. Dos Passos circulated it among a small group of
Jefferson specialists.[26] Madison Hemings's twenty-two-hundred-word
memoir became a central item of evidence in the Hemings affair. In a
scholarly article Dumas Malone and Steven H. Hochman conceded
that Hemings had spoken sincerely, but they dismissed outright his
claim that Jefferson was his father. They described the newspaper editor, Wetmore, as a biased abolitionist, a wily anti-Jeffersonian who had
manipulated Hemings—"quite clearly, the story was solicited and published for a propagandist purpose"—but they did not discuss the text in
detail.[27] In *The Jefferson Image in the American Mind* (1960), Merrill
Peterson disparaged the Hemings memoir as a manifestation of the old
"miscegenation legend" engendered by "the hatred of the Federalists"
and "the campaign of British critics to lower the prestige of American
democracy by toppling its hero from his pedestal."[28]

Madison's memoir found one very influential believer. Fawn Brodie
turned the Jeffersonian world on its ear in 1974 with the publication of
Thomas Jefferson: An Intimate History. The author of three previous biographies, Brodie maintained that Jefferson and Sally Hemings enjoyed
an intense, passionate, but necessarily secret love affair for more than
thirty years. She took Madison Hemings at his word when he claimed
Jefferson was the father of Hemings's children.[29]

While Hemings descendants rejoiced at Brodie's biography, many
scholars denounced it not only for the author's conclusions but for her
method, which rested heavily on psychoanalytic interpretation. Brodie
brought smirks to some scholarly faces, for example, when she theorized

that Jefferson must have had Hemings on his mind when he toured the fields of France and commented on the "mulatto" color of the soil.[30]

To counter the avalanche of negative publicity that engulfed Jefferson after the publication of Brodie's biography, Dumas Malone dramatically released a long-suppressed document that, he said, proved Jefferson's innocence; it was a letter Ellen Randolph Coolidge had written to her husband in 1858 asserting that Jefferson's nephew Samuel Carr had fathered Sally Hemings's children. Ellen did not want her accusation against her cousin to become public. In the portion of her letter she wished her husband to show around, Ellen vaguely laid the blame for Monticello's "yellow children" on the plantation's "Irish workmen" and "dissipated young men in the neighborhood who sought the society of the mulatresses." And indeed, Ellen's letter had been kept private by her descendants for more than a century, perhaps because of her somewhat slanderous remark that her cousin Sam Carr was a "keeper of a black seraglio." Harold Jefferson Coolidge, Jefferson's great-great-great-grandson, had allowed Brodie to read the letter but to quote only selected passages, and he resented Brodie's interest in Jefferson's alleged black progeny: "I am distressed that the subject which seems to interest you most relates to the controversial matter of Mr. Jefferson's children and I can assure you categorically that this is not a subject which I wish to have raised by making use of quotations from the letters of Ellen Coolidge."[31]

When Brodie's book appeared, Coolidge granted Malone permission to publish Ellen's entire letter in *The New York Times*.[32] Rising up as a voice from the grave, it instantly became the central text for those who believed that Jefferson was not the father. Malone himself later hedged, saying in 1984 that he refused to believe Jefferson and Hemings had a long-term affair but that "it might have happened once or twice."[33]

Then came Barbara Chase-Riboud's book *Sally Hemings: A Novel* (1979), portraying the Jefferson-Hemings relationship as "an extraordinary and fascinating love story," in the author's words.[34] Though Brodie's biography and Chase-Riboud's novel swayed millions of minds, the academy, especially the corps of Jefferson specialists, budged hardly at all. It seemed that the Hemings-Jefferson mystery was ultimately insoluble and would forever remain mired in scholarly dispute. But science caught up with history.

The fabled lost tsarina of Russia and a filmmaker both had hidden hands in the dramatic DNA revelation that one of Sally Hemings's children had a blood tie to Jefferson's family. In 1995 the director James Ivory released a film titled *Jefferson in Paris*, dramatizing a passionate affair between the mature Jefferson and the adolescent Hemings. Around the time of the film's release, the topic of DNA testing was a hot one in Jefferson's hometown of Charlottesville because a DNA test had recently cracked the world-famous case of a local woman named Anna Anderson Manahan. For decades Manahan had claimed to be Anastasia, daughter of the tsar murdered by the Bolsheviks, Nicholas II. The tsar's surviving relatives, including members of the British royal family, gave blood samples to be compared with tissue taken from Manahan before her death. When the results showed she did not have the royal DNA, a great story was ruined by science, and Manahan was posthumously ushered into the pantheon of fakers.

A number of people suggested, half-jokingly, that it might be time to "dig up Jefferson," extract some cells from whatever was left of him, and settle the Hemings business once and for all. During a dinner-party conversation in Charlottesville in 1996 at the home of Dr. Eugene Foster, a retired pathologist, a guest named Winifred Bennett floated the idea that DNA testing might resolve the Hemings controversy.

Intrigued by his dinner guest's suggestion, Dr. Foster took the DNA idea to officials at Monticello, who put him in touch with Herbert Barger, a passionate genealogist married to a collateral descendant of Jefferson's, "a first cousin, six generations removed," as Barger described her.[35] Barger took up the case eagerly, as he felt confident that DNA would exonerate the Founder. Conducting a proper DNA analysis required locating a sufficient number of Hemings and Jefferson descendants for a valid sampling. Blood samples had to come from direct descendants along an unbroken male line. Sally Hemings's youngest son, Eston, had one male descendant who consented to be tested.[36]

Thomas Jefferson had no legitimate son who survived to adulthood, but with Barger's help Dr. Foster was able to obtain blood samples from male descendants of Jefferson's uncle Field Jefferson. Descendants of the paternal grandfather of Peter and Samuel Carr—the nephews whom the Jefferson family blamed for the Hemings "yellow children"—also consented to be tested.

The results, announced in the November 5, 1998, issue of *Nature* under the headline "Jefferson Fathered Slave's Last Child," stunned historians and the public: Eston Hemings *had* been fathered by a Jefferson. For historians, the DNA revelation was the equivalent of discovering a lost continent. Madison Hemings, once ridiculed as an abolitionist tool, had apparently been vindicated, as had Fawn Brodie. DNA also suggested that the solemn statement by Jefferson's grandchildren that one of the Carr brothers had fathered Hemings's children was untrue; the Carrs could not have fathered Eston.[37]

Dr. Foster and his coauthors were careful not to overstate their findings. They wrote, "The simplest and most probable explanations for our molecular findings are that Thomas Jefferson, rather than one of the Carr brothers, was the father of Eston Hemings Jefferson." But they also conceded:

We cannot completely rule out other explanations of our findings based on illegitimacy in various lines of descent. For example, a male-line descendant of Field Jefferson could possibly have illegitimately fathered an ancestor of the presumed male-line descendant of Eston. But in the absence of historical evidence to support such possibilities, we consider them to be unlikely.

The accompanying historical analysis by Eric S. Lander and Joseph Ellis ran under the subheading "DNA analysis confirms that Jefferson was indeed the father of at least one of Hemings' children."[38]

Before long a backlash began to take shape. Several weeks later *Nature* published letters complaining that "the authors did not consider all the data at hand in interpreting their results. No mention was made of Thomas Jefferson's brother Randolph (1757–1815), or of his five sons," and that "any male ancestor in Thomas Jefferson's line, white or black, could have fathered Eston Hemings." Responding to the criticism, the authors allowed, "The title assigned to our study was misleading in that it represented only the simplest explanation of our molecular findings."[39]

By a bizarre historical coincidence, the Hemings DNA findings emerged at the precise moment when another American president, William Jefferson Clinton, was under fire in a scandal involving the White

House intern Monica Lewinsky. In his analytical article in *Nature*, Ellis drew a straight line between the two scandals:

> Politically, the Thomas Jefferson verdict is likely to figure in upcoming impeachment hearings on William Jefferson Clinton's sexual indiscretions, in which DNA testing has also played a role. The parallels are hardly perfect, but some are striking. . . . Our heroes—and especially Presidents—are not gods or saints, but flesh-and-blood humans, with all of the frailties and imperfections that this entails.

Proposing a moral equivalence between Thomas Jefferson and Bill Clinton enraged conservatives, who began suggesting that the timing of the DNA announcement had been manipulated to help Clinton.[40] At the very least, as William Safire charged in an essay titled "Sally-gate," the DNA announcement had handed the Clinton White House a powerful talking point: "That's the White House party line: everybody did it. If Jefferson impregnated a young slave and refused to comment on Callender's story, what's the big deal about Clinton dallying with young women and lying under oath about it? The historian's spin: We are all Federalists; we are all sinners; so forget this impeachment stuff."[41] An NBC correspondent commented: "The White House must be smiling. After all, if Bill Clinton's favorite President could end up on Mount Rushmore and the $2 dollar bill despite being sexually active with a subordinate, it might put Mr. Clinton's conduct with a certain intern in a different light."[42]

Soon after the DNA announcement, Monticello's president, Daniel P. Jordan, appointed a staff research committee "to gather and assess critically all relevant evidence about the relationship between Thomas Jefferson and Sally Hemings." In January 2000 the committee issued its report, which Jordan summarized at a press conference: "Although paternity cannot be established with absolute certainty, our evaluation of the best evidence available suggests the strong likelihood that Thomas Jefferson and Sally Hemings had a relationship over time that led to the birth of one, and perhaps all, of the known children of Sally Hemings."[43]

This announcement truly changed the Jeffersonian landscape. Both Daniel Jordan and Monticello's chief historian, Lucia Stanton, had previously gone on record expressing strong doubt that Jefferson had fathered Hemings's children; Jordan had called it "a moral impossibility."[44] But the DNA findings had compelled them to take a fresh look at the historical material and caused them to reverse their position. By and large, the academic community concurred. For example, the eminent historian of slavery Philip Morgan wrote, "In an earlier work, I accepted too readily the conventional wisdom that one of the Carr nephews fathered Sally's children. . . . The weight of evidence now tilts heavily in [Jefferson's] direction and the burden of proof has dramatically shifted."[45]

Herbert Barger, who had assisted in gathering the DNA samples for the tests, indefatigably fired off lengthy, impassioned letters of protest whenever a newspaper or magazine referred to the Hemings-Jefferson link as a fact. He succeeded in persuading *The Washington Post* to admit that its reporting on the story required a clarification. The newspaper's ombudsman wrote: "The Post often has failed to make clear what is fact (DNA testing shows that a Jefferson fathered Eston Hemings but not which Jefferson), what is speculation and what is convenient."[46]

Barger's seemingly lonely effort was just the beginning of a counter-surge. A group of Jefferson's admirers established the Thomas Jefferson Heritage Society in 2000 to defend the Founder. They formed up under the flag, reflecting the liberal-conservative split in opinion over the interpretation of the DNA, perhaps caused but certainly widened by Joseph Ellis's comparison of Jefferson to Clinton. In the foreword to a book of essays titled *The Jefferson-Hemings Myth: An American Travesty*, the society's president referred to it as "a group of concerned businessmen, historians, genealogists, scientists, and patriots."[47] David N. Mayer, professor of law and history at Capital University and author of a book about Jefferson's constitutional thought, characterized the Monticello report as "a politically correct history. It reaches the conclusion that a lot of people would like it to reach."[48]

The campaign against Monticello's conclusion centered on the core point that a number of Jeffersons could have been the father of Eston Hemings. "There were at least seven close relatives who could have been the father, the most likely being Thomas Jefferson's younger brother, Randolph," wrote Reed Irvine. Even Ann Coulter, not known as a historian, had that exculpatory fact at her fingertips: "There were 25

Jefferson males with the same DNA alive when Hemings conceived her last son. Seven of them were at Monticello during the relevant time period."[49] The Jefferson biographer Alf Mapp Jr. was willing to go even further in exonerating Jefferson: "As of this date [2008], though another member of the Jefferson family may have fathered children by Sally Hemings, there is no available evidence that Thomas Jefferson did."[50]

Professors Mapp and Mayer became two of the thirteen academics who formed the Scholars Commission on the Jefferson-Hemings Matter in 2000 "to reexamine the issue carefully and issue a public report." This group included well-known historians and political scientists such as Lance Banning, Harvey C. Mansfield, Forrest McDonald, and Jean Yarbrough. Three Ivy League colleges were represented along with the University of North Carolina, Stanford, Bowdoin, and other top-tier universities. The commission was led by Robert F. Turner, associate director at the Center for National Security Law, University of Virginia School of Law.[51] They came to a conclusion quite different from that of the Monticello committee. As Turner described it: "The scholars' conclusions ranged from 'strong skepticism' about the allegation to a conviction that the charge was 'almost certainly false.'" One member, Forrest McDonald, Distinguished University Research Professor at the University of Alabama, said, "I have studied the subject as thoroughly as I could. . . . Thomas Jefferson was simply not guilty of the charge."[52]

In a July 4, 2001, opinion piece in *The Wall Street Journal*, Turner lamented the free fall in Jefferson's standing in a Gallup opinion poll, a decline he blamed on the Hemings affair and on "a cultural struggle taking place in contemporary academia."[53] He quoted Ellis's oft-repeated observations that, among academics, Jefferson is "the dead-white-male who matters most" and the "most valued trophy in the cultural wars." He insisted that Jefferson was "probably getting a bum rap" and pointed the finger at Jefferson's "less cerebral" brother Randolph, who "would seem to be a far more likely candidate for Eston's paternity than the aging president. . . . Randolph is documented by a 19th-century slave account to have spent his evenings at Monticello playing his fiddle among the slaves and 'dancing half the night.'"

Turner also cited "the eyewitness testimony of Jefferson's highly respected overseer, Edmund Bacon," which he said "may be the single most important piece of evidence in the case." In Bacon's account, "[Jefferson] freed one girl [Harriet] some years before he died, and there was a great deal of talk about it. She was nearly as white as anybody and very beautiful. People said he freed her because she was his own daughter. She was not his daughter; she was ———'s daughter. I know that. I have seen him come out of her mother's room many a morning when I went up to Monticello very early."[54] That ellipsis—"she was ———'s daughter"—has tantalized and taunted generations of Jefferson scholars. Because the original notes from Bacon's interview have never come to light, no one knows whom Bacon was talking about.

But it is easy to show that Bacon's account is false: it is contradicted by the calendar. Harriet Hemings was born in 1801 at Monticello, but Bacon did not begin work at Monticello until September 1806, so he could not have witnessed Harriet's father, whoever he was, leaving Sally Hemings's room. (Bacon stated that he began to live at Monticello in December 1800, but Jefferson kept careful records of hirings and payments to employees and contractors, and there is no mention of Bacon until 1806; it is almost inconceivable that Bacon was present before then unless he did nothing, drew no pay, and for five and a half years kept such a low profile that he entirely eluded Jefferson's notice.) Throughout his memoir Bacon exaggerated his closeness to Jefferson, and I can only conclude that the loyal overseer was willing to fabricate a phantom lover in order to protect the reputation of his old boss.*

Turner also focused on one more piece of evidence that hadn't been adequately explained. The Monticello blacksmith Isaac Granger had remarked in his memoir that "Old Master's brother, Mass Randall, was a mighty simple man: used to come out among black people, play the fiddle and dance half the night; hadn't much more sense than Isaac."[55] Randolph Jefferson lived on a plantation in Buckingham County, some twenty miles from Monticello, but Isaac's remark implies that Randolph was a frequent visitor to Monticello's slave quarter. This intriguing piece of evidence—supporting the core of the defenders' arguments—

---

*If Bacon got dates and children mixed up and was referring to the late summer of 1807, when Eston was conceived, he has Monticello's architecture against him. Sally Hemings did not have a "room" at Monticello when Eston was conceived. She was then living in a cabin on Mulberry Row. The row of rooms called the south dependency was not completed until 1809, and Hemings moved into her room some time after that.

could not be easily brushed off. Nothing in the Monticello records suggests Randolph's frequent presence on the mountain, but Isaac Granger was there, an eyewitness. And "used to come" implies something that happened frequently or habitually. It holds open the door for Randolph being the father of Sally Hemings's children.

One advantage of living in Charlottesville is that the town is awash in Jeffersonian items, such as the slender brown volume I happened to spot in the window of an antiquarian bookstore. It was the rare, 1951 edition of Isaac Granger's *Memoirs of a Monticello Slave*. In 1967, Monticello's director, James Bear, published a scholarly version of Granger's memoir with footnotes and an index under the title *Jefferson at Monticello*; everyone naturally uses this modern edition. I had noticed that Granger's text contained many confusing leaps of subject matter, non sequiturs that could not be easily explained. But when I looked at the 1951 edition, many of the non sequiturs suddenly made sense: they came at chapter breaks in the original manuscript that Bear ignored when having the text retypeset for his edition, in which chapters dealing with different subjects were run together without any page or line breaks in a continuous text.[56]

A vitally important piece of information had been obscured by the architecture of this book. When I looked at the paragraph describing Randolph's visits to a slave quarter in the 1951 edition, I could clearly see that it was in a section where Granger describes family activities and events that took place *away from Monticello*. The blacksmith was talking about Randolph's frolics not along Monticello's Mulberry Row but in the slave quarter at Randolph's *own* plantation in the next county. He knew about Randolph's activities because Monticello slaves, including members of Granger's own family, often visited his plantation. Everyone relies on the newer edition with all its useful scholarly apparatus, but when I examined the original book, the strongest evidence for "Uncle Randolph's" paternity vanished.[57]

Sally Hemings retains her hold on the American imagination not just as an irritant to Jefferson's admirers but as a profoundly subversive figure. Like an American Cassandra, cursed never to be believed, she has kept alive the fear that there may be parts of our past we do not know, or do not want to know, but that never go away—a whole secret history. Her story suggests the unsettling, painful truth that the gulf between masters and slaves was an illusion, that it had been fabricated, then laboriously sustained even as the idea of race became blurred, obsolete, and then unsustainable, as it did at Monticello, that in slavery time the country developed a system to generate power and wealth that was not just oppressive but insane.

The Man in the Iron Mask

"I am of a mixed breed . . . [a] Mongrel," said an illustrious American in a speech in 1881. It was not Frederick Douglass or Booker T. Washington but Samuel Clemens who made that claim. He was addressing the annual banquet of the Pilgrim Society, an organization founded on principles of genealogical purity and dedicated to preserving the idea that America was a white man's nation. Invited to address their gathering, Clemens skewered them, their forebears, and their triumphalism: "Those Pilgrims were a hard lot. They took good care of themselves, but they abolished everybody else's ancestors."

Gathering into one lineage all the outcasts of American history, Clemens stood before the Pilgrim sons presenting himself as the archetype of the true American, an amalgam of the wretched genealogical refuse of Indians, Quakers, witches, and Africans: "The first slave brought into New England out of Africa by your progenitors was an ancestor of mine—for I am of a mixed breed, an infinitely shaded and exquisite Mongrel. . . . [M]y complexion is the patient art of eight generations."[1] Clemens spoke figuratively—he was not literally the descendant of Quakers, witches, and slaves—but his metaphorical language was all the more powerful: he was speaking a truth about the country, an old truth long suppressed by a founding myth that had "abolished everybody else's ancestors." But the abolition was incomplete, there were survivors, and they carried their parallel genealogies.

Clemens offered not a soothing dream of multiculturalism but a vision of violent genealogical conquest by which all identities but

Anglo-Saxon had been eradicated. He was speaking not just about race but about power, and power's yearning to cleanse itself. As John Adams wrote to Jefferson, "Power always thinks it has a great soul and vast views beyond the comprehension of the weak; and that it is doing God's service when it is violating all His laws."[2]

Jefferson constantly moved the boundaries on his moral map to make the horrific tolerable to him. In the deleted passages of the Declaration of Independence, he vehemently denounced the slave trade as an "execrable commerce" in which "men are bought and sold." But not long after, finding it financially expedient, he sold slaves repeatedly, on a large scale. The execrable commerce somehow became less execrable. In the 1760s, Jefferson had argued a court case declaring it "wicked" that a white man be held in servitude just because deep in his lineage he had some black blood. The very idea of a white man held in bondage just like a black man struck him as a horrible, nightmarish entrapment, a foul species of evil. But by the 1790s, exactly that was going on at Monticello. Jefferson and his family could not conceive of themselves doing anything that was evil. So they redefined evil. A few favorite black people would be exceptionally well treated; a very few, those with kinship ties, would be smuggled out one way or another. But in the meantime the family on the summit was haunted by the sight of white relatives in slavery to them.

In ways that no one completely understands, Monticello became populated by a number of mixed-race people who looked astonishingly like Thomas Jefferson. We know this not from what Jefferson's detractors have claimed but from what his grandson Jeff Randolph openly admitted. According to him, not only Sally Hemings but another Hemings woman as well "had children which resembled Mr. Jefferson so closely that it was plain that they had his blood in their veins." Resemblance meant kinship; there was no other explanation. Since Mr. Jefferson's blood was Jeff's blood, Jeff knew that he was somehow kin to these people of a parallel world.

Jeff said the resemblance of one Hemings to Thomas Jefferson was "so close, that at some distance or in the dusk the slave, dressed in the same way, might be mistaken for Mr. Jefferson." This is so specific, so vivid—"at some distance or in the dusk"—that Jeff had to be relating a likeness he had seen many times and could not shake the memory of.

We can imagine one of these encounters, a scene at twilight with Jeff, age eighteen, walking out onto the terrace after dinner. The view to the west is glorious as the sun falls below the Blue Ridge Mountains, sixty miles in the hazy distance. Muffled sounds of conversation and music emanate from the house and mingle with the rising night sounds of the forest. The small town of Charlottesville lies in darkness in the valley below. From the terrace—the ambiguous boundary line between the Jefferson world above and the slave world below—Jeff gazes down onto a path and sees the tall figure of his grandfather striding purposefully, head and shoulders erect, the famous profile clearly distinguishable even in the fading light. There's something odd about the clothes, but no matter. We then hear a sound from behind Jeff, and he turns, startled, to see Mr. Jefferson approaching him from the house. Jeff looks down to see his grandfather still on the path, receding into the distance. He turns and the real grandfather is on the terrace with him. Mr. Jefferson claps his hand on Jeff's shoulder and comments on the soft beauty of a Virginia night in early spring. Jeff peers into the darkness, and the man below has vanished.

We can see Jefferson's double appearing at the periphery of a family event, standing at a respectful distance; or suddenly striding into view, not quite in focus; or seen from the terrace playing the fiddle with his head thrown back, just like Mr. Jefferson. We can see the Randolphs seeing the double, and we observe that they make no comment, appear to take no notice, unless perhaps a Randolph is alone and can give a long curious look without being noticed. This double was someone they could not avoid seeing but were not supposed to notice. In fact, Jeff Randolph saw the double many times. He haunted Monticello.

Jeff described an incident of the two realms colliding. The moment of collision would make a powerful little film because the camera is adept at capturing suspense and astonishment. The incident occurred at dinner in the elegant dining room. Jefferson was there, along with Jeff Randolph and his mother, Martha Randolph, and her other children, and a guest. We see and hear the people at the table as Mr. Jefferson discourses brilliantly. The camera rises slightly, and we see, moving silently behind the diners, the double, bearing a fresh platter of food and heading for Mr. Jefferson. We see the double's face and that of the honored guest as he listens intently to Mr. Jefferson's remarks. An inner voice tells the guest, *Don't look, don't raise your eyes, you do not want to know.* But of course he looks up, and our hearts freeze. The camera focuses on Jeff for the reaction shot, since he in fact wrote about this very moment: "in one instance, a gentleman dining with Mr. Jefferson, looked so startled as he raised his eyes from the latter to the servant behind him, that his discovery of the resemblance was perfectly obvious to all."

The guest must have been a Northerner or a foreigner. Local friends, drilled in the social protocol of the "peculiar institution," noticed the slaves who resembled Mr. Jefferson but never breached protocol by mentioning them. A University of Virginia professor who often visited Monticello with a colleague said that they "saw what others saw" but never heard the topic discussed. "An awe and veneration was felt for Mr. Jefferson among his neighbors which . . . rendered it shameful to even talk about his name in such a connexion." Still, what the professor saw vexed him, and he pondered the connection "in his own secret mind," the locked and silent chamber.[3]

In the 1850s, Jeff Randolph took the biographer Henry Randall around Monticello, filling the writer's astonished ear with stories of the parallel family who lived on the mountain. Jeff said that his grandfather made no attempt to conceal the resemblance between himself and his slaves. He told Randall that Sally Hemings "was a house servant and her children were brought up house servants—so that the likeness between master and slave was blazoned to all the multitudes who visited this political Mecca."

The biographer was amazed at these revelations. Not being a Southerner, he was unaccustomed to the notion of slaves resembling the master's family. He could not comprehend that Jefferson tolerated this daily display of miscegenation. "Why on earth," he asked, didn't Jefferson "put these slaves who looked like him out of the public sight"? Jeff replied that his grandfather "never betrayed the least consciousness of the resemblance." He went on to say that he had no doubt that his mother "would have been very glad to have them removed" but that everyone so "venerated" Jefferson that none dared to "broach such a topic to him." Jefferson's power was such that he imposed his own reality on this little familial empire. "What suited him, satisfied [us]," Randolph said.[4]

Jefferson exerted an extraordinary level of psychological control over his family to keep his version of reality in place and the parallel realm unexamined. His great-granddaughter Sarah Randolph said that Jefferson never talked about anything he didn't want to talk about. An unsympathetic acquaintance wrote not of reticence or taciturnity but of "that frigid indifference which forms the pride of his character."[5] Frigid indifference forms a useful shield for a public character against his political enemies, but Jefferson deployed it against his own daughter Martha, who was deeply upset by the sexual allegations against her father and wanted a straight answer—*Yes or no?*—an answer he would not deign to give.

Sharper than a serpent's tooth is a thankless father's indifference, but Jefferson knew he could expect his daughter's devotion and felt no need to make explanations. As a grown woman, Martha remained the daughter, and she never became a confidante, even when scandal engulfed the family. She unburdened herself to her children. "My mother, as she has often told me, was very indignant, even exasperated," the granddaughter Ellen wrote. One day Martha and Jefferson's private secretary confronted Jefferson with a widely published, highly insulting poem about him and Hemings. In silence, Jefferson "smiled at their annoyance."[6]

Jefferson could smile, but his daughter could not. She "took the Dusky Sally stories much to heart," Jeff Randolph said. Jefferson's silence about his mixed-race children split them off from reality. Though it was a species of schizophrenia to which Southern families had become accustomed, denial yielded not comfort but only anxiety, and from anxiety there erupted rage at the "yellow children," who were blamed for it all.

Another moment arrived when the parallel world broke through the barrier. In 1822, Jefferson freed Sally Hemings's two oldest children, Beverly and Harriet, then aged twenty-four and twenty-one. He did this furtively, through an intermediary (the ever-loyal Edmund Bacon), and without the required legal authorization, which would have attracted attention; but even so, he could not escape notice and suspicion. Bacon recalled the departure of Harriet: "He freed one girl some years before he died, and there was a great deal of talk about it. . . . by Mr. Jefferson's direction I paid her stage fare to Philadelphia, and gave her fifty dollars."[7] Harriet's brother Beverly left the same year. Even though "there was a great deal of talk about it" in Charlottesville, at Monticello all was silence, or evasion. In the Farm Book, Jefferson wrote the words "run away [18]22" and "run. 22" next to their names.[8] The $50, plus stage fare, that he gave Bacon for Harriet was a large sum, yet Jefferson made no note of it in his accounts.

The family detected Jefferson's hidden hand at work, and they also knew that his entries about Harriet and Beverly in the Farm Book were just a cover story. Ellen said that it was her grandfather's decision to allow the two Hemingses "to withdraw quietly from the plantation" and that "it was called running away." Jefferson freed them because they were "sufficiently white to pass for white."* It was his "principle" to do this, she said. The alternative—to acknowledge that these people were her grandfather's children—was unthinkable: "The thing will not bear telling. There are such things, after all, as moral impossibilities."

Jefferson went to his grave without giving his family any denial of the Hemings charges, so they had no weapon to fire and no shield for defense when stories about his mixed-race offspring continued to circulate, stories that always tormented his daughter Martha. On her deathbed in 1836, Martha called her sons Jeff and George Wythe Randolph to her side. She enjoined them "always to defend the character of their grandfather." She told Jeff to look in the Farm Book, where the birth dates of the slaves were kept, and directed him to find the birth of the slave "who most resembled Mr. Jefferson." Jeff found the entry—and maddeningly for history did not disclose the identity of this man. Martha asserted that Hemings and Jefferson had been apart from each other for fifteen months before the birth of that child, and "she bade her sons remember this fact."[9]

Martha had found comfort in fraud, because the Farm Book and other records show that Jefferson was present at Monticello every time Sally Hemings conceived, and there is no indication that Hemings was ever away from Monticello at those times. Challenging the Jeffersonian paternity of just one Hemings child in any case would not get her father

---

*Ellen went on to say: "I remember four instances of this, three young men and one girl, who walked away and staid away—their whereabouts was perfectly known but they were left to themselves—for they were white enough to pass for white."

off the hook, but apparently Martha's intent was to give her children *some* deniability.[10]

In the 1960s a University of Virginia scholar scrutinized the entries in the Farm Book, counting to nine on his fingers as he tried and failed to duplicate Martha's result. He wrote to another specialist, offering advice on how to draft a delicate footnote conceding as obliquely and obscurely as possible that Jefferson's daughter had not told the truth to her sons: "The only embarrassing thing to phrase will be a footnote pointing out that Martha was wrong in saying that Jefferson was not at Monticello 9 months before the birth of each of Sally's children. Perhaps you could say it this way: 'In attempting to refute a libel, Martha made a misstatement.'"[11]

When Jeff Randolph took Henry Randall around Monticello in the 1850s and told him that two Hemings women had children who resembled Jefferson, he also said that he knew the identities of the real fathers of the mixed-race Hemings children. Randall wrote down what Jeff told him:

> Mr. Jefferson had two nephews, Peter Carr and Samuel Carr whom he brought up in his house. They were the sons of Mr. Jefferson's sister and her husband Dabney Carr. . . . Sally Henings was the mistress of Peter, and her sister Betsey* the mistress of Samuel—and from these connections sprang the progeny which resembled Mr. Jefferson. Both the Henings girls were light colored and decidedly goodlooking. . . . their connexion with the Carrs was perfectly notorious at Monticello, and scarcely disguised by the latter—never disavowed by them. Samuel's proceedings were particularly open.[12]

Samuel Carr was a convenient scapegoat because, in fact, he did have a black family. He fathered several children with a free woman of color, Judath Barnett, and this black family lived in a settlement of free blacks north of Charlottesville that came to be known as Free State. Its very

---

*Randall mistakenly used the spelling "Henings." More important, his account is muddled on a major point: Sally Hemings had a *niece* named Betsy and a *sister* named Betty, and it remains unclear which woman Jeff had in mind; possibly Jeff's statement was clear and Randall garbled the conversation in recalling it.

existence was a rebuke and a repudiation of Thomas Jefferson's insistence that free blacks could not live side by side with whites. By the time Jeff pinned the blame for the Hemings children on his Carr cousin, Samuel was in his grave, and his mixed-race family had decamped for more secure freedom in Ohio.

Possibly, Jeff Randolph knew the truth about his grandfather's "proceedings" and kept it hidden from the women in the family. Jeff told his sister Ellen that Samuel and Peter Carr had admitted their guilt to him in a tearful confession sometime in the second decade of the nineteenth century. But if that were so, why didn't Jeff tell his mother on her deathbed and relieve her torment?

Before we pass judgment on Jeff Randolph, there are additional factors to consider. Like his father, Colonel Thomas Mann Randolph, Jeff was forced into the role of buffer and middleman, handling the dirty business. Like his father, he was caught between Jefferson and the women in the family, who were blind in their devotion to Jefferson. He always had to consider the feelings of his mother and sisters while bowing to his grandfather, and simultaneously he had to make everything run.

Jeff's account hints at a sympathy for his enslaved relatives—a dangerous sentiment for a slave master—and hints also at a divide in the family. His sister Ellen called these people—unquestionably her own blood kin—the "yellow children" and spoke of them with disdain as "a race of half-breeds. . . . The thing will not bear telling."[13] We sense feelings of astonishing intensity and relentlessness. At Monticello the "yellow children" lived in the glare of those hostile feelings every day. No act of loyalty or devotion could mitigate those feelings, because for Ellen the mere existence of these children defiled the reputation of her grandfather. This is strikingly different from Jeff, who spoke of the Hemingses neutrally, even sympathetically.

Jeff had connections to the African-American community his sister might not have known about, and at almost the same time he was making his revelations to the biographer about the mixed-race children of Monticello, he offered crucial help to a Charlottesville "black" family trying to cross the legal line into whiteness. Around 1835 a free mulatto woman named Ann Foster, a property owner who lived near the University of Virginia, gave birth to a son she named Clayton Randolph

Foster. Her bestowing the name Randolph proves nothing by itself, but an obscure court record from the 1850s is intriguing: "Upon evidence of Thomas J. Randolph . . . Susan Catharine Foster and Clayton Randolph Foster, children of Ann Foster, are [declared by the court to be] not negroes in the meaning of the act of assembly."[14]

To give such evidence, Jeff had to prove to the court's satisfaction that he had authoritative knowledge of sufficient white blood in the Foster lineage to have them declared "not negroes." At the very least, Jeff knew this mixed-race family very well. He was less inclined than his sister to revile such people as "a race of half-breeds," knowing as he did the peculiar geography of the parallel world that Jefferson's ideology compelled them to deny.

Jeff offered the same help to the grandchildren of Mary Hemings Bell, doing what he could to rescue a few people from the system. These rescues present themselves as psychological mini-dramas, with hints of secret blood ties, hidden identities, and a redemptive climax; they suggest hidden grief endured by the masters, consciences we cannot perceive until we learn to read the secret signs.

The insanity of this world is apparent in the story of the Fosters, who walked into the Albemarle County courthouse as black people and left as whites, their true genealogy abolished. And the brutality of this world is apparent in the nature of the evidence Jefferson's partisans offered for his innocence of the charges James Callender had made against him. One of Jefferson's supporters blithely admitted that rape was common at Monticello: "In gentlemen's houses everywhere, we know that the virtue of unfortunate slaves is assailed with impunity. . . . Is it strange, therefore, that a servant of Mr. Jefferson's, at a home where so many strangers resort . . . should have a mulatto child? Certainly not."[15]

Ellen Randolph made a similar admission. She wrote that young white men in the vicinity of Monticello regarded the slave quarter as their bordello: "There were dissipated young men in the neighborhood who sought the society of the mulatresses and they . . . were not anxious to establish any claim of paternity in the results of such associations." Ellen may have been referring to her brother Jeff's school friends, who were "intimate with the Negro women," according to Edmund Bacon.[16] The silent implication was that the black women were immoral, but Jeff Randolph defended the character of slaves: "There was as much decency of deportment and as few illegitimates [among the slaves] as among the laboring whites elsewhere; as many lived in wedlock from youth to age without reproach."[17]

But in his grandfather's case, Jeff Randolph and the partisans who followed him put on the iron mask of denial, knowing the immense symbolic importance of keeping the Founder pure. That image of purity has been a potent talisman, a charm against knowledge of a past in which virtue was assailed on all sides, a talisman against everything that cannot bear telling.

"I Only Am Escaped Alone to Tell Thee"

Madison Hemings bequeathed a narrative that changed American history when he stated bluntly, in an 1873 newspaper interview, that Thomas Jefferson was "my father." When his recollections came to wide attention in 1974 thanks to Fawn Brodie's *Thomas Jefferson: An Intimate History,* they collided with the modern imperative to find redemption almost everywhere we look.[1]

In an extraordinary cultural transformation, the memoir that Merrill Peterson had disparaged in the 1960s as "the Negroes' pathetic wish for a little pride" has been refashioned into a comforting myth of a secret cross-racial romance. Brodie washed Jefferson clean of any stain when she wrote, "If the story of the Sally Hemings liaison be true, as I believe it is, it represents not scandalous debauchery . . . but rather a serious passion that brought Jefferson and the slave woman much private happiness over a period lasting thirty-eight years."[2] She suggested that Jefferson was neither a "brooding celibate" nor, "as some blacks today believe," a monstrous "debaucher." In Brodie's view Jefferson himself was a victim who endured as much travail as anyone over the affair: "It also brought suffering, shame, and even political paralysis in regard to Jefferson's agitation for emancipation." Turning to Sally Hemings, Brodie stressed the romantic, saying that Hemings "was certainly lonely in Paris, as well as supremely ready for the first great love of her life."[3]

This is a story that deeply appeals to modern sensibilities; looking into Jefferson's inner life will lead us to a redemptive vision: "His ambivalences seem less baffling; the heroic image remains untarnished and his genius undiminished. And the semi-transparent shadows do tend to disappear."[4] Brodie averted her gaze from some of the truths her work had uncovered, and she also fell victim to an impulse she had detected in other Jefferson biographers who "protect by nuance, by omission, by subtle repudiation, without being in the least aware of the strength of their internal commitment to canonization."[5] Determined to prove not just that Jefferson was the father of Hemings's children but that he was in love with Hemings, Brodie took what she wanted from Madison's recollections and ignored evidence that contradicted her thesis.

In Brodie's wake came the novelist Barbara Chase-Riboud, whose *Sally Hemings: A Novel* of 1979 enchanted millions of readers, seduced the press, and created an utterly fantastic image of Sally Hemings in the popular mind, perhaps indelibly. Chase-Riboud said, "I ended up admiring their love, their fierce defense of their children, how they were allowed to run away. . . . Plus she might have influenced him on his politics."[6] But Chase-Riboud was correct when she said that the Hemings story possesses "symbolic, almost mythic dimensions. Tragedy and secrecy, ambiguity and hypocrisy—all these elements combine in the story. It is truly an allegory of the social and psychic dramas of the races in America."[7]

Madison Hemings's recollections are much more than an item of evidence in the Hemings-Jefferson controversy. They take us deep into the psychology of slavery at Monticello. In telling his life story, Madison did not begin with his famous father, as one might expect. Instead, he went back to the remote past, unfolding a narrative as it had been told and retold in the Hemings family. It is a story of origins, of beginnings, and of the archetypes of the New World in distant times. It is a story of the first father and the beginning of amalgamation, the amazement of whites and blacks at the first mixed-race people, and the overthrow of the father. In just a few lines, it evokes the feel of myth.

A British mariner known only as Captain Hemings came to Virginia's shores in the 1730s and fathered a child by a slave. When he learned of the existence of this child, a daughter, the captain tried to purchase her from her owner, John Wayles (Jefferson's father-in-law), but Wayles "would not part with the child, though he was offered an extraordinarily large price for her." It is notable that Madison begins his story with the white ancestor who acknowledged paternity of his daughter, which Jefferson never did.

The captain persisted: "Being thwarted in the purchase, and determined to own his own flesh and blood he resolved to take the child by force or stealth." Captain Hemings laid a plan to kidnap the child and her mother, but "leaky fellow servants" revealed the plot to Wayles, who locked the mother and child away in his house.* The captain sailed away from Virginia, never to see his daughter again. That daughter was Elizabeth Hemings, Madison's grandmother, the matriarch of Monticello's Hemingses.

These events had taken place more than a century and a quarter before Madison's telling of them. The story must have been repeated many times in the Hemings family. It points to a deep, abiding sense of dislocation and loss and to the struggle of the slaves to comprehend people who regarded children as cash and severed blood ties with "no compunctions of conscience":

> I have been informed that it was not the extra value of that child over other slave children that induced Mr. Wales to refuse to sell it, for slave masters then, as in later days, had no compunctions of conscience which restrained them from parting mother and child of however tender age, but he was restrained by the fact that just about that time amalgamation began, and the child was so great a curiosity that its owner desired to raise it himself that he might see its outcome.

In the contest between the father and the master, the master wins and keeps the mixed-race child out of base curiosity, to observe it as if it were a joke of nature. The first master defeats the first father, makes him disappear, and sets himself in the father's place. That is the dark heart of this foundation story. The master's ultimate prize is to take the girl as his concubine and establish, perversely, a perpetual lineage in slavery. He fathers children with her and passes them to the next master: Wayles had six children by Elizabeth Hemings, and they went

---

*In this brief remark, Madison hints at divides within the slave community, with some willing to betray others to curry favor with the master.

into Jefferson's inheritance. Mastery inverted the strongest bond of humanity—with the enslaver becoming the father—a vision alien to whites but part of the historical DNA of African-Americans.

Our human yearning for immortality expresses itself in children, but fathering children by a slave condemned the offspring to slavery, perpetuating not just the master's lineage but the master's power. It is the ultimate expression of mastery to hold power after death, because for the master life is power and power is life. Faulkner made this demented species of power a central theme in *Absalom, Absalom!*, which tells in kaleidoscopic episodes the story of a determined plantation master who exiles his son and depicts mastery not as a peculiarly Southern phenomenon but as the American enterprise gone mad.[8]

In Madison's account, his mother broke the power of the masters when she broke the lineage of enslavement established by John Wayles. When his mother went to France as the companion of Jefferson's daughter, she

> became Mr. Jefferson's concubine, and when he was called back home she was *enciente* [pregnant] by him.* He desired to bring my mother back to Virginia with him but she demurred. She was just beginning to understand the French language well, and in France she was free, while if she returned to Virginia she would be re-enslaved. So she refused to return with him.

So Jefferson offered her a deal to get her to return: "To *induce* her to do so, he promised her extraordinary privileges [emphasis added]." Furthermore, he "made a solemn pledge that her children should be freed at the age of twenty-one years." So she returned "in consequence of his promises, on which she implicitly relied."[9]

"Extraordinary privileges" echoes the "extraordinarily large price" Captain Hemings had offered Wayles. Sally Hemings succeeds where Captain Hemings had failed. She lays hold of the future, but only by consenting to become the master's concubine: she sacrifices herself for her children. What is missing from Madison's account is a declaration of love. A transaction has taken place, not a love affair.

---

*The newspaper misspelled it; the correct spelling is *enceinte*.

Madison was a forthright speaker; he did not shrink from saying that his grandmother had children by four different men. He reported bluntly that his mother became Jefferson's "concubine," a harsh word to use of one's mother, and he used the same word of his grandmother's relationship with John Wayles. Elsewhere in his recollections Madison describes in warm terms the emotional bond between Thomas Jefferson and his wife, Martha: "intimacy sprang up between them which ripened into love." This is vastly different from "my mother became Mr. Jefferson's concubine."

Madison's wife, Mary McCoy, was the granddaughter of a slave and a slave master. Madison described her lineage this way: "Her grandmother was a slave, and lived with her master, Stephen Hughes, near Charlottesville, as his wife. She was manumitted by him, which made their children free born." He pointedly did not use the word "wife" in his account of his mother's relationship with Jefferson. Madison said that Jefferson was "affectionate" toward his grandchildren, but he did not say that about Jefferson's relationship with his mother.

Jefferson maintained tight emotional control over his family on the summit. A descriptive letter to his daughter Martha has a commanding tone:

> I now see our fireside formed into a groupe, no member of which has a fibre in their composition which can ever produce any jarring or jealousies among us. No irregular passions, no dangerous bias, which may render problematical the future fortunes and happiness of our descendants.[10]

In contrast to that group clustered around the fireside, every time the Hemings children gazed up at the mansion, they confronted an existential either-or: *I am/am not a Jefferson. I am/am not white/black.* Madison's account suggests that they endured a peculiarly deep estrangement from Jefferson: "he was affectionate toward his white grandchildren," but toward his black offspring "he was very undemonstrative. . . . He was not in the habit of showing partiality or fatherly affection to us children." Madison did not offer a single anecdote about Jefferson. His impressions of him were vague and general—distant glimpses of the master on his terrace and in the shops—and one wonders whether he ever saw Jefferson up close or ever heard him say a word. In their accounts the former slaves Israel Jefferson and Isaac Granger, especially the latter, tell more about Jefferson than his son does. Madison's recollections, aside from making his lineage known, "do not suggest that he identified with Jefferson in any way," as the Monticello historian Lucia Stanton puts it.[11]

In place of affection the Hemings children received their promised privileges. When they were very young, they were exempted from labor. Madison and his siblings "were permitted to stay about the 'great house,' and only required to do such light work as going on errands. Harriet learned to spin and to weave in a little factory on the home plantation. . . . We were always permitted to be with our mother, who was well used." Her only tasks were "to take care of his chamber and wardrobe, look after us children and do such light work as sewing." Madison regarded this as the fulfillment of the promise Jefferson made in Paris that Sally would receive extraordinary privileges. It also speaks to the harshness of life for Monticello's ordinary slaves. Apparently, it was extraordinary for children to be with their mothers.

Another of Madison's remarks leaps out. The Hemings children knew that eventually they would be released, so they felt "free from the dread" of knowing they would be slaves all their lives "and were measurably happy." But the certainty of eventual freedom came with a price. All the Hemings siblings reached their twenties without marrying or having children, which was unusual. But because they all knew that one day they would be leaving the mountain, they had to be free from encumbrances. Jefferson might not manumit a spouse; he might keep children, as he had kept some of Mary Hemings's children.

Sally Hemings talked about her French trip all the time. "I have often heard her tell about it," Edmund Bacon recalled. To him and other white listeners she is likely to have given a sanitized travelogue of the wonders of an ocean voyage, of the great city of London, where she stayed with John and Abigail Adams, of the great city of Paris, where she was free because there was no slavery. Her family would have known what choices Sally Hemings made in Paris and what she had given up.

Hemings brought back from Paris a mysterious token of her time there. It is hard to say exactly what it means. Excavating the site of Sally Hemings's cabin on Mulberry Row, archaeologists found a French ointment jar in household trash behind the cabin and estimated that it had been thrown away there in 1809. It is not so surprising that she would have held on to this little keepsake, but the puzzle is, why did she throw it away after holding on to it for twenty years? The year 1809 was when Hemings moved from that cabin to her room in the Monticello dependency; it was the year Jefferson retired from the presidency and the year when his extended white family settled in with him permanently at Monticello. To Hemings, somehow the events of that year must have broken off something she associated with Paris, or represented an end, or a dashing of hopes that she finally realized were unrealistic. As the Randolphs gathered around the fireside with the paterfamilias, she grasped Jefferson's feelings about his family ties. Her treaty would be fulfilled, but there would never be a recognition of her, only silence and denial.

Madison learned to read and write when he "induced" the white children to teach him. There is a clue in his recollections to a book they used in their lessons. A great deal of attention has focused on Madison's use of the French word *enceinte* (pregnant), which Jefferson's defenders have pounced on as evidence that his statement was written by the newspaper editor S. F. Wetmore. Madison might have learned the word from his mother, but a more intriguing possibility is that when Jefferson's grandchildren taught him, they used Jefferson's favorite novel, Laurence Sterne's *Tristram Shandy*, where the word *enceinte* appears on an early page.[12] The novel opens with a ribald joke about the moment of conception, but the joke would have carried a special double entendre in the mind of a child of Sally Hemings:

> I WISH either my father or my mother, or indeed both of them, as they were in duty both equally bound to it, had minded what they were about when they begot me; had they duly considered how much depended upon what they were then doing; . . . —Had they duly weighed and considered all this, and proceeded accordingly,—I am verily persuaded I should have made a quite different figure in the world.

As Madison read those lines, he would only have to lift his eyes to his young Randolph tutor to get an idea of what a different figure he might have made—someone known openly and honestly to the world as a sprig of Jefferson's tree.

Jefferson wrote in *Notes on the State of Virginia* that when he gazed into the faces of dark-skinned slaves, he saw nothing but "eternal monotony . . . that immoveable veil of black which covers all the emotions." But the light-skinned faces of his Hemings children—his own face barely veiled—would have unsettled him, so he kept them at a physical and emotional distance.

When Harriet Hemings left Monticello to head north forever in 1822, Jefferson had his overseer Bacon give her the traveling money.* He did not share a final, intimate moment with his daughter to hand her the money himself. Perhaps he had never acknowledged her existence and did not want to start then. He wrote "run" (for "runaway") next to Harriet's name in the Farm Book, so his daughter appeared in his records as a fugitive.

Madison did not mention that his father talked to him about going free, but Jefferson did talk about manumission with at least two other slaves who were freed in his will: his butler, Burwell Colbert, and the blacksmith Joseph Fossett.

After Jefferson's death Madison and Eston Hemings took their mother to live in Charlottesville, where their racial identity oscillated along the either-or axis according to the eyes and intentions of whites. The 1830 census taker listed all of them as white, but when a special census of free blacks was taken three years later, they were classified as mulatto.[13] Their racial identity may have shifted because the special 1833 census, ordered by Virginia's government after the Nat Turner uprising in 1831, enumerated free blacks for the purpose of determining how many of them were willing to immigrate to Africa. The census taker may have pushed them to leave by making them officially mulattoes.†

In providing some background to Madison's memoir, Dumas Malone noted the fierce "anti-Negro sentiment" that Hemings confronted in his new home in Ohio: "The county seat was so hostile to black settlement that as late as 1888 . . . a Negro had never been allowed to live within

---

*Similarly, he had used a go-between for another personal transaction, sending his farm manager to tell Mary Hemings he was taking two of her children.
†Of the 452 free blacks in Albemarle County, none expressed the desire to leave the country of their birth.

the town limits." This extreme hostility Madison endured in Ohio may explain the element of family tension in his memoir. He was the only surviving Hemings child willing to make a public statement about their origins, and he was the only Hemings-Jefferson offspring who still regarded himself as black.* Madison's siblings had entered the realm of denial. Eston and his family had decided to cross over into the white world; Beverly and Harriet had long since crossed over, as Madison described in surprising detail:

> Beverly left Monticello and went to Washington as a white man. He married a white woman in Maryland, and their only child, a daughter, was not known by the white folks to have any colored blood coursing in her veins. Beverly's wife's family were people in good circumstances.
>
> Harriet married a white man in good standing in Washington City, whose name I could give, but will not, for prudential reasons. She raised a family of children, and so far as I know they were never suspected of being tainted with African blood in the community where she lived or lives. . . . She thought it to her interest, on going to Washington, to assume the role of a white woman, and by her dress and conduct as such I am not aware that her identity as Harriet Hemings of Monticello has ever been discovered.[14]
>
> Eston married a colored woman in Virginia, and moved from there to Ohio, and lived in Chillicothe several years. In the fall of 1852 he removed to Wisconsin, where he died a year or two afterwards. He left three children.

Proud of his African blood, Madison seemed disappointed and even bitter that his siblings passed into the white world, notably in his remark that Harriet "thought it to her interest . . . to assume the role of a white woman." Because his siblings had all crossed the color line into whiteness and silence, this story and others like it were buried and

---

*Some of his children and their descendants passed for white and lost contact with their African-American kin. His son Thomas, serving as a white officer in the Union army, was captured and died in the Confederate prison at Andersonville.

denied, even by the offspring of the hidden unions. The slave era was over, and the truth of that era would be lost if Madison did not speak up, as if to say, as Ishmael does in *Moby-Dick*: "I only am escaped alone to tell thee."

After Jefferson's death Sally Hemings moved into a house in Charlottesville with her sons Madison and Eston, then in their early twenties. They had been freed in Jefferson's will, but she had not been; the will didn't even mention her. In the appraisement of slaves after Jefferson's death, Hemings, then just over fifty, had been adjudged an old woman of no value. Sally was "given her time" by Jefferson's daughter, an informal, quasi-manumission by which Sally could legally remain in Virginia but was not required to provide any further service. In his will Jefferson asked his executors to petition the Virginia legislature to grant permission to Madison and Eston to remain in the state, which was done. Without this special permission, they would have been required to leave the commonwealth under the provisions of the 1806 removal law.

A year after Sally Hemings's death in 1835, the brothers left Charlottesville for Ohio with their wives and children. *The Cleveland American* reported the presence of an unnamed mixed-race child of Thomas Jefferson's in 1845, stating, "Notwithstanding all the services and sacrifices of Jefferson in the establishment of the freedom of this country, his own son, now living in Ohio, is not allowed a vote, or an oath in a court of justice!"[15] Though Eston won esteem by his skill as a musician and his sterling character, his race irredeemably condemned him. According to a newspaper article published after his death: "notwithstanding all his accomplishments and deserts, a great gulf, an impassable gulf" separated Eston Hemings and white people, "even the lowest of them." Another newspaper account was blunt: "a nigger was a nigger in those days and that settled it."[16]

Eston crossed the line into whiteness around 1850. He moved his family from Ohio, where they were well known, to Madison, Wisconsin, where they were not, dropped the name Hemings for Jefferson, and passed as a white person, as did his wife and three children. Eston was remembered in one newspaper account as "Quiet, unobtrusive, polite and decidedly intelligent." The account continued, "he was soon very well and favorably known to all classes of our citizens, for his personal appearance and gentlemanly manners attracted everybody's attention to him."

He could not conceal his remarkable resemblance to Thomas Jefferson. "It was rumored," said one newspaper in 1902, "that he was a natural son of President Thomas Jefferson, a good many people accepted the story as truth, from the intrinsic evidence of his striking resemblance to Jefferson."[17] One of Eston's acquaintances, on a trip to Washington with several other men from Ohio, was stunned when the group came to a statue of the third president: "'Gentlemen, who in Chillicothe looks the most like that statue?' I asked. Instantly came the unanimous answer, 'Why, Eston Hemings!'" The man who noticed Eston's "striking" likeness to the statue pointedly asked Eston about it, and Eston responded that his mother "belonged to Mr. Jefferson . . . and she never was married."

A friend of Eston's son Beverly either guessed a Thomas Jefferson connection or was told about it. When Beverly Jefferson died in 1908, the *Chicago Tribune*'s obituary did not mention descent from Jefferson, but shortly afterward it printed the following letter: "His death deserves more than a passing notice, as he was a grandson of Thomas Jefferson, father of the doctrines of the democratic party, hence one of the FFV [First Families of Virginia]. Beverly Jefferson was one of God's noblemen— gentle, kindly, courteous, charitable. He was friendly to everybody in his home city, and he will be missed there quite as much or more, perhaps, than any other citizen."[18]

Choosing the surname Jefferson might seem an odd way to hide one's identity, but Eston's features made it impossible to deny that he had some blood tie to the third president. His twentieth-century descendants believed they were descended from an unnamed Jefferson "uncle," most likely a cover story devised in the late nineteenth century to hide the family's descent not so much from Thomas Jefferson as from Sally Hemings. If it became known they were descended from Hemings, they would no longer be white people, but colored.

The secrets buried in slavery time formed a minefield; the borderland of the parallel worlds was literally deadly, as I discovered from an article dating to World War I from *The Washington Post*, "Drafted Man, Classed as Colored, Commits Suicide in an Ohio Camp." The article reported an incident involving one Alfred Lord, a white twenty-seven-year-old Ohio man drafted to serve in the army in the fall of 1917. "I'm ready," he told a reporter as he climbed aboard a train in his hometown of Mineral City with 105 other young men, their departure hailed by a large, flag-waving crowd of well-wishers. When the army physician examined him at the induction camp in Chillicothe, something did not seem quite right: "the surgeon did not pass him. Instead he called in other surgeons. They, too, examined Lord. There were whispered conferences. 'We are sorry to tell you this,' one of the surgeons said, finally, 'but there is evidence that there is negro blood in your veins. You will have to go into a negro regiment.' Lord . . . although of dark complexion, always had thought himself white, and . . . had associated with white men all his life. . . . That night he committed suicide."[19] The article did not say what sign revealed his Negro blood. In any case, Lord changed in a blink from being one thing to being another, an instantaneous and fatal metamorphosis.

Eston's son John Wayles Jefferson, white enough to attain the rank of lieutenant colonel in the Eighth Wisconsin Infantry, lived through such an instant of icy terror when he encountered a childhood friend who knew his carefully hidden background as a colored man in another state, another time. The acquaintance recalled that the colonel "begged me not to tell the fact that he had colored blood in his veins, which he said was not suspected by any of his command."[20]

When Monticello's historians went to interview Hemings descendants, they found photographs from the early twentieth century of Eston's grandson and a friend dressed as pickaninnies, wearing blackface and striking comical "colored" poses, including ogling white girls with the sort of leer that would get a real black man lynched. The grandson had been raised by his grandmother, Eston's wife, who was born in Virginia under slavery. Either the photographs were savagely ironic—the make-believe pickaninny had no idea he was descended from slaves—or the young man *did* know and the little joke bespoke a savage self-hatred.[21]

The brutal racial order split the Hemings family apart and drove some of them underground. The Monticello historians found that Madison's son "disappeared and may be the source of stories among his sisters' descendants of a mysterious and silent visitor who looked like a white man, with white beard and blue, staring eyes. He slipped in and out of town to visit older family members but never formed ties with the younger generations."[22] The family said that two of Madison's sons never married "perhaps because of concerns about revealing skin color" in their offspring. Some of the grandsons passed for white; their sisters remained black, and though they all lived in southern Ohio they dared not meet—"we never heard from them," one descendant told the historians. A great-grandson of Madison Hemings's passed as a swarthy European, "adopting a variety of European accents along with his fictitious identities." In need of help and care in his final days, he sought out his sister, who took him in, to the bafflement of her children: "We didn't understand who [he] was because [he] had an Italian accent. . . . And then we found out actually he was our uncle. And that [he] had crossed over, he had been white."

Another descendant of Madison Hemings's related a bitter moment in his grandmother's life, when she was not notified of the death of her brother, who had passed for white and married a white woman years before. He had remained in touch, however, through cards and phone calls on certain meaningful occasions. His new family did not send word across the color line until months after he died, perhaps to ensure that no part of the black family appeared at the funeral. One descendant told the historians, "The blacks don't like it because you're light-skinned and the whites know you're black so you're just stuck there." Another added, "They used to call us white niggers."[23]

The distant figure of Jefferson hovers over this world like the god of a Deist universe, the supreme being who set events in motion and then departed, with his offspring "left to the guidance of a blind fatality," struggling in the world their own father had created.

"The Effect on Them Was Electrical"

At its extreme edge American idealism, with its relentless pursuit of justice, induces a kind of giddiness. A petition that a group of abolitionists submitted to Congress during Jefferson's presidency noted that while "cruelties and horrors" beset Europe, "a beneficent and overruling Providence has been pleased to preserve for our country the blessings of peace, to grant us new proofs of his goodness, and to place us in a condition of prosperity, unrivalled in the records of history." Surely, they went on, a reciprocal obligation is imposed: a "nation so crowned with the blessings of peace, and plenty, and happiness" must "manifest its gratitude . . . by acts of justice and virtue."[1] One such act unfolded in the following manner.

On the first day of April in 1819 a group of seventeen slaves left a plantation in the mountains south of Charlottesville, not far from Monticello, bound for a distant destination. They had been forbidden to carry much baggage and been told they could only take items they would need on a journey. A black man, a fellow slave, was in charge of them. It was not at all unusual for slave drivers to be black men, and this caravan would not have excited much notice at a time when the roads of Virginia were full of "gangs of Negroes, some in irons," on their various melancholy ways to slave markets. This group of five adults and twelve children had not been told where they were going.[2]

Riding in wagons, the slaves headed west across the Blue Ridge, then turned north to follow the Great Wagon Road up the Valley of Virginia. Along the way, a white man galloped up to check on the party's progress.

He was their master, a wealthy, politically prominent Virginian. Several of the slaves were ill, which delayed the party, so the owner rode ahead. In Maryland the wagons turned west along the National Road (today's Route 40), reaching the Monongahela River after a trek of some 280 miles.

The master had arrived at the Monongahela ahead of his slaves, and there he purchased two flat-bottomed boats, sixty feet long and twelve feet wide, on which the party embarked. Because his slaves were all mountain people who knew nothing of boats, the owner hired a river pilot but had to put him off at Pittsburgh because the man was constantly drunk. At Pittsburgh the Monongahela joins the Ohio River, the great water route to the West and a dividing line between slavery and freedom. On its left bank lay Virginia and then Kentucky, slave states, while on the right stretched the shores of Ohio, which was free.

As the master later remembered, the landscape seemed extraordinarily beautiful that April under a bright sun and cloudless sky, with the pale green foliage of spring emerging on the banks as they floated gently past. Altogether, it was "a scene . . . in harmony with the finest feelings of our nature," as he later wrote in a memoir.

The master deliberately chose this stunning panorama as the backdrop to reveal their destination. He ordered the boats lashed together, assembled the people, and "made them a short address": "I proclaimed in the shortest & fullest manner possible, that they were no longer Slaves, but free—free as I was, & were at liberty to proceed with me, or to go ashore at their pleasure."

The master later wrote that "the effect on them was electrical." The people stared at him and then at each other, "as if doubting the accuracy or reality of what they heard." A profound silence settled upon them. Then, as they slowly grasped the truth of what they had heard, they began to laugh—"a kind of hysterical, giggling laugh"—and then to cry, and then fell again into silence. "After a pause of intense and unutterable emotion, bathed in tears, and with tremulous voices, they gave vent to their gratitude and implored the blessing of God."

The owner had a further announcement. He said that in recompense for their past services to him, upon their arrival at their destination, the free state of Illinois, he would give each head of a family 160 acres of land. He would settle near them. To the gift of land, "all objected, saying I had done enough for them in giving them their freedom," insisting they would happily delay their emancipation and remain his slaves until they had comfortably established him in his new home. But the master refused the offer. He said that he had "thought much of my duty & of their rights" and "had made up my mind to restore to them their immediate & unconditional freedom; that I had long been anxious to do it." Indeed, when the party reached Illinois, "I executed & delivered to them Deeds to the land promised them."

Along with their freedom and the gift of land, a heavy burden was about to descend on the freed people, the master remarked, and so he availed himself "of the deck scene to give the Negroes some advice." He expressed

a great anxiety that they should behave themselves and do well, not only for their own sakes, but for the sake of the black race held in bondage; many of whom were thus held, because their masters believed they were incompetent to take care of themselves, & that liberty would be to them a curse rather than a blessing. My anxious wish was that they would so conduct themselves, as to show by their example, that the descendants of Africa were competent to take care of & govern themselves, & enjoy all the blessings of liberty, & all the other birthrights of man; & thus promote the universal emancipation of that unfortunate & outraged race of the human family.

The emancipator was Edward Coles, a thirty-two-year-old member of a very prominent Virginia family. Dolley Madison was his cousin, and among the Virginians whom the Coles family counted as friends and patrons were Patrick Henry, James Monroe, James Madison, and Thomas Jefferson.

In the massive landscape of slavery, the emancipation of seventeen people may not seem like a significant event. But its symbolism was and is enormous. Coles's emancipation of these slaves was regarded as a cornerstone of the foundation of Illinois. A painting of the event on the river hangs in the capitol rotunda in Springfield, titled *Future Governor Edward Coles Freeing His Slaves While Enroute to Illinois 1819.* In 1822, Coles ran for governor of the state (it was only the second gubernatorial election there) specifically to beat back attempts to make Illinois a slave state, and he narrowly won.

The event is also significant because it was preceded by a debate between Coles and Thomas Jefferson about freeing the enslaved people. Jefferson told Coles *not* to do it, but Coles was determined to give up slave-owning "whatever might be the sacrifices of pecuniary interest, or personal convenience." The difficulties and sacrifices it required were, he declared, nothing but "dust in the balance when weighing the consolation and happiness of doing what you believe right."[3] In the twilit Jeffersonian moral universe, Coles's act blazes and reminds us what American idealism looks like.

Coles had concluded that slavery had to be eradicated when he was a student at the College of William and Mary, Jefferson's alma mater. One of his professors was the Episcopal bishop James Madison (second cousin of the future president). As Coles wrote in a memoir:

> I can never forget [Bishop Madison's] peculiarly embarrassed manner, when lecturing & explaining the rights of man, I asked him, in the simplicity of youth, & under the influence of the new light just shed on me—if this be true how can you hold a slave— how can man be made the property of man? He frankly admitted it could not be rightfully done, & that Slavery was a state of things that could not be justified on principle, & could only be tolerated in our Country, by . . . the difficulty of getting rid of it.

These arguments failed to impress Coles, who had imbibed what Jefferson called "the gas of liberty." Coles said, "I do not believe that man can have a right of property in his fellow man, but on the contrary, that all mankind are endowed by nature with equal rights."[4] At every opportunity he peppered the bishop with ethical queries worthy of the Stoa of the Athenians, or the dining room of Monticello:

> Was it right to do what we believed to be wrong, because our forefathers did it? They may have thought they were doing right, & their conduct may have been consistent with their ideas of propriety. Far different is the character of our conduct, if we believe we do wrong to do what our forefathers did. As to the diffi-

culty of getting rid of our slaves, we could get rid of them with much less difficulty than we did the King of our forefathers. Such inconsistency on our part, & such injustice to our fellow-man, should not be tolerated because it would be inconvenient or difficult to terminate. We should not be deterred by such considerations, & continue to do wrong because wrong had been done in times past; nor ought a man to attempt to excuse himself for doing what he believed wrong, because other men thought it right.

Above all Coles believed in the responsibility of the individual. If you had principles, you had to act by them. Rather than following "the will of the majority," the individual must obey "what he believed to be the will of God, and felt to be the dictates of right deeply implanted in his nature."

As he persisted in his debates with the bishop-professor, Coles found that "in theory" the bishop agreed with him, "but I could not convince him he was bound to carry out his theory, & to act up to his principles, by giving freedom to his Slaves." Bishop Madison looked to the legislature to abolish slavery, as did Jefferson. George Washington expressed the same wish for years, until, weary of waiting for the political climate to change, he decided to defy convention and act on his own to free his slaves.

Coles agreed that he too would prefer a general emancipation sanctioned by the state, but if the people of Virginia

> neglected to do their duty, & tolerated a state of things which was in direct violation of their great fundamental doctrines, I could not reconcile it to my conscience & sense of propriety to participate in it; and being unable to screen my self under such a shelter, from the peltings & upbraidings of my own conscience, and the just censure, as I conceived, of earth & heaven, I could not consent to hold as property what I had no right to.[5]

He kept his intentions secret because he had not yet received title to the slaves allotted to him, and he believed that if his father discovered his intentions, he would not pass title to the slaves.[6] But as soon as his father died, Coles told his family of his intention to free his slaves. They argued against the "folly of throwing away property which was necessary to my comforts, and which my parents all their lives had been labouring to acquire." How would he support himself?

Despite the objections of his family, Coles said his resolution remained "fixed & unalterable": his "aversion to living in the midst and witnessing the horrors of slavery" compelled him to action. Deeply reluctant to leave his home and family, he considered remaining in Virginia and freeing his slaves on his home ground, retaining them as paid free laborers.[7] But his friends were "indignant" at the very idea of it, ominously warning that both he and his freed slaves "would be considered and treated as pests of society, and every effort made to persecute, to injure, and to extirpate us."[8]

Edward's brother Isaac had served as President Jefferson's private secretary, and on Isaac's recommendation Jefferson's successor, James Madison, offered Edward that post in 1809. Eager to put his emancipation plan into action immediately, Coles agonized over accepting the president's offer and decided to reject it so that he could the more quickly free his slaves. Riding into Charlottesville to post his letter turning down the offer, Coles encountered James Monroe, who urged him to accept the job, which, he argued, would familiarize him with the leaders of the western states and provide the necessary background information for an emancipation. Monroe told Coles that "it was particularly desirable that I should associate with non-slaveholding people," whose "habits & customs were so different" from what he had been accustomed to in Virginia, with its "peculiar state of society." (It is interesting that Monroe believed not only that slave and non-slave societies were very different but that it was Virginia that was "peculiar.")[9] At Monroe's urging, Coles took the post, and he later went to Russia as President Madison's special envoy to Tsar Alexander I.

In Madison's White House, Coles felt the giddy sense of luxury at the crest of American society: "the ease and self indulgence of being waited on . . . the luxuries of the table &c &c, in which children are usually brought up by the rich planters of the Southern states, had been . . . increased and confirmed as a habit in me, by a residence of more than five years in the family of the President of the United States." First at home, and then at the White House, Coles said, he received a "double schooling" in the "great & protracted indulgence in the highest walks of ease and luxury in this Country." Later, when he lived without servants, the memory of that ease and luxury "made me feel more sensibly my diminished means of living, & especially the want of being waited on."[10]

Travelers remarked on the laziness slavery induced in white people of all classes. In his *American Geography* the New England clergyman and geographer Jedidiah Morse noted the "dissipation of manners [that] is the fruit of indolence and luxury, which are the fruit of the African slavery."[11] Conversing with "the indolent masters" of Virginia, the French journalist Brissot de Warville heard all their reasons for the impossibility of freeing slaves: "they fear that if the Blacks become free, they will cause trouble; on rendering them free, they know not what rank to assign them in society; whether they shall establish them in a separate district, or send them out of the country. These are the objections which you will hear repeated every where against the idea of freeing them." Brissot de Warville regarded all of this as a tissue of rationalizations, believing that the real obstacle was "the character, the manners and habits of the Virginians. They seem to enjoy the sweat of slaves. They are fond of hunting; they love the display of luxury, and disdain the idea of labour."[12]

Coles's service to Madison only strengthened his determination to carry out an emancipation. Riding through the capital, on numerous occasions President Madison and Coles passed coffles of slaves chained up for the auction block or for the dreaded journey farther south. Coles had the nerve to needle the president on his luck that no foreigners happened to be riding with them: "I have taken the liberty to jeer him, by congratulating him, as the Chief of our great Republic, that he was not then accompanyed by a Foreign Minister, & thus saved the deep mortification of witnessing such a revolting sight in the presence of the representative of a nation, less boastful perhaps of its regard for the rights of man, but more observant of them."[13]

While working at the White House, Coles turned his thoughts to his deferred emancipation plan and decided to recruit an ally, a renowned advocate of liberty who would certainly lend his support, Thomas Jefferson. In July 1814, Coles took up his pen with "hesitation" and "embarrassment" to call Jefferson's attention to "a subject of such magnitude, and so beset with difficulties . . . a general emancipation of the slaves of

Virginia." Expressing "the highest opinion of your goodness and liberality," Coles quickly came to his point: "My object is to entreat and beseech you to exert your knowledge and influence in devising and getting into operation some plan for the gradual emancipation of slavery."

Referring to Jefferson as one of "the revered fathers of all our political and social blessings" and extolling the "valor, wisdom and virtue [that] have done so much in ameliorating the condition of mankind," Coles then sharpened his pen and thrust it straight at the Founder: "it is a duty, as I conceive, that devolves particularly on you, to put into complete practice those hallowed principles contained in that renowned Declaration, of which you were the immortal author, and on which we founded our right to resist oppression and establish our freedom and independence."

Coles did not ask Jefferson to free his slaves immediately, but to formulate a general emancipation plan for Virginia and lay it before the public, backed by his immense prestige. Referring to Jefferson's "great powers of mind and influence," Coles urged him to put forth a plan "to liberate one-half of our fellow beings from an ignominious bondage to the other."[14]

Jefferson put him off. Although slavery presented "a moral reproach to us" and "the love of justice and the love of country" demanded emancipation, he could detect no "serious willingness to relieve them & ourselves from our present condition of moral & political reprobation."[15]

Jefferson said he was waiting for signs of "progress of public sentiment"—signs of slave owners (there was no other "public") changing their minds. "I had always hoped that the younger generation . . . would have sympathized with oppression wherever found, and proved their love of liberty beyond their own share of it," he wrote, though he had in his hands a letter from a member of the younger generation. He insisted that the right moment had not yet arrived because progress "has not been sufficient." He soothed Coles about the delay: "Yet the hour of emancipation is advancing, in the march of time. It will come." Rejecting the idea that individuals should act on their own, he opined that the only way to bring about emancipation was for the legislature to set a date after which all slaves born in Virginia would be trained to take care of themselves—and then be exiled.

Emancipation, he went on, required "a gradual extinction of that species of labour & substitution of another, [to] lessen the severity of the shock which an operation so fundamental cannot fail to produce." The shock, he thought, would be felt both by the Virginia economy and by the freed people. He repeated language he had used twenty-five years earlier: "Brought from their infancy without necessity for thought or forecast, [black people] are by their habits rendered as incapable as children of taking care of themselves, and are extinguished promptly wherever industry is necessary for raising young. In the mean time they are pests in society by their idleness, and the depredations to which this leads them."

He understood why Coles had approached him "as the person who should undertake this salutary but arduous work," but he insisted he was too old. "This enterprise is for the young. . . . It shall have all my prayers, & these are the only weapons of an old man." He urged Coles not to leave Virginia but to "reconcile yourself to your country and its unfortunate condition" and to work "softly but steadily" to bring about the day of emancipation:

> come forward in the public councils, become the missionary of this doctrine truly christian; insinuate & inculcate it softly but steadily, through the medium of writing and conversation; associate others in your labors, and when the phalanx is formed, bring on and press the proposition perseveringly until its accomplishment. . . . And you will be supported by the religious precept, "be not weary in well-doing."*

Believing in the unique capacity of a great leader, Coles wrote to Jefferson again, insisting that he was one of "the only persons who have it in their power effectually to arouse and enlighten the public sentiment, which in matters of this kind ought not to be expected to lead, but to be led." Coles agreed that the public was sunk in apathy and

---

*Jefferson's startling assemblage of Christian aphorisms in this letter—"It shall have all my prayers"; "become the missionary of this doctrine truly christian"; "be not weary in well-doing"— is striking because Coles made no religious references in his initial letter but, rather, a thoroughly secular appeal based on justice and human rights. Possibly, Jefferson had heard from James Madison that Coles was religious, and Jefferson thought Coles could be deflected by images of Christian patience.

inertia, weighted by "habit and interest." It could be jolted from its stupor only by someone such as Jefferson, someone who possessed "a great weight of character, and on whom there devolves in this case a most solemn obligation." To Jefferson's protest that he was too old to take up the cause, Coles riposted: "Your time of life I had not considered as an obstacle to the undertaking. Doctor Franklin, to whom, by the way, Pennsylvania owes her early riddance of the evils of slavery, was as actively and as usefully employed on as arduous duties after he had past your age as he had ever been at any period of his life."*[16]

That was the end of the correspondence. The revolutionary refused to take up the torch, and Coles turned his thoughts to Illinois.

Several years earlier Jefferson had received another powerful and practical appeal to join in an emancipation "experiment" from his former private secretary in Paris, William Short, whom Jefferson called his "adoptive son." Sixteen years younger than Jefferson, Short attended William and Mary, where he studied law under George Wythe as Jefferson had. Short was one of the founders of the Phi Beta Kappa Society and one of America's early millionaires. His father left him a substantial inheritance, which he invested shrewdly in land, canals, and, later, railroads. A relative of Jefferson's wife, he had been a guest at Monticello in the 1770s and 1780s, including the day in 1781 when British raiders ascended the mountain and nearly captured the Founder and when the Jefferson family fled to Poplar Forest. He was at Poplar Forest during the weeks when Jefferson worked on his *Notes on the State of Virginia*—a significant coincidence. For almost certainly Jefferson discussed his ideas, including his racial theories, with Short.

Jefferson noticed that his protégé possessed "a peculiar talent for prying into facts." In 1788 in France, Short visited a château that Jefferson had also visited, and commented on the labor system that had struck Jefferson as a possible replacement for American slavery—the métayage, or sharecropping, system. In two letters written to Jefferson five years apart, in 1793 and 1798—long after Jefferson had returned to

---

*Nor was Jefferson too old to take up the arduous, years-long task of establishing the University of Virginia, an accomplishment he put on his tombstone.

America but when Short was still in Europe—Short turned *Notes on the State of Virginia* around, deploying Jefferson's Enlightenment language in that book to demolish Jefferson's "suspicions" about black inferiority and racial mixing.

In 1793 he seized on a passing remark Jefferson had made in their correspondence—"We are beginning in Virginia to think of tenanting our lands"—and used it as the opening gambit for a discussion of métayage and freeing slaves. He asked Jefferson if "by tenanting you mean that humane and philanthropic system of [renting farms] to the slaves." This was what Jefferson had indeed proposed in 1789 when he told Edward Bancroft of his plan to settle some of his slaves on farms alongside German immigrants. Jefferson had not carried out that plan, but Short contemplated doing it himself:

> I think those who have the misfortune to own slaves, should for the sake of humanity make the experiment. When I shall return to America it is my intention to preach this not only by precept but by example—and for this purpose I intend purchasing a small number—it is a subject my mind goes much on—I have already formed the rules to be observed for exciting in these people the idea of property and the desire to acquire it, which I think would be easily done.

Acting as Short's agent, which he did for the many years when Short lived in Europe, in 1795 Jefferson purchased a thirteen-hundred-acre plantation near Monticello called Indian Camp, later known as Morven.* Short approached the moral problem of slavery as a businessman would, with a free-market approach—"exciting in these people the idea of property and the desire to acquire it." He did not share Jefferson's racial views; indeed, he thought he saw signs of "the perfectibility of the black race" and believed that slaves could, given the chance, work their way out of slavery. For him, the notion of turning slaves into free tenants "seems . . . to unite the very ideas which are formed to give the

---

*It was sold in 1813 to a merchant who renamed it Morven. In 1988, Morven became the residence of John Kluge, for a time the wealthiest person in the United States. In 2001 he bequeathed the property to the University of Virginia.

most heartfelt satisfaction to a pure and virtuous mind—viz. an union of the purest principles of humanity with the prosperity of one's country."

Short was convinced that owners would make more money from renting land to free blacks than from compelling enslaved blacks to work the same acres. He told Jefferson that if a few owners were to try the experiment, keep careful track of their expenses and profits, and publish the results in the newspapers, slaveholders would see that it was in their financial interest to free their slaves. He emphasized the profit motive: "The only way to bring men . . . to desire an event is to show that they have an interest in it. I wish the slaveholders to be attacked by proofs that their interest would not suffer." He expected such an undertaking to encounter difficulties, but they would be overcome: "Whatever may be the result of the first essays, time & repetition will I think infallibly shew the advantage of free, above forced, labor."

The historian Billy Wayson, a close student of the financial dealings between Jefferson and Short, sees the latter as an important transitional figure. Old-line Virginians measured wealth in land, slaves, and honor; Short expresses the emerging mode of capitalism. And it was the capitalist in this pair who argued for using the free market and incentives to end slavery in Virginia.[17]

Like Coles, Short believed in the power of a leader, suggesting that someone of Jefferson's talent and stature could get the experiment started: "Let the enlightened & virtuous citizens, who toil for public instruction, turn the public mind towards this subject, & endeavour to demonstrate that the owners of slaves would gain in point of interest by the change." His letter combined an appeal to Jefferson's Enlightenment principles with a large dose of flattery. He wrote of "a penetrating genius capable of diving into the bosom of futurity"; he said that "this great & momentous object, the transformation of 700,000 slaves into free citizens, [required] the talents of the statesman, the philosopher, the philanthrope, in short all who have any regard to the interests of their country or the rights of humanity." His syntax suggests numerous people, but he knew that Jefferson saw himself as the combination of all those personae.

Short proposed an eminently workable plan for freeing the slaves who were "the most industrious & most ripe for liberty"—allow one day of the week, "or any other portion of their time," in which the slaves could earn money to purchase themselves.[18] Short suggested that the Virginia legislature could pass a law requiring owners to try this plan. He did not say it, but the implication was clear that Jefferson could put this program in place on his own at Monticello. Jefferson made no reply.

Having lived with Jefferson in Paris, Short had gotten to know Sally Hemings and may well have been aware of Jefferson's relationship with her when he boldly attacked Jefferson's core objection to emancipation—his professed aversion to miscegenation. In a startling discourse on the *beauty* of racial mixture, Short compared the loveliness that could be attained by racial mingling to "the perfect mixture of the rose & the lilly." If black people were set free, he foresaw a "gradual mixture" with the happy result that "all of our Southern inhabitants should advance to the middle ground between their present color & the black." The extraordinary word in that sentence is "advance"—a direct challenge to Jefferson's contention that mixing degraded his race. To this also, Jefferson made no reply.

As Edward Coles was making final preparations for his trek to Illinois in the early months of 1819, Jefferson actually had in hand the means to free some Monticello slaves and send them to new lives under Coles's leadership. His old friend the Revolutionary War hero Thaddeus Kosciuszko had died in 1817, leaving the will that bequeathed Jefferson funds to free his slaves and purchase land and farming equipment for them to begin a life on their own. In the spring of 1819, Jefferson pondered what to do about this bequest. Kosciuszko had made him executor of the will, so Jefferson had a legal duty, as well as a personal obligation to his deceased friend, to carry out the terms of the document.*

These terms came as no surprise to Jefferson. He had helped Kosciuszko draft the will, which states, "I hereby authorize my friend, Thomas Jefferson, to employ the whole [bequest] in purchasing Negroes from his own or any others and giving them liberty in my name."

---

*Jefferson asked his friend General John Hartwell Cocke, the owner of Bremo plantation in nearby Fluvanna County, to take over the execution of the will, but Cocke declined.

Kosciuszko's estate had grown to nearly $20,000, and this money was Jefferson's for the taking. But he refused it, even though it would have relieved the debt hanging over him while also relieving him, in part at least, of the "moral reproach" of slavery.[19]

Coles, Kosciuszko, and William Short all saw the appalling corruption of slavery and its burgeoning power. The only force that could turn the tide was, they believed, the sacred, incorruptible idealism of the Revolution. A leader wielding that instrument could conquer any evil—and so they turned to Jefferson. "All mankind are endowed by nature with equal rights," Coles wrote to Jefferson. No one knew this language better than Jefferson—indeed, he had helped to create it—and he replied to Coles, in kind, that "the flame of liberty had been kindled in every breast, & had become as it were the vital spirit of every American." But note the past-perfect tense: he was evoking a Revolutionary spirit that had come and gone. His supplicants did not realize how much Jefferson had changed.

If Jefferson had accepted Kosciuszko's bequest, as much as half of it would have gone not to Jefferson but, in effect, to his slaves—to the purchase price for land, livestock, equipment, and transportation to get them started in a place such as Illinois or Ohio. Moreover, the slaves most suited for immediate emancipation—smiths, coopers, carpenters, the most skilled farmers—were the very ones whom Jefferson most wanted to keep. He also shrank from any public identification with the cause of emancipation.

As U.S. minister to France in the 1780s, Jefferson had begun to see slave labor as the most powerful and most convenient engine of the American enterprise. With a class of slaves, the United States could produce the commodities (tobacco and rice) needed to pay down the country's debt to Great Britain. And then in the next decade, on his home ground, Jefferson began to perceive the pure financial value of owning slaves. Farming would always be a species of "gambling," in his memorable image, but the ownership of slaves, and the existence of a robust secondary market for slaves, provided not only a safety net but an investment opportunity.

We have seen how he worked out his 4 percent formula—the annual increase in the value of his slaveholdings. It had long been accepted that slaves were assets that could be seized for debt, but Jefferson turned this around when he used slaves as collateral for that very large loan he took out from the Dutch banking house in order to rebuild Monticello. He pioneered the monetizing of slaves, just as he pioneered the industrialization and diversification of slavery with his nailery, textile factory, coopering shop, short-lived tinsmithing business, and gristmill. Far from regarding slaves as childlike and incompetent, he realized they were highly amenable to training in specialized skills, and he put into effect a long-term program to staff his plantation with skilled people for decades. He took the 1789 emancipation plan he had outlined in Paris—which would train slaves to prepare them for citizenship—and turned it on its head.

Nevertheless, Jefferson's reputation as an emancipator has remained more or less intact. "No Virginian (and probably no American) did more than Thomas Jefferson to oppose slavery," writes Robert Turner of the University of Virginia School of Law.[20] This belief that he was a frustrated emancipator rests in large part on the letters he wrote to progressives who questioned him about emancipation—or at any rate on the snippets from these letters that have received wide circulation thanks to the modern publication of Jefferson's papers. Many of them have been compiled on the Monticello website under the rubric "Quotations on Slavery and Emancipation." Beautifully composed, in stirring, evocative prose, the letters make inspiring reading.

The language of these letters is remarkably uniform from the 1780s to his death in 1826, and remarkably similar to the conversation Jefferson had with the Duke de La Rochefoucauld-Liancourt at Monticello in 1796. Jefferson forcefully states his personal commitment to the ideal of emancipation: in the online compendium he mentions his willingness to sacrifice anything for emancipation in four different documents. He states his concern for the welfare of his slaves while saying that the black people remain incompetent. He alludes to the horror of racial mixing. Whenever someone presents him with evidence of intelligence and achievement among black people, he dismisses the evidence.

In replying to Coles, Jefferson reached far back into the past, repeating the old rumor from the 1770s that a Quaker experiment in freeing slaves had failed miserably, that the Quakers "had set free a parcel of lazy, worthless negroes."[21] In fact, the Quaker emancipation and many others just like it in Delaware and Maryland had been extremely successful, but Jefferson continued to circulate the useful fiction that blacks "are by their habits rendered as incapable as children of taking care of themselves." The historian William W. Freehling writes that in Delaware and Maryland "black freedmen formed an orderly working class," but in the minds of Jefferson and other slaveholders "the phenomenon of orderly free blacks *could* not happen and therefore *had* not happened."[22]

When Jefferson walked around Philadelphia in company with Kosciuszko in the 1790s, he encountered a thriving class of free black Americans. As the historian Richard Newman writes: "A census of the free black community conducted by Pennsylvania abolitionists in 1790 . . . found stable black families, hard-working people of color, and a desire among free blacks and newly liberated enslaved people to master both literacy and marketable skills."[23] As we have seen, at Monticello he had mechanics capable of building him a carriage, capable of comprehending and making real his designs for woodwork (which he adjudged the finest in the country), skilled at smithing, painting, glazing, coopering, and so on. His cooks, trained at the White House by French professionals, could easily have made a living as free people. Moreover, these skills were all the more valuable to him, as to all Virginia's planters, because white artisans were so scarce, so costly, and so often drunk. According to one estimate, by the mid-nineteenth century about 80 percent of Virginia's artisans were enslaved or free blacks.[24] Nothing could be more convenient than owning an entire community of skilled working people. Having seen all this with his own eyes, Jefferson continued to speak of the "imbecility" of blacks.[25]

In his letters and in his conversations Jefferson blamed slavery on the slaves. On an 1807 visit to Monticello a British diplomat, Augustus John Foster, was treated to a disquisition on African-American stupidity:

> He told me, also, that the Negroes have, in general, so little foresight that though they receive blankets very thankfully from their masters on the commencement of winter and use them to keep off the cold, yet when the warm weather returns they will frequently cast them off, without a thought as to what may be-

come of them, wherever they may happen to be at the time, and then not seldom lose them in the woods or the fields from mere carelessness.[26]

In fact, the slaves had no blankets, because Jefferson's overseers had not distributed any. In a memorandum to a new overseer, a year before the diplomat's visit, Jefferson wrote, "I allow them a best striped blanket every three years. Mr. Lilly had failed in this; but the last year Mr. Freeman gave blankets to one-third of them."[27] Jefferson knew one thing to be true but said another to a credulous outsider.

In one instance, Jefferson admitted to a friend that a response he had given to a French progressive was not entirely honest. In the summer of 1808, Henri Grégoire, bishop of Blois, sent Jefferson a copy of his new book, *De la littérature des Nègres*, later translated into English as *An Enquiry Concerning the Intellectual and Moral Faculties and Literature of Negroes*. As its title implies, Grégoire's *Enquiry* sought to discredit the notion of black inferiority through a survey of literary achievements. Jefferson responded fulsomely:

> Be assured that no person living wishes more sincerely than I do, to see a complete refutation of the doubts I have myself entertained and expressed on the grade of understanding allotted them by nature, and to find that in this respect they are on par with ourselves. . . . On this subject they are gaining daily in the opinions of nations, and hopeful advances are making towards their re-establishment on an equal footing with the other colors of the human family. I pray you therefore to accept my thanks for the many instances you have enabled me to observe of respectable intelligence in that race of men, which cannot fail to have effect in hastening the day of their relief.

But to a friend who also knew Grégoire, Jefferson said that he was utterly unimpressed by the anthology, which was the product, he thought, of the bishop's "credulity," which was why, he added, "I wrote him . . . a very soft answer."[28]

Jefferson claimed he was waiting to find what he called a "natural aristocrat" among the blacks, a scholar such as himself. When candidates did present themselves—the poet Phillis Wheatley and the mathematician Benjamin Banneker—Jefferson dismissed and derided their achievements. In *Notes* he had advanced the idea that black people were "in reason much inferior" because he had never known of a black person "capable of tracing and comprehending the investigations of Euclid." But when Coles went to Illinois, he took enslaved farmers and made them yeomen; Kosciuszko had farmers in mind. Neither looked for Euclidean scholars.

Always, Jefferson told his supplicants to look toward the future with hope. The day of emancipation was coming. It would arrive when white people experienced "a revolution in public opinion," as he wrote to yet another correspondent who brought up emancipation. But in an 1805 letter to an intimate, his private secretary, William Burwell, he wrote, "I have long since given up the expectation of any early provision for the extinguishment of slavery among us."[29] The governments of all the Southern states were in the hands of slaveholders whose sense of justice and morality was defined not by the soaring language of the Revolution but by their pocketbooks. Among this class, Jefferson said to Burwell, "interest is morality." As a senator from Georgia declared: "You cannot prevent slavery—neither laws moral or human can do it. Men will be governed by their interest, not the law."[30]

Around the time that Coles was struggling to settle his freed people in Illinois, Jefferson wrote to a congressman expressing sentiments that Coles might have written: "I can say, with conscious truth, that there is not a man on earth who would sacrifice more than I would to relieve us from this heavy reproach"—he meant the moral reproach of slavery. "The cession of that kind of property, for so it is misnamed, is a bagatelle which would not cost me a second thought."[31] But to his son-in-law he wrote just eight weeks later: "I consider a woman who brings a child every two years as more profitable than the best man of the farm. What she produces is an addition to the capital."[32] And when he was mulling over what he would do about Kosciuszko's will, he wrote to a manager:

> a child raised every 2. years is of more profit than the crop of the best laboring man. in this, as in all other cases, providence has made our duties and our interests coincide perfectly. . . . with respect therefore to our women & their children I must pray you

to inculcate upon the overseers that it is not their labor, but their increase which is the first consideration with us.[33]

Jefferson composed one of his most famous metaphors to express his fear of a murderous slave rebellion: "we have the wolf by the ears and feel the danger of either holding or letting him loose."[34] But Jefferson also thought of the slave as a creature that inexhaustibly produces gold. His wolf metaphor has been widely published, but an unpublished letter written in 1810 records another remark that is less known: upon learning that a relative thought of selling his slaves, Jefferson said that "it wou'd never do to destroy the goose."[35]

Jefferson deployed his most soaring language not where it would do the most good—in a public campaign to awaken the conscience of the slaveholders—but to soothe would-be emancipators while he deflected their petitions. The truth was that slavery would end not when South Carolina planters suddenly started to sing "Amazing Grace" but when it ceased to be profitable, and Jefferson helped to make that day recede into the very, very distant future as vast new territories opened up just over the horizon. When in 1803 Jefferson acquired Louisiana for the United States and doubled the size of the country, the question arose: Would we have slavery in this new land? As the Senate began debate on the purchase, President Jefferson sent a secret note to his floor manager, instructing the senator to insert a clause in the bill for establishing a government in Louisiana: "Slaves shall be admitted into the territory."[36]

17

"Utopia in Full Reality"

On the summit of Monticello, Jefferson arranged everything beautifully. But outside the plantation's gates, devils prowled. His daughter saw them: "the country is over run with those trafickers in human blood the negro buyers."[1] The black people of Virginia had been fully monetized. From Albemarle County and other places in the Old South, coffles of people were driven west and south. Between 1810 and 1861, a million slaves were taken to the interior in a forced migration "dwarfing the transatlantic slave trade that had carried Africans" to America, as Ira Berlin has written.*[2]

At its extreme edge the pursuit of happiness bends morality as gravity bends light. With the free market in people fully open and unrestricted, Jefferson's grandson Jeff Randolph was aghast at a peculiarly vile "branch of profit" being avidly pursued: "It is a practice, and an increasing practice, in parts of Virginia, to rear slaves for market," he said in 1832. He rose before Virginia's legislature to ask, with soaring oratory such as his grandfather could have unleashed but did not: "How can an honorable mind, a patriot, and a lover of his country, bear to see this Ancient Dominion, rendered illustrious by the noble devotion and

---

*The historian Steven Deyle writes: "The United States banned the African slave trade but not slavery itself, opening the door to the development of an even larger American trade in slaves. Virginia slave owners used their extensive political power in the early Republic to promote this new traffic, which quickly answered their needs. The domestic slave trade transformed southern society, making human chattel the most valuable form of property in the South" (Deyle, "'Abominable' New Trade").

patriotism of her sons in the cause of liberty, converted into one grand menagerie, where men are to be reared for the market, like oxen?"[3]

This is the narrative beneath Manifest Destiny, a realm of actuality experienced by people at the bottom of American society and viewed only in fragments by those above them, an actuality that formed its own narrative and that survives perpetually: African-American music, James Baldwin wrote more than a century later, "begins on the auction block."[4]

As early as the 1780s, Jefferson had his eye on the vast "country before us," which lay waiting for Americans "to fill with people and with happiness."[5] Chafing at the borders that restrained expansion, he wrote in 1801, during the first year of his presidency:

> it is impossible not to look forward to distant times, when our rapid multiplication will expand itself beyond those limits, & cover the whole Northern, if not the Southern continent with a people speaking the same language, governed in similar forms, & by similar laws: nor can we contemplate, with satisfaction, either blot or mixture on that surface.[6]

The time was not so distant.

The following year, President Jefferson received reports that Spain intended to hand over to France its enormous Louisiana territory, including the important port of New Orleans. A crisis arose when Spain transferred the territory to France and, in October 1802, restricted American trade through New Orleans. Jefferson ordered the U.S. minister in Paris, Robert Livingston, to open negotiations with Napoleon to buy the city and the region surrounding it. France responded with an offer to sell the entire territory, and by the end of 1803 the huge Louisiana Purchase came into American hands. For $15 million the United States acquired some 827,000 square miles of land from the Mississippi River to the Rocky Mountains.

When Jefferson had written in 1801 that no "blot or mixture" could be allowed to mar the surface of the West, he meant, of course, the presence of blacks. But in Paris, Livingston observed that "slavery alone can fertilize those colonies," so Jefferson reversed his policy of racial exclusion.[7] As President Jefferson and Congress considered how to absorb and govern the new territory, Jefferson instructed Senator John

Breckinridge of Kentucky (a Virginia native who was shortly to become Jefferson's attorney general) to allow African-American slaves in the territory, thus becoming, as Robert McColley writes, "the father of slavery in Louisiana."[8]

Slavery already existed in Louisiana. The Spanish had slaves, so did the French, and so did Americans who had crossed into Spanish territory to establish plantations. They imported slaves from Africa and the Caribbean, and they loudly demanded that no restrictions be placed on this commerce, insisting that "African laborers" were "all important to the very existence of our country." Without them, "cultivation must cease."[9]

Just a few years earlier, in 1798, Congress had debated the question of allowing slavery into Mississippi when it had been acquired by treaty from Spain. Confronted by human-rights arguments that slavery was "an evil in direct hostility to the principles of our Government," slaveholders countered with soothing arguments about "amelioration" and "diffusion." A Virginia senator explained: "if the slaves of the Southern States were permitted to go into the Western country . . . there would be a great probability in ameliorating their condition, which could never be done whilst they were crowded together as they are now in the Southern States." Jefferson's protégé Senator Wilson Cary Nicholas of Virginia added that Congress would be "doing a service" to the slaves by admitting them to Mississippi because "in time it might be safe to carry into effect the plan which certain philanthropists have so much at heart . . . the emancipation of this class of men."[10] Only from the mouth of a slaveholder could the word "philanthropist" come out as a taunt.

But when Louisiana beckoned, ameliorating the condition of blacks was not on the planters' minds. They sent an open letter to Congress describing the nature of the labor they wanted done. The levees on the Mississippi River "can only be kept in repair by those whose natural constitutions and habits of labor enable them to resist the combined efforts of a deleterious moisture, and a degree of heat intolerable to whites. . . . [T]he labor is great." Jefferson had a letter from a planter describing the territory as a "vast swamp unfit for any creatures outside of fishes, reptiles, and insects." Senator Jonathan Dayton of New Jersey said: "Slavery must be tolerated, it must be established in that country, or it can never be inhabited. White people cannot cultivate it."[11] A

Georgia senator, himself a rice planter, said that restricting slavery in Louisiana "will depreciate . . . lands there fifty per cent."[12]

South Carolina, anticipating a bonanza and taking the lead, as it would in 1861, reopened the international slave trade at Charleston even before the Louisiana Purchase was finalized. The traders knew that the Constitution authorized an end to the international slave trade in 1808, and they seized the day.

As slavery loomed over Louisiana, no less a figure than Thomas Paine—he of "These are the times that try men's souls"—wrote directly to his old Revolutionary comrade in 1805, begging President Jefferson not to bring "poor negroes to work the land in a state of slavery and wretchedness."[13] At this fresh moment of decision, one man might change the course of events. In his letter Paine summoned the ghost of Jefferson's old self:

> I recollect when in France that you spoke of a plan of making the negroes tenants on a plantation, that is, allotting each negroe family a quantity of land for which they were to pay to the owner a certain quantity of produce. I think that numbers of our free negroes might be provided for in this manner in Louisiana. The best way that occurs to me is for Congress to give them their passage to New Orleans, then for them to hire themselves out to the planters for one or two years; they would by this means learn plantation business, after which to place them on a tract of land as before mentioned. A great many good things may now be done.

But the question of the status of free blacks in the new American possession had already been decided.

The governor in New Orleans, William Claiborne, reported his concern about a long-established militia organization, the Free Colored Battalion of New Orleans, which had fought in the Patriot cause against the British during the Revolution. This free black militia carried out many important tasks: they were the ones who, when floods threatened the levees, turned out to make them stronger; they fought fires in New Orleans; they chased runaway slaves. When the militia dispatched a letter to Claiborne praising "the Justice and Liberality" of the American character and declaring their own "sincere attachment to the Government of the United States," to which "we shall offer our services with fidelity and Zeal," their offer reached the highest level of the government.[14] Jefferson and his cabinet decided to allow the militia to believe, for the moment, that the justice and liberality of the United States would descend on them; in his notes of a cabinet meeting Jefferson recorded the decision that the militia "be confirmed in their posts, and treated favorably, till a better settled state of things shall permit us to let them neglect themselves."[15] But more than benign neglect was to occur: the aspirations of the free blacks in New Orleans were to be crushed.

The congressional debate over slavery in Louisiana presented Jefferson with an opportunity. For a brief time, the political will existed in Congress to stem the tide of slavery; an outright ban on slave importations—in a proposed bill that was not supported by the president—just barely failed to pass. Two decades earlier, Jefferson the younger radical had written the terms of the Ordinance of 1784, banning slavery in any new territory of the United States: "After the year 1800 . . . there shall be neither slavery nor involuntary servitude." Such a law would have put slavery on a timetable; those who held slaves would have had sixteen years to figure a way out of it. But the ordinance—which would have included Mississippi and Alabama—failed to pass in the Continental Congress when just one delegate from New Jersey missed the vote due to illness. Jefferson himself wrote that "the fate of millions unborn" had been determined by the absence of this one man.

After the 1784 limitation on slavery failed to pass, as the historian Joyce Appleby has written, Jefferson "backed away from attacking the institution as his power to do something about it increased."[16] As president, Jefferson could have proposed something similar for Louisiana—an emancipation plan with a horizon of fifteen, twenty, or twenty-five years, permitting slavery to "fertilize" the province but then requiring that it diffuse itself into oblivion, as he said he wanted to happen. But no such message emanated from the White House.

Congress defied Jefferson, allowing the movement of slaves into Louisiana but with a set of restrictions that outraged slaveholders. The laws approved in 1804 "held out promise for severely curbing the growth of slavery in the western reaches of the new American empire," as one historian summarizes them. The importation of slaves was allowed, but not by traders, only by an actual owner, "a citizen of the United States, removing into said Territory for actual settlement." If a Virginian wished to open a sugar plantation manned by his slaves, he had to go and be there himself. Furthermore, the law forbade an owner to sell his slaves in Louisiana.[17]

Those already in the territory blustered, threatened secession, and raised the dire image of their welcoming Napoleon back to Louisiana, for they could see the congressional intent to ban slavery in the future. On the other hand, Congress knew that only slaveholders had the ready cash to establish new Louisiana plantations quickly.[18] In response to pressure from slave owners, and equally enormous pressure to have the territory settled as quickly as possible with American citizens in a "torrent of emigration," Congress added a sunset clause allowing the restrictions to expire after one year. John Quincy Adams remarked sardonically, "slavery in a normal sense is an evil; but as connected with commerce it has important uses."[19]

"Diffusion" might have worked had President Jefferson put some muscle into the temporary restrictions on slavery. Without such an effort, however, diffusion led not to the weakening of slavery but to the opposite—the strengthening of slavery and the weakening of the Union. As Ira Berlin writes, "Slaveholders drove small farmers . . . to the margins, [and] in the absence of competitors, slaveholders solidified their rule."[20] In William Freehling's assessment the Louisiana Purchase, with its "gigantic massing of slaves," resulted in a "republican catastrophe." As large planters surged into the territory, "little of the richest Louisiana or Arkansas dirt remained for Jefferson's backbone of liberty, slaveless white farmers."[21]

Some years later John Drayton, the South Carolina governor who had campaigned to get slavery into Louisiana, expressed "the firm conviction that a separate confederacy of the slave-holding States is the object now aimed at & will be steadily pursued." The necessary elements for such a confederacy were already in place, he said: "its chivalric population, its valuable products & an unrestrictic [sic] commerce" would create "utopia in full reality."[22] His image of a "chivalric" society is revealing and chilling: slaveholders had an extraordinarily romantic view of themselves, seeing themselves not as slave drivers but as knights, though they rode on the backs of slaves.

Jefferson, in his capacity as secretary of state, had been in charge of the patent office when Eli Whitney sent in his plans for the cotton gin in 1793. He was transfixed. He peppered the inventor with questions: "How many hands"—meaning how many slaves—"does it take to operate this machine?" "What quantity of cotton has it cleaned?" When Whitney received his patent for the cotton engine, Jefferson called it the most important invention the nation had produced. He had seen the future.

Jefferson saw slavery as congruent with his Enlightenment conception of the world and a quasi-religious vision that he articulated from time to time. Pious Christians denounced him as an atheist, but Jefferson did have a deistic belief in the workings of God; he could see the hand of the deity, for example, in the evident prosperity of the United States. In his first inaugural address he spoke of "acknowledging and adoring an overruling Providence which *by its dispensations* proves that it delights in the happiness of man here and his greater happiness hereafter [emphasis added]." Near the conclusion of the address he returned to that theme: "May that Infinite Power which rules the destinies of the universe, lead our councils to what is best, and give them a favorable issue for your peace and prosperity."

On his home ground in Virginia and at Monticello, Jefferson saw divine agency in the "increase" of black children, his human assets: "a child raised every 2. years is of more profit than the crop of the best laboring man. in this, as in all other cases, providence has made our duties and our interests coincide perfectly." He ordered his manager to take special care in the treatment of the "breeding" women.[23] There is little or no distance between this "providential" calculation and "the branch of profit" Jeff Randolph reviled—"to rear slaves for market"— but Jefferson had thoroughly rationalized what he was doing.

The business of slavery was conducted in such a "sooty atmosphere" that morality vanished in the smoke. Near the end of 1815, Jefferson sold a three-year-old girl from Monticello named Sally, the daughter of Aggy, to his overseer at Poplar Forest, Jeremiah Goodman, for $150.[24] Jefferson and Goodman agreed that Sally would remain with her mother at Monticello. It seemed strange that an overseer would spend $150 to own a girl who lived ninety miles away, but in later records Sally turns up with the surname Goodman, so the overseer was buying his own daughter. A year and a half later Goodman changed his mind: he wanted to sell Sally back to Jefferson for $180, so the two men decided that the sale was "annulled." One day Sally had a father; the next day she did not. In such a world, such things happen and no one is responsible. The founding has many fathers, but slavery is an orphan.

The long list of people who begged Jefferson to do something about slavery includes resounding names—Lafayette, Kosciuszko, Thomas Paine—along with the less-known Edward Coles, William Short, and the Colored Battalion of New Orleans. They all came to Jefferson speaking the Revolution's language of universal human rights, believing that the ideals of the Revolution actually meant something.

Deeply reluctant to judge a Founder as wanting in moral force, modern commentators retreat to a range of adjectives such as "flawed," "human," "contradictory," "paradoxical," "compartmentalized," while preserving for Jefferson what the historian Alan Taylor calls "a fundamental core of naive innocence."[25] But at Jefferson's core there lay a fundamental belief in the righteousness of his power. Jefferson wore racism like a suit of armor, knowing that it would always break the sharpest swords of the idealists.

Lafayette had a powerful insight, detecting in slaveholders a combination of "prejudices, Habits, and Calculations."[26] This combination acted as their engine, in place of a conscience. Racism ratified their power, as did the dispensations of Providence. They were precursors of the Ayn Rand protagonist of the twentieth century. One of Rand's admirers wrote gratefully to her that she had "the courage to tell the masses . . . you are inferior and all the improvements in your condition which you simply take for granted you owe to the effort of men who are better than you." Rand herself composed a sentence that could have come from the pen of a Southern planter: "The man at the bottom who, left to himself, would starve in his hopeless ineptitude, contributes nothing to those above him, but receives the bonus of all their brains."[27]

Jefferson fashioned a system at Monticello that worked supremely well; he lacked for nothing in the many long years he lived there before, during, and after his presidency. And yet the consensus among historians has been that he was weighted down and eventually dragged under by slavery. Ellis expressed this consensus when he wrote:

> His lifestyle, his standard of living itself at Monticello, were all dependent upon the institution of slavery. . . . It was an ironic form of dependence, because he went bankrupt, as did a significant percentage of the planter class in Virginia, in the late eighteenth and nineteenth centuries. Slavery in Virginia was not working as an economic institution.[28]

Such assessments come from a close study of what Jefferson said, but not from the evidence of his ledgers. "I am not fit to be a farmer with the kind of labour we have," he once famously complained. But then we find him reporting in 1800 that "my nailery . . . still flourishes greatly, employing 16. boys at a clear profit of about 4. to 500£ annually." Feeling pinched, he "executed a mortgage to you on 80. slaves, which at a sale would fetch 4000£." He settled one debt in installments, "the last of which will be paid off by this year's crop"—a crop that was of course planted, cultivated, and harvested by his black slaves. Would white men have done better, produced more? Actually, no: he found white tenant farmers, when he could locate any, to be lazy and pigheaded, leaving the fields "in a slovenly and disgusting state; and to get the tenants to aim at something better is extremely difficult. . . . it is easy enough to get tenants if you will let them destroy the land."[29]

We simply cannot believe Jefferson's complaints about his slaves, which fit into his pattern of shifting blame to others for his own mistakes and weaknesses. During his presidency Jefferson averred that the slave's "burden on his master [is] daily increasing," yet as the economic historian Steven Hochman has found, "during his presidency Jefferson's nailery and his farms provided an income that should have met reasonable expectations. The debit side of Jefferson's balance sheet was where he had his problems."

In 1801, the first year of his presidency, Jefferson overspent his salary by some $8,600, earning $25,000 and spending $33,636.84. He laid out $3,100 for a new carriage and horses, wishing to have "first-rate" steeds, and, Hochman adds, "a particularly large item was $2,797.38 for wines."[30] Debt never prevented Jefferson from doing anything he wanted to do. He built Monticello and then rebuilt it on a grander scale; then he built his Poplar Forest mansion; then he spent some $30,000 on a mill and canal near Monticello. The historian Herbert E. Sloan writes, "Had he not poured some $30,000 into his flour mill and local navigation improvements, he might have withstood some of the pressures that crushed him."[31] The consensus must be turned around: with Jefferson miring himself in debt, his slaves kept him afloat.

The blow that finally destroyed Jefferson's finances came not from the supposedly burdensome slaves, whose labors were financing his lifestyle and the modernization of his plantation, but from his in-law Wilson Cary Nicholas, the former senator. In 1818, when Nicholas was heavily invested in land speculations, he asked Jefferson to co-sign a $20,000 note—and then promptly went bankrupt. Even so, Jefferson managed to stagger along at Monticello.

At its extreme edge idealism becomes rude, and so it was when the Marquis de Lafayette visited Monticello in 1824, on his final, highly emotional, triumphal tour of the nation he helped to create, and he pressed Jefferson about his failure to do anything to end slavery. Before modern commentators deride any criticism of Jefferson as rank "presentism," they should consider the appeal that came from the lips of Lafayette, a hero very much of that time.

When Lafayette arrived at Monticello, he fell into Jefferson's arms. An enormous throng, gathered on the lawn of the mansion, settled into a profound silence as the two heroes embraced and wept. In the following weeks the old friends took daily carriage rides around the mountain, driven by a slave, Israel Gillette Jefferson, who left a memoir: "I well recollect a conversation he had with the great and good Lafayette, when he visited this country . . . as it was of personal interest to me and mine."[32] He continued:

> On the occasion I am now about to speak of . . . the conversation turned upon the condition of the colored people—the slaves. . . .
> [M]y ears were eagerly taking in every sound that proceeded from the venerable patriot's mouth.
> Lafayette remarked that he thought that the slaves ought to be

free; that no man could rightly hold ownership in his brother man; that he gave his best services to and spent his money in behalf of the Americans freely because he felt that they were fighting for a great and noble principle—the freedom of mankind; that instead of all being free a portion were held in bondage (which seemed to grieve his noble heart). . . . Mr. Jefferson replied that he thought the time would come when the slaves would be free, but did not indicate when or in what manner they would get their freedom. He seemed to think that the time had not then arrived.

At Jefferson's death, his slaves paid the price for the master's first-rate acquisitions and his relative's speculations in western lands. The families of Jefferson's most devoted servants were split apart. Onto the auction block went Caroline Hughes, the nine-year-old daughter of Jefferson's gardener Wormley Hughes. Also sold away from her family was Isabella Fossett, age eight. One family was divided up among eight different buyers, another family among seven buyers.[33]

Joseph Fossett, the Monticello blacksmith, was among the handful of slaves freed in Jefferson's will, but Jefferson left Fossett's family enslaved. In the six months between Jefferson's death and the auction of his property, Fossett tried to strike bargains with white families in Charlottesville to purchase his wife and six of his seven children. His oldest child (born, ironically, in the White House itself) had already been given to Jefferson's grandson. Fossett found sympathetic buyers for his wife, his son Peter, and two other children, but he watched the auction of three young daughters to different buyers. One of them, seventeen-year-old Patsy, immediately escaped from her new master, a University of Virginia official.

Joseph Fossett spent ten years at his anvil and forge earning the money to buy back his wife and children. By the late 1830s he had the cash in hand to reclaim Peter, then about twenty-one, but the owner reneged on the deal. Compelled to leave Peter in slavery and having lost three of their daughters, Joseph and Edith Fossett departed Charlottesville for Ohio around 1840.

Jefferson said that free blacks and whites could not live "under the same government," but even during his lifetime they were doing so right in Albemarle County. Just north of Charlottesville a family of free blacks owned more than two hundred acres in the settlement that expanded and came to be known as Free State. One free black who lived there, Zachariah Bowles, occasionally worked at Monticello. He married one of Jefferson's most important household servants, Critta Hemings. After Jefferson's death his grandson Francis Eppes purchased Mrs. Bowles and immediately set her free so that she could live with her husband. Their landholdings were substantial, amounting to nearly one hundred acres.

For decades historians have been trying without success to discover what happened to Jefferson's two missing children, Harriet and Beverly Hemings, who left Monticello in 1822 with their father's consent. Harriet and Beverly apparently never told their families about their lineage. The safest thing to do was to disappear and abolish your genealogy. When the DNA findings of a link between Jefferson and Hemings made headlines around the world in 1998, no descendants of theirs emerged to claim kinship.

The last known sighting of Beverly Hemings occurred in Petersburg, Virginia, about twenty miles south of Richmond, in the early 1830s. After successfully creating a new identity, Beverly returned incognito to the land of slavery and boldly made a very public appearance— giving a demonstration of the new scientific sensation, ballooning.[34]

The antebellum equivalent of a space shuttle launch, balloon ascents drew enormous, awestruck crowds, so this aeronaut ran the risk of being recognized. But he must have had enough confidence in his new identity, and more confidence in the fact that he looked white, to reenter Virginia like a spy venturing into an occupied country. Beverly's metamorphosis from plantation slave to aviation pioneer is truly extraordinary. We know of his balloon ascent from an allusion to it in the memoir of the Monticello blacksmith Isaac Granger, who witnessed the event; it may have been the one advertised in the July 3, 1834, Petersburg *American Constellation*—"A 4th of July Balloon Ascension" by "a splendid balloon, 30 feet high, and 58 feet in circumference."

Beverly's new life as a balloonist brings to mind a seemingly trivial detail in the Monticello records: he had worked there as a cooper, a maker of barrels. Barrels were a valuable commodity, and Jefferson had his slaves produce them for sale off the plantation. Coopering was also a key skill in ballooning. Balloonists had to fabricate an intricate but sturdy system of wooden barrels, which they filled with water and a carefully measured amount of sulfuric acid. The ensuing reaction within the casks, which had to be very tightly made, produced hydrogen gas. Leather pipes directed the hydrogen into the balloon. Thus the successful ascent of a balloon depended on the quality of the chemistry and the coopering.[35]

Not having seen his family for some ten years or more, Beverly must have sent advance word of the balloon ascent to his brother Madison Hemings, who turned up from Charlottesville. Madison was legally a free man, but he was living in the land of slavery and was yoked by the restrictions fastened on free people of color. Beverly was legally still a slave because Jefferson had never freed him, but ironically Madison saw him in his post-Monticello life as an aeronaut, doing something that not only attained the height of adventure but symbolized human liberation. A contemporary poem paid envious tribute to one early balloonist, an Icarus who never fell:

> He's gone off to glory, where he's free from all sorrow,
> If he's not there to-night, he'll be there to-morrow,
> And Heaven I'm sure has forgiven his sin,
> For I saw the sky open, and saw him pop in.[36]

Beverly disappeared so thoroughly from the historical record that he might as well have popped into the sky. He had achieved in fact what the balloon poet could only imagine—a vanishing.

18

Jefferson Anew

All societies can lose their moorings.
—*William Styron*

Thomas Jefferson quite consciously shaped his legacy. Like many other of our Founding Fathers, he organized and stored his voluminous correspondence to preserve his point of view for the future. But with equal deliberation and care he made alterations to Monticello during his presidency, knowing that when he retired, influential visitors would ascend his mountain and describe to others what they'd seen. He redesigned the entrance hall as a museum displaying objects that supported the portrait of him as an American *philosophe* with wide-ranging intellectual interests and many notable accomplishments. With displays of dazzling, exotic artifacts brought back from the West by Lewis and Clark, he drew attention to the Louisiana Purchase, by which he had not only doubled the size of the United States but made real the dream of establishing a continent-wide empire of liberty.

Slavery could ruin the image. As mentioned earlier, Jefferson's initial design of the mansion "removed from sight as much as possible" all functions that would appear "less agreeable." His redesign of the Monticello landscape further hid slavery from visitors. A new approach road, less direct than the old one, "skirted the main agricultural endeavors [and] avoided all the domestic and industrial sites," writes Sara Bon-Harper, one of Monticello's archaeologists. With the new arrangement of trees and roads, Jefferson could control almost everything his guests saw.[1] There would be no accidental glimpses of overseers and slaves. Jefferson's plan, Bon-Harper continues, "effectively shielded the visitor from any views of industry or enslavement." A guest who arrived via the new road in 1809, Margaret Bayard Smith, sensed that something was missing: "No vestige of the labour of man appeared; nature seemed to hold an undisturbed dominion. . . . I cast my eyes around, but could discern nothing but untamed woodland."[2]

The correspondence Jefferson saved has allowed posterity to portray him as an implacable enemy of slavery and a frustrated emancipationist, thanks to his fervent early views on the subject and thanks to the "soft answers" he sent to his abolitionist correspondents to soothe and baffle them. Meanwhile, in the public sphere, where he came to wield enormous power and influence, he did nothing to hasten slavery's end during his terms as a diplomat, secretary of state, vice president, and twice-elected president or after his presidency. After his death, when the Virginia Assembly fruitlessly bandied about emancipation plans, a pro-slavery legislator mockingly noted Jefferson's absence from this field of battle, but his mockery expressed a truth: "When Hercules died, there was no man left to lift his club."[3]

The difficult truth is that for decades Jefferson skillfully played both sides of the slavery question, maintaining his reputation as a liberal while doing nothing. One letter from 1796, long overlooked, caused excitement and confusion among specialists when it was rediscovered in 1997, for in it Jefferson seemed to favor the education of slave children—in integrated schools. It's worth looking closely at what he wrote, keeping in mind that Jefferson the lawyer always worded his correspondence meticulously. After conjuring the possibility of "instruction of the slaves . . . mixed with those of free condition," he added that it was questionable whether such a plan should be extended beyond slave children "destined to be free"—an all-important clause.[4] Given that in 1796 *no* slaves were destined to be free, this "proposal" cannot even be called hypothetical. Jefferson could only have had in mind that joyous (to him) day in the remote, misty future when ships would assemble to take the black people away; he was writing about the education they would receive before their exile.* The seemingly radical, farseeing plan turns out to be just another soft answer, in this case addressed to Robert Pleasants, a Virginia Quaker who had in fact already set his slaves free (in 1782) and established a school (in 1784) for free black children.

---

*How remote was that day? In 1832 the Virginia legislature considered a statewide emancipation plan that would come to fruition in 1910.

Jefferson's image-making has been effective. In a 1995 analysis of Jefferson's record on race and slavery, Alexander O. Boulton insisted that Jefferson, "throughout the entire course of his life, maintained an abiding faith in an antislavery philosophy in his words and actions. It is difficult to understand Jefferson's ardent critique of all forms of authority and oppression without including his fervent antislavery beliefs."[5]

Boulton did not specify what "actions" Jefferson had taken, though he mentioned Jefferson's "thought," his "faith," his "beliefs" in general. Jefferson would have been delighted to read Boulton's essay, as it precisely conveys the impression he wished to propagate in his ample library of "soft answers." Jefferson would have been doubly delighted at the essay's title, "The American Paradox," signifying a condition of bafflement. George Ticknor, a visitor from Boston, had already in 1815 noted that in conversation Jefferson displayed a "love of paradox."[6]

Not so very long ago most historians thought that Jefferson's reputation would be permanently shredded if it were proved that he fathered children by Sally Hemings. John Chester Miller of Stanford declared in 1977 that if Jefferson did have an affair with Hemings, then he "deserves to be regarded as one of the most profligate liars and consummate hypocrites ever to occupy the presidency."

> To give credence to the Sally Hemings story . . . is to infer that there were no principles to which he was inviolably committed, that what he acclaimed as morality was no more than a rhetorical facade for self-indulgence, and that he was always prepared to make exceptions in his own case when it suited his purpose. In short, beneath his sanctimonious and sententious exterior lay a thoroughly adaptive and amoral public figure—like so many of those of the present day. Even conceding that Jefferson was deeply in love with Sally Hemings does not essentially alter the case: love does not sanctify such an egregious violation of his own principles and preachments and the shifts and dodges, the paltry artifices, to which he was compelled to resort in order to fool the American people.[7]

But when Typhoon Hemings hit the SS *Jefferson*, something miraculous occurred: the great vessel heeled over, then slowly righted itself and steamed majestically on its way, flying new flags of multiculturalism

My problem with Gordon Reed

and amelioration. Writers redefined the "adaptive and amoral" Jefferson as the lover of Sally Hemings and the secret, tormented father of a multiracial family. A leading Jefferson scholar, Peter Onuf of the University of Virginia, writes, "If anything, Jefferson's stock rebounded," because "Jefferson as lover—no matter how unequal the lovers' power—is a more sympathetic character than Jefferson the owner and exploiter of his fellow human beings." He asks, "Was . . . Jefferson's image shining more brightly than ever?"[8]

Onuf's discussion appeared in a 2010 collection of essays titled *Seeing Jefferson Anew: In His Time and Ours.* As one reviewer of the book suggested, "The emerging consensus about Jefferson's relationship with Sally Hemings has tended to alleviate some of the tension between Jefferson as apostle of liberty and Jefferson as slaveholder." Sally Hemings, having "humanized" her master, to a large extent now dominates the representation of Jefferson as a slaveholder. The same reviewer noted, "Hemings appears early and often in this book. . . . She has as many page citations in the index as Alexander Hamilton, James Madison, and Jefferson's wife, Martha—combined. Clearly, we have entered a new phase in Jefferson studies, and Hemings has a lead role."[9]

To shift into this new phase requires, however, an enormous act of forgetting. Yes, the four Hemings children were, as Madison Hemings said, "free from the dread of having to be slaves all our lives long," but the six hundred other African-Americans who labored for Jefferson were never free from that dread. Peter Fossett, put on the block and sold "like a horse," humanizes what the historian Walter Johnson has rightly called "an economy in which everything was for sale: productive and reproductive labor but also sex and sentiment." Fossett puts a face on "the obscene synthesis of humanity and interest, of person and thing, that underlay so much of Southern jurisprudence, the market in slaves, the daily discipline of slavery."[10] That was the synthesis Jefferson formulated when he said that Providence had made his interests and duties coincide.

Forgotten also is Jefferson's blunt rationalization for enslaving African-Americans. Augustus John Foster, who visited Jefferson at Monticello in 1807, reported that "he considered them to be as far inferior to the rest of mankind as the mule is to the horse, and as made to carry burthens."[11]

Peter Onuf writes of "the problematic image of the democratic founder who was profoundly hostile to slavery but could never extricate himself from an institution that guaranteed the welfare and well-being of his 'country,' Virginia."[12] But Jefferson never tried to extricate himself. The record of his actions suggests that he formulated a grand synthesis by which slavery became integral to the empire of liberty. Jefferson saw that slavery could build a bridge to a profitable future, that slavery reliably produced working capital both for aristocratic planter families like his own and for energetic strivers like his overseer Edmund Bacon. Shrewd, frugal, and an instinctive acquisitor, Bacon accumulated slaves and marched them into new land in Kentucky, where he established a prosperous farm. Not once did Jefferson urge Bacon to relinquish slavery as he had pushed Edward Coles to give up his emancipation plan.

In *American Sphinx*, Joseph Ellis mapped Jefferson's mind as a labyrinth of "capsules or compartments" arranged "to keep certain incompatible thoughts from encountering one another."[13] But Ellis's labyrinth may represent our minds more than Jefferson's, for it is we who compartmentalize certain historical realities in order to preserve an innocent image of our beginnings. Thus David Brooks wrote in *The New York Times* in 2008: "The people who created this country built a moral structure around money. . . . The result was quite remarkable. The United States has been an affluent nation since its founding. But the country was, by and large, not corrupted by wealth."[14] The fact that slavery was the underpinning of much of America's founding wealth must be in a different compartment.

The syntax that biographers and historians use when they write about Jefferson is revealing. In books, articles, blogs, and websites, he strides across the American stage as a potent, overpowering actor: he built Monticello, he wrote the Declaration of Independence, he engineered the Louisiana Purchase. But when it comes to slavery, suddenly Jefferson is not an active force but the pawn of historical forces beyond his control; he becomes a victim. Verbs go from the active to the passive voice; he is trapped by convention, by society, by laws, by his family, by debt. On the subject of debt, a historian writes, "The old patriarch's financial burdens . . . were staggering." Were those burdens the result of Jefferson's faulty planning? Were they his responsibility? No. His debts were "brought on chiefly by the failure of his estate to handle his large obligations," which is to say that his farms and the workers on them somehow let him down.[15]

The biographer Merrill Peterson wrote in 1970 of Jefferson's extraordinary versatility "exploding in all directions. . . . Others might be content with what was; he could think only in terms of what should be." Though it was considered "folly" to put a mansion on a hilltop, Jefferson would not be deterred: "He was born with an irrepressible urge to build." When he dreamed of creating a great university in Virginia, he "built from the ground up" despite intense opposition. Yet on the subject of slavery, Peterson depicts Jefferson as hamstrung: "Until the institution itself could be extinguished, slavery was an evil he had to live with." Jefferson knew that his overseers beat his slaves, including children, but Peterson absolves the master: "There were limits to his own superintendence." With pathbreaking financial acumen Jefferson monetized his slaves and negotiated a very large foreign loan using slaves as collateral, but in Peterson's account Jefferson's slaves "were mortgaged," as if some anonymous clerk had arranged the loan.[16]

Sometimes the instinct to exonerate does its work by subtly softening the facts. When the University of Virginia Library put the will of Thaddeus Kosciuszko on display, the will in which he left Jefferson money specifically to free his slaves, the explanatory wall panel turned Kosciuszko's clear stipulation into a mere recommendation, noting that the will "named Jefferson the executor, suggesting that he use the money to liberate his slaves at Monticello." Moreover, it added that "Jefferson would have been forbidden to do so by Virginia law," although that is not true: freed slaves had to leave Virginia within a year of their manumission, but there was no legal bar to freeing them, nor to their being educated.

Many writers on slavery today have emphasized the "agency" of the enslaved people, insisting that we pay heed to the efforts of the slaves to resist their condition and assert their humanity under a dehumanizing system.[17] But as slaves gain "agency" in historical analyses, the masters seem to lose it. As the slaves become heroic figures, triumphing over their condition, slave owners recede as historical actors and are replaced by a faceless system of "context" and "forces." So we end up with slavery somehow afloat in a world in which nobody is responsible.

One historian writes about Monticello's slaves as if they had no master: "There is every indication that they grasped the baleful position they had been born into, and knew that forces were actively working to keep them down."[18]

In this newly orthodox narrative the slaves appear as keepers of the American flame, providing profiles in courage and cherishing the Revolutionary ideal of liberty in their hearts, while Thomas Jefferson and all the masters and mistresses he represents are somehow mired, stuck, ensnared, or blind. The slaves redeem the epoch of the "peculiar institution" by transforming it into one marked by their heroism.

Instead of thinking about Jefferson and his slaves as an "ironic," "paradoxical," or "complex" subject, perhaps we should train ourselves to say "perverse." It is indeed a perverse irony if enslaved Americans have risen from the dead to save Jefferson one more time.

Jefferson's stirring antislavery pronouncements of the 1770s and 1780s reflect his leading role in a surge of American progressivism. Assessing "the critical period between 1776 and 1787," David Waldstreicher writes, "The Continental Congress had intermittently moved against the slave trade and nearly banned slavery from the new northwestern territories. A consensus existed in many, perhaps most parts of the country that slavery was inconsistent with American revolutionary principles and ought to be consigned to the dustbin of history."[19] During that window of political opportunity and heady idealism, Virginia passed its remarkably liberal manumission law of 1782, and two years later Jefferson proposed his ban on slavery in the western and southern territories—the measure that failed by one vote.

As he composed *Notes on the State of Virginia*, Jefferson sensed a deflation of Revolutionary fervor: "From the conclusion of this war we shall be going down hill." He feared that once they returned to business as usual, Americans would care less about abstractions such as Revolutionary ideals: "They will forget themselves, but in the sole faculty of making money, and will never think of uniting to effect a due respect for their rights. The shackles, therefore, which shall not be knocked off at the conclusion of this war, will remain on us long, [and] will be made heavier and heavier."

The haunting image of shackles growing heavier was prophetic. The black people were doomed to perpetual shackles once they became financial instruments. Jefferson was not the only planter to discern the "silent profit." As slaveholders in the new nation grasped that not only the labor of slaves but their increase would support the plantation system indefinitely, they exulted at the prospect before them. One Deep South planter declared: "owing to the operation of this institution [slavery] upon our unparalleled natural advantages, we shall be the richest people beneath the bend of the rainbow."[20] And so the slaves were doubly doomed when Jefferson allowed slavery into Louisiana.

From the time he began composing *Notes* until the end of his life, Jefferson assumed the role of Great Communicator on slavery, defending himself and his country against all challengers. As luminaries such as Lafayette and Thomas Paine discovered, debating Jefferson would always prove fruitless. A shrewd and relentless lawyer, he composed briefs for the defense containing "just enough of the semblance of morality to throw dust into the eyes of the people," to borrow his own words.[21] In their entirety Jefferson's rationalizations amount to nothing compared with his perfectly clear presidential order to admit slavery to the Louisiana Territory. Later in his life Jefferson mocked abolitionists for "wasting Jeremiads on the miseries of slavery" and more or less went over to arguing that slavery was a positive good. Describing what he could see from his terrace—Mulberry Row's "ameliorated" cabins, where his enslaved relatives lived—he claimed in 1814 that American slaves were better fed and clothed than England's workers and "labor less"—an argument that to this day is the trump card for slavery's retrospective apologists.[22]

In the 1790s, as Jefferson was mortgaging his slaves to build Monticello, George Washington was trying to scrape together the financing to free his slaves at Mount Vernon, which he finally ordered in his will, to be carried out "without evasion, neglect or delay." He proved that emancipation was not only possible but practical, and he overturned all the Jeffersonian rationalizations. Jefferson insisted that a multiracial society with free black people was impossible, but Washington did not think so. Never did Washington suggest that black people were inferior or that they should be exiled; nor did it occur to him that people must be "capable of tracing and comprehending the investigations of Euclid," as Jefferson stipulated, in order to deserve citizenship.

It is curious that we accept Jefferson as the moral standard of the Founders' era, not Washington. Perhaps it is because the Father of His Country left a troubling legacy: his emancipation of his slaves stands not as a tribute but as a rebuke to his era, and to the prevaricators and profiteers of the future, and declares that if you claim to have principles, you must live by them. Americans like to believe, however, as Reinhold Niebuhr wrote in *The Irony of American History*, that "we are (according to our traditional theory) the most innocent nation on earth."[23] Jefferson perpetually murmurs absolution over compromise, delay, and evasion, offering a transcendent innocence that is impervious to reality.

That is why he has survived the Sally Hemings scandal. He had struck a deal with a sixteen-year-old girl and made the grown woman stick to it for the rest of her life, knowing she would sacrifice her body and soul to save her children. Every day she cleaned his bedroom. Every day their son Madison counted the months until he would get free of that place and that man, his father, the master and enslaver. But when this sorry history came before the public in our own time, Jefferson's stock rose—because we wanted it to. Jefferson's unchangeable symbolic role is to make slavery safe.[24] Only a supremely powerful totem can guard our collective memory on this score, shining brilliantly enough to avert our gaze from the traffickers in human blood roaming outside the gates.

Notes

Introduction: "This Steep, Savage Hill"

1. Ticknor, *Life, Letters, and Journals*, p. 34; Richard Rush, Oct. 9, 1816, quoted in Stein, *Worlds of Thomas Jefferson at Monticello*, p. 50. This paragraph is based on the opening of my 1984 essay on Monticello in *Mansions of the Virginia Gentry*, p. 118.
2. "Education: The Power of the Mind," Monticello.org, quoting Charles Bullock, 1948.
3. "Once the Slave of Thomas Jefferson," *Frontline*, "Jefferson's Blood," PBS.org; "Peter Fossett, the Venerable Ex-Slave." Fossett used the word "friends" with its old meaning: benefactors. Thus TJ's granddaughter once spoke of her wish to "befriend" a slave.
4. Levy, *First Emancipator*, p. 178.
5. Whitman, "Spanish Element in Our Nationality," p. 386.
6. Freeman, *George Washington*, vol. 1, p. 6.
7. Morgan and Nicholls, "Slaves in Piedmont Virginia," pp. 248, 251.
8. Eric Slauter, "The Declaration of Independence and the New Nation," in *Cambridge Companion to Thomas Jefferson*, p. 21.
9. Davis, *Problem of Slavery in the Age of Revolution*, pp. 174, 179.
10. TJ to Edward Bancroft, Jan. 26, 1788, in *Papers*, vol. 14.
11. Quoted in McColley, *Slavery and Jeffersonian Virginia*, p. 125.
12. Lander and Ellis, "Founding Father."
13. Lottie Bullock, quoted in Stanton, "Other End of the Telescope," p. 146. Stanton notes that Bullock's mother "had been raised by a Hemings descendant in Charlottesville."
14. Notes on Arthur Young's letter to George Washington, June 18, 1792, in *Papers*, vol. 24. Original document: TJ to George Washington, June 18, 1792, "Notes on Mr. Young's Letter," General Correspondence, 1651–1827, Thomas Jefferson Papers, Series 1, image 734, Library of Congress, http://memory.loc.gov/ammem /collections/jefferson_papers/.
15. TJ to Madame Plumard de Bellanger, April 25, 1794, in *Papers*, vol. 28.
16. Washington to Alexander Spotswood, Nov. 23, 1794, in *Writings of George Washington from the Original Manuscript Sources*, vol. 34, p. 47, http://etext.virginia .edu/washington/fitzpatrick/.

17. Davis, "Enduring Legacy of the South's Civil War Victory." Another scholar who has noted the slave owners doing all they could to increase the enslaved population is Catherine Clinton, "'Southern Dishonor': Flesh, Blood, Race, and Bondage," in Bleser, *In Joy and in Sorrow*, pp. 53–55. Fogel, *Slavery Debates*, p. 27: "During the decade of the 1970s, the growing mountains of evidence finally made it obvious that the profitability of slavery was increasing, not declining, on the eve of the Civil War. Moreover, the sharp rise in the purchase price of slaves relative to their rental price meant that slave owners were never more confident about the future of their system than they were during the last half of the 1850s."

18. The sanitized version is in Betts, *Thomas Jefferson's Farm Book*, Thomas Mann Randolph to TJ, Jan. 31, 1801, p. 443; full text: Martha Jefferson Randolph and Thomas Mann Randolph to TJ, postscript, Jan. 31, 1801, in *Papers*, vol. 32; "ideal rural community": Francis L. Berkeley Jr., introduction to *Farm Book*, p. xviii.

19. Baker, "Memoirs of Williamsburg, Virginia."

20. Stanton, *Free Some Day*, p. 142.

21. Niebuhr, *Reinhold Niebuhr on Politics*, p. 284.

22. Ellis, "Philadelphia Story." Joyce Appleby writes, "The paradox is so blatant, there is probably another answer." Appleby, *Thomas Jefferson*, p. 142.

23. Melville, "Benito Cereno," p. 306.

1. *"Let There Be Justice"*

1. Lucia Stanton, "Jefferson's People," in *Cambridge Companion to Thomas Jefferson*, p. 95.

2. Adams, *Jefferson's Monticello*, pp. 75, 76 caption 65.

3. Thomas Jefferson Randolph Memoirs, version 2, no. 1397.

4. Beiswanger, *Monticello in Measured Drawings*, p. 37.

5. Quoted in Beiswanger, "Thomas Jefferson and the Art of Living Out of Doors."

6. Anna Maria Thornton, quoted in Howard, *Dr. Kimball and Mr. Jefferson*, p. 146.

7. TJ to Charles Clay, Aug. 23, 1811, in *Papers*, Retirement Series, vol. 4.

8. Quoted in Malone, *Jefferson the Virginian*, p. 149.

9. Bear, *Jefferson at Monticello*, pp. 72, 71.

10. Ibid., p. 11. Isaac Granger has hitherto been known as Isaac Jefferson, and his memoir of life at Monticello was published under that name, but the surname Jefferson may have been applied to him by the memoir's nineteenth-century editor. Recent research by Monticello's historian Lucia Stanton indicates that the blacksmith's surname was actually Granger.

11. Ibid., p. 71.

12. TJ to Benjamin Austin, Jan. 9, 1816, in Peterson, *Thomas Jefferson: Writings*, p. 1370.

13. Stanton, *Free Some Day*, p. 105.

14. Harrison and Burke, *Two Monticello Childhoods*, pp. 4–5.

15. Stanton, *Free Some Day*, p. 138.

16. "Lafayette's Visit to Monticello (1824)," account of Israel Jefferson, Monticello.org.

17. Dain, *Hideous Monster of the Mind*, p. 4.

18. Langhorne, "Black Music and Tales from Jefferson's Monticello," p. 60.

19. TJ to Thomas Mann Randolph Jr., June 8, 1803, Library of Congress.

20. Daugherty, *Way of an Eagle*, p. 232.
21. TJ moved Sally Hemings and his cooks out of Mulberry Row into rooms underneath the terrace, but he never got around to fixing up Mulberry Row. Kelso, *Archaeology at Monticello*, pp. 44–46.
22. Bear and Stanton, *Jefferson's Memorandum Books*, vol. 1, pp. 36–37. McLaughlin, *Jefferson and Monticello*, pp. 154–55. The slaves worked for nothing; the contractor and their owner took the wages.
23. D'Souza, *What's So Great About America*, p. 113.
24. Bear and Stanton, *Jefferson's Memorandum Books*, vol. 1, p. 37. TJ made a slight error, writing "ruet" instead of "ruat," so the actual meaning is "let justice be done, the sky will fall."
25. Ibid., pp. 245–47.
26. Quoted in Rhys Isaac, "The First Monticello," in Onuf, *Jeffersonian Legacies*, p. 85.
27. He was remembering the journey when his family moved from Albemarle County to another plantation near Richmond, when TJ was two. Sarah N. Randolph, *Domestic Life of Thomas Jefferson*, p. 23.
28. Susan Kern, lecture, Jefferson Library, International Center for Jefferson Studies, Sept. 12, 2006; Kern, *Jeffersons at Shadwell*, pp. 75–77.
29. *Notes on the State of Virginia.*
30. TJ to Edward Coles, Aug. 25, 1814, in *Papers*, Retirement Series, vol. 7.
31. Tucker, *Blackstone's Commentaries*, app. p. 66.
32. TJ to Edward Coles, Aug. 25, 1814.
33. Argument in the case of *Howell v. Netherland*, in Ford, *Works of Thomas Jefferson*, vol. 1.
34. Randolph, "Edmund Randolph's Essay on the Revolutionary History of Virginia," April 1935, p. 122.
35. Malone, *Jefferson the Virginian*, p. 188.
36. Ibid., pp. 180–82, 184, 187.
37. Quoted in Maier, *American Scripture*, p. 112.
38. Randolph, "Edmund Randolph's Essay on the Revolutionary History of Virginia," July 1935, p. 216.
39. Stephen A. Conrad, "Putting Rights Talk in Its Place," in Onuf, *Jeffersonian Legacies*, p. 269. Ronald L. Hatzenbuehler writes that in *Summary View*, "Jefferson attacked the existence of slavery in Virginia because it was inconsistent with liberty" and in so doing split with his Virginia peers "in a significant way." Hatzenbuehler, *"I Tremble for My Country,"* p. 51.
40. Randolph, "Edmund Randolph's Essay on the Revolutionary History of Virginia," July 1935, pp. 216, 215.
41. Jean Yarbrough writes: "In the original draft, Jefferson makes it clear that he considers slaves to be men. . . . By virtue of their membership in the human race, all men possess certain inalienable rights. That Jefferson means to include the slaves is clear from the original version, where he attributes to the slaves 'the most sacred rights of life and liberty,' which rights they enjoy by virtue of their 'human nature.'" Yarbrough, "Race and the Moral Foundation of the American Republic," p. 95.
42. Miller, *Wolf by the Ears*, p. 9.

43. Quoted in David Brion Davis, "The Problem of Slavery," in Paquette and Ferleger, *Slavery, Secession, and Southern History*, p. 22.
44. Miller, *Wolf by the Ears*, p. 30.
45. Becker, *Declaration of Independence*, pp. 239–40; Thelen, "Reception of the Declaration of Independence," in Gerber, *Declaration of Independence*, p. 206.

2. Pursued by the Black Horse

1. Randall, *Life of Thomas Jefferson*, vol. 1, p. 63.
2. Ibid., pp. 62–65. The severe 1772 storm is known as the "Washington-Jefferson Storm" because both men recorded it in their notes.
3. A family named Eppes had owned Elizabeth Hemings, and she came into Wayles's possession, aged about eleven, when he married Martha Eppes, his first wife: Kukla, *Mr. Jefferson's Women*, pp. 68, 118. The name of Elizabeth Hemings's mother is believed to be Parthena. Barbara Heath came to this conclusion by analyzing the names of Betty Hemings's children and grandchildren, noting the appearance of Thena and Thenia, common nicknames for Parthena. She then found "Parthena" among the Wayles slaves.
4. In his memoir the blacksmith Isaac Granger remarked, "Folks said that these Hemingses was old Mr. Wayles's children." Sally Hemings's son Madison said the same thing: "Elizabeth Hemings grew to womanhood in the family of John Wales, whose wife dying she (Elizabeth) was taken by the widower Wales as his concubine, by whom she had six children—three sons and three daughters, viz.: Robert, James, Peter, Critty, Sally and Thena. These children went by the name of Hemings." The overseer Edmund Bacon said that the Hemingses were "old family servants and great favorites." Bear, *Jefferson at Monticello*, p. 4.
5. TJ to Archibald Thweatt, May 29, 1810, in *Papers*, Retirement Series, vol. 2.
6. Ibid.
7. Stanton, *Free Some Day*, p. 19.
8. Ibid., pp. 21–22.
9. *Farm Book*, plates 5–9.
10. TJ wrote the names of the white workers Fossett, Nelson, Rise, and Walker.
11. McLaughlin, *Jefferson and Monticello*, p. 101; "Monticello: stone house (slave quarters), recto, September 1770, by Thomas Jefferson," N38; K16 (electronic edition), *Thomas Jefferson Papers: An Electronic Archive*. The individuals mentioned included Jenny, Suck, Scilla, Dinah, and Ursula.
12. Kelso, *Archaeology at Monticello*, pp. 64, 96; McLaughlin, *Jefferson and Monticello*, pp. 143–45.
13. TJ to Thomas Mann Randolph Jr., Oct. 19, 1792, in *Papers*, vol. 24.
14. McLaughlin, *Jefferson and Monticello*, p. 188.
15. Martha Wayles Skelton Jefferson, Household Accounts, images 24, 27, Library of Congress.
16. Bear, *Jefferson and Monticello*, p. 3.
17. Vail, *De la littérature et des hommes de lettres des États Unis d'Amérique*. I am grateful to Jane Foster for her translation of the Vail account.
18. Langhorne, "Black Music and Tales from Jefferson's Monticello," p. 60.
19. Bear, *Jefferson and Monticello*, p. 3.

20. Ibid., p. 5.
21. Hemings, "Life Among the Lowly."
22. Thomas Jefferson Randolph Memoirs, version 2, no. 1397.
23. *Freedman's Friend*, Dec. 1868.
24. Kranish, *Flight from Monticello*, p. 266.
25. Ibid., p. 283.
26. Randall, *Life of Thomas Jefferson*, vol. 1, pp. 337–39.
27. Kranish, *Flight from Monticello*, p. 286.
28. Bear, *Jefferson at Monticello*, p. 8.

3. "We Lived Under a Hidden Law"

1. TJ to James Madison, May 25, 1810, in *Papers*, Retirement Series, vol. 2.
2. TJ to D'Anmours, Nov. 30, 1780, in *Papers*, vol. 4.
3. Wilson, "Evolution of Jefferson's *Notes on the State of Virginia*."
4. McColley, *Slavery and Jeffersonian Virginia*, p. 115.
5. *Virginia Gazette*, Aug. 20, 1772, p. 1, http://research.history.org/DigitalLibrary /VirginiaGazette/VGbyYear.cfm. Also quoted in Boulton, "American Paradox," p. 470.
6. *Notes on the State of Virginia*. All direct quotations from *Notes* in this chapter are from the searchable UVA etext: http://etext.virginia.edu/toc/modeng/public/JefVirg .html.
7. Mill, *Basic Writings*, p. 134.
8. Wolf, *Race and Liberty in the New Nation*, pp. 1–2, 4–5.
9. Ibid., pp. 6–7, 17–19; Zuckerman, *Almost Chosen People*, p. 196. As he often did, TJ contrived to have things both ways. Having thrown in his lot with the reactionaries in the 1780s, he retroactively denounced them in 1814 as benighted, self-interested people from whom "nothing was to be hoped." He said they cared only for property rights and looked upon black people as animals. TJ to Edward Coles, Aug. 25, 1814, in *Papers*, Retirement Series, vol. 7.
10. Quoted in Boulton, "American Paradox," p. 469.
11. Boswell and Croker, *Life of Samuel Johnson*, p. 461.
12. Quoted in Wilson, "Evolution of Jefferson's *Notes on the State of Virginia*," p. 124.
13. Jordan, *White over Black*, pp. 287, 519.
14. Rush, *Address to the Inhabitants of the British Settlements in America, upon Slave-Keeping*, p. 3.
15. Bruce Dain remarks: "Jefferson had to dismiss a Wheatley. One instance of substantial black reason or imagination would upset his whole scheme." Dain, *Hideous Monster of the Mind*, p. 34. David Waldstreicher writes: "Wheatley posed a special problem for Thomas Jefferson. He must have been aware that enlightened figures like Voltaire and Rush had already cited Wheatley's poetry in the ongoing, international . . . debate about race, nature, and slavery. . . . His vituperative response to Wheatley suggests the threat that her poems and her public actions . . . posed for Jefferson." Waldstreicher, "Wheatleyan Moment," p. 545. David Grimsted dissects TJ's derision of Wheatley in "Anglo-American Racism and Phillis Wheatley's 'Sable Veil,' 'Length'ned Chain,' and 'Knitted Heart,'" pp. 338–444.
16. Wheatley, *Complete Works*, p. 89.

17. TJ to Clark, Jan. 1, 1780, in *Papers*, vol. 3.
18. TJ to Chastellux, June 7, 1785, in *Papers*, vol. 8.
19. Thomas Jefferson, *Writings of Thomas Jefferson*, ed. Lipscomb and Bergh, vol. 16, p. 452.
20. Ibid., vol. 10, p. 363.
21. Thomas Mann Randolph Jr., Notes on the Genealogy of Pocahontas, n.d., Thomas Jefferson Papers Series 6, Randolph Family Manuscripts, 1790–1889, Library of Congress.
22. Bear, *Jefferson at Monticello*, p. 85.
23. As McColley notes, Virginians "could command the sympathy of outsiders simply by showing the right attitudes." McColley, *Slavery and Jeffersonian Virginia*, p. 114.
24. Barker, "Unraveling the Strange History of Jefferson's *Observations sur la Virginie*," p. 140.
25. Pybus, *Epic Journeys of Freedom*, p. 105. See also Pybus, "Jefferson's Faulty Math."
26. Holton, *Forced Founders*, p. 143.
27. Kranish, *Flight from Monticello*, pp. 254–55.
28. Ibid., p. 253.
29. Ibid., p. 270.
30. Short to TJ, Feb. 27, 1798, in *Papers*, vol. 30.
31. Kukla, *Mr. Jefferson's Women*, pp. 69–70.
32. Armstrong, undated marginal annotation on *Notes on the State of Virginia*, p. 240. I am grateful to John Winthrop Aldrich, who remembered this annotation made by his great-great-great-great-grandfather and provided me with a copy.
33. Quoted in Edmund S. Morgan, *American Slavery, American Freedom*, p. 380.
34. John Kern, "Henry County: Dry Bridge Rosenwald School and Bassett Furniture, Inc.: 'We Lived Under a Hidden Law,'" lecture, Virginia Forum, 2010.
35. Peterson, *Jefferson Image in the American Mind*, p. 187.

4. *"The Hammer or the Anvil"*

1. Randall, *Life of Thomas Jefferson*, p. 345.
2. *Farm Book*, plate 29.
3. These departures "had the hallmarks of well-planned, premeditated action," writes the historian Cassandra Pybus in "Jefferson's Faulty Math," pp. 245–46. *Farm Book*, plate 29; Stanton, *Free Some Day*, pp. 52–55. Though TJ asserted that Cornwallis "carried off" his people, implying that the British had forced his slaves to abscond, in the Farm Book he wrote that Black Sal and her children "joined the enemy." He may have made inquiries among the remaining slaves and found that Sal had gone of her own accord. Three men named Robin, Barnaby, and Harry and a boy named Will fled Monticello for the British camp at Elk Hill. Barnaby, a blacksmith, died; after Robin and Will returned to Monticello, TJ sold them; Harry was one of three slaves "never more heard of." "Jefferson's Statement of Losses to the British at His Cumberland Plantations in 1781" [Jan. 27, 1783], in *Papers*, vol. 6.
4. TJ to Jean Nicolas Démeunier, June 26, 1786, in *Papers*, vol. 10.

5. TJ to Charles Bellini, Sept. 30, 1785, in *Papers*, vol. 8.
6. Ellis also refers to TJ's "highly developed network of interior defenses." Ellis, *American Sphinx*, pp. 149–50, 177; Miller, *Wolf by the Ears*, p. 163; Brodie, *Thomas Jefferson*, pp. 371–72.
7. TJ to James Monroe, deleted portion, May 20, 1782, in *Papers*, vol. 6.
8. Wiencek, *Imperfect God*, p. 268.
9. Price to TJ, July 2, 1785, in *Papers*, vol. 8.
10. TJ to Price, Aug. 7, 1785, in *Papers*, vol. 8.
11. Hochman, "Thomas Jefferson," p. 180.
12. Thomas Jefferson, "Argument in the Case of Howell vs. Netherland," in Ford, *Works of Thomas Jefferson*, vol. 1.
13. TJ to Angelica Schuyler Church, Nov. 27, 1793, in *Papers*, vol. 27.
14. Thomas Jefferson, "The Article on the United States in the *Encyclopédie méthodique*; Additional Questions of M. de Meusnier, and Answers," [ca. Jan.–Feb. 1786], in *Papers*, vol. 10.
15. TJ to Alexander McCaul, April 19, 1786, in *Papers*, vol. 9.
16. Pybus, *Epic Journeys of Freedom*, pp. 104–105, 240–41n4.
17. TJ to Francis Eppes, July 10, 1788, in *Papers*, vol. 13.
18. TJ to Nicholas Lewis, July 29, 1787, in *Papers*, vol. 11.
19. TJ discusses the legal intricacies of the Wayles debt in TJ to Eppes, July 10, 1788. Even if the Wayles slaves had somehow been responsible for the debt, the slaves TJ inherited from his parents certainly were not, yet TJ called upon them to labor harder as well.
20. The other fourteen people might have been the so-called privilege slaves, the commission that Wayles and his partner were entitled to take; or they escaped or died before sale.
21. When TJ and two other heirs took possession of the Wayles estate, they decided to assume Wayles's debt personally, believing that they could pay it off, rather than leaving it as part of the estate. It was not a bad strategy, but it turned out to be a mistake. Sloan, *Principle and Interest*, pp. 14–26.
22. Sloan, ibid., p. 24, refers to TJ's generalized sense of victimization by the war, the weather, the market, the merchants in England, and so on. In a 1785 letter TJ blamed British merchants for getting Americans into debt by offering "good prices and credit to the planter, till they got him more immersed in debt than he could pay without selling his lands or slaves." TJ to Nathaniel Tracy, Aug. 17, 1785, in *Papers*, vol. 8.

5. The Bancroft Paradox

1. TJ to Montmorin, July 23, 1787, in *Papers*, vol. 11; Nettels, *Emergence of a National Economy*, p. 49.
2. As the U.S. trade representative in Paris, "Jefferson knew that he represented South Carolina as well as Virginia; his efforts to find new markets for American products, including rice, had increased his awareness of the importance of slave labor in the national economy," as David Brion Davis writes. Davis, *Problem of Slavery in the Age of Revolution*, p. 178; Waldstreicher, *Runaway America*, p. 231.
3. Adams, *Paris Years of Thomas Jefferson*, pp. 134–35.

4. Ibid., p. 7. "Your republic has instructed us," wrote another Frenchman to TJ, "and your institutions will perhaps one day establish in our country that which English and American philosophers have thus far only led us to hope for." Pulley, "Thomas Jefferson at the Court of Versailles," p. 27.

5. Adams, *Paris Years of Thomas Jefferson*, p. 150.

6. Pulley, "Thomas Jefferson at the Court of Versailles," p. 69.

7. TJ to Brissot de Warville, Aug. 16, 1786, in *Papers*, vol. 10.

8. Quoted in Adams, *Paris Years of Thomas Jefferson*, pp. 134–35.

9. Ibid., pp. 136–37.

10. "Jefferson's Notes from Condorcet on Slavery," n.d., in *Papers*, vol. 22.

11. Popkin, *Third Force in Seventeenth-Century Thought*, pp. 51, 52.

12. Quoted in Adams, *Paris Years of Thomas Jefferson*, p. 139.

13. TJ to Démeunier [June 26, 1786], in *Papers*, vol. 10. Adams, *Paris Years of Thomas Jefferson*, pp. 137, 147.

14. "A Bill Concerning Slaves," in Ford, *Works of Thomas Jefferson*, vol. 2.

15. Pulley, "Thomas Jefferson at the Court of Versailles," p. 49.

16. TJ to Brissot de Warville, Feb. 11, 1788, in *Papers*, vol. 12.

17. Waldstreicher, *Runaway America*, p. 219.

18. Adams, *Paris Years of Thomas Jefferson*, pp. 11–12, 187.

19. Pulley, "Thomas Jefferson at the Court of Versailles," p. 40.

20. D'Souza, *What's So Great About America*, p. 113.

21. Bancroft to TJ, Sept. 16, 1788, in *Papers*, vol. 14.

22. Ibid.

23. Wolf, *Race and Liberty in the New Nation*, p. 54.

24. McColley, *Slavery and Jeffersonian Virginia*, pp. 158–59.

25. Wolf, *Race and Liberty in the New Nation*, pp. 31–33.

26. Thomas Jefferson, "Notes of a Tour Through Holland and the Rhine Valley," March 3, 1788, in *Papers*, vol. 13.

27. TJ to Short, April 9, 1788, in *Papers*, vol. 13.

28. TJ to Edward Coles, Aug. 25, 1814, in *Papers*, Retirement Series, vol. 7.

29. TJ to Jean Nicolas Démeunier [June 26, 1786].

30. Short to TJ, Oct. 7, 1793, in *Papers*, vol. 27.

31. "Jefferson's Notes from Condorcet on Slavery," n.d., in *Papers*, vol. 14.

6. *"To Have Good and Human Heart"*

1. TJ to Lewis, July 11, 1788, in *Papers*, vol. 13.

2. Sarah N. Randolph, *Domestic Life of Thomas Jefferson*, pp. 152–53; Randall, *Life of Thomas Jefferson*, vol. 1, pp. 552–53, cites the recollections of the enslaved gardener Wormley Hughes. TJ's daughter Martha, who was in the carriage, described the event; Hughes corroborated most of the details in a conversation with Randall, though Hughes said nothing about devotion.

3. Malone, *Jefferson and the Rights of Man*, p. 246.

4. TJ to Mary Jefferson Eppes, Jan. 17, 1800, in *Papers*, vol. 31. In the ensuing decades TJ made numerous arrivals at Monticello, and there is no record of the slaves repeating this emotional welcome.

5. Martha Jefferson to TJ, May 3, 1787, in *Papers*, vol. 11.

6. TJ was prescient: ten years later he had to put up money to save the plantation from creditors. Thomas Mann Randolph could never get out from under the mortgage, and eventually his son Thomas Jefferson Randolph sold the property. Wayson, "Martha Jefferson Randolph," p. 276.

7. Ibid., pp. 201–202, 206, 209.

8. Martha Jefferson Randolph to TJ, June 23, 1798, in *Papers*, vol. 30.

9. TJ to Thomas Mann Randolph Sr., Feb. 4, 1790, in *Papers*, vol. 16. TJ had inherited the property from John Wayles through his late wife. Marriage Settlement for Martha Jefferson, Feb. 21, 1790, in *Papers*, vol. 16. Gaines, *Thomas Mann Randolph*, p. 29.

10. TJ to James Monroe, deleted portion, May 20, 1782, in *Papers*, vol. 6.

11. TJ to Lewis, Dec. 19, 1786, in *Papers*, vol. 10.

12. TJ to Randolph Jefferson, Sept. 25, 1792, in *Papers*, vol. 24.

13. *Jefferson Encyclopedia*, s.v. "Moldboard Plow," Monticello.org.

14. TJ to Charles Willson Peale, April 17, 1813, in *Farm Book*, p. 47.

15. *Notes on the State of Virginia.*

16. *Jefferson Encyclopedia*, s.v. "Threshing Machine," Monticello.org.

17. *Farm Book*, plate 77.

18. Ibid.

19. Senile corps: TJ to Thomas Mann Randolph, Jan. 29, 1801, in *Papers*, vol. 32; Lucia Stanton, "Those Who Labor for My Happiness," in Onuf, *Jeffersonian Legacies*, p. 155.

20. TJ to Jean Nicolas Démeunier, April 29, 1795, in *Papers*, vol. 28.

21. TJ to William Short, April 13, 1800, in *Papers*, vol. 31.

22. Stanton, "Those Who Labor for My Happiness," pp. 154–55.

23. Martin, "Mr. Jefferson's Business," p. lix.

24. Bear, *Jefferson at Monticello*, pp. 85–86.

25. TJ to Démeunier, April 29, 1795.

26. TJ to James Lyle, July 10, 1795, in *Papers*, vol. 28.

27. TJ to William Temple, April 26, 1795, in *Papers*, vol. 28.

28. *Farm Book*, plate 46.

29. La Rochefoucauld-Liancourt, *Travels Through the United States of North America*, vol. 2, p. 157.

30. Stanton, "Those Who Labor for My Happiness," p. 174n24.

31. Ibid., p. 152.

32. TJ to Banneker, Aug. 30, 1791, in *Papers*, vol. 22.

33. Deed of Mortgage of Slaves to Van Staphorst & Hubbard, May 12, 1796, in *Papers*, vol. 29.

34. TJ to Van Staphorst and Hubbard, Feb. 28, 1796, in *Papers*, vol. 28.

35. La Rochefoucauld-Liancourt, *Travels Through the United States of North America*, vol. 2, p. 138.

36. Malone, *Jefferson and the Ordeal of Liberty*, p. 179.

37. Christopher Morris offers a fascinating analysis in "Articulation of Two Worlds."

38. Aside from being expensive, skilled white workers were not always reliable (many of them drank), and there were few of them; TJ told La Rochefoucauld-Liancourt that "there were not four stone masons in the whole county of Albemarle." McLaughlin, *Jefferson and Monticello*, p. 70.

39. Weld, *Travels Through the States of North America*, vol. 1, p. 147.
40. George Washington described the Revolution as a struggle "for the purpose of rescuing America from impending Slavery." Washington to Chastellux, May 7, 1781, in Fitzpatrick, *Writings of George Washington*, vol. 22.
41. Edmund S. Morgan, "Heart of Jefferson."
42. Preliminary Will of Tadeusz Kosciuszko [before May 5, 1798], in *Papers*, vol. 30.

7. What the Blacksmith Saw

1. Randolph to Nicholas Trist, Nov. 2, 1818, Papers of the Trist, Randolph, and Burke families, accession no. 10487. The incident took place at Morven, owned by David Higginbotham.
2. TJ to Jeremiah Goodman, March 5, 1813, in *Papers*, Retirement Series, vol. 5.
3. TJ to Jeremiah Goodman, Jan. 6, 1815, in *Papers*, Retirement Series, vol. 8.
4. Bear, *Jefferson at Monticello*, p. 23.
5. TJ to Lewis, July 11, 1788, in *Papers*, vol. 13.
6. Memorandum for Nicholas Lewis, ca. Nov. 7, 1790, in *Papers*, vol. 18.
7. TJ to Randolph, Feb. 3, 1793, in *Papers*, vol. 25.
8. Bear and Stanton, *Jefferson's Memorandum Books*, vol. 1, p. 334; Stanton, *Free Some Day*, pp. 33, 36; Hochman, "Thomas Jefferson," p. 72; TJ to Archibald Thweatt, May 29, 1810, in *Papers*, Retirement Series, vol. 2; McLaughlin, *Jefferson and Monticello*, pp. 103–104; William Page's salary, Bear and Stanton, *Jefferson's Memorandum Books*, vol. 2, p. 934.
9. TJ to Randolph, Feb. 3, 1793, in *Papers*, vol. 26.
10. During the Revolution, TJ brought in a British deserter, an alcoholic who lasted two years in the job.
11. Randolph to TJ, April 22, 1798, in *Papers*, vol. 30. When Smith George was ill in 1798 and 1799, the nail boys' productivity plummeted. TJ to John McDowell, Oct. 22, 1798, in *Papers*, vol. 30; TJ to McDowell, March 21, 1799, in *Papers*, vol. 31.
12. Stanton, *Free Some Day*, pp. 45–46, 48, 51, 170n73; Bear, *Jefferson at Monticello*, pp. 23–24. Campbell did not prepare the 1847 interview for publication until 1871.
13. Bear, *Jefferson at Monticello*, p. 6.
14. Ibid.
15. Ibid., p. 4.
16. Ibid., p. 18.
17. Ibid., p. 12.
18. Gaye Wilson, lecture, Jefferson Library, International Center for Jefferson Studies, Sept. 2006.
19. Bear, *Jefferson at Monticello*, pp. 19, 23, 18, 19.
20. Ibid., p. 19.
21. Ibid., p. 13.
22. Ibid., p. 17. In 1797, Polly married her cousin John Wayles Eppes.
23. Ibid., pp. 15–16.
24. Stanton, *Free Some Day*, pp. 33–34; Bear, *Jefferson at Monticello*, pp. 3, 18–19.
25. Bear, *Jefferson at Monticello*, pp. 14–15.
26. Statement of Nailery Profits, Sept. 30, 1797, in *Papers*, vol. 29. McLaughlin, *Jefferson and Monticello*, p. 112; Stanton, *Free Some Day*, p. 34.

27. Bear, *Jefferson at Monticello*, p. 23.
28. Randolph to TJ, Jan. 13, 1798, in *Papers*, vol. 30.
29. Randolph to TJ, Feb. 26, 1798, in *Papers*, vol. 30.
30. TJ to Randolph, April 19, 1798, in *Papers*, vol. 30.
31. Randolph to TJ, April 29, 1798, in *Papers*, vol. 30.
32. Randolph to TJ, June 3, 1798, in *Papers*, vol. 30.
33. Martha Jefferson Randolph to TJ, Jan. 30, 1800, in *Papers*, vol. 31. Martha Randolph applied this description to Ursula's symptoms but said the symptoms were the same as Smith George's.
34. The healer, referred to in letters as both a "doctor" and a "conjuror," lived near Randolph Jefferson's plantation, Snowden, just across the James River from Scottsville.
35. Martha Jefferson Randolph to TJ, Jan. 30, 1800, in *Papers*, vol. 31.
36. TJ to Thomas Mann Randolph, Feb. 4, 1800, in *Papers*, vol. 31; TJ to Maria Jefferson Eppes, Feb. 12, 1800, in *Papers*, vol. 31. Martha wrote that after Jupiter died, the doctor "absconded" and she thought he should be prosecuted for murder. The healer may have given Jupiter a compound known as nux vomica, a common preparation in colonial times, containing strychnine. In low doses strychnine is a tonic, but in high doses it produces seizures, including the grand mal convulsions that apparently killed Jupiter. Communication from Anthony L. McCall, M.D., Ph.D., FACP, James M. Moss Professor of Diabetes, University of Virginia Health System.
37. Stanton, *Free Some Day*, pp. 33, 50; Randolph to TJ, April 12, 1800, in *Papers*, vol. 31. Benjamin Franklin's grandson Dr. William Bache, who lived near Monticello, was summoned to take care of Ursula when TJ expressed his concern.
38. Communication from David J. Stone, M.D.
39. Stanton, *Free Some Day*, p. 50.
40. In his memoir Isaac says nothing about his wife and children. Bear, *Jefferson at Monticello*, p. 16; Stanton, *Free Some Day*, pp. 49–50.

8. What the Colonel Saw

1. TJ to James Dinsmore, Dec. 1, 1802, no. 6540, TJ Papers, University of Virginia. Bear, "Mr. Jefferson's Nails."
2. TJ to John Strode, June 5, 1805, Library of Congress. TJ was asking Strode to recommend an overseer.
3. TJ to William Wirt, 1815, quoted in McLaughlin, *Jefferson and Monticello*, p. 127.
4. Kern, *Jeffersons at Shadwell*, pp. 141, 325n37; Bear and Stanton, *Jefferson's Memorandum Books*, vol. 1, p. 177n54.
5. Kern, *Jeffersons at Shadwell*, p. 140.
6. www.wisconsinhistory.org/museum/artifacts/archives/001446.asp.
7. Account Book Kept by Thomas Jefferson and Others, no. 186-a. II, "The Est. of Thomas Jefferson Esqr. in Account with Nicholas Lewis," April 9, 1791. The purchase was made after TJ's return from France when he was in Philadelphia; Lewis was still managing Monticello. At first I thought these might have been horse collars, but those items are identified in TJ's records as "leather collars" or "horse collars," and Lewis would have been similarly specific.

8. TJ to Thomas Mann Randolph, Aug. 26, 1811, in *Farm Book*, p. 149.
9. Randolph to TJ, March 27, 1792, in *Papers*, vol. 23.
10. TJ to Randolph, April 19, 1792, in *Papers*, vol. 23; TJ to Randolph, Feb. 18, 1793, in *Papers*, vol. 25.
11. TJ to Randolph, April 19, 1792.
12. Randolph to TJ, April 22, 1798, in *Papers*, vol. 30.
13. TJ to Randolph, Jan. 25, 1798, in *Papers*, vol. 30.
14. Randolph to TJ, Feb. 26, 1798, in *Papers*, vol. 30.
15. Stanton, *Free Some Day*, pp. 42–43.
16. Randolph to TJ, Jan. 13, 1798, in *Papers*, vol. 30; TJ to Randolph, Jan. 25, 1798, in *Papers*, vol. 30; TJ to Randolph, May 3, 1798, in *Papers*, vol. 30; Stanton, *Free Some Day*, pp. 36–40.
17. TJ to Stevens Thomson Mason, Oct. 27, 1799, in *Papers*, vol. 31.
18. TJ to James Monroe, July 10, 1796, in *Papers*, vol. 29.
19. Hochman, "Thomas Jefferson," pp. 211–13.
20. Stanton, "Looking for Liberty," p. 651; Moss and Moss, "Jefferson Miscegenation Legend in British Travel Books," pp. 257–58; Brodie, *Thomas Jefferson*, p. 370. Anonymous letter: McLaughlin, *Jefferson and Monticello*, pp. 96–97, 100.
21. La Rochefoucauld-Liancourt, *Travels Through the United States of North America*, vol. 2, p. 162.
22. Bear and Stanton, *Jefferson's Memorandum Books*, vol. 2, p. 934n.
23. Eppes to TJ, Feb. 10, 1803, no. 1397, Small Special Collections Library, University of Virginia.
24. TJ to Thomas Mann Randolph, June 24, 1793, in *Papers*, vol. 26.
25. TJ to James Madison, Aug. 16, 1810, in *Papers*, Retirement Series, vol. 3; Bear and Stanton, *Jefferson's Memorandum Books*, vol. 2, p. 1251n.
26. Martha Jefferson Randolph and Thomas Mann Randolph to TJ, postscript, Jan. 31, 1801, in *Papers*, vol. 32.
27. Francis L. Berkeley Jr., introduction to *Farm Book*, p. xviii.
28. McLaughlin, *Jefferson and Monticello*, p. 112.
29. Peterson, *Thomas Jefferson and the New Nation*, p. 535.
30. Ibid., pp. 529, 534.
31. Ellis, *American Sphinx*, p. 149; Malone, *Jefferson the Virginian*, p. 163.
32. Randolph to TJ, April 12, 1800, in *Papers*, vol. 31.
33. Randolph to TJ, ca. April 19, 1800, in *Papers*, vol. 31.
34. TJ to Randolph, Jan. 23, 1801, in *Papers*, vol. 32.
35. Randolph concluded, "Such is the sound sense cleverness & energy of Lillie." Randolph to TJ, Jan. 31, 1801, in *Papers*, vol. 32.
36. TJ to Dinsmore, Dec. 1, 1802, no. 6540, TJ Papers, University of Virginia; Bear, "Mr. Jefferson's Nails."
37. Randolph to TJ, May 30, 1803, TJ Papers, University of Virginia; TJ to Randolph, June 8, 1803, in *Farm Book*, p. 19; Stanton, *Free Some Day*, p. 77; McLaughlin, *Jefferson and Monticello*, p. 113. Stanton states that Cary was a friend of the runaway James Hubbard and suggests that Cary too might have been planning to run away; if so, Colbert's prank deranged Cary's plans.
38. Martha Jefferson Randolph to TJ, Nov. 30, 1804, in *Family Letters*, p. 264.
39. Bear and Stanton, *Jefferson's Memorandum Books*, vol. 2, p. 1108.

40. TJ to Jones and Howell, May 16, 1804, in *Farm Book*, p. 445.

41. Oldham to TJ, Nov. 26, 1804, quoted in Stanton, *Free Some Day*, p. 116. I have corrected Oldham's spelling.

42. On July 20, 1805, TJ wrote to Oldham, who was then in Richmond: "I am informed that James Hemings my servant has put himself under your superintendance until he can hear from me on the subject of his return. I can readily excuse the follies of a boy and therefore his return shall ensure him an entire pardon. During my absence hereafter I should place him with Johnny Hemings and Lewis at house joiner's work. If you will get him a passage in the Richmond stage I will get Mr. Higginbotham to pay his fare on his arrival at Milton." It seems that Hemings briefly considered the offer, then thought better of it and disappeared (TJ to Oldham, July 20, 1805, Massachusetts Historical Society, Boston). A small note in TJ's records indicates that years later Jimmy Hemings did come back to the mountain, probably to see his family. TJ gave him a tip for finding the lost eyepiece of his telescope. But he never again came under TJ's control. McLaughlin, *Jefferson and Monticello*, pp. 113–15.

43. TJ to John Strode, June 5, 1805, Library of Congress; TJ to Randolph, June 5, 1805, Library of Congress.

44. Randolph to Nicholas Trist, Nov. 2, 1818, Papers of the Trist, Randolph, and Burke families, accession no. 10487.

45. Bear, *Jefferson at Monticello*, p. 98.

46. Alexis de Tocqueville, *Democracy in America*, http://xroads.virginia.edu/~HYPER /DETOC/home.html.

47. Waldstreicher, *Runaway America*, p. 185.

48. "Dillwyn Park Would Hold Memories of Struggle," p. A6, quoting Wilbert Dean.

49. Randolph to Nicholas Trist, Nov. 2, 1818.

50. Onuf, *Jefferson's Empire*, p. 9; Bob Dylan, "Lonesome Day Blues," in *"Love and Theft."*

9. A Mother's Prayers

1. Hannah's letter, *Farm Book*, pp. 41–42.

2. *Farm Book*, plates 9, 31.

3. TJ to Edmund Bacon, Poplar Forest, Nov. 29, 1817, quoted in Martin, "Mr. Jefferson's Business," p. 156.

4. Yancey to TJ, Oct. 20, 1819, in *Farm Book*, pp. 44–45.

5. Yancey to TJ, Oct. 14, 1819, in *Farm Book*, pp. 304–5.

6. Yancey to TJ, Oct. 20 and 26, 1819, in *Farm Book*, pp. 44–45; Oct. 14, 1819, p. 305.

7. Elizabeth Trist to Nicholas P. Trist, Nov. 28, 1822, Nicholas Philip Trist Papers, Library of Congress; transcription: Monticello.org, Family Letters Digital Archive, http://retirementseries.dataformat.com/Search.aspx. Trist wrote that Billy "horribly mutilated" the man's face.

8. *Richmond Enquirer*, Nov. 22, 1822, p. 1.

9. Henry Brown was a relative of Nicholas P. Trist, the husband of TJ's granddaughter Virginia; Jacob White was the overseer.

10. Wilson C. Nicholas Jr. to Thomas Jefferson Randolph, Jan. 31, 1823, March 2, 1824, accession no. 1397, box 4, Edgehill-Randolph Papers; Horn, *Thomas Jef-*

ferson's Poplar Forest, pp. 101–102; Stanton, *Free Some Day*, p. 85. The story of Hannah's Billy is difficult to reconstruct, and McLaughlin's account (*Jefferson and Monticello*, pp. 114–16) is partially incorrect, confusing Hannah's Billy with William "Billy" Hern. Stanton, *Free Some Day*, p. 85. Bedford County Court Order Book, vol. 18, pp. 318–19.

11. Elizabeth Trist to Nicholas P. Trist, Oct. 2, 1822, Nicholas Philip Trist Papers, Library of Congress, transcription: Family Letters Digital Archive.

10. *"I Will Answer for Your Safety . . . Banish All Fear"*

1. Harrison and Burke, *Two Monticello Childhoods*, p. 4.
2. Margaret Bayard Smith's Account of a Visit to Monticello, July 29, 1809, in *Papers*, Retirement Series, vol. 1.
3. Neiman, "Sub-floor Pits, Slave-Quarter Architecture, and the Social Dynamics of Chesapeake Slavery."
4. Neiman, "Changing Landscapes."
5. Ibid.
6. Ibid.
7. Bear, *Jefferson at Monticello*, pp. vi, 31.
8. www.monticello.org/archaeology/survey/site22.html.
9. Stanton, *Free Some Day*, pp. 74–77.
10. www.monticello.org/plantation/work/nailmaking.html; Daniel Bradley to TJ, Sept. 7, 1805, Massachusetts Historical Society, Boston; TJ to Daniel Bradley, Oct. 6, 1805, in *Farm Book*, pp. 20–21; Stanton, *Free Some Day*, pp. 75–76.
11. Stanton, *Free Some Day*, p. 83.
12. Bear, *Jefferson at Monticello*, pp. 97–99.
13. TJ to Reuben Perry, May 10, 1811, in *Papers*, Retirement Series, vol. 3.
14. Stanton, *Free Some Day*, pp. 80–82; Towler, "Albemarle County Court Orders."
15. Martin, "Mr. Jefferson's Business," p. xxxix.
16. Bear, *Jefferson at Monticello*, p. 80.
17. Ibid., p. 71.
18. Ibid., p. 97.
19. Bacon to TJ, May 19, 1819, quoted in Martin, "Mr. Jefferson's Business," p. xxxviii.
20. Bear, *Jefferson at Monticello*, p. 90.
21. Ibid., pp. 92–93.
22. Neiman, McFaden, and Wheeler, "Archaeological Investigation of the Elizabeth Hemings Site." In the summer of 2007 the archaeology team found evidence of other slave houses near this site.
23. Ibid., p. 8.
24. Ibid., p. 54. The tea set is on display at the Visitor Center.
25. Crawford: Getting Word Project File, interview, March 26, 2001, quoted in Bon-Harper, Neiman, and Wheeler, "Monticello's Park Cemetery," p. 9; visitors' question: ibid., p. 1.
26. Philip D. Morgan, *Slave Counterpoint*, p. 642.
27. Gawalt, "Jefferson's Slaves."
28. The Grangers also received seven pecks of cornmeal—the stuff of the hoecakes

that formed the staple of a bland diet. Bear, *Jefferson at Monticello*, p. 54; Sorensen, "Taking Care of Themselves."
29. TJ to Edward Coles, Aug. 25, 1814, in *Papers*, Retirement Series, vol. 7.
30. TJ to William A. Burwell, Jan. 28, 1805, in *Farm Book*, p. 20.

11. *"To Serve You Faithful"*

1. "With Respect to the three Jobs Stewart was to do I beleave it will be impossople
   to Get him to do them The old man has never done one or not more than one days
   work since you Left heare. He is Eternally drunk and like a mad man." Bacon to
   TJ, Nov. 8, 1807, in Martin, "Mr. Jefferson's Business" p. 59. "A very fine workman":
   Bear, *Jefferson at Monticello*, p. 102.
2. Quoted in Susan R. Stein, "Dining at Monticello: The 'Feast of Reason,'" in
   Fowler, *Dining at Monticello*, p. 74.
3. The French chef at the White House used a similar stove and wrote to TJ, "I am
   worried about the charcoal." Working with charcoal stoves was a recognized haz-
   ard, but there is no record of Monticello cooks becoming ill. Etienne Lemaire to
   TJ, Sept. 17, 1804, translation courtesy of Lucia Stanton.
4. The restorers followed a detailed inventory of cooking equipment drawn up by
   James Hemings before he left TJ's service. Dianne Swann-Wright, "African
   Americans and Monticello's Food Culture," in Fowler, *Dining at Monticello*, p. 42.
5. Justin A. Sarafin, "Like Clockwork: French Influence in Monticello's Kitchen," in
   Fowler, *Dining at Monticello*, pp. 25–26.
6. George Ticknor, Feb. 1815, in *Life, Letters, and Journals*, vol. 1, p. 36.
7. Fowler, *Dining at Monticello*, pp. 1, 7.
8. Elizabeth V. Chew, "Carrying the Keys: Women and Housekeeping at Monticello," in ibid., pp. 33–34.
9. Fowler, *Dining at Monticello*, p. 3.
10. Lucia Stanton, "Nourishing the Congress: Hospitality at the President's House,"
    in ibid., pp. 8, 11–13.
11. Stanton, "'A Well-Ordered Household'," p. 13.
12. Ibid., p. 10.
13. Freeman to TJ, April 1804, dated as received April 18, Library of Congress; Deed
    of John Freeman's Indenture to James Madison, in *Papers*, Retirement Series,
    vol. 1.
14. Freeman to TJ, March 2, 1809, Library of Congress.
15. Stanton, "'A Well-Ordered Household,'" p. 19.
16. TJ to Martha Jefferson Randolph, Jan. 27, 1803, in *Family Letters*, p. 242; www
    .history.com/this-day-in-history/presidents-child-born-in-white-house; www.msnbc
    .msn.com/id/28109794/ns/politics-white_house/t/blacks-white-house-slavery
    -service/#.TyvwUS01tu8; www.whitehouse.gov/about/first-ladies/marthajefferson
    (accessed Feb. 4, 2012).
17. Bear and Stanton, *Jefferson's Memorandum Books*, vol. 2, p. 1069.
18. *Family Letters*, pp. 229n2, 295n4.
19. Lemaire to TJ, Aug. 17, 1802, transcript of translation by Lucia Stanton, Jefferson
    Library, International Center for Jefferson Studies.

20. *Farm Book*, plate 129; Bear and Stanton, *Jefferson's Memorandum Books*, vol. 2, p. 1077; Stanton, "'A Well-Ordered Household,'" p. 11 caption.
21. Stanton, "'A Well-Ordered Household,'" pp. 9, 21n35.
22. TJ to Joseph Dougherty, Sept. 6, 1807, quoted in ibid., p. 12.
23. TJ to Dougherty, July 31, 1806, in *Farm Book*, p. 22.
24. Stanton, "'A Well-Ordered Household,'" p. 11.
25. TJ to Lewis, April 12, 1792, in *Papers*, vol. 23.
26. TJ to Bell, Sept. 25, 1792, in *Papers*, vol. 24.

12. The Double Aspect

1. Quoted in Justus, *Down from the Mountain*, p. 150.
2. Bear, *Jefferson at Monticello*, pp. 99–100.
3. Lucia Stanton, "Those Who Labor for My Happiness," in Onuf, *Jeffersonian Legacies*, pp. 152–53.
4. Ibid., p. 151.
5. Self and Stein, "Collaboration of Thomas Jefferson and John Hemings," p. 236.
6. Stanton, *Free Some Day*, p. 136.
7. Ibid., pp. 135–36.
8. TJ to Thomas Mann Randolph, May 19, 1793, in *Papers*, vol. 26.
9. Stanton, *Free Some Day*, p. 136.
10. TJ to Richard Richardson, memorandum [ca. Dec. 21, 1799], in *Papers*, vol. 31, note.
11. Bear, *Jefferson at Monticello*, p. 54.
12. Ibid., pp. 101–102.
13. Stanton, *Free Some Day*, pp. 71, 137.
14. TJ to Richardson, memorandum, in *Papers*, vol. 31; Langhorne, *Monticello*, p. 228.
15. Stanton, *Free Some Day*, pp. 121, 137; TJ to Martha Jefferson Randolph, Aug. 24, 1819, in *Family Letters*, p. 431.
16. Stanton, *Free Some Day*, p. 137.
17. Horn, *Thomas Jefferson's Poplar Forest*, p. 40.
18. TJ to Ellen Coolidge, Nov. 14, 1825, in *Family Letters*, p. 461; Martha J. Randolph to Ellen Coolidge, Nov. 16, 1825, Family Letters Digital Archive, Thomas Jefferson Foundation, Inc., http://retirementseries.dataformat.com; Bear and Stanton, *Jefferson's Memorandum Books*, vol. 2, p. 1391.
19. Cornelia Jefferson Randolph to Virginia Jefferson Randolph Trist, Nov. 7, 1814, Family Letters Digital Archive, Thomas Jefferson Foundation, Inc., http://retirementseries.dataformat.com
20. Ellen (Eleanora) Wayles Randolph Coolidge to Martha Jefferson Randolph, [Poplar Forest], [Nov. 1816?], Family Letters Digital Archive.
21. Quoted in Self and Stein, "Collaboration of Thomas Jefferson and John Hemings," p. 233.
22. TJ to Dinsmore, Nov. 15, 1808, Library of Congress.
23. TJ to Dinsmore, April 13, 1817, Jefferson and others, Sixty-Eight Letters to and from Jefferson.
24. TJ to Dinsmore, June 25, 1817.

25. TJ to Dinsmore, Sept. 26, 1810, in *Papers*, Retirement Series, vol. 3.
26. Langhorne, *Monticello*, p. 227.
27. Stanton, *Free Some Day*, p. 137.
28. Bear and Stanton, *Jefferson's Memorandum Books*, vol. 2, pp. 1026, 1265, 1275, 1328, 1352.
29. *Papers*, Retirement Series, vol. 1, pp. 192–93n; vol. 3, p. 520n.
30. Bacon wrote such a pass for Hubbard. Bear, *Jefferson at Monticello*, p. 98.
31. Bear, "Hemings Family of Monticello," p. 80.
32. Stanton, *Free Some Day*, p. 104.
33. TJ to Martha Jefferson Randolph, Aug. 8, 1790, in *Papers*, vol. 17.
34. Bear and Stanton, *Jefferson's Memorandum Books*, vol. 2, pp. 923–24.
35. Deed of Manumission for Robert Hemings, Dec. 24, 1794, in *Papers*, vol. 28; Stanton, *Free Some Day*, p. 118; TJ to Thomas Mann Randolph, Dec. 26, 1794, in *Papers*, vol. 28.
36. Martha Jefferson Randolph to TJ, Jan. 15, 1795, in *Papers*, vol. 28.
37. When Robert died in 1819 at age fifty-seven, Martha wrote to her father that "Poor old Robert Hemming is dead." Bear, "Hemings Family of Monticello," pp. 80–81; *Farm Book*, p. 451.
38. TJ to William Short, May 7, 1784, in *Papers*, vol. 7.
39. McLaughlin, *Jefferson and Monticello*, pp. 220–22.
40. Bear and Stanton, *Jefferson's Memorandum Books*, vol. 2, p. 808n7.
41. Ibid., p. 819.
42. Dianne Swann-Wright, "African Americans and Monticello's Food Culture," in Fowler, *Dining at Monticello*, p. 40; *Farm Book*, p. 15; Bear, "Hemings Family of Monticello," p. 82.
43. TJ to James Barbour, May 11, 1821, Library of Congress.
44. Communication from Leni Sorensen.
45. Lucia Stanton, "Nourishing the Congress: Hospitality at the President's House," in Fowler, *Dining at Monticello*, p. 189n4; Stanton, *Free Some Day*, pp. 125–29; Bear, "Hemings Family of Monticello," p. 84.
46. Langhorne, *Monticello*, p. 108.
47. Bear and Stanton, *Jefferson's Memorandum Books*, vol. 1, p. 371.
48. Randall, *Life of Thomas Jefferson*, vol. 1, pp. 337–39.
49. Monroe quoted in Stanton, *Free Some Day*, p. 104; TJ to Martha Jefferson Randolph, Aug. 8, 1790, in *Papers*, vol. 17; TJ to Hylton, July 1, 1792, in *Papers*, vol. 24.
50. There is no mention of Martin in the Memorandum Book after TJ's return from France.
51. TJ to Hylton, Nov. 22, 1792, in *Papers*, vol. 24. TJ was at Monticello from July 22 to September 27, and Martin is not mentioned in his household accounts. Bear and Stanton, *Jefferson's Memorandum Books*, vol. 2, pp. 877–78.
52. TJ to Martha Jefferson Randolph, Jan. 22, 1795, in *Papers*, vol. 28.
53. When Robert was sold to Dr. Stras, it was noted in the Memorandum Book, but Martin's sale was not; nor is there a record of his death. Some sources state that Martin Hemings died in 1807, but that is an error based on a misreading of TJ's records; there was another Martin who died in 1807.
54. Bear, *Jefferson at Monticello*, p. 4.

13. America's Cassandra

1. Turner, *Jefferson-Hemings Controversy*, pp. 355–56.
2. Fleming, *Intimate Lives of the Founding Fathers*, pp. 409–16.
3. The Woodson family oral history states that Tom Woodson was Sally Hemings's first child; but Madison Hemings never mentioned Tom Woodson, and the DNA test did not find any link between the Woodson and the Jefferson families. Joseph Fossett's descendants have claimed that he was TJ's son, but Madison Hemings, speaking of himself and his Hemings siblings, insisted, "We were the only children of his by a slave woman."
4. Durey, *With the Hammer of Truth*, p. 160.
5. Joshua D. Rothman, *Notorious in the Neighborhood*, p. 30; Burton, *Jefferson Vindicated*, p. 30.
6. Burton, *Jefferson Vindicated*, pp. 12–13.
7. Setlock, "Thomas Jefferson and Sally Hemings"; Arthur E. Sutherland, book review of *A Brief Narrative of the Case and Trial of John Peter Zenger* by James Alexander and Stanley Nider Katz, *Harvard Law Review* 77, no. 4 (Feb. 1964), pp. 789–90; historictrials.freeservers.com/Crosswell/wasp.htm.
8. Durey, *With the Hammer of Truth*, pp. 55, 124.
9. Transcription from Monticello website. Callender adopted a high moral tone in his assault on TJ for sexual misconduct, but he was no friend of African-Americans. The same issue of the *Recorder* carried an advertisement on the front page offering a $10 reward for a runaway slave named Fanny, and another ad offered for sale "A *light, active* negro boy." Potential buyers were advised to "enquire of the Printers."
10. *Richmond Examiner*, Sept. 25, 1802, in McMurry and McMurry, *Jefferson, Callender, and the Sally Story*, p. 53; Joshua D. Rothman, *Notorious in the Neighborhood*, p. 35.
11. *Richmond Examiner*, Sept. 25, 1802, in McMurry and McMurry, *Jefferson, Callender, and the Sally Story*, pp. 53–54; Durey, *With the Hammer of Truth*, p. 161.
12. Ellis, *American Sphinx* (1996 ed.), "Appendix: Note on the Sally Hemings Scandal." Ellis revised the appendix for subsequent editions. The 1996 version is on the Monticello website: www.pbs.org/wgbh/pages/frontline/shows/jefferson/cron/1996sphinx.html.
13. Jon Kukla examines this subject in depth and reproduces several original documents. Kukla, *Mr. Jefferson's Women*, pp. 189–98.
14. Brodie, *Thomas Jefferson*, p. 350.
15. Ibid., p. 360.
16. Durey, *With the Hammer of Truth*, pp. 160, 168, 170.
17. Brodie, *Thomas Jefferson*, p. 374; *Richmond Examiner*, July 20 and 27, 1803; McMurry and McMurry, *Jefferson, Callender, and the Sally Story*, p. 100.
18. Brodie, *Thomas Jefferson*, pp. 356, 374.
19. *Richmond Examiner*, July 20, 1803; Brodie, *Thomas Jefferson*, p. 370; Durey, *With the Hammer of Truth*, pp. 131, 166–71, 176.
20. *Report of the Research Committee on Thomas Jefferson and Sally Hemings*, p. F5; Burton, *Jefferson Vindicated*, pp. 133–34.
21. I am grateful to Jon Kukla for providing his transcriptions of the Cocke Diary, from the Cocke Papers, box 188, MSS no. 640. TJ's defenders question Cocke's

truthfulness, claiming that he nursed a grudge against TJ for a variety of reasons, one being that his roof leaked because he had followed a Jeffersonian design: "He was probably jealous and resentful." Burton, *Jefferson Vindicated*, pp. 94–96.

22. Lanier and Feldman, *Jefferson's Children*, p. 19. A TJ defender has alleged that the exclamation is a later interpolation by an unknown person, but the handwriting is identical to that on the rest of the page.

23. In his 1874 biography James Parton briefly brought up the Hemings story in order to dismiss it. Parton, *Life of Thomas Jefferson*, p. 569.

24. Hemings, "Life Among the Lowly"; Israel Jefferson, "Reminiscences of Israel Jefferson," in Brodie, *Thomas Jefferson*, p. 481. Israel Jefferson's original last name is now known to have been Gillette; he adopted the Jefferson surname at the urging of the Albemarle County clerk. Jeff Randolph's unsent letter: Justus, *Down from the Mountain*, pp. 148–52. McMurry and McMurry, *Anatomy of a Scandal*, p. xxxi.

25. Brodie, *Thomas Jefferson*, p. 476; Lucia Stanton and Dianne Swann-Wright, "Bonds of Memory: Identity and the Hemings Family," in Lewis and Onuf, *Sally Hemings and Thomas Jefferson*, p. 176; "Extract from a letter Fiske Kimball to Gibboney," Oct. 28, 1938, Genealogical data pertaining to the Hemings family of Monticello, MSS 6636 6636-a 6636-b 6636-c, Special Collections, University of Virginia. Quite possibly, Kimball made his remark not out of any prejudice of his own but from an awareness of the prejudice of his recipient.

26. Dos Passos was then writing *The Head and Heart of Thomas Jefferson*. Malone and Hochman, "Note on Evidence," p. 523. McMurry and McMurry, *Anatomy of a Scandal*, p. xxxi.

27. They wrote, "Our concern here . . . is with the circumstances of its appearance rather than its contents." Malone and Hochman, "Note on Evidence," pp. 524, 526.

28. Peterson, *Jefferson Image in the American Mind*, pp. 186–87. In addition to the Madison Hemings memoir, Peterson was discounting kinship claims by the Fossett family that had appeared in *Ebony* magazine.

29. Brodie also gave tentative credence to James Callender's allegation that TJ had been the father of "President Tom," supposedly the firstborn child of Sally Hemings, even though Madison Hemings made no mention of a brother named Tom in his memoir, listing his siblings as Beverly, Harriet, and Eston. He said his mother became pregnant in France by TJ and that the infant died at Monticello shortly after its birth. Brodie explained the contradiction by speculating that Tom had left Monticello before Madison's birth and that Sally wished to keep Tom's existence a secret even from his siblings to protect Tom's new identity. But Brodie rejected claims by Joseph Fossett's descendants that he was TJ's son. Brodie, *Thomas Jefferson*, pp. 292, 558n45.

30. Ibid., pp. 229–30.

31. Ibid., pp. 292, 439, 536n21; Harold Coolidge to Brodie, Dec. 14, 1970, in Bringhurst, "Fawn Brodie's *Thomas Jefferson*," p. 441.

32. Ellen (Eleanora) Wayles Randolph Coolidge to Joseph Coolidge, Oct. 24, 1858, Monticello.org, Family Letters Digital Archive, http://familyletters.dataformat.com/default.aspx. Ellen's letter was published in *Proceedings of the American Antiquarian Society* 84, pt 1 (April 1974), pp. 65–72, and in *New York Times*, May 18, 1974.

33. *New York Times*, July 4, 1984, p. C9.

34. Dabney and Kukla, "Monticello Scandals," p. 61.
35. Herbert Barger website: http://jeffersondnastudy.com/ (accessed Dec. 7, 2011).
36. No descendants of Beverly Hemings could be found—he had disappeared into the white world—and Madison had no living direct male descendants.
37. The DNA findings brought not just revelation but destruction. Fawn Brodie's "vindication" had been partial and very ambiguous. Though she thought there had been a "President Tom" Woodson born of Hemings and TJ in 1790, the DNA evidence proving that the Woodsons had no blood tie to the Jeffersons suggested to some that "President Tom" might never have existed, that James Callender had lied or been misled by his sources, and that Brodie had chased a phantom. In any case, Brodie, who died long before the DNA tests, had not been entirely convinced that the Woodson family was descended from President Tom: "The tie relating Thomas Woodson to Jefferson and Sally Hemings is not yet binding, but further research may uncover the essential links. The tenacious Woodson family oral history cannot be discounted just because all the links have not yet appeared." Brodie, "Thomas Jefferson's Unknown Grandchildren." The strength of the Woodson family's oral history suggests that they have some connection to the Monticello community.
38. Lander and Ellis, "Founding Father."
39. *Nature*, Jan. 7, 1999, p. 32.
40. As one of Jefferson's defenders wrote: "The new 'evidence' was rushed to press in the middle of the congressional impeachment inquiry of Bill Clinton. Prof. Ellis actively opposed the impeachment effort, and he repeatedly used his new position to draw parallels in defense of Mr. Clinton." Turner, "Truth About Jefferson."
41. Safire, "Sallygate."
42. Media Research Center, *CyberAlert*, Nov. 3, 1998, www.mrc.org/cyberalerts/1998/cyb19981103.asp#2.
43. Daniel P. Jordan, statement on the *Report of the Research Committee on Thomas Jefferson and Sally Hemings*, Jan. 26, 2000; "Jefferson Likely Dad of Slave Child," Associated Press, Jan. 26, 2000.
44. Daniel Jordan quote: www.pbs.org/jefferson/archives/interviews/jordan.htm.
45. Philip D. Morgan, "Interracial Sex in the Chesapeake," in Lewis and Onuf, *Sally Hemings and Thomas Jefferson*, p. 78. One member of Monticello's staff committee, White McKenzie Wallenborn, M.D., dissented from the majority view. He contended in his minority report that TJ had denied the Hemings allegations, and he concluded, "The historical evidence is not substantial enough to confirm nor for that matter to refute his paternity." In a later statement he wrote that the Monticello committee's conclusion had opened the door to "the campaign by leading universities (including Thomas Jefferson's own University of Virginia), magazines, university publications, national commercial and public TV networks, and newspapers to denigrate and destroy the legacy of one of the greatest of our founding fathers and one of the greatest of all of our citizens." In Dr. Wallenborn's view a more accurate conclusion would have been that "it is still impossible to prove with absolute certainty whether Thomas Jefferson did or did not father any of Sally Hemings's five children." *Thomas Jefferson Foundation DNA Study Committee Minority Report*, April 12, 1999; *Reply to Thomas Jefferson Foundation Response to*

   the *Minority Report to the DNA Study Committee,* 2nd revision, June 29, 2000; both at Monticello.org.

46. Shipp, "Reporting on Jefferson," p. B06.
47. Coates, *Jefferson-Hemings Myth,* p. 9.
48. Thomas, "Report That Jefferson Fathered Slave's Children Disputed."
49. The Irvine and Coulter articles, and many others, are archived at http://jefferson dnastudy.com/.
50. Mapp wrote, "If Alive, He Still Would Be Ahead of Our Time."
51. For nearly a decade the *Final Report of the Scholars Commission on the Jefferson-Hemings Matter, April 12, 2001* was available only online, and many of its files became unreadable. Robert Turner's 2011 print edition includes all the original scholarly views plus a lengthy analysis by Turner. Although the group boasted a professor of biochemistry and biophysics, its glaring weakness was the absence of any specialist on Southern history, plantation history, or African-American history.
52. Individual Views of Prof. Forrest McDonald, in Turner, *Jefferson-Hemings Controversy,* p. 311.
53. Turner, "Truth About Jefferson."
54. Turner, *Jefferson-Hemings Controversy,* p. 14; Bear, *Jefferson at Monticello,* p. 102.
55. Bear, *Jefferson at Monticello,* p. 22.
56. Isaac Jefferson, *Memoirs of a Monticello Slave,* p. 35. The original, handwritten setting copy of the manuscript, dating to the 1870s, is online: www2.lib.virginia .edu/small/collections/tj/memoirs.html.
57. When TJ's daughter and grandchildren were searching for any scrap of evidence that might exonerate TJ on the Hemings charge, they never mentioned Randolph as a possible father. The grandchildren placed the blame on their cousins the Carr brothers. Although some twenty-five male Jeffersons resided in Virginia in the years when Sally Hemings was having children, nearly all of them lived at great distances from Monticello, and no credible evidence suggests that any of them were on the mountain at the right time to be the father of a Hemings. If Randolph did father the Hemings children, he did so without leaving any evidence of his visits to the mountain. Even TJ's staunch defender Cynthia H. Burton conceded this point in her book, *Jefferson Vindicated*: "Not enough is known to definitely place Randolph at Monticello when all the Hemings children were conceived" (p. 60). At the time Eston Hemings was conceived, TJ had invited his brother Randolph to visit. Born on May 21, 1808, Eston was conceived between August 15 and September 12, 1807, according to Burton's calculations (ibid., table preceding p. 38, p. 58). TJ arrived at Monticello from Washington on August 4. Four days later he was handed a letter from Randolph, who asked him for money to pay for some seed Randolph was buying for Monticello. On August 12, TJ sent him the money with a note saying that their sister was at Monticello "and we shall be happy to see you also" (Mayo, *Thomas Jefferson and His Unknown Brother,* pp. 20–21). The letter from Randolph had been hand delivered to Monticello by Randolph's son Lewis in July, but in his August 12 reply TJ made no mention of Lewis's presence at Monticello, which he certainly would have done to keep Randolph apprised of his son's movements, a customary feature of the era's correspondence. (Another factor argues against Lewis: he was about fifteen years younger

than Sally Hemings.) Lewis must have left Monticello before TJ arrived on August 4—so Lewis could not have been the father of Eston. Did Randolph act on the invitation to visit? In his letter TJ enclosed the $20 cash payment Randolph had asked for, indicating that TJ did not expect to see his brother at Monticello anytime soon. Visits very often leave some kind of trace—a note in the accounts for a sum of money paid, received, or lent; a follow-up "thank you for coming" letter; or a mention in a letter to someone else that "Uncle Randolph has been here." But no record refers to Randolph actually visiting Monticello in August or September 1807.

14. The Man in the Iron Mask

1. http://etext.virginia.edu/railton/onstage/pilgrims1.html.
2. Quoted in Niebuhr, *Irony of American History*, p. 21.
3. Henry Randall to James Parton, June 1, 1868, transcribed in Brodie, *Thomas Jefferson*, p. 497.
4. Ibid., pp. 494–96.
5. This was the notorious James Callender. Durey, *With the Hammer of Truth*, p. 159.
6. Quoted in Burton, *Jefferson Vindicated*, p. 80.
7. Bear, *Jefferson at Monticello*, p. 102. I have omitted a portion of Bacon's remarks, which I will take up later.
8. *Farm Book*, plate 130.
9. Henry Randall to James Parton, transcribed in Brodie, *Thomas Jefferson*, pp. 495–96.
10. Ibid. Cynthia Burton suggests that Hemings might have been away from Monticello at a Carr farm, but her evidence is not compelling. Years later Jeff Randolph related what his mother had said to Randall, who passed Martha's refutation along to another biographer, James Parton. Randall claimed to Parton that he had independently verified Martha's research: "It so happened when I was afterwards examining an old account book of the Jeffersons I came pop on the original entry of this slaves birth: and I was then able from well known circumstances to prove the fifteen months separation . . ." Here, at that spot in Randall's sentence, generations of scholars have held their breath, tantalized. Randall continued: "but those circumstances have faded from my memory. I have no doubt I could recover them however did Mr. Jefferson's vindication in the least depend upon them." The minutest inquiries into plantation records and calendars have failed to turn up the "well known circumstances."
11. John Cook Wyllie to James A. Bear Jr., May 6, 1966, "Genealogy of Betty Hemmings Compiled by John Cook Wyllie, Genealogical Data Pertaining to Hemings," Wyllie Papers.
12. There is confusion over which Carr brother was supposedly the lover of Sally Hemings. In this passage, Randall says that Jeff Randolph identified Peter Carr as Hemings's lover; in Ellen Coolidge's 1858 letter to her husband she identifies Samuel Carr. It is more likely that Samuel was the one they both had in mind. Ellen wrote her letter immediately after her conversation with Jeff when her memory of the details would have been fresh. Randall wrote his letter twelve years after

his conversation with Jeff Randolph, so it is likely Randall got the Carr brothers mixed up. But to further complicate the issue, in an 1873 letter Jeff wrote, "The paternity of these persons was admitted by two others," meaning *both* of the Carr brothers.

13. Ellen Wayles Randolph Coolidge to Joseph Coolidge, Oct. 24, 1858, Family Letters Digital Archive, Thomas Jefferson Foundation, Inc., http://retirementseries.data format.com. The transcription in early editions of Gordon-Reed, *Thomas Jefferson and Sally Hemings*, pp. 258–60, was erroneous and inadvertently misleading; in a reprint of 2003 these errors were corrected.

14. Towler, "Albemarle County Court Orders," Albemarle County Minute Book, 1856–59, Oct. 6, 1857, p. 190. This record is among the fascinating discoveries made by Sam Towler in the Albemarle County courthouse.

15. *Richmond Examiner*, Sept. 25, 1802, in McMurry and McMurry, *Jefferson, Callender, and the Sally Story*, pp. 53–54; Durey, *With the Hammer of Truth*, p. 161.

16. Bear, *Jefferson at Monticello*, p. 88. Jeff Randolph disputed Bacon's story.

17. Thomas Jefferson Randolph Memoirs, version 2, no. 1397.

15. "I Only Am Escaped Alone to Tell Thee"

1. Hemings, "Life Among the Lowly." The Brodie transcription, *Thomas Jefferson*, pp. 471–76, is the most reliable in print, with only minor, inconsequential errors.

2. Brodie, *Thomas Jefferson*, p. 32.

3. Ibid., p. 228.

4. Ibid., p. 32.

5. Ibid., p. 30.

6. Trescott, "Hemings Affair," pp. B1, B6.

7. Dabney and Kukla, "Monticello Scandals," p. 61.

8. Robert Towne dramatized and updated this brand of mastery in the film *Chinatown*, when an aged tycoon, Noah Cross, in one coup seizes control of both the water supply and the young granddaughter he has incestuously fathered. When the detective Jake Gittes asks the magnate, who already has more wealth than he can possibly use, what more he could possibly desire, Cross replies, "The *future*, Mr. Gittes. The future." At the moment when, in a horrifying spasm of violence, Cross wins everything he covets, he symbolically wraps his hand around the eyes of his daughter-granddaughter to shut out the knowledge of how she came to be and how she came into his possession; she must be made blind.

9. One scholar expressed doubt there was a "treaty" at all: Philip D. Morgan, "Interracial Sex in the Chesapeake," in Lewis and Onuf, *Sally Hemings and Thomas Jefferson*, p. 84n45. Jon Kukla raises the possibility that the affair began not in France but at Monticello in 1793 or 1794: *Mr. Jefferson's Women*, pp. 125–33.

10. TJ to Martha Jefferson Randolph, June 8, 1797, in *Papers*, vol. 29.

11. Lucia Stanton and Dianne Swann-Wright, "Bonds of Memory: Identity and the Hemings Family," in Lewis and Onuf, *Sally Hemings and Thomas Jefferson*, p. 174.

12. Burton, *Jefferson Vindicated*, pp. 123–24. I am grateful to David Kalergis for his observation that Madison may have learned the word from *Tristram Shandy*.

13. Stanton and Swann-Wright, "Bonds of Memory," p. 182n5.

14. There was a tradition among some African-American families from Charlottesville that Harriet returned there after TJ's death and started a family, but the
evidence they offered in the 1940s is extremely garbled and calls for further
research. Pearl Graham, Notes on an Interview with Three Descendants of Thomas
Jefferson, July 28, 1948, typescript graciously provided by Lucia Stanton. Graham,
"Thomas Jefferson and Sally Hemings," pp. 98–100. Brodie, *Thomas Jefferson*,
pp. 554–55n47.
15. Quotation from *Cleveland American*, reprinted in *Liberator*, Dec. 19, 1845, in
Stanton and Swann-Wright, "Bonds of Memory," p. 165.
16. Stanton and Swann-Wright, "Bonds of Memory," p. 164.
17. "A Sprig of Jefferson Was Eston Hemings," *Scioto Gazette*, Aug. 1, 1902, quoted in
Frontline website "Jefferson's Blood," www.pbs.org/wgbh/pages/frontline/shows
/jefferson/cron/1902sprig.html, also quoted in Leary, "Sally Hemings's Children,"
pp. 172–73. According to this account, which appeared nearly fifty years after
Eston's death, "There came from Monticello, Virginia, to Chillicothe, a remarkably fine looking colored man and his family. Eston Hemings was of a light bronze
color, a little over six feet tall, well proportioned, very erect and dignified; his
nearly straight hair showed a tint of auburn."
18. Fawn M. Brodie, "Thomas Jefferson's Unknown Grandchildren," *Getting Word:
The Newsletter* (Winter 2007/2008), p. 2.
19. "Drafted Man, Classed as Colored, Commits Suicide in an Ohio Camp," Sept. 29,
1917, p. 4; Sept. 30, 1917, p. 3.
20. Stanton and Swann-Wright, "Bonds of Memory," p. 169.
21. Ibid., p. 162.
22. Ibid., pp. 166–67.
23. Ibid., p. 171.

16. *"The Effect on Them Was Electrical"*

1. Petition of the American Convention for Promoting the Abolition of Slavery, quoted
in Adam Rothman, *Slave Country*, p. 27.
2. Ketcham, "Dictates of Conscience," p. 52; Ress, *Governor Edward Coles*, pp. 11–17.
3. Ress, *Governor Edward Coles*, p. 34.
4. Monroe, "Edward Coles, Patrician Emancipator," www.lib.niu.edu/2005/iht
1210502.html.
5. Ketcham, "Dictates of Conscience," pp. 47–48.
6. Coles, "Emancipation," Oct. 1827, p. 1. I am very grateful to Bruce Carveth for
generously providing copies of his Coles material. Coles knew he could ease his
conscience simply by asking his father for some other property, but he reasoned
that the effect would be merely to perpetuate the enslavement of his allotted inheritance "as if I had sold the portion of them which I should otherwise have
inherited."
7. He considered and abandoned the idea of keeping the freed people in Virginia,
evading the removal law "by not having the free papers recorded," and formalizing
the emancipation in his will so that the freed people would be protected in case
of his sudden death.
8. Coles, "Emancipation," pp. 2–3.

9. Coles, "Autobiography," n.p.
10. Ibid.
11. Morse, *American Geography*, pp. 390–91.
12. Brissot de Warville, quoted in Poole and Buchanan, *Anti-Slavery Opinions Before the Year 1800*, www.gutenberg.org/files/23956/23956-h/23956-h.htm.
13. Ress, *Governor Edward Coles*, pp. 42–43; Ketcham, "Dictates of Conscience," p. 52.
14. Coles to TJ, July 31, 1814, in *Papers*, Retirement Series, vol. 7.
15. TJ to Coles, Aug. 25, 1814, in *Papers*, Retirement Series, vol. 7.
16. Coles to TJ, Sept. 26, 1814, in *Papers*, Retirement Series, vol. 7.
17. Billy Wayson, lecture, Jefferson Library, International Center for Jefferson Studies, May 2011.
18. Short to TJ, Feb. 27, 1798, in *Papers*, vol. 30.
19. Kosciuszko wrote three more wills in Europe after leaving the United States. These dealt mainly with his property in Europe, though he did decide in 1806 to leave $3,700 from the U.S. funds to his American godson, Kosciuszko Armstrong (son of John Armstrong Jr., U.S. minister to France). He corresponded with TJ in 1817 and reiterated that his intention to free slaves with his American funds remained "fixed." Kosciuszko believed that his European wills would in no way affect his American will, but TJ's refusal to execute Kosciuszko's will left it in limbo, an attractive prize for litigants. Armstrong and other claimants tried and failed to invalidate the emancipation will in a U.S. suit in 1823, giving TJ a second chance, but he did nothing. Two decades later another suit succeeded, and the U.S. will was declared invalid by the Supreme Court. Had TJ acted as his friend had wished, several enslaved families would have been liberated and become landowners in a free state. Mizwa, "Kosciuszko's 'Fortune' in America and What Became of It," pp. 1–3.
20. Turner, "Did Jefferson Sleep with Sally Hemings?"
21. *Life and Ancestry of Warner Mifflin*, pp. 84, 79, 85.
22. Freehling, *Reintegration of American History*, p. 188.
23. Richard Newman, "Good Communications Corrects Bad Manners," in Hammond and Mason, *Contesting Slavery*, p. 77.
24. Fogel, *Slavery Debates*, p. 39.
25. TJ to Benjamin Banneker, Aug. 30, 1791, in *Papers*, vol. 22.
26. Foster, *Jeffersonian America*, pp. 148–49.
27. TJ to Edmund Bacon, memorandum Fall 1806, in *Farm Book*, p. 25.
28. TJ to Grégoire, Feb. 25, 1809, in Peterson, *Thomas Jefferson: Writings*, p. 1202; TJ to Joel Barlow, Oct. 8, 1809, in *Papers*, Retirement Series, vol. 1.
29. TJ to Burwell, Jan. 28, 1805, in "Quotations on Slavery and Emancipation," www.monticello.org/site/jefferson/quotations-slavery-and-emancipation.
30. Brown, "Senate Debate on the Breckinridge Bill," p. 347.
31. TJ to John Holmes, April 22, 1820, in "Quotations on Slavery and Emancipation," www.monticello.org/site/jefferson/quotations-slavery-and-emancipation.
32. TJ to John Wayles Eppes, June 30, 1820, in *Farm Book*, p. 26.
33. TJ to Joel Yancey, Jan. 17, 1819, in *Farm Book*, p. 43.
34. TJ to Lydia Sigourney, July 18, 1824, in "Quotations on Slavery and Emancipation," www.monticello.org/site/jefferson/quotations-slavery-and-emancipation.

35. Elizabeth Trist to Catharine Wistar Bache, Dec. 28, 1810, Family Letters Digital Archive, Thomas Jefferson Foundation, Inc., http://retirementseries.dataformat .com.
36. Scanlon and Gallatin, "A Sudden Conceit," p. 152.

17. *"Utopia in Full Reality"*

1. Martha Jefferson Randolph to Ellen W. Randolph Coolidge, Aug. 2, 1825, Family Letters Digital Archive, Thomas Jefferson Foundation, Inc., http://retirementseries .dataformat.com.
2. Berlin, *Generations of Captivity*, p. 161.
3. Thomas J. Randolph, *Speech of Thomas J. Randolph*, p. 17.
4. Baldwin, *Cross of Redemption*, p. 152.
5. *Notes on the State of Virginia*.
6. TJ to James Monroe, Nov. 24, 1801, in *Papers*, vol. 35.
7. Jed Handelsman Shugerman, "The Louisiana Purchase and South Carolina's Reopening of the Slave Trade in 1803," pp. 272–73.
8. McColley, *Slavery and Jeffersonian Virginia*, p. 125.
9. Hammond, *Slavery, Freedom, and Expansion*, p. 48.
10. Adam Rothman, *Slave Country*, pp. 24–26.
11. Ibid., pp. 31–32; Brown, "Senate Debate on the Breckinridge Bill," p. 345.
12. Brown, "Senate Debate on the Breckinridge Bill," p. 347.
13. Paine to TJ, Jan. 25, 1805; TJ to Paine, June 5, 1805, Jefferson Papers, Library of Congress.
14. Taylor, *From Timbuktu to Katrina*, p. 75.
15. Hammond, *Slavery, Freedom, and Expansion*, p. 47.
16. Appleby, *Thomas Jefferson*, p. 136.
17. Hammond, *Slavery, Freedom, and Expansion*, pp. 44–45.
18. Ibid., pp. 30, 39–47.
19. Brown, *Constitutional History*, p. 215.
20. Berlin, *Many Thousands Gone*, p. 9.
21. William W. Freehling, "The Louisiana Purchase and the Coming of the Civil War," in Levinson and Sparrow, *Louisiana Purchase and American Expansion*, pp. 72–73.
22. William Cabell Rives to James Madison, April 18, 1833, http://rotunda.upress .virginia.edu/founders/default.xqy?keys=FOEA-print-02-02-02-2721.
23. TJ to Joel Yancey, Jan. 17, 1819, in *Farm Book*, p. 43.
24. TJ to Jeremiah Goodman, Nov. 30, 1815, July 20, 1817, in *Farm Book*, pp. 40–41.
25. Taylor, "American Abyss," p. 390.
26. Quoted in Burstein, *Jefferson's Secrets*, p. 142.
27. Ludwig von Mises, letter to Ayn Rand, Jan. 23, 1958, http://hessenflow.wordpress .com/2011/04/23/ludwig-von-mises-letter-to-ayn-rand/; Ayn Rand, *Atlas Shrugged*, p. 975.
28. Interview with Joseph Ellis. www.pbs.org/wgbh/pages/frontline/shows/jefferson /interviews/ellis.html.
29. TJ to William Short, April 13, 1800, in *Papers*, vol. 31.
30. Hochman, "Thomas Jefferson," pp. 223–25. The historian Billy Wayson remarked to me that TJ was "a genius at finance." He tapped numerous supplies of credit,

including the banks he professed to loathe, and skillfully juggled and refinanced his loans.

31. Ibid., p. 238; Sloan, *Principle and Interest*, p. 11.
32. Israel Jefferson quoted in Brodie, *Thomas Jefferson*, p. 481.
33. Stanton, *Free Some Day*, pp. 144–45.
34. Isaac Granger said: "Sally had a son named Madison, who learned to be a great fiddler. He has been in Petersburg twice: was here when the balloon went up— the balloon that Beverly sent off." Bear, *Jefferson at Monticello*, p. 4.
35. Crouch, *Eagle Aloft*, pp. 25, 172.
36. *Liberty Hall and Cincinnati Gazette*, January 8, 1835.

18. Jefferson Anew

1. In the 1790s he purchased the side of the adjacent mountain, Montalto, that could be seen from Monticello, cleared its trees, planted meadows, and set sheep to grazing there to create a pastoral vista.
2. Bon-Harper, "Contrasting Worlds," pp. 4–5.
3. Peterson, *Jefferson Image in the American Mind*, p. 49.
4. TJ to Robert Pleasants, Aug. 27, 1796, in *Papers*, vol. 29.
5. Boulton, "American Paradox," p. 473.
6. Ticknor, *Life, Letters, and Journals*, p. 35.
7. Miller, *Wolf by the Ears*, pp. 156, 176.
8. Peter S. Onuf, "Thomas Jefferson and American Democracy," in Boles and Hall, *Seeing Jefferson Anew*, p. 14.
9. Kevin Butterfield, Review of Boles, John B.; Hall, Randal L., eds., *Seeing Jefferson Anew: In His Time and Ours*. H-Law, H-Net Reviews. April 2011. www.h-net.org /reviews/showrev.php?id=31509.
10. Walter Johnson, "Inconsistency, Contradiction, and Complete Confusion: The Everyday Life of the Law of Slavery," *Law & Social Inquiry* 22, no. 2 (Spring 1997), p. 413.
11. Foster, *Jeffersonian America*, p. 149. Also quoted in Lucia Stanton, "Those Who Labor for My Happiness," in Onuf, *Jeffersonian Legacies*, p. 163.
12. Onuf, "Scholars' Jefferson," p. 675.
13. Ellis, *American Sphinx*, p. 104.
14. David Brooks, "The Great Seduction," *New York Times*, June 10, 2008.
15. "Jefferson Lottery," Monticello.org.
16. Peterson, *Thomas Jefferson and the New Nation*, pp. 23, 538, 149, 535, 534.
17. Johnson, "On Agency"; Morris, "Articulation of Two Worlds."
18. Gordon-Reed, *Hemingses of Monticello*, p. 405.
19. Phillips, *American Negro Slavery*, pp. 184–85.
20. Waldstreicher, *Runaway America*, p. 232.
21. TJ to David Bailey Warden, Dec. 26, 1820, in Ford, *Works of Thomas Jefferson*, vol. 12.
22. TJ to Charles Pinckney, Sept. 30, 1820, in Ford, *Works of Thomas Jefferson*, vol. 12; TJ to Thomas Cooper, Sept. 10, 1814, in "Quotations on Slavery and Emancipation," www.monticello.org/site/jefferson/quotations-slavery-and-emancipation.
23. Niebuhr, *Irony of American History*, p. 23.

24. In an essay about the implications of the DNA tests that linked TJ to Sally
    Hemings, Gordon Wood writes of the national "symbolic memory," saying that
    "distortions of heritage are precisely what many people want and perhaps need in
    order to keep the past alive and meaningful. We critical historians thus tamper
    with popular heritage at our peril." Gordon Wood, "The Ghosts of Monticello," in
    Lewis and Onuf, *Sally Hemings and Thomas Jefferson*, pp. 31–32.

Bibliography

Jefferson's Papers

Unless otherwise noted, all citations to Thomas Jefferson's letters and other papers are to the online, electronic edition: *The Papers of Thomas Jefferson Digital Edition*, ed. Barbara B. Oberg and J. Jefferson Looney (Charlottesville: University of Virginia Press, Rotunda, 2008). This digital edition is available on the website "The Founders Online" through the National Archives at http://founders.archives.gov/. The text of the digital edition is arranged chronologically, making page-number citations unnecessary. Citations will give the item's date and volume number. This edition, still in progress, does not yet include all of Jefferson's papers.

Jefferson's orthography has vexed modern editors. My extracts from Jefferson's writings generally preserve his unorthodox spelling and his preference for lowercase letters at the start of sentences. In some instances I have capitalized words for readability and clarity of meaning.

Most of Jefferson's original papers are held at the Library of Congress. Images of these documents, and some transcriptions, are available at http://memory.loc.gov/ammem/collections/jefferson_papers/.

The Massachusetts Historical Society also holds a major collection of Jefferson's papers. The society has placed online Jefferson's Farm Book, architectural drawings, and other papers in a searchable edition with images of the original pages: *Thomas Jefferson Papers: An Electronic Archive* (Boston: Massachusetts Historical Society, 2003), http://www.thomasjeffersonpapers.org/.

Thomas Jefferson's Farm Book, ed. Edwin Morris Betts (Charlottesville, Va.: Thomas Jefferson Memorial Foundation, 1953), includes a facsimile of the original Farm Book along with several hundred pages of selected papers. Citations to the facsimile are denoted by plate numbers; citations to papers are denoted by page numbers. The original Farm Book is in the collections of the Massachusetts Historical Society. For unknown reasons at an unknown time by an unknown person, numerous leaves of the original Farm Book were removed, including an extremely important page (p. 25) listing slaves sold or given away by Jefferson. This page and others have surfaced in other collections.

Other Jefferson papers, as well as many important papers of his extended family, are in the Albert and Shirley Small Special Collections Library, University of Virginia. It is useful to consult "A Calendar of the Jefferson Papers of the University of Virginia," http://ead.lib.virginia.edu/vivaxtf/view?docId=uva-sc/viu00007.xml.

Citations to "Ford" are to the online publication: *The Works of Thomas Jefferson*, ed. Paul Leicester Ford, Federal Edition (New York: G. P. Putnam's Sons, 1904–5); http://oll.libertyfund.org/index.php?option=com_staticxt&staticfile=show.php%3Ftitle=1734&Itemid=28; http://oll.libertyfund.org/?option=com_staticxt&staticfile=show.php%3Ftitle=1734.

Thomas Jefferson, *The Writings of Thomas Jefferson*, ed. Andrew Adgate Lipscomb and Albert Ellery Bergh (Washington, D.C.: Thomas Jefferson Memorial Association of the United States, 1903), Google Books. Print source: *Thomas Jefferson: Writings*, ed. Merrill Peterson (New York: Library of America, 1984).

All quotations from Jefferson's *Notes on the State of Virginia* are taken from the searchable online edition: http://etext.virginia.edu/toc/modeng/public/JefVirg.html. Print source: Thomas Jefferson, *Notes on the State of Virginia*, ed. David Waldstreicher (Boston: Bedford/St. Martin's, 2002).

Madison Hemings Memoir

Monticello's website has the only accurate transcription of Hemings's memoir as published in 1873; it was posted late in 2012: www.monticello.org/getting-word/people/madison-hemings. All earlier published versions are incorrect in one way or another. The one in Brodie, *Thomas Jefferson*, pp. 471–76, is the most reliable in print, although it does have errors. The one in editions prior to 2013 of Gordon-Reed, *Thomas Jefferson and Sally Hemings*, drops a phrase and a sentence, inadvertently garbling the meaning of two important passages; alerted to these problems by this author, Gordon-Reed made corrections for new printings of her book. Other sources using erroneous transcriptions include Lewis and Onuf, *Sally Hemings and Thomas Jefferson*, app. A, pp. 255–58; the Frontline website "Jefferson's Blood"; and the printed version of the 2000 Monticello Hemings report. (A legible image of the entire original newspaper article, "Life Among the Lowly, No. 1," *Pike County Republican* (Ohio), March 13, 1873, has always been difficult to obtain. A partial image is available at www.loc.gov/exhibits/jefferson/images/vc11.jpg.)

Books and Dissertations

Adams, William Howard. *Jefferson's Monticello*. New York: Abbeville Press, 1983.
———. *The Paris Years of Thomas Jefferson*. New Haven, Conn.: Yale University Press, 1997.
Appleby, Joyce. *Thomas Jefferson*. New York: Times Books, 2003.
Baldwin, James. *The Cross of Redemption: Uncollected Writings*, ed. Randall Kenan. New York: Vintage, 2011.
Bear, James A., Jr., ed. *Jefferson at Monticello*. Charlottesville: University of Virginia Press, 1967.
Bear, James A., Jr., and Lucia C. Stanton, eds. *Jefferson's Memorandum Books*. 2 vols. Princeton, N.J.: Princeton University Press, 1997.
Becker, Carl. *The Declaration of Independence: A Study in the History of Political Ideas*. New York: Harcourt, Brace and Company, 1922.

Beiswanger, William L. *Monticello in Measured Drawings*. Charlottesville, Va.: Thomas Jefferson Memorial Foundation, 1998.

Berlin, Ira. *Generations of Captivity: A History of African-American Slaves*. Cambridge, Mass.: Belknap Press of Harvard University Press, 2003.

————. *Many Thousands Gone*. Cambridge, Mass.: Belknap Press of Harvard University Press, 1998.

Bleser, Carol, ed. *In Joy and in Sorrow: Women, Family, and Marriage in the Victorian South, 1830–1990*. New York: Oxford University Press, 1991.

Boles, John B., and Randal L. Hall, eds. *Seeing Jefferson Anew: In His Time and Ours*. Charlottesville: University of Virginia Press, 2010.

Boswell, James, and John Wilson Croker. *The Life of Samuel Johnson, LL.D.: Including a Journal of a Tour to the Hebrides*. New York: George Dearborn, 1833.

Brodie, Fawn M. *Thomas Jefferson: An Intimate History*. New York: W. W. Norton, 1974.

Brown, Everett S. *The Constitutional History of the Louisiana Purchase 1803–1812*. Berkeley: University of California Press, 1920. www.archive.org/stream/constitutionalhi00browrich/constitutionalhi00browrich_djvu.txt.

Burstein, Andrew. *Jefferson's Secrets: Death and Desire at Monticello*. New York: Basic Books, 2005.

Burton, Cynthia H. *Jefferson Vindicated: Fallacies, Omissions, and Contradictions in the Hemings Genealogical Search*. Keswick, Va.: Cynthia H. Burton, 2005.

The Cambridge Companion to Thomas Jefferson. Edited by Frank Shuffleton. Cambridge, U.K.: Cambridge University Press, 2009.

Coates, Eyler Robert, ed. *The Jefferson-Hemings Myth: An American Travesty*. Charlottesville, Va.: Jefferson Editions, 2001.

Conrad, Joseph. *Heart of Darkness*. Chestertown, Md.: Chester River Press, 2008.

Cooper, John Milton, Jr., and Thomas J. Knock, eds. *Jefferson, Lincoln, and Wilson: The American Dilemma of Race and Democracy*. Charlottesville: University of Virginia Press, 2010.

Crouch, Thomas D. *The Eagle Aloft: Two Centuries of the Balloon in America*. Washington, D.C.: Smithsonian Institution Press, 1983.

Dain, Bruce. *A Hideous Monster of the Mind: American Race Theory in the Early Republic*. Cambridge, Mass.: Harvard University Press, 2002.

Daugherty, Sonia. *The Way of an Eagle: An Intimate Biography of Thomas Jefferson and His Fight for Democracy*. New York: Oxford University Press, 1941. Reprinted as *Thomas Jefferson: Fighter for Freedom and Human Rights*. New York: Ungar, 1961.

Davis, David Brion. *The Problem of Slavery in the Age of Revolution, 1770–1823*. Ithaca, N.Y.: Cornell University Press, 1975.

D'Souza, Dinesh. *What's So Great About America*. Washington, D.C.: Regnery, 2002.

Durey, Michael. *With the Hammer of Truth: James Thomson Callender and America's Early National Heroes*. Charlottesville: University Press of Virginia, 1990.

Ellis, Joseph J. *American Sphinx*. New York: Vintage Books, 1998.

The Family Letters of Thomas Jefferson. Edited by Edwin Morris Betts and James Adam Bear Jr. Columbia: University of Missouri Press, 1966.

Finkelman, Paul. *Slavery and the Founders: Race and Liberty in the Age of Jefferson*. Armonk, N.Y.: M. E. Sharpe, 2001.

Fleming, Thomas. *The Intimate Lives of the Founding Fathers*. New York: HarperCollins, 2009.

Fogel, Robert William. *The Slavery Debates, 1952–1990: A Retrospective*. Baton Rouge: Louisiana State University Press, 2003.

Foster, Augustus John. *Jeffersonian America: Notes on the United States of America Collected in the Years 1805–6–7 and 11–12 by Sir Augustus John Foster, Bart*. Edited by Richard Beale Davis. San Marino, Calif.: Huntington Library, 1954.

Fowler, Damon Lee, ed. *Dining at Monticello*. Charlottesville, Va.: Thomas Jefferson Foundation, 2005.

Freehling, William W. *The Reintegration of American History: Slavery and the Civil War*. New York: Oxford University Press, 1994.

Freeman, Douglas Southall. *George Washington: A Biography*. 7 vols. New York: Charles Scribner's Sons, 1948–57.

Gaines, William H., Jr. *Thomas Mann Randolph*. Baton Rouge: Louisiana State University Press, 1966.

Gordon-Reed, Annette. *The Hemingses of Monticello: An American Family*. New York: W. W. Norton, 2008.

————. *Thomas Jefferson and Sally Hemings: An American Controversy*. Charlottesville: University Press of Virginia, 1997.

Hammond, John Craig. *Slavery, Freedom, and Expansion in the Early American West*. Charlottesville: University of Virginia Press, 2007.

Hammond, John Craig, and Matthew Mason, eds. *Contesting Slavery: The Politics of Bondage and Freedom in the New American Nation*. Charlottesville: University of Virginia Press, 2011.

Harrison, Ellen Wayles Randolph, and Martha Jefferson Trist Burke. *Two Monticello Childhoods: Anniversary Dinner at Monticello, October 14, 1976, in Memory of Thomas Jefferson*. Charlottesville, Va.: Thomas Jefferson Memorial Foundation, 1976.

Hatzenbuehler, Ronald L. *"I Tremble for My Country": Thomas Jefferson and the Virginia Gentry*. Gainesville: University Press of Florida, 2006.

Hochman, Steven Harold. "Thomas Jefferson: A Personal Financial Biography." Ph.D. diss., University of Virginia, 1987.

Holton, Woody. *Forced Founders: Indians, Debtors, Slaves, and the Making of the American Revolution in Virginia*. Chapel Hill: University of North Carolina Press, 1999.

Horn, Joan L. *Thomas Jefferson's Poplar Forest: A Private Place*. Forest, Va.: Corporation for Jefferson's Poplar Forest, 2002.

Howard, Hugh. *Dr. Kimball and Mr. Jefferson: Rediscovering the Founding Fathers of American Architecture*. New York: Bloomsbury, 2006.

Jefferson [Granger], Isaac. *Memoirs of a Monticello Slave, as Dictated to Charles Campbell in the 1840's by Isaac, One of Thomas Jefferson's Slaves*. Charlottesville: University of Virginia Press, 1951.

Jordan, Winthrop D. *White over Black: American Attitudes Toward the Negro, 1550–1812*. Chapel Hill: University of North Carolina Press, 1968.

Justus, Judith P. *Down from the Mountain: The Oral History of the Hemings Family: Are They the Black Descendants of Thomas Jefferson?* Perrysburg, Ohio: Jeskurtara, 1990.

Kelso, William M. *Archaeology at Monticello: Artifacts of Everyday Life in the Plantation Community*. Charlottesville, Va.: Thomas Jefferson Memorial Foundation, 1997.

Kennedy, Roger G. *Mr. Jefferson's Lost Cause: Land, Farmers, Slavery, and the Louisiana Purchase*. New York: Oxford University Press, 2003.

Kern, Susan. *The Jeffersons at Shadwell*. New Haven, Conn.: Yale University Press, 2010.

Kranish, Michael. *Flight from Monticello: Thomas Jefferson at War*. New York: Oxford University Press, 2010.

Kukla, Jon. *Mr. Jefferson's Women*. New York: Knopf, 2007.

Langhorne, Elizabeth. *Monticello: A Family Story*. Chapel Hill, N.C.: Algonquin Books, 1987.

Lanier, Shannon, and Jane Feldman. *Jefferson's Children: The Story of One American Family*. New York: Random House, 2000.

La Rochefoucauld-Liancourt, François-Alexandre-Frédéric. *Travels Through the United States of North America, the Country of the Iroquois, and Upper Canada, in the Years 1795, 1796, and 1797*. London, 1800.

Leichtle, Kurt E., and Bruce G. Carveth. *Crusade Against Slavery: Edward Coles, Pioneer of Freedom*. Carbondale: Southern Illinois University Press, 2011.

Levinson, Sanford, and Bartholomew H. Sparrow, eds. *The Louisiana Purchase and American Expansion, 1803–1898*. Lanham, Md.: Rowman & Littlefield, 2005.

Levy, Andrew. *The First Emancipator: The Forgotten Story of Robert Carter, the Founding Father Who Freed His Slaves*. New York: Random House, 2005.

Lewis, Jan, and Peter S. Onuf, eds. *Sally Hemings and Thomas Jefferson: History, Memory, and Civic Culture*. Charlottesville: University Press of Virginia, 1999.

Maier, Pauline. *American Scripture: Making the Declaration of Independence*. New York: Knopf, 1997.

Malone, Dumas. *Jefferson and the Ordeal of Liberty*. Boston: Little, Brown, 1962.

———. *Jefferson and the Rights of Man*. Boston: Little, Brown, 1951.

———. *Jefferson the Virginian*. Boston: Little, Brown, 1948.

Martin, Russell Lionel, III. "Mr. Jefferson's Business: The Farming Letters of Thomas Jefferson and Edmund Bacon, 1806–1826." Ph.D. diss., University of Virginia, 1994.

Mayo, Bernard. *Thomas Jefferson and His Unknown Brother*. Charlottesville: University Press of Virginia, 1981.

McColley, Robert. *Slavery and Jeffersonian Virginia*. Urbana: University of Illinois Press, 1973.

McLaughlin, Jack. *Jefferson and Monticello: The Biography of a Builder*. New York: Henry Holt, 1988.

McMurry, Rebecca L., and James F. McMurry, Jr. *Anatomy of a Scandal: Thomas Jefferson & the Sally Story*. Shippensburg, Pa.: White Mane Books, 2002.

———. *Jefferson, Callender, and the Sally Story: The Scandalmonger and the Newspaper War of 1802*. Toms Brook, Va.: Old Virginia Books, 2000.

Melville, Herman. "Benito Cereno." In *Billy Budd, Sailor, and Other Stories*. Edited by Harold Beaver. Baltimore: Penguin, 1970.

[Mifflin, Warner]. *Life and Ancestry of Warner Mifflin*. Compiled by Hilda Justice. Philadelphia: Ferris & Leach, 1905.

Mill, John Stuart. *The Basic Writings of John Stuart Mill: On Liberty, the Subjection of Women, and Utilitarianism*. New York: Modern Library, 2002.

Miller, John Chester. *The Wolf by the Ears: Thomas Jefferson and Slavery*. Charlottesville: University Press of Virginia, 1991.

Morgan, Edmund S. *American Slavery, American Freedom: The Ordeal of Colonial Virginia*. New York: W. W. Norton, 1975.

Morgan, Philip D. *Slave Counterpoint: Black Culture in the Eighteenth-Century Chesapeake and Lowcountry*. Chapel Hill: University of North Carolina Press, 1998.

Morris, Thomas D. *Southern Slavery and the Law, 1619–1860*. Chapel Hill: University of North Carolina Press, 1996.

Morse, Jedidiah. *American Geography; or, A View of the Present Situation of the United States of America*. London, 1792.

Nettels, Curtis P. *The Emergence of a National Economy, 1775–1815*. New York: Holt, Rinehart and Winston, 1962.

Niebuhr, Reinhold. *The Irony of American History*. New York: Charles Scribner's Sons, 1952.

———. *Reinhold Niebuhr on Politics: His Political Philosophy and Its Application to Our Age as Expressed in His Writings*. Edited by Harry R. Davis and Robert C. Good. New York: Scribner, 1960.

Norwood, Kyle Bentley. "'After Glory Run': Slave Life at Thomas Jefferson's Bedford County Plantation, 1800–1830." Master's thesis, University of New Mexico, 1994.

Onuf, Peter S. *Jefferson's Empire: The Language of American Nationhood*. Charlottesville: University Press of Virginia, 2000.

———. *The Mind of Thomas Jefferson*. Charlottesville: University of Virginia Press, 2007.

———, ed. *Jeffersonian Legacies*. Charlottesville: University Press of Virginia, 1993.

Onuf, Peter S., and Leonard J. Sadosky. *Jeffersonian America*. Malden, Mass.: Blackwell, 2002.

Paquette, Robert Louis, and Louis A. Ferleger, eds. *Slavery, Secession, and Southern History*. Charlottesville: University Press of Virginia, 2000.

Parton, James. *Life of Thomas Jefferson, Third President of the United States*. Boston: James R. Osgood, 1874.

Peterson, Merrill D. *The Jefferson Image in the American Mind*. New York: Oxford University Press, 1960.

———. *Thomas Jefferson and the New Nation: A Biography*. New York: Oxford University Press, 1970.

Phillips, Ulrich Bonnell. *American Negro Slavery: A Survey of The Supply, Employment and Control of Negro Labor As Determined By The Plantation Régime*. New York: D. Appleton and Company, 1918.

Poole, William Frederick, and George Buchanan. *Anti-Slavery Opinions Before the Year 1800*. Cincinnati: Robert Clarke & Co., 1873. Project Gutenberg EBook. www.gutenberg.org/files/23956/23956-h/23956-h.htm.

Popkin, Richard Henry. *The Third Force in Seventeenth-Century Thought*. Leiden: E. J. Brill, 1992.

Pulley, Judith Poss. "Thomas Jefferson at the Court of Versailles: An American *Philosophe* and the Coming of the French Revolution." Ph.D. diss., University of Virginia, 1966.

Pybus, Cassandra. *Epic Journeys of Freedom*. Boston: Beacon Press, 2006.

Rand, Ayn. *Atlas Shrugged*. New York: Signet, 1957.

Randall, Henry Stephens. *The Life of Thomas Jefferson*. New York: Derby & Jackson, 1858.

Randolph, Sarah N. *The Domestic Life of Thomas Jefferson.* New York: Harper & Brothers, 1871.

Randolph, Thomas J. *Speech of Thomas J. Randolph, in the House of Delegates of Virginia, on the Abolition of Slavery.* Richmond, 1832. www.archive.org/details /speechofthomasjr1832rand.

Reed, B. Bernetiae. *The Slave Families of Thomas Jefferson.* Greensboro, N.C.: Sylvest-Sarah, Inc. 2007.

Report of the Research Committee on Thomas Jefferson and Sally Hemings. Thomas Jefferson Foundation, Jan. 2000, Monticello.org.

Ress, David. *Governor Edward Coles and the Vote to Forbid Slavery in Illinois, 1823– 1824.* Jefferson, N.C.: McFarland, 2006.

Rothman, Adam. *Slave Country.* Cambridge, Mass.: Harvard University Press, 2005.

Rothman, Joshua D. *Notorious in the Neighborhood: Sex and Families Across the Color Line in Virginia, 1787–1861.* Chapel Hill: University of North Carolina Press, 2003.

Rush, Benjamin. *An Address to the Inhabitants of the British Settlements in America, upon Slave-Keeping.* Norwich [Conn.]: Reprinted and sold by Judah P. Spooner, 1775.

Sloan, Herbert E. *Principle and Interest: Thomas Jefferson and the Problem of Debt.* Charlottesville: University Press of Virginia, 1995.

Stanton, Lucia. *Free Some Day: The African-American Families of Monticello.* Charlottesville, Va.: Thomas Jefferson Foundation, 2000.

———. *Slavery at Monticello.* Monticello Monograph Series. Charlottesville, Va.: Thomas Jefferson Memorial Foundation, 1996.

Stein, Susan R. *The Worlds of Thomas Jefferson at Monticello.* New York: Abrams, 1993.

Taylor, Quintard, Jr. *From Timbuktu to Katrina: Readings in African-American History.* Boston: Thomas Wadsworth, 2008.

Ticknor, George. *Life, Letters, and Journals of George Ticknor.* Boston: Houghton Mifflin, 1909.

Tocqueville, Alexis de. *Democracy in America.* Edited by Bruce Frohnen. Washington, D.C.: Regnery, 2002.

Tucker, St. George. *Blackstone's Commentaries.* Philadelphia: William Young Birch and Abraham Small, 1803.

Turner, Robert F., ed. *The Jefferson-Hemings Controversy: Report of the Scholars Commission.* Durham, N.C.: Carolina Academic Press, 2011.

Vail, Eugene A. *De la littérature et des hommes de lettres des États Unis d'Amérique.* Paris, 1841.

Waldstreicher, David. *Runaway America: Benjamin Franklin, Slavery, and the American Revolution.* New York: Hill & Wang, 2004.

Warville, Jacques-Pierre Brissot de. *New Travels in the United States of America.* London, 1794.

[Washington, George]. *The Writings of George Washington from the Original Manuscript Sources, 1745–1799.* Edited by John C. Fitzpatrick. Vol. 34. http://etext .virginia.edu/washington/fitzpatrick/.

Wayson, Billy Lee. "Martha Jefferson Randolph: The Education of a Republican Daughter & Plantation Mistress, 1782–1809." Ph.D. diss., University of Virginia, 2008.

Weld, Isaac. *Travels Through the States of North America.* Vol. 1. London, 1799.

Wheatley, Phillis. *Complete Works.* Edited by Vincent Carretta. New York: Penguin, 2001.

Whitman, Walt. "The Spanish Element in Our Nationality." In *Complete Prose Works*. Philadelphia: David McKay, 1892.

Wiencek, Henry. *An Imperfect God: George Washington, His Slaves, and the Creation of America*. New York: Farrar, Straus and Giroux, 2003.

———. *Mansions of the Virginia Gentry*. Birmingham, Ala.: Oxmoor House, 1988.

Wills, Garry. *"Negro President": Jefferson and the Slave Power*. Boston: Houghton Mifflin, 2003.

Wolf, Eva Sheppard. *Race and Liberty in the New Nation: Emancipation in Virginia from the Revolution to Nat Turner's Rebellion*. Baton Rouge: Louisiana State University Press, 2006.

Zuckerman, Michael. *Almost Chosen People: Oblique Biographies in the American Grain*. Berkeley: University of California Press, 1993.

Manuscripts

Armstrong, John, Jr. Undated marginal annotation on *Notes on the State of Virginia*. London: John Stockdale, 1787. Rokeby Collection, courtesy of John Winthrop Aldrich.

Baker, Eliza. "Memoirs of Williamsburg, Virginia." Report taken by Elizabeth Hayes of a conversation between Eliza Baker and the Reverend Dr. W. A. R. Goodwin, May 4, 1933. Dr. W. A. R. Goodwin Records, Colonial Williamsburg Archives, Williamsburg, Va.

Bedford County Court Order Book.

John Hartwell Cocke Papers. Albert and Shirley Small Special Collections Library, University of Virginia.

Coles, Edward. "An Autobiography." Coles Collection, Pennsylvania Historical Society.

———. "The Emancipation." Coles Collection, Pennsylvania Historical Society.

Edgehill-Randolph Papers. Albert and Shirley Small Special Collections Library, University of Virginia.

[Jefferson, Thomas]. Account Book Kept by Thomas Jefferson and Others. Thomas Jefferson Memorial Foundation, Miscellaneous Box, 1767–1852. #186-a. II. "The Est. of Thomas Jefferson Esqr. in Account with Nicholas Lewis," April 9, 1791. Albert and Shirley Small Special Collections Library, University of Virginia.

Jefferson, Thomas, and others. Sixty-Eight Letters to and from Jefferson, 1805–17. Electronic Text Center, University of Virginia Library. http://etext.virginia.edu/toc/modeng/public/Jef1Gri.html.

Papers of the Trist, Randolph, and Burke families, Albert and Shirley Small Special Collections Library, University of Virginia.

Randolph, Thomas Jefferson. Memoirs, version 2. University of Virginia (typescript available at the Jefferson Library, Robert H. Smith International Center for Jefferson Studies).

Wyllie Papers. Albert and Shirley Small Special Collections Library, University of Virginia.

Articles

Barker, Gordon S. "Unraveling the Strange History of Jefferson's *Observations sur la Virginie*." *Virginia Magazine of History & Biography* 112, no. 2 (2004).

Bear, James A., Jr. "The Hemings Family of Monticello." *Virginia Cavalcade* 29, no. 2 (Autumn 1979).

———. "Mr. Jefferson's Nails." *Magazine of Albemarle County History* 16 (1958), pp. 47–52.

Beiswanger, William L. "Thomas Jefferson and the Art of Living Out of Doors." *Magazine Antiques*, April 2000.

Bon-Harper, Sara. "Contrasting Worlds: Plantation Landscapes at Monticello." Paper presented at the 2010 Annual Meeting of the Society for Historical Archaeology.

Bon-Harper, Sara, Fraser Neiman, and Derek Wheeler. "Monticello's Park Cemetery." Monticello Department of Archaeology Technical Report Series, no. 5 (2003).

Boulton, Alexander O. "The American Paradox: Jeffersonian Equality and Racial Science." *American Quarterly* 47, no. 3 (Sept. 1995).

Bringhurst, Newell G. "Fawn Brodie's *Thomas Jefferson*: The Making of a Popular *and* Controversial Biography." *Pacific Historical Review* 62, no. 4 (Nov. 1993).

Brodie, Fawn M. "Thomas Jefferson's Unknown Grandchildren." *American Heritage* (Oct. 1976). www.americanheritage.com/content/thomas-jefferson%E2%80%99s -unknown-grandchildren?nid=53472.

Brown, Everett S. "The Senate Debate on the Breckinridge Bill for the Government of Louisiana, 1804." *American Historical Review* 22, no. 2 (Jan. 1917).

Dabney, Virginius, and Jon Kukla. "The Monticello Scandals: History and Fiction." *Virginia Cavalcade* 29, no. 2 (Autumn 1979).

Deyle, Steven. "An 'Abominable' New Trade: The Closing of the African Slave Trade and the Changing Patterns of U.S. Political Power, 1808–60." *William and Mary Quarterly*, 3rd ser., 66, no. 4 (2009).

Ellis, Joseph J. "Philadelphia Story." *American Heritage* 60, no. 2 (Summer 2010).

Furstenberg, François. "Beyond Freedom and Slavery: Autonomy, Virtue, and Resistance in Early American Political Discourse." *Journal of American History* 89, no. 4 (March 2003).

Gawalt, Gerard W. "Jefferson's Slaves: Crop Accounts at Monticello, 1805–1808." *Journal of the Afro-American Historical and Genealogical Society* 13, nos. 1–2 (Spring/Fall 1994).

Getting Word: The Newsletter.

Graham, Pearl M. "Thomas Jefferson and Sally Hemings." *Journal of Negro History* 46, no. 2 (1961).

Grimsted, David. "Anglo-American Racism and Phillis Wheatley's 'Sable Veil,' 'Length'ned Chain,' and 'Knitted Heart.'" In *Women in the Age of the American Revolution*, edited by Ronald Hoffman and Peter J. Albert. Washington, D.C., 1989.

Johnson, Walter. "Inconsistency, Contradiction, and Complete Confusion: The Everyday Life of the Law of Slavery." *Law & Social Inquiry* 22, no. 2 (Spring 1997).

———. "On Agency." *Journal of Social History* 37, no. 1 (2003).

Ketcham, Ralph L. "The Dictates of Conscience: Edward Coles and Slavery." *Virginia Quarterly Review* 36, no. 1 (Winter 1960).

Lander, Eric S., and Joseph J. Ellis. "Founding Father." *Nature*, Nov. 5, 1998, pp. 13–14.

Langhorne, Elizabeth. "Black Music and Tales from Jefferson's Monticello." *Folklore and Folklife in Virginia* 1 (1979).

Leary, Helen F. M. "Sally Hemings's Children: A Genealogical Analysis of the Evidence." *National Genealogical Society Quarterly* 89, no. 2 (Sept. 2001).

Malone, Dumas, and Steven H. Hochman. "A Note on Evidence: The Personal History of Madison Hemings." *Journal of Southern History* 41, no. 4 (Nov. 1975).

Mizwa, Stephen P. "Kosciuszko's 'Fortune' in America and What Became of It." *Kosciuszko Foundation Monthly Newsletter*, April 1956.

Monroe, Dan. "Edward Coles, Patrician Emancipator." Illinois Periodicals Online. www.lib.niu.edu/2005/iht120502.html.

Morgan, Edmund S. "The Heart of Jefferson." *New York Review of Books*, Aug. 17, 1978.

Morgan, Philip D., and Michael L. Nicholls. "Slaves in Piedmont Virginia, 1720–1790." *William & Mary Quarterly* 46, no. 2 (April 1989).

Morris, Christopher. "The Articulation of Two Worlds: The Master-Slave Relationship Reconsidered." *Journal of American History* 85, no. 3 (Dec. 1998).

Moss, Sidney P., and Carolyn Moss. "The Jefferson Miscegenation Legend in British Travel Books." *Journal of the Early Republic* 7, no. 3 (Autumn 1987).

Neiman, Fraser D. "Changing Landscapes: Slave Housing at Monticello." www.pbs.org/saf/1301/features/archeology.htm.

———. "Sub-floor Pits, Slave-Quarter Architecture, and the Social Dynamics of Chesapeake Slavery." Lecture, Central Virginia Social History Group, March 25, 1997.

Neiman, Fraser D., Leslie McFaden, and Derek Wheeler. "Archaeological Investigation of the Elizabeth Hemings Site." Charlottesville, Va.: Thomas Jefferson Foundation, 2000.

Onuf, Peter S. "The Scholars' Jefferson," *William and Mary Quarterly*, 3rd ser., 50, no. 4 (Oct. 1993).

Pybus, Cassandra. "Jefferson's Faulty Math: The Question of Slave Defections in the American Revolution." *William and Mary Quarterly*, 3rd ser., 62, no. 2 (April 2005).

Randolph, Edmund. "Edmund Randolph's Essay on the Revolutionary History of Virginia." *Virginia Magazine of History and Biography* 43, no. 2 (April 1935), no. 3 (July 1935).

Scanlon, James E., and Albert Gallatin. "A Sudden Conceit: Jefferson and the Louisiana Government Bill of 1804." *Louisiana History: The Journal of the Louisiana Historical Association* 9, no. 2 (Spring 1968).

Self, Robert L., and Susan R. Stein. "The Collaboration of Thomas Jefferson and John Hemings: Furniture Attributed to the Monticello Joinery." *Winterthur Portfolio* 33, no. 4 (Winter 1998).

Setlock, Joelene McDonald. "Thomas Jefferson and Sally Hemings: When Oral Traditions, DNA, and Corroborating Evidence Collide." www.ohiou.edu/~glass/vol/1/11.htm.

Shugerman, Jed Handelsman. "The Louisiana Purchase and South Carolina's Reopening of the Slave Trade in 1803," *Journal of the Early Republic* 22, no. 2 (2002).

Sorensen, Leni. "Taking Care of Themselves: Food Production by the Enslaved Community at Monticello." *Repast: Quarterly Publication of the Culinary Historians of Ann Arbor* 21, no. 2 (Spring 2005), online resource.

Stanton, Lucia. "Looking for Liberty: Thomas Jefferson and the British Lions." *Eighteenth-Century Studies* 26, no. 4 (Summer 1993).

———. "Monticello to Main Street: The Hemings Family and Charlottesville." *Magazine of Albemarle County History* 55 (1997).

———. "The Other End of the Telescope." *William and Mary Quarterly*, 3rd ser., 57, no. 1 (Jan. 2000).

————. "'A Well-Ordered Household': Domestic Servants in Jefferson's White House." *White House History* 17 (2006).

Taylor, Alan. "American Abyss." *Review in American History* 25, no. 3 (1997).

Thelen, David. "Reception of the Declaration of Independence." In *The Declaration of Independence: Origins and Impact,* edited by Scott Douglas Gerber. Washington, D.C.: CQ Press, 2002.

Towler, Sam. "Albemarle County Court Orders Concerning Slavery Issues from 1800–1865." *Central Virginia Heritage* 21, no. 3 (Winter 2004).

Waldstreicher, David. "The Wheatleyan Moment." *Early American Studies* 9, no. 3 (Fall 2011).

Wilson, Douglas L. "The Evolution of Jefferson's *Notes on the State of Virginia*." *Virginia Magazine of History & Biography* 112, no. 2 (2004).

Yarbrough, Jean. "Race and the Moral Foundation of the American Republic: Another Look at the Declaration and the *Notes on Virginia*." *Journal of Politics* 53, no. 1 (Feb. 1991).

Newspaper Articles

Coulter, Ann. "Jefferson Met Hemings in Vietnam." *Jewish World Review,* June 21, 2001. http://jeffersondnastudy.com/.

Davis, David Brion. "The Enduring Legacy of the South's Civil War Victory." *New York Times,* Aug. 26, 2001.

"Dillwyn Park Would Hold Memories of Struggle." Media General News Service, Charlottesville *Daily Progress,* Nov. 28, 2007.

"Drafted Man, Classed as Colored, Commits Suicide in an Ohio Camp." *Washington Post,* Sept. 29, 1917, p. 4, 1917.

Irvine, Reed. "Mainstream Media Allows Smear of Washington, but Not Bill Clinton." *Insight on the News,* Aug. 9, 1999. http://findarticles.com/p/articles/mi_m1571/is_29_15/ai_55426745/.

Mapp, Alf. "If Alive, He Still Would Be Ahead of Our Time." www.tjheritage.org/editorials.html.

"Peter Fossett, the Venerable Ex-slave, Well Known Among the Best Families of Cincinnati, Talks of Olden Times." Unidentified Cincinnati newspaper, n.d. [July 1900?].

Safire, William. "Sallygate." *New York Times,* Nov. 2, 1998.

Shipp, E. R. "Reporting on Jefferson." *Washington Post,* May 30, 1999.

Thomas, Alice. "Report That Jefferson Fathered Slave's Children Disputed." *Columbus Dispatch,* Aug. 27, 2000.

Trescott, Jacqueline. "The Hemings Affair." *Washington Post,* June 15, 1979.

Turner, Robert F. "Did Jefferson Sleep with Sally Hemings?," History News Network, Aug. 8, 2005. http://hnn.us/articles/825.html.

————. "The Truth About Jefferson." *Wall Street Journal,* July 4, 2001.

Virginia Gazette. http://research.history.org/DigitalLibrary/VirginiaGazette/VGbyYear.cfm.

Music

Bob Dylan, *"Love and Theft."* Columbia Records, 2001.

Acknowledgments

Anyone writing about Jefferson and slavery is profoundly indebted to the pathbreaking research and writings of Cinder Stanton, Shannon Senior Historian at the Thomas Jefferson Foundation. She broke the seals on many hidden histories. I have known Cinder for some twenty years, and my debt to her is enormous. Our interpretations may diverge, but I remain deeply grateful for her generous, unstinting assistance.

I was able to launch the research for this book as a resident fellow at the Robert H. Smith International Center for Jefferson Studies, down the road from Monticello. I am grateful to Daniel P. Jordan, former president of the Thomas Jefferson Foundation. A staunch believer in the Jeffersonian principle of free inquiry, Dan urged me to apply for a fellowship even when I said that I did not know what I would find and that my conclusions might not be to everyone's liking. At ICJS I owe special thanks to Dr. Andrew Jackson O'Shaughnessy, Saunders Director; Mary Scott-Fleming, Director of Enrichment Programs; Jack Robertson, Foundation Librarian; Anna Berkes, Research Librarian; Leah Stearns, Digital Library Project Coordinator; Endrina Tay, Associate Foundation Librarian for Technical Services; and Eric Johnson, Library Services Coordinator.

For their many courtesies and help I thank Leslie Greene Bowman, President of the Thomas Jefferson Foundation; Susan R. Stein, Richard Gilder Senior Curator and Vice President for Museum Programs; Justin Sarafin, Dependencies Project Coordinator; Elizabeth V. Chew, Associate Curator of Collections; Gaye Wilson, Research Historian; and Derek

Wheeler, Research Archaeologist. I send special thanks to Leni Sorenson, Monticello's African-American Research Historian, for sharing her illuminating, vital new research, and to Fraser D. Neiman, Director of Archaeology, and Sara Bon-Harper, Archaeological Research Manager, both of whom led me on treks around the mountain and continue to unlock Monticello's stories.

I benefited greatly from my conversations with the staff at the Jefferson Papers, who shared their insights and research. I thank J. Jefferson Looney, Editor-in-Chief, Papers of Thomas Jefferson: Retirement Series; Catherine Coiner Crittenden, Senior Digital Technician; Lisa A. Francavilla, Managing Editor; Robert F. Haggard, Senior Associate Editor; Ellen C. Hickman, Assistant Editor; and Christine Sternberg Patrick, Assistant Editor.

Much of the heaviest work for this book took place in the old Custom House by the river in Chestertown, Maryland, where I was extremely fortunate to hold the first Patrick Henry Writing Fellowship at the C.V. Starr Center for the Study of the American Experience, at Washington College. The fellowship was generously endowed by the late Margaret Henry Penick Nuttle. I thank the marvelous people at the Starr Center—Adam Goodheart, Hodson Trust–Griswold Director; Jill Ogline Titus, Associate Director; Jenifer Endicott Emley, Center Coordinator; and Michael Buckley, Program Manager. My thanks also to Baird Tipton, former president of Washington College, and Kenneth Schweitzer, Director of American Studies. My stay in Chestertown was immeasurably enriched by meeting Kathleen Jones, Joan and Richard Ben Cramer, Jeremy Rothwell, Alexa and Stu Cawley, and Margaret Nuttle Melcher. I thank Ted Widmer, Director of the John Carter Brown Library, who took me around the Starr Center when he was ensconced there.

My fellowship at the Virginia Foundation for the Humanities has provided crucial resources and equally crucial interactions with an ever-changing community of scholars. I thank Robert C. Vaughan, President, for his constant support and encouragement. At just the right time for me, the foundation attracted the distinguished William Freehling to its door. His wise counsel has been of inestimable value.

I owe thanks to other scholars and friends, including Billy Wayson, Dianne Swann-Wright, Cassandra Pybus, Sue Perdue, Jon Kukla,

Bruce Carveth, David Stone, Tony McCall, Sam Towler, Daniel Bluestone, Chris Tilghman, Prinny Anderson, Susan Hutchison, Tatiana van Riemsdijk, John Winthrop Aldrich, and James A. Bear, Jr. For his help on the history of ballooning, I thank Tom D. Crouch, Senior Curator, Division of Aeronautics, National Air and Space Museum, Smithsonian Institution. I have warm memories of the late Gene Foster, the DNA trailblazer, who gave advice and encouragement. I thank Jane Foster for her translations and advice.

My heaven-sent editor, Elisabeth Sifton, patiently nurtured a book that seemed to go on endlessly, and then Jesse Coleman skillfully brought it to the light of day. My agent and comrade, Howard Morhaim, watched, waited, and encouraged. At the start, he warned me that this would be a very hard book to write, and he was correct. An old friend, Judy Vale, emerged from the past at a critical moment.

To my son, Henry, I send thanks for reading the manuscript and for his assurances that I had not run off the rails. As he sets off on his own historical journeys, I would offer encouragement if I thought he needed it, but his light already burns brightly. To my wife, Donna, who read every page of every draft during the long, winding, arduous trek, I send my love always.

Charlottesville
March 2012

Index

slavery/slaves (*cont.*)
  newspaper notices for, 130, 147;
  "passing" by (color line), 45–46, 50,
  54, 95, 171, 179, 214, 226–31,
  264–65; personal loyalty of, 38–42,
  51–52, 54–55, 56; plantation culture
  of, 60–61, 255, 257–58, 274;
  poisoning of, 110–11, 122, 131;
  popular attitudes toward, 19–20;
  population of, 155, 226, 248;
  pregnancies of, 166–72; "privilege,"
  283*n*; productivity of, 20–22, 47, 50,
  92–94, 113–25, 283*n*, 286*n*; profit
  from, 8–9, 10, 33–34, 67–68, 71,
  86–92, 93, 96–97, 109, 114, 124,
  246–47, 250, 258–62, 270–71, 274,
  278*n*; as property, 9, 22–25, 37,
  38–39, 50–51, 60–64, 67, 68–69,
  96–97, 124–25, 130–31, 246–47,
  258–62, 271–75, 281*n*; quasi-freedom
  of, 174–87; racist views on, 5, 7, 21,
  22–23, 25, 27–28, 43–61, 76–83, 87,
  89–90, 94–95, 97, 124*n*, 157, 212,
  242–49, 258–64, 270, 271–75, 281*n*;
  rape of, 47, 217; rebellions by, 54–56,
  81, 130, 226, 251; re-enslavement of,
  166–72, 256–57; religious background
  of, 128, 129, 130, 146–47, 179;
  religious opposition to, 48, 66, 80,
  241*n*, 247–48, 259; during Revolution,
  48–49, 54–56, 63–64, 68, 69–70,
  106–107, 182–83, 256, 273; sale of,
  3–5, 10, 32, 51–57, 66, 70–71, 89–90,
  96–97, 103, 111–12, 121–22, 130–31,
  148, 150, 164–66, 172, 174, 185, 186,
  210, 230–32, 239, 254, 259–60,
  263–64, 270, 274, 282*n*, 293*n*;
  skilled, 85–86, 95–98, 103–12,
  174–87, 247–48; skin color of, 45–46,
  50, 54, 95, 130, 168, 171, 179, 186,
  198–99, 214, 215, 216–17, 226–31,
  264–65; smallpox contracted by,
  55–56, 63–64, 69, 70; social impact
  of, 45–46, 97–98, 123–25, 238–39,
  253–54, 258; in Southern states, 6,
  28, 66–67, 78–80, 85, 90–91,
  101–102, 251, 253–54, 255, 270, 274;

  suicide of, 101–102, 124–25, 182–83,
  229–30; in territories, 251, 253–59,
  274; theft by, 130, 145–46, 171*n*; tips
  given to, 107, 108; trade in, 27–28, 45,
  66, 71, 76, 142, 230–32, 253–59, 273;
  training of, 7, 9–10, 53–54, 58–59,
  85–86, 91–98, 103–12, 174–87, 223,
  247–48; "transporting" of, 130, 131,
  146; trials of, 130–31; wages paid to,
  79, 91–92, 102, 104, 109, 164, 172,
  174, 176, 179, 184, 190; as wet nurses,
  35, 36, 92, 166; white artisans and
  farmers compared with, 57–59,
  74–75, 97, 248, 258, 261, 285*n*
Sloan, Herbert E., 262
Smith, Margaret Bayard, 136–37
Society of Friends of the Blacks, 77
Solomon (slave), 128
Somerset decision (1772), 45
Sophocles, 189
Sorensen, Leni, 155–57, 161, 162
South Carolina, 6, 67, 75, 251, 256, 283*n*
Spain, 254, 255
Stanton, Lucia, 111, 178, 182, 202–203,
  224
Sterne, Laurence, 225–26
Stewart, William, 120–21, 176, 291*n*
Stras, George, 180, 293*n*
Stratford Hall plantation, 154
Styron, William, 267
sub-floor pits, 141–42
*Summary View of the Rights of British
  America, A* (Jefferson), 6, 26–27
Supreme Court, U.S., 301*n*
swept yards, 139–40

Tarleton, Banastre, 41
taxation, 6, 56, 181
Taylor, Alan, 260
tenant farmers, 80, 82–83, 242–44, 250
Thomas Jefferson: An Intimate History
  (Brodie), 198–99, 219–20
*Thomas Jefferson: Fighter for Freedom
  and Human Rights* (Daugherty), 19–20
Thomas Jefferson Heritage Society, 203
Thomson, Charles, 50